IMPERIAL
CHINA

and Its Southern Neighbours

The **Nalanda-Sriwijaya Centre (NSC)** at the Institute of Southeast Asian Studies, Singapore, pursues research on historical interactions among Asian societies and civilizations. It serves as a forum for comprehensive study of the ways in which Asian polities and societies have interacted over time through religious, cultural, and economic exchanges and diasporic networks. The Research Series provides scholars with an avenue to present the outcome of their research and allows an opportunity to develop new or innovative approaches in the sphere of intra-Asian interactions.

The **Institute of Southeast Asian Studies (ISEAS)** was established as an autonomous organization in 1968. It is a regional center dedicated to the study of socio-political, security and economic trends and developments in Southeast Asia and its wider geostrategic and economic environment. The Institute's research programmes are the Regional Economic Studies (RES, including ASEAN and APEC), Regional Strategic and Political Studies (RSPS), and Regional Social and Cultural Studies (RSCS).

ISEAS Publishing, an established academic press, has issued more than 2,000 books and journals. It is the largest scholarly publisher of research about Southeast Asia from within the region. ISEAS Publishing works with many other academic and trade publishers and distributors to disseminate important research and analyses from and about Southeast Asia to the rest of the world.

IMPERIAL CHINA

CHINA

and Its Southern Neighbours

Edited by
**Victor H. Mair and
Liam C. Kelley**

ISEAS

INSTITUTE OF SOUTHEAST ASIAN STUDIES
Singapore

First published in Singapore in 2015 by
ISEAS Publishing
Institute of Southeast Asian Studies
30 Heng Mui Keng Terrace, Pasir Panjang
Singapore 119614

E-mail: publish@iseas.edu.sg   • Website: bookshop.iseas.edu.sg

The responsibility for facts and opinions in this publication rests exclusively with the authors and their interpretations do not necessarily reflect the views or the policy of the publisher or its supporters.

ISEAS Library Cataloguing-in-Publication Data

Imperial China and Its Southern Neighbours / edited by Victor H. Mair and Liam C. Kelley.
1.   China—Civilization
2.   Political culture—China—History.
3.   China—Relations—Southeast Asia.
4.   Southeast Asia—Relations—China.
5.   Southeast Asia—Economic integration.
6.   China—Relations—Middle East.
7.   Middle East—Relations—China.
I.   Mair, Victor H., 1943-
II. Kelly, Liam.
III. International Conference on Imperial China and Its Southern Neighbours (2012 : Singapore)
DS721 I34   2015

ISBN 978-981-4620-53-6 (soft cover)
ISBN 978-981-4620-54-3 (E-book PDF)

Typeset by International Typesetters Pte Ltd
Printed in Singapore by Markono Print Media Pte Ltd

CONTENTS

Preface   vii

The Contributors   xi

1. Introduction: Imperial China Looking South   1
    Wang Gungwu

2. Layers of Meaning: Hairstyle and Yue Identity in Ancient   16
    Chinese Texts
    Erica F. Brindley

3. Sinicization and Barbarization: Ancient State Formation at   43
    the Southern Edge of Sinitic Civilization
    Nam C. Kim

4. Clothes Make the *Man*: Body Culture and Ethnic Boundaries   80
    on the Lingnan Frontier in the Southern Song
    Sean Marsh

5. What Makes a Chinese God? Or, What Makes a   111
    God Chinese?
    Hugh R. Clark

6. Dragon Boats and Serpent Prows: Naval Warfare and   140
    the Political Culture of China's Southern Borderlands
    Andrew Chittick

 7. Inventing Traditions in Fifteenth-Century Vietnam   161
    Liam C. Kelley

 8. Epidemics, Trade, and Local Worship in Vietnam, Leizhou   194
    Peninsula, and Hainan Island
    Li Tana

 9. Southeast Asian Primary Products and Their Impact   214
    on Chinese Material Culture in the Tenth to
    Seventeenth Centuries
    Derek Heng

10. New Evidence on the History of Sino–Arabic Relations: 239
    A Study of Yang Liangyao's Embassy to the
    Abbasid Caliphate
    Rong Xinjiang

11. The Peacock's Gallbladder: An Example of Tibetan   268
    Influence in Late Imperial China
    Rebecca Shuang Fu and Xiang Wan

12. Transformation of the Yunnanese Community along   291
    the Sino–Burma Border During the Nineteenth and
    Early Twentieth Centuries
    Yi Li

13. How the North Tried to Pacify the South Through   316
    Ritual Practices: On the Origins of the Guan Suo Opera
    in the Nineteenth Century
    Sylvie Beaud

14. Realms within Realms of Radiance, Or, Can Heaven   338
    Have Two Sons? Imperial China as *Primus Inter Pares*
    among Sino-Pacific Mandala Polities
    Andrew J. Abalahin

Index   371

PREFACE

This volume is composed of papers presented at the international conference on "Imperial China and Its Southern Neighbours", organized by the Nalanda-Sriwijaya Centre, Institute of Southeast Asian Studies (ISEAS), Singapore, and held at ISEAS on 28–29 June 2012.

The northern periphery of China, from the late Neolithic and the Bronze Age up to modern times, has been carefully scrutinized, both by Chinese scholars and foreign researchers. Even traditional Chinese sources, such as the standard histories, devote considerable attention to the peoples, cultures, and states of the northern and northwestern border regions of the Chinese heartland. Since the Chinese state began in the northern portion of its current configuration and received demonstrable, formative inputs from the north and northwest, it is understandable that correspondingly greater attention would be paid to the north than to the south, particularly during the early periods of the development of the Chinese nation. In contrast, the southern rim of China has been relatively poorly studied, despite the fact that the languages, ethnic groups, and cultures of the south are every bit as complex, interesting, and important as those of the north.

In this conference, we aimed to remedy this disparity by giving due emphasis to the south as a vital region of social, economic, and cultural interaction between Sinitic and non-Sinitic peoples. First, however, we had to recognize that "the south" has not been a fixed entity or a static, well-defined region during the last three millennia of Chinese history. Rather, it has been defined by a continuously changing, amorphous boundary with the north. Indeed, there has been a gradual encroachment of the north upon the south. This was already documented in modern scholarship more than half a century ago by Harold J. Wiens, *China's March Toward the Tropics* (1954, also published under at least one other title), and C.P. Fitzgerald, *The Southern Expansion of the Chinese People* (1972).

A dramatic change occurred around the time of the fall of the Western Jin Dynasty (265–316) and the founding of the Eastern Jin Dynasty (317–420). This was a time of crisis in the northern heartland, one that was precipitated by climatic distress and consequent geopolitical realignments. The net effect was to catapult large numbers of northerners southward, quickening the pace of expansion and assimilation.

The aim of this conference was to go beyond the bare facts of history in an attempt to understand the dynamics of north-south interaction and exchange. Through examination of art, literature, material culture, trade patterns, and other cultural and economic manifestations, we sought to show that the communication between north and south was by no means unidirectional and that it had profound consequences for diverse aspects of society throughout East Asia, Southeast Asia, and beyond. For example, much of what is referred to as Taoist religion actually consists of elements and practices transmitted from the south. Another salient characteristic of late medieval Chinese culture was tea drinking, but this too was brought from the "barbarian" south. Such conspicuous instances of the northern assimilation of southern culture prompt us to ask precisely what were the mechanisms whereby such aspects of culture were transmitted and what were the processes by means of which they became a part of the national culture.

We wish to emphasize that, although we began with the premise of an originally northern-based China interacting with and encroaching upon the south, it was not our intention for this to be a China-centred conference. Instead, we also wished to investigate how the south viewed the north and assimilated aspects of northern culture. Only through a balanced approach that gives due recognition both to the north and to the south do we feel that full justice can be done to the theme of our conference.

This conference brought together scholars who work on various groups living in the southern reaches of China and in South Asia and Southeast Asia. Our focus was not restricted to contiguous land masses only, but also took into account the burgeoning ocean trade and migration that have occurred during the last two millennia and more. Naturally, both insular and continental societies have been taken into consideration.

We do not want to give the impression that our subject area is one of virgin territory. Indeed, much valuable scholarship on the relationship between the north of China and the south has accumulated during the last couple of centuries. A good indication of the state of our field may be by consulting the classic work by Wang Gungwu entitled, *The Nanhai Trade: Early Chinese Trade in the South China Sea* (1954) and the collection of materials in *China and Southeast Asia*, Routledge Library on Southeast Asia, in six volumes (2009). Nonetheless, we feel that the time is ripe to take stock of the current level of knowledge and bring to bear new bodies of evidence from diverse disciplines.

The overall purpose of our conference was to better understand the nature of the societies and cultures that lie to the south of the Chinese heartland and to bring the south into the mainstream of historical studies. We believe that the papers that have been brought together in this volume achieve these goals in a respectable fashion and hope that others will find them to be of use in pursuing further research on this compelling macro region.

We would like to thank the following for assistance in organizing the conference and preparing the volume: Tansen Sen, Geoff Wade, Caixia Lu, Joyce Zaide, and Paula Roberts.

Victor H. Mair
University of Pennsylvania

THE CONTRIBUTORS

Andrew J. Abalahin is an independent scholar in the Philippines. He has a PhD in Southeast Asian history from Cornell University and has taught at San Diego State University.

Sylvie Beaud is an anthropologist affiliated at the Center for Ethnology and Comparative Sociology (Nanterre, France) and at the Maison franco-japonaise (Tokyo, Japan). Her research focuses on identity, kinship and the role of ritual in propaganda in China. She is currently preparing a book based on her doctoral dissertation titled, *Masks on Parade. Han Identity in the Interplay of Politics and Ritual: The Case of the Guan Suo Opera (Yunnan, China)*.

Erica F. Brindley is Associate Professor of History and Asian Studies at Pennsylvania State University. She specializes in ancient Chinese intellectual history, philosophy, and culture, focusing especially on topics that relate to the body, psychology, cosmos, identity, and the self. She is the author of numerous books and articles, including *Individualism in Early China: Human Agency and the Self in Thought and Politics; Music, Cosmology, and the Politics of Harmony in Early China*; and *Ancient China and the Yue: Perceptions and Identities on the Southern Frontier, c.400 BCE – 50 CE*.

Andrew Chittick, the E. Leslie Peter Professor of East Asian Humanities and History at Eckerd College in St. Petersburg, Florida, has developed and led the college's East Asian Studies programme since 1998. His primary research focus is on the society, culture, and military history of the Chinese medieval southern dynasties. He is the author of *Patronage and Community in Medieval China: The Xiangyang Garrison 400–600 CE*, as well as a chapter on the southern dynasties in the forthcoming *Cambridge History of China, Volume 2: The Six Dynasties*. He has also studied and taught on Southeast Asian history and early Sino–Southeast Asian relations, Asian environmental history, and the history and contemporary practice of dragon boat racing.

Hugh R. Clark is Professor of History and East Asian Studies at Ursinus College, Pennsylvania. He is the author of *Community, Trade, and Networks: Southern Fujian from the 3rd to the 13th Centuries* (1991) and *Portrait of a Community: Society, Culture, and the Structures of Kinship in the Mulan River Valley from the Late Tang Through the Song* (2007), and has published numerous articles on the history of southern Fujian province across the late Tang and Song. His most recent work, *The Sinitic Encounter with the Southeast through the First Millennium CE*, will be published in Fall 2015.

Rebecca Shuang Fu focuses on Chinese literature and textual culture in the first millennium, and Turfan and Dunhuang manuscripts (200–1000) in particular. At the same time, she also has a broad range of interests in social history, art history, popular religion and culture, current archaeology, history of writing, and women's and gender studies. Her current book project, *Women's Literacy Practices in Late Medieval China (600–1000)*, traces women's engagement and involvement in text-based activities back to the second half of the first millennium, a period during which the written word played an ever-increasing role in people's day-to-day lives. Drawing on certain types of primary materials underutilized in the field of medieval Chinese literature, such as Turfan and Dunhuang manuscripts, the book's interdisciplinary approach brings into focus the generally overlooked category of non-elite women. Rebecca Shuang Fu received her PhD from the University of Pennsylvania in 2015.

Derek Heng is Associate Professor of Humanities and Head of Studies (History) at Yale-NUS College and Head of Nalanda-Sriwijaya Centre, Institute of Southeast Asian Studies, Singapore. He specializes in the trans-regional history of Maritime Southeast Asia and the South China Sea during the first and early second millennia AD, and is the author of *Sino–Malay Trade and Diplomacy in the Tenth Through the Fourteenth Century* (2009). He has also authored a number of articles on the Chinese material remains recovered from archaeological sites in Southeast Asia, which have appeared in the *Journal of Sung-Yuan Studies*, *International History Review*, *Journal of Southeast Asian Studies* and *International Journal of Maritime History*. He has also edited three volumes on the history and historiography of Singapore's past, including *Singapore in Global History* (2011) and *New Perspectives and Sources on the History of Singapore: A Multi-Disciplinary Approach* (2006). He is currently working on new methods in integrating archaeological data from Southeast Asia with Chinese digital textual databases.

Liam C. Kelley is Associate Professor of History at the University of Hawaii at Manoa where he teaches courses on Southeast Asian history. His research focuses on pre-modern Vietnamese history and Sino–Vietnamese cultural relations. He is the author of *Beyond the Bronze Pillars: Envoy Poetry and the Sino–Vietnamese Relationship* (2005) and various articles on pre-modern Vietnamese history.

Nam C. Kim is Assistant Professor of Anthropology at the University of Wisconsin-Madison, and his archaeological research is concerned with violence, ancient cities, states, and Vietnam. In recent years he has been directing field investigations working with Vietnamese colleagues at Co Loa, one of the earliest prehistoric cities of the region. Dr Kim is the author and co-author of various articles in international refereed journals, including "The Role of Coercion and Warfare in the Rise of State Societies in Southern Zambezia" (2015), "Cultural Landscapes of War and Political Regeneration" (2013), "Lasting Monuments and Durable Institutions: Labor, Urbanism, and Statehood in Northern Vietnam and Beyond" (2013), "Angels, Illusions, Hydras, and Chimeras: Violence and Humanity" (2012), and "Co Loa: An Investigation of Vietnam's Ancient Capital" (2010).

Li Tana is a Senior Fellow of the School of Culture, History, and Language, College of Asia and Pacific Studies, Australian National University. She is interested in the maritime history of Vietnam and the history of overseas Chinese. Her recent project is the environmental history of the Red River Delta of the last thousand years. Her works include *The Nguyen Cochinchina* (1998), *Water Frontier*, co-edited with Nola Cooke (2004), *Tongking Gulf Through History*, co-edited with Nola Cooke and James A. Anderson (2010); *Anthony Reid and the Study of the Southeast Asian Past*, co-edited with Geoff Wade (2012).

Yi Li is a Post-doctoral Fellow at the History Programme, School of Humanities and Social Sciences, Nanyang Technological University, Singapore, where she teaches history of modern Southeast Asia and conducts research on the colonial/post-colonial history of the Chinese community in Burma/Myanmar. Her research interests include British Imperial history, European colonies in Southeast and South Asia, overseas Chinese communities, and the history of Burma/Myanmar. Her doctoral thesis, "Local and Transnational Institutions in the Formation of Chinese Migrant Communities in Colonial Burma", was completed at SOAS, University of London, in 2012.

Victor H. Mair, Professor of Chinese Language and Literature at the University of Pennsylvania, has taught there since 1979. He specializes in Buddhist popular literature as well as the vernacular tradition of Chinese fiction and the performing arts. Beginning in the early 1990s, Professor Mair has led an interdisciplinary research project on the Bronze Age and Iron Age mummies of Eastern Central Asia. Among other results of his efforts during this period are six documentaries for television (Scientific American, NOVA, BBC, Discovery Channel, History Channel, and German Television), a major international conference, numerous articles, and a book, *The Tarim Mummies: Ancient China and the Mystery of the Earliest Peoples from the West* (2000). He is also the author of numerous other publications (including several anthologies from Columbia University Press) and is the editor of *Sino-Platonic Papers*, the ABC Chinese Dictionary Series (University of Hawai'i Press), and the Cambria Sinophone World Series. He blogs frequently for Language Log.

Sean Marsh is a doctoral candidate in the Department of History at the University of California, Davis, and is writing a dissertation on local geographies, ethnographic discourse, and the colonization of the southern frontier during the Song Dynasty. He has published two articles: "Simple Natives and Cunning Merchants: Song Representations of Frontier Trade in Guangxi", *Asia Major* (2014), and "'A Country of Gentlemen': Koryo and the Huizong Court in the *Xuanhe fengshi Gaoli tujing*", *Journal of the Southwest Conference on Asian Studies* (2008).

Rong Xinjiang is Professor of History and Director of the Center for Research on Ancient Chinese History at Peking University. His main research interests include China's cultural contacts with the outside world during the Han-Tang period, the Silk Road (overland and maritime), the history of the Sui and Tang dynasties, and the history of Central Asia. He has extensive publications on these topics in Chinese, English, and Japanese, including, in English, *Eighteen Lectures on Dunhuang*, translated by Imre Galambos (2013).

Dr **Xiang Wan** is currently a postdoctoral researcher at Peking University. He received his PhD degree at the University of Pennsylvania in 2013. His field of research covers the history and prehistory of the Silk Road, especially the period of the Roman Empire and the Kushan Empire. He also works on the histories and cultures of various nationalities in the frontier of China. Making use of documentary as well as unearthed sources, Dr Wan has published articles about the image of ancient Chinese in the eyes of the Western people, travelogues in India written by Chinese Buddhist pilgrims, the end of the Kushan Empire, and the transition of power to the Hunnic invaders in northern Indian subcontinent. His PhD dissertation, focusing on the domestication and use of the horse in ancient China, reviews meticulously the rise of equestrian powers in East Asia and its influence on the steppe of Eastern Eurasia.

Wang Gungwu is University Professor, National University of Singapore, Emeritus Professor of Australian National University, and former Vice-Chancellor, University of Hong Kong. He received his B.A. (Hons.) and M.A. degree from the University of Malaya (Singapore), and his PhD from the University of London (SOAS). His books since 2000 include *The Chinese Overseas: From Earthbound China to the Quest for Autonomy* (2000); *Anglo-Chinese Encounters since 1800: War, Trade, Science and Governance* (2003); *Renewal: The Chinese State and New Global History* (2013).

1

INTRODUCTION
Imperial China Looking South

Wang Gungwu

Sixty years ago, a newly unified China was established, and its new leaders began to look southwards afresh. What they saw was a region that had been transformed by five centuries of a global maritime trade that eventually spawned several European empires. During that period, and especially in the nineteenth century, the earlier trading empires of the sixteenth to eighteenth centuries evolved into national empires as nation-states developed out of feudal and absolute monarchies. Some, like those of Britain and France, were greatly enriched and strengthened by the scientific and industrial revolutions and their large capitalist enterprises spread across the globe. By the first half of the twentieth century, however, the rival empires in Europe had turned on themselves, and this led them to fight two world wars. In the Asia that they had dominated since the early nineteenth century, their destructive conflicts produced many revolutionary changes, for example, the rise of a modern Japanese empire, the destruction of imperial China, new divisions on the Indian subcontinent and, at the end of the Second World War, the emergence of Southeast Asia as a self-conscious region with nationalist leaders who were dedicated to the task of building nation-states out of former colonial territories. The region's newfound self-awareness was enhanced by the common experience, for three and a half years during the Second World War, of having been under the dominance of a single, the Japanese, empire. This was the first time that the various kingdoms and ports and their peoples had ever come more or less under the control of one imperial power.

By the time China was reunified in 1949, some of the leaders of the countries to China's south were beginning to discover that they could together develop a distinctive identity for the region, and that it was in their interest to consider doing so as soon as they could. Spurred by anti-colonial movements that embarked on the task of nation building, inspired by modern concepts of sovereignty, freedom, equality, and economic development, their leaders and scholars found new perspectives from which to examine the history of China's relations with the region. For a while, the new countries were divided by the Cold War. This allowed the ideologies of the two superpowers, the United States and the Soviet Union, to determine the terms of division. It was a divide that was aggravated by a bitter hot war fought in the former French Indochina, one that inevitably affected all the states of Southeast Asia. Given the naval power of the United States, the anti-communist forces could, for most of the three decades between 1945 and 1975, control the coastal waters south from Taiwan to the Philippines, northern Borneo, the Malay Peninsula, Thailand, and what had been French Indochina.

It was in this context that the history of trading relations between China and the kingdoms of the Nanhai (the Chinese equivalent to the South China Sea until modern times) attracted my attention in 1953. The subject was not new but had been studied largely in the context of using Chinese sources to throw light on the early history of Southeast Asia. The starting point was the exciting archaeological finds that proved that the region had a long and remarkable history. As more cultural artifacts were found, ranging from the monumental remains of Angkor Wat and Borobodur to beautiful examples of Dong-son drums and the discoveries at the ancient port of Oc-Eo, the realization that Chinese texts contained materials that could illuminate the findings and describe the rulers and peoples of the polities that produced them aroused much excitement, especially among French and Dutch scholars. In particular, the fields of ethnology and historical geography were enriched. We began to see the outlines of earlier sets of interstate relations behind the extensive cultural interactions that were built on a regular maritime trade.

My attention was focused on the rise of imperial China along the northern coasts of the South China Sea. The arrival of northern armies under the Qin and Han dynasties at the turn of the third century BC to port cities like what is now Hanoi and Guangzhou changed the terms and nature of both political and economic relations. On the one hand, the hinterlands of the two cities came under imperial rule; on the other, relations beyond those ports across the Nanhai meant connecting the personalized ties between rulers that characterized the tributary trade that China encouraged. Following the imperial official recognition of each of these rulers, regular visits became normal, and brief notes on the trade began to appear in Chinese records and, eventually, in documents about exotic places and peoples. Combing through those notes and records led me to understand the pattern of each relationship and the major changes that occurred when there were power shifts in China as well as in the coastal kingdoms of the region. I was especially interested in the first phases of these relationships and, in my study, *The Nanhai Trade: Early Chinese Trade in the South China Sea*, wrote on the major features that determined how imperial China viewed the south.

A great deal has happened in the world of scholarship since *The Nanhai Trade* was written in 1954. Obviously, the ancient Nanhai was nothing like what the South China Sea has become, and both China and the littoral states around that sea have changed a great deal during the past six decades. Historians have found more documents to examine, and other records have been further combed for additional snippets of information. Even more significant have been the archaeological finds on land and the cargoes that have survived in the wrecks discovered under the seas nearby. In addition, those artifacts have been thoroughly scrutinized with the latest technological devices. There has indeed been remarkable progress and we know a lot more than we ever did. But how much that has led to better understanding of imperial China's relations with the polities and peoples in the south remains an open question.

Consider the various paradigms that have been introduced to package all those centuries of development. For example, there are narratives of the wars between Vietnam and China and the regular turbulence on the borders separating Yunnan from Burma. At sea as well as overland, the connections were based largely on a growing multilateral trade, with sizeable human migrations southwards at different times. In modern times, much of the conversation, using the vocabulary of Western scholarship, has been about empires and colonies. Separately, for Chinese officials until the late nineteenth century, there were efforts to retain the tributary system under which diplomatic and trading relations were traditionally conducted. Each of these paradigms stimulated particular areas of scholarship. Recently, there has been much work done about the complex factors that entered into culture contacts, especially in mercantile plural societies. These are accompanied by a fresh interest in the integrative and assimilation processes that follow when generations of peoples are led to live close to one another. There are also new questions about foreign tutelage where political and economic changes have to be made. In addition, there are claims for local genius that transformed foreign ideas and institutions when they became localized. And, with new nations forming, there are, not least, sensitive questions of autonomy and independence related to the position of ethnic identities and the protection of their minorities' rights. For the leaders in China and the new nations of Southeast Asia, the affirmation of sovereignty has become central and, for some, this would include the issue of political participation and the development of distinctive democratic practices. Clearly, depending on which paradigm is chosen as the central focus, the story of imperial China and the south could be told very differently.

The conference title referring to imperial China highlights an important paradigm. It can be taken to refer to a political China that takes many shapes and forms. It brings to the fore the China after Qin Shihuang unified territories from the Great Wall to the coastal lands of the East and South China Seas. Also, during the two millennia since, there could have been several Chinas. Half the ruling houses of China were not originally people whom historians would call "Chinese". It is possible, albeit anachronistically, to describe some successful dynastic houses as, for example, Turko-Mongol, Tibetan or Jurchen-Manchu, speakers of non-

Sinitic languages like those from the Altaic or Tungusic linguistic families. At another level, one could point to different groups of believers operating at elite levels of Chinese society, Nestorian Christians, Jews, Zoroastrians, and Manichaeans, among others. Yet others were Buddhist, Islamic, Lamaist, or shamanist, before they encountered the "Chinese" worlds of Taoist, Confucian, and the Sinicized Buddhist. And, looking southwards, northern Chinese migrants adapted to a range of local deities and practices that were eventually incorporated as new markers of Chineseness.

The Chinese official record had always asserted that the southern edges of the Qin-Han Empire reached the mountainous *southwest* consisting of peoples of distinct ethnic groups. To their east, in the lowlands, were various Yue or Viet peoples. Most of them, except for those in northern Vietnam who eventually became independent, were incorporated into the Chinese cultural family. Beyond that were maritime peoples who came to China to trade, and they could choose whether or not they wanted to be part of the enlarged Chinese community.

When I started in 1953, I had taken the conventional view that hundreds of tribes in the Yellow and Yangzi river valleys interacted for centuries, migrating, mixing, trading, and fighting, until they packaged a set of shared values that characterized a distinct *huaxia* culture. This is the culture we identify as "Chinese." By the third century BC, this had blossomed into the "Hundred Schools" that reflected the brilliant discourses among the leading thinkers of the age. Among the best known among them were Confucius and his disciples, the activists led by Mozi, the followers of Laozi and Zhuangzi and, perhaps the most powerful in governance, the Legalists who drew their inspiration from Shang Yang and Han Fei.

After the Han rulers conquered the south, they imposed their increasingly Confucian culture on the people there. From the first century BC to the seventh century AD, the non-Han of the south were forced to absorb official political culture and ethical values together with the new ideas that came from India brought there by the Buddhists. Together with Taoist formulations that responded to the Buddhist challenge, the new body of ideas was able to encompass local belief-systems, rituals, and practices. After a few centuries, that combination had become strong enough to contribute richly to the formation of Han Chinese civilization. In other words, the belief-systems added new symbols and images to the larger mix of what became identified as Chinese. What I did not know was how much the southern indigenes had given and what was accepted into the cultures that we call "Chinese".

Between the Qin-Han and the Manchu Qing dynasties, three major streams of thought shaped China's master narrative that coloured all ideas of what was or was not *huaxia* culture. The Taoists preferred to leave the origins of this culture open, while the Confucians stuck to the texts anointed by Confucius and used them to determine what qualified people to become Chinese. In contrast, the Chinese who turned to Buddhism were prepared to look beyond borders. As Buddhists, they had no difficulty relating themselves to the "Western Heaven" (西天) that connected them to India and Central Asia. The fact of such different viewpoints shows that there have always been many ways of approaching that Chinese narrative. The chapters in this volume testify to the wide range of viewpoints about what happened over the centuries. The richness of current scholarship that focuses on what lies beneath the idea of Imperial China is most encouraging. What more lies below what we know today? What are the perspectives that have guided the progress since I began sixty years ago?

I shall offer a brief survey of four perspectives that influence the study of the relations between China and its southern neighbours. The first is the Sinocentric Chinese perspective. The second comes from the opposite direction, looking north, from both the maritime south and the overland southwest. The third comes from the distant West but represents modern national efforts to envisage universal history. With the fourth, I shall look to a broader perspective that contains a bundle of social science initiatives. They all have one thing in common: they confirm the attraction of history, and are linked to people who make history, who write and study it, who decide how history may be used, and who try to determine what the dominant historical narrative should be.

The Sinocentric Perspective

I was born and brought up in Southeast Asia but taught at home to see Chinese history and culture from within, what I later learnt was a Sinocentric view. The Chinese historical record was my starting point with which to understand how the Chinese saw their neighbours and what they knew about the world. At the colonial English school where I received my formal education, I was taught the history of Britain and its Empire. This confirmed for me that starting from inside and looking out, whether from within China or Britain, was the norm. The story began with Britons, Romans, Anglo-Saxons, and Normans, and went on to how the United Kingdom expanded to dominate Asia during the past two hundred years. Thanks to that national-imperial perspective, I learnt about the larger world that was once the global British Empire. We were especially drawn to all the places marked red on the map.

In other words, I thought my homegrown Sinocentric approach was normal, quite comparable to the Anglocentric view. At the National Central University in Nanjing where I was enrolled for more than a year in 1947–48, both the traditionalist and the nationalist versions of Sinocentric history were put before me. It showed that one centric vision can evolve into another, and people can have parallel perspectives if they want. It also endorsed what I took to be the norm — the Chinese, like the British, can claim that their respective perspective on history is legitimate.

Over the decades, this Sinocentric narrative has moved away from that in the official histories compiled by Confucian literati. Historians within and outside China have used existing sources to rewrite history in new ways. Some have been influenced by European methodology; others have been specifically drawn to Marxist analyses. But they remain close to Chinese sources that are seen as Sinocentric. The modified narrative still says that the Qin-Han conquests marked a systematic beginning through deep cultural penetration by Chinese from the north. The majority Yue south of the Yangzi did retain much of their culture for a while. But, when Turco-Mongol and Tibetan forces invaded northern China and large numbers of families migrated south with their armed retainers, fundamental changes began to take place. After several centuries, the descendants of northern families with their Han culture had created what they as settled southerners saw as a distinctive Tang culture (that of the Tangren or Tang people).

After the fall of the Tang, the kingdoms in the south received more immigrants, and the southern elites affirmed their position as Chinese. Their culture became, in their eyes, increasingly more authentic than that in the north. They thought the peoples and cultures from the steppes had diluted what was Chinese. The country now needed the southerners to maintain a balanced Chinese vision.

This perspective can be compared with the Vietnamese view that saw their culture as more authentic than the northern Chinese, especially after the Mongol conquest and also when the Manchu Qing dynasty ruled China. Comparing "Tangren" and Vietnamese portrayals can tease out some of the subtleties in the Sinocentric perspective. What is fascinating is that the Sinocentric model could describe when and how Mongol and Manchu intrusions were domesticated and their dynasties accommodated in the Chinese narrative. That inclusive process has been used to suggest how the current narrative established in Asia after a century of Western dominance may delineate how future global history is written. For the histories of southern China and Vietnam, however, the key difference rests on the fact that the Tangren provinces of China accepted the northern perspective while the Vietnamese were free to cultivate their own.

It is now acknowledged that, after the Ming, there were exceptional moments when southern Chinese experienced remarkable changes, whether on land or at sea. The Ming consolidated control over Yunnan, the former lands of the Dali state that Mongol Yuan had destroyed and, about the same time, attempted to intervene in Vietnam's internal affairs. Later, coastal Chinese like Zheng Chenggong brought Taiwan into the fold. The vitality of southern Chinese was severely tested when the Manchu and their allies conquered all of China. The record shows that those in the south resisted the invaders much more strongly than in the north. Furthermore, in the twentieth century, it was the southerners who began to shape a new national consciousness. The sense of Chinese oneness, bolstered by modern ideas of the sovereign nation-state, was also strongly supported by merchants, workers, and other sojourners in Southeast Asia. Thus, step by step, China's relations with its southern neighbours acquired new dimensions.

The Sinicization perspective reminds us how long the process of becoming Chinese took. Until now, large numbers of peoples in China's southwest remain wedded to their own ways. But, with more direct interventions today from a powerful central government, that process has been speeded up and resisting it is likely to become more difficult. How will this affect the Sinocentric story? As Chinese historians confront other historical perspectives, will it be told differently? Let me turn to the perspective of China's southern neighbours. I shall call it the northward perspective.

The Northward Perspective

The key point here is that this perspective was based on a weak sense of recorded history. China's southern neighbours countered the Chinese historical narrative largely with silence. When I was young, such a northward perspective was never recognized. At university, I learnt that there were very few records extant that could tell us what its southern neighbours thought of China. Most of the time, we depend on what Chinese officials had compiled about what southern peoples experienced of China's wealth and power. These materials touched on wars and commerce, changing tributary conditions, and culture-contacts that included the peoples in Guangxi, Guizhou, Yunnan, and the northern regions of Vietnam, Laos, and Myanmar and some of the littoral kingdoms of the South China Sea. The first full account was the *Man Shu* of Fan Zhuo, concerning the state of Nan Zhao in Yunnan in the ninth century. Another very full one was that of Zhou Daguan, the *Zhenla fengtuji* written four centuries later. All others were brief summaries or fragments of lost works. In any case, they do not represent southern perspectives, merely what the Chinese officials thought were worth noting.

The earliest northward perspective came from Vietnam, and that was deeply influenced by Sinocentric records. Vietnamese historians retrospectively interpreted early Chinese official accounts to recapture their ancient past. They also used that framework to account for the hierarchical relations with China and provided the Vietnamese with a proto-nationalist perspective. Later, with new narratives introduced by Christian missionaries and French colonial historians, that Vietnamese version of Sinocentrism has been discarded and replaced by modern nationalist historiography. There is little evidence of an indigenous historical perspective.

There are Thai and Burmese perspectives in their respective chronicles, but references to China were largely limited to the few official contacts they had, especially when they touched on possible Chinese help to sort out local wars and political matters like the occasional succession problem.

In the Malayo-Javanese world, it is remarkable how little has so far been found in their records about relations with China, whether diplomatic or commercial, before the twentieth century. In retrospect, it is possible to speculate what the rulers and officials of these kingdoms might have thought of China. For example, reading Chinese histories "against the grain", as recent Southeast Asian historians have done with colonial records, is one way to point to what northward perspectives might have been like.

After the sixteenth century, European historical jottings can be used to help us portray some Southeast Asian experiences of dealing with Chinese merchants. But, except for the peoples in China's southwest, notably those along the borders of Myanmar and Laos, and with China's exceptional relationship with Vietnam, imperial China was hardly present in the region down to the twentieth century. It was only after the coming of European empires that Southeast Asians sought to build a coherent northward perspective for themselves. This is still work in progress.

The Universal History Perspective

The third perspective refers to the modern national narrative that was extended to cover the history of the world.

Lacking strong history-writing traditions, China's southern neighbours are open to new approaches to history. When the Europeans arrived, new commercial needs shaped a perspective that was connected to an emerging worldview. This Europe-based knowledge system produced a dominant narrative that gradually replaced what there was of local but poorly articulated perspectives. By the nineteenth century, the nation-state empires of Western Europe had been strengthened by a global capitalist economy. This led to the quest for a paradigm of universal history. However, as I discovered when I was introduced to the history of the British Empire, the idea of that universal history itself has behind it strong national narratives. When looked at closely, the idea may be suffused with a specifically French, German, or Anglo-American imperial imagination.

For the nation-building states of Southeast Asia, this universal history founded on the national histories of major European powers is attractive. It has a distinguished pedigree and may be traced back to the histories of Herodotus and Thucydides and the trajectories of Greek and Roman empires. Also, the salvation faiths that shaped the outlooks of the Jews, Christians, and Muslims gave it a linear and progressive timeline that provided post-Renaissance Europe with a master narrative. That was later revised to suit the secular nation-state approach in history writing. The global impact of the European states added to its appeal, as can be seen in the speed at which various Asian leaders chose to use it to reframe their own histories. The Japanese took the lead in the late nineteenth century and inspired the Chinese, Koreans, and others, now very much including the new generation of nationalist leaders among China's southern neighbours.

Thus, when former colonies became new nations after the Second World War and sought to emulate the states of the West, it is easy to understand why they adopted this master narrative. Two main strategies are being used, the first turning the colonial records against the imperialists by reading them "against the grain"; the second, digging deep into each country's past for authentic features to define the nation. In so doing, they can reinterpret their historical relations with China, both when China was strong and when China was weak. This includes a perspective on China siding with communist powers during the Cold War and China as a successful model of state capitalism. Although that was after the end of imperial China, the narrative can be read back into China's imperial past.

The new master narrative was based on the sovereignty and legitimacy of nation-states. The origins of each state were traced back to the remote past, claiming that it was destined to become what it is today. The approach has political and emotional appeal, but it draws on subjective judgements of what parts of the past are necessary to support what constitutes the national ideal today. It can be argued that this serves one of the basic needs of human society. Most people want a sense of belonging, to be comfortable and secure in a collective identity. It is therefore natural to seek a global order in which all nations can be assured of peace and prosperity as the end of history. Once this is accepted as the universal answer to world order, national histories should conform to this master narrative. To accept the rules governing such an international order then becomes the test of a country's good will and sincerity. Any power that does not pass the test could be declared an outcast that should be contained if not punished. In short, the dominant master narrative holds the moral high ground.

For the neighbours south of China, such an approach could be used to read back into the past. It did not matter if their local traditions were Hindu-Buddhist, Muslim, Confucian, or Christian. As long as they are embedded in the country's nationalist aspirations, they can help revive the past. The Sinocentric notes found in Chinese records can now be modified or discarded. The universal history narrative can counter any viewpoint that does not support the interests of the nation-state. Where China is concerned, its southern neighbours can employ this paradigm to rewrite their histories altogether.

Ironically, this same perspective has also been used to support a narrow Sinocentric perspective, one that uses the Sinicization process to promote the modern Chinese nation-state. I first saw this emerging in the 1930s, when the nationalist narrative that had been aroused by anti-imperialist sentiments was greatly aggravated by the Japanese invasion of China. It was for a while opposed by internationalism, also taken from Europe though seen by some as something of a Western heresy. The form of that internationalism was represented by the communist ideal. But the latter vision failed, in part because the nationalist narrative superimposed on the Sinocentric perspective was too powerful. The post-Maoist adjustment to the modern universal narrative has returned to its nationalist base in the hope of redesigning a new kind of multinational state.

Now that the dominant narrative can challenge the Sinocentric and bolster a new northward perspective, it is likely to produce historical interpretations that can aggravate national sentiment for the foreseeable future. Such a development could result in more misunderstanding and strife that will do little to enhance historical scholarship. Can this be avoided? As long as the sovereign nation is the primary loyalty, it probably cannot. In that case, can we build a platform that frees the historians of both China and its neighbours from increasing suspicion, fear, and anger?

This leads me to my fourth perspective, one that, for want of a more accurate label, I shall call the New History perspective, which is a little like saying, Let a hundred flowers bloom!

The New History Perspective

In the 1950s, I thought the British version of universal history was comparable, if not parallel, to the Sinocentric claim to project a universalist *Tianxia*, or All under Heaven. However, two other perspectives caught my attention. One included for me "New History" and social history, equally innovative and impressive. James Harvey Robinson had stressed intellectual and cultural progress that called for the application of multidisciplinary research, and G.M. Trevelyan talked of "history with the politics left out". The second was economic history with a political agenda. This began with Karl Marx in Western Europe and was associated with violent action. When I was in Nanjing, I observed how the idea of class revolution became the driving force that overturned the Chinese world. After 1949, PRC historians were exhorted to follow this agenda and some effort was made to try to rid China of its Sinocentric perspective.

I was reminded of this fourth perspective when Ho Ping-ti, the distinguished historian, died in 2012. When he was young, his ambition had been to master the social sciences he learnt from the West and rewrite all of Chinese history with a new set of instruments. If he had been interested in China's southern neighbours, that meant he would have moved away from the Sinocentric view. But that ambition also suggested that he would reject the universal narrative of the nationalist historians. He was familiar with the work of Max Weber and other contemporaries who brought social science dimensions to enrich the way to look at history.

The debates that Weber and others like him initiated took New History far beyond what Robinson had envisaged but nevertheless produced many blossoms. The vision of what the social scientific approach could do for history has been inspirational. Although historians have found it difficult to shake off the dominant narrative centred on the nation-state, the increasingly varied efforts of generations of New History advocates have increased the breadth and depth of historical explanation. No longer would narratives hinge so much on what men did for nation-states; no longer would international relations be only about peace and war. The gates are open for the study of other actors: workers and subalterns, women, human security, the environment, including everything that did not depend on the alluring discourse of power and wealth.

Where China and its southern neighbours are concerned, the past half-century has seen some social science flowers blooming among younger historians trained in the West. In China and Southeast Asia, there is still unease if not resistance, in part because of traditional disciplinary divides, but in part also because the emphasis on theoretical and quantitative skills does not attract historians. Of course, opening wide to New History extends the number of approaches to successful history writing. But the criteria for excellence are also demanding in new ways. For historians to learn enough so that they can distinguish the fruitful from the facile may not be easy. To master appropriate methodologies and apply them to localized historical data requires highly critical skills. And, to adapt theories drawn from other societies and use unfamiliar paradigms for local phenomena is risky and can be controversial. It is obvious that there is no shortage of reasons why many historians still hesitate to employ this perspective.

Furthermore, for China and its southern neighbours, there is no meeting of minds. On the one hand, Chinese historians have only recently moved away from Marxist certainties. Now they face a medley of methods and theories derived from Western experiences that few as yet know how to employ. This has meant that even the best scholars on China's relations with its southern neighbours tend to stay within the Sinocentric tradition. On the other hand, historians of the neighbouring states are still encouraged to work with their nationalist paradigm. As a result, the social sciences have added little to what the historians of China and its neighbours can share.

The new history perspective has so far not been attractive in the region. In China, the Sinocentric perspective remains strong. In the south, the local historians either neglect historical research because they do not think it important or prefer the nationalist response against imperial history and are content to claim that response as universal. These perspectives will continue to predominate as long as the interests of nation-states remain primary.

In that context, you can see why the papers collected in this volume are so appealing. Most of the topics examined here reach out in new directions. And a multiplicity of perspectives is explored by using a wide range of local and transnational data without being tied down to political or cultural borders. There are some subjects here that someone half a century ago might have thought of studying, but the approaches and methodologies used and the theoretical insights that are being tested today would not have been possible at that time. As I look back at the immense amount of work that has been done during the past decades, I feel there has been an awakening followed by shouts of self-discovery. I sense a borderless spirit at work in the papers offered in this volume. Perhaps the multifaceted perspectives of New History have inspired some of the many-splendoured blossoms gathered here.

2

LAYERS OF MEANING
Hairstyle and Yue Identity in Ancient Chinese Texts

Erica F. Brindley

Human physical appearance can often be read in terms of one's personal identity or as markers and statements of social norms, cultural values, or responses to one's environment.

In ancient China, a society especially attuned to the ritual regulations that served as the backbone of its ethical and political system, an individual's physical appearance and comportment had significance in educated discourse and social interaction. In particular, hairstyle signaled a variety of social distinctions and was full of cultural meaning. Mark Lewis, following the work of anthropologists such as E.R. Leach and Gananath Obeyesekere, has persuasively demonstrated that hair "is a key social marker and symbol in most cultures, indicating gender, class, age, character, social role, and degree of civilization".[1] In Zhou culture, adults bound their hair. Ceremonies to confirm coming to adulthood involved changing one's hairstyle to mark the transition to a new stage of life: a capping ceremony was held for men, and a similar ceremony of pinning the hair was held for women.[2] It should come as no surprise, then, that the hairstyles of alien peoples did not go unnoticed in the textual record.

This chapter examines the meanings associated with three hairstyles characteristic of ethnic Yue outsiders: unbound hair, sheared hair, and the mallet-shaped bun. In particular, we look at peoples associated with the "Yue" 越 ethnonym, who were subsumed under the following categories: (1) Yue peoples from the ancient states of Wuyue 吳越, and (2) Yue peoples who might be grossly categorized as belonging to the so-called "Hundred Yue" (Baiyue 百越). Before proceeding, I will clarify some of the complicated ways in which ancient authors referred to such Yue peoples.[3] Authors often used different terms interchangeably; in one passage they might refer to the Yue, in another, we see them calling the same people "Manyi" 蠻夷, "Yi" 夷, or "Man" 蠻. As we will see from the sources discussed below, the type of nomenclature used depends on context and historical period. As dizzying as the array of names appears to be, there are some basic patterns; there appear to be sufficient cultural, material, and linguistic connections among all the following groups referred to as "Yue" to justify studying them as a single mega-cultural identity.

For the most part, in this chapter, I highlight two somewhat distinct groups and eras of Yue: the Wuyue of the East and Southeast, dating to the mid-Zhou period, who lived in or near the present-day provinces of Jiangsu, Zhejiang, and Fujian; and the Hundred Yue, who were situated in the Zhejiang-Fujian corridor, as well as farther south, in and around the present-day provinces of Guangdong, Guangxi, and even northern Vietnam. Authors from the late Zhou began to invoke this latter umbrella term, the "Hundred Yue", to refer to variations that existed among the Yue peoples and cultures at the same time that they appeared to be unified: they were all Yue. "Hundred Yue" also appears to be more of an ethnonym than the geopolitical reference, "Wuyue", which conjures up an earlier time.

Wuyue has largely political but also cultural and ethnic associations. "Wuyue" refers to two distinct but culturally related states that appear in the textual record around 576 BC (for Wu) and the early fifth century BC (for Yue).[4] These states were located in the southeast of the East Asian

mainland, in the regions associated with the southern reaches of the ancient
Yi peoples near Lake Tai and modern-day Shanghai and Zhejiang. The
term "Yi" is a Sinitic designation for ancient groups of peoples who seem
to have inhabited and dominated the eastern spheres of the continent, as
far north as the Shandong peninsula, and farther south along the coast.
Although this term later comes to refer to "barbarians" in general, it is
mostly used during the pre-imperial (pre-Qin and Han) times in reference
to a specific group of people, not to "barbarians" in general. It is also
completely distinct from contemporary ethnic groups known as the Yi in
Southwest China.

    While a precise relationship still needs to be established between groups
referred to as "Yi" and "Yue", they appear to be linked. Some scholars
have suggested a connection — if not kinship relationship — between the
ancient Yi who were prevalent during Shang and early Zhou times in the
Shandong region and just south of there, and the cultures, peoples, and
languages of the state of Yue of mid-Zhou times.[5] In ancient sources, the
Yue peoples of the Wuyue regions appear to be associated with Eastern
Yi (Dongyi 東夷) peoples.

    During early imperial (Qin-Han) times, the Southeast regions of
southern Zhejiang and northern Fujian came together under many names,
but in general, the peoples were referred to by contemporary scholars as
Minyue (閩越). In Warring States and Qin-Han texts, such geopolitical
and ethnographic terms as Minyue, Yue Donghai 越東海, Dong'ou 東甌,
Minzhong 閩中 Dongyue 東越, and Manyi were variously used to describe
the Yue peoples who inhabited this region.

    The Hundred Yue, also a subcategory of "Yue" peoples and cultures,
were associated more generally with regions south of the Yangzi and
along the southern coast from Zhejiang and Fujian to northern Vietnam.
The terms "Manyi" (or "Man") and "Southern Man" 南蠻 peoples
are sometimes used in the record to describe southerners in general
and appear to be used synonymously with the reference to the Hundred
Yue ranging from Zhejiang to Vietnam, across the entire stretch of
the Southlands.[6] And lastly, just as Minyue was associated with the
Southeast during early imperial times, the Guangdong, Guangxi, and
Vietnam regions were generally associated with the Southern Yue (Nanyue
南越) peoples.

The descriptions of hairstyle that we examine all stem from the perspective of the Central States outsider, and they all date to the Warring States and early imperial period. By evaluating the extent to which certain hairstyles were used to stereotype, exaggerate, and/or denigrate foreigners such as the Yue, and by analyzing the various layers of cultural meaning associated with each style, I provide a metric for understanding the ways in which the Yue may have been perceived by peoples from the Central States. Cultural analysis of this sort will also reveal cases in which references to Yue hairstyles were merely a rhetorical shorthand, reflecting not a factual ethnographic description but a Central States ignorance about Yue people and cultures. We thus gain insight into the degree to which the Central States elite possessed accurate or deep knowledge about Yue peoples and cultures.

Unbound Hair (*Pifa* 被髮)

Two related markers — that of "unbound hair" (*bei* 被 read as *pi* 披; "exposed", "opened", or loose hair) and "sheared hair" (*duanfa* 斷髮) — are associated with the Yi and Yue peoples of the East and South. Based on connotations and early uses of the word *pi* 被, "to wear", unbound hair may have implied that the hair hung down over the neck and shoulder, as one would wear a robe or cape. This would have been quite different from the latter formulation, sheared hair, which presumably described hair that did not extend beyond the neck.[7] Even though the two phrases differ from each other, the custom of cutting off one's hair appears to be linked to wearing it loose or unbound, and often, the two phrases are used interchangeably in stock descriptions of certain Yue peoples. We will first examine each of these two hairstyles separately, and only later will we ask what it means for these two styles to be so closely enmeshed.

What were the connotations of keeping one's hair loose, or unbound, in Zhou culture? In the *Analects*, Confucius famously discusses Guan Zhong 管仲, a seventh century BC minister to the then overlord of the Zhou regions, Duke Huan of Qi 齊桓公, saying that "if it were not for Guan Zhong, we would all be leaving our hair unbound and fastening our garments on the left" 微管仲, 吾其被髮左衽矣.[8] While this quote likely refers to Qi's successful exploits against northwestern, non-Zhou others (sometimes referred to as the "Rong" 戎), Confucius's sentiment — namely, that Guan Zhong saved them from such unseemly, barbaric habits — rings clear. Here, ethnic otherness, along with a concomitant sense of the cultural superiority of the self and one's own ways, is partly expressed through unbound hair.

In the *Liji*, we have confirmation that both western and eastern (Yi) tribes could each be characterized as having "unbound hair". This passage is worth quoting in full so as to gain a sense of how cultural difference was delineated by geographical region through the five directions (north, south, east, west, and centre), and how each group was characterized by a few key, physical markers:

中國戎夷, 五方之民, 皆有其性也, 不可推移. 東方曰夷, 被髮文身, 有不火食者矣. 南方曰蠻, 雕題交趾, 有不火食者矣. 西方曰戎, 被髮衣皮, 有不粒食者矣. 北方曰狄, 衣羽毛穴居, 有不粒食者矣.

The peoples of the five directions, including those from the Central States, Rong and Yi, all have their natures, which they cannot be pushed to alter. In the east they are called the Yi. They wear their hair unbound and tattoo their bodies. There are some who eat food that has not been cooked. In the south they are called the Man.[9] They carve into their foreheads and are pigeon-toed. There are some who also eat food that has not been cooked. In the west they are called the Rong. They wear their hair unbound and dress in skins. There are some who do not eat grains. In the north they are called the Di. They wear animal and bird skins and dwell in caves. There are some who also do not eat grains.[10]

It is clear from this passage that keeping one's hair unbound, in and of itself, was not a trait that could identify a person from Yue, as opposed to a person from the Rong tribes. However, when the two traits of unbound hair and tattooing the body were combined, this was indisputably thought to be a signature of the Yue peoples. Notably, the only time hair is mentioned as a marker of identification in this entire passage is when it is "unbound"; no other hairstyle seems to elicit comment or consideration. This suggests the transgressive, non-normative nature of "unbound hair", as opposed to hair that is fixed in a different style from that of the people from the Central States (or Huaxia 華夏). It appears that what mattered most was the act of doing something to one's hair, which implies extra work, attention, effort, and artifice, as opposed to letting it hang loose in its natural state.

References to loose and unbound hair do not only appear as ethnic markers. Not infrequently, they represent transgression and everything that seems to go with the act of going beyond or breaking through cultural norms. As Mark Lewis puts it, wearing one's hair unbound "invariably denotes figures outside the human community: barbarians, madmen, ghosts, and immortals".[11] By examining usages in the literature that link unbound or sheared hair to paranormal, extra-human beings, we gain a better sense of how the Central States peoples would have perceived such an appearance and what they may have implied when mentioning it in relationship to the Yue.

The transgressive connotations of unbound hair are clearly linked to perceptions of the Yue ethnic other throughout Warring States literature. In stories about the legendary figure of Wu Zixu 伍子胥, this occurs quite frequently.[12] Authors often discuss the occasion on which Wu escapes from Chu to the state of Wu, where he "unbound his hair and begged for food in Wu" 被髮乞食於吳.[13] This reference makes clear use of the widespread knowledge that the Wu-Yue peoples kept their hair unbound, and points to hairstyle in order to quickly denote how Wu Zixu had crossed over into a foreign culture as well as social class (that of a beggar). It imparts a poignant portrayal of a man down on his luck, who not only enters new geographic space, but also engages in a physical transition of the body. In his new form, Wu must embrace an odd, perhaps humiliating custom just as he must accept poverty. Indeed, the image is powerful because it points to a double transformation at both the cultural and social levels. Intriguingly, it does not point to a degradation of his moral fibre, so in one sense, the normative values of honesty and righteousness were preserved in the process.

A passage in the *Mencius* drives home the opposite point: that to keep one's hair unbound was considered not only unseemly, but morally depraved as well:

今有同室之人鬬者, 救之, 雖被髮纓冠而救之, 可也. 鄉鄰有鬬者, 被髮纓冠 而往救之, 則惑也, 雖閉戶可也.

Now, if people in the same room with you are fighting, you should stop them. If you do so while wearing but a cap tied over your unbound hair, it is permissible. However, if others are fighting in the village or vicinity, and you went to stop them while wearing but a cap tied over your unbound hair, you would be misguided. In such a case, shutting your door [and not going out to help] would even be allowable.[14]

According to this passage, it is only acceptable to appear publicly with unbound hair — and a simple cap over it — if there is an emergency directly in front of your person and your aid is required. Any other situation dictates that you hide yourself and your unbound hair, and that you do not provide aid, even if the fighting is occurring outside your house. In short, sporting unbound hair was not merely a serious social faux pas; it signified an utter breach of ritual comportment and so, in a sense, a lack of moral integrity.

As Lewis has already noted about the importance of hairstyle in ancient China, "The binding of one's hair marked membership in civilized society, and variations in style indicated differences in status."[15] A glimpse of the hundreds of different styles of hair worn by the terracotta soldiers found in the tomb of Qin Shihuang, the First Emperor of Qin, attests to the ways in which such markers could indicate difference in rank and culture of origin. It is interesting to note that there is not a single terracotta soldier with unbound hair, even though it has been argued that the many hairstyles of the soldiers represent the diversity of peoples over whom the First Emperor ruled. Presumably, the First Emperor would have expected the soldiers of his army to conform to a minimal standard of hair dressing while active on duty. While certainly military rules of personal upkeep were likely to have been different than civilian protocols, the lack of any soldier with unkempt, unbounded hair may still support the general notion that this hairstyle marked disorder and transgression in the Zhou context.

It does not take a great leap of the imagination to link unbound hair with an unbounded mind. Many usages of the phrase "unbounded hair" occur in stories about the legendary figure Jizi 箕子, the grand tutor of Zhou 紂, who was the last king of the Shang Dynasty. In order to avoid execution, Jizi allegedly "wore unbounded hair and pretended to be crazy" 被髮而佯狂.[16] In the Han text, *Wuyue chunqiu*, the same statement is said about Wu Zixu, and in the *Yuejueshu*, about the Yue minister, Fan Li 范蠡.[17] Phrases such as "wore unbounded hair and sang crazily" 被髮而狂歌, occur in the literature to alert one to the transgressive behaviour of lunatics.[18]

Of course, the figure of the crazy man is not always a negative one in ancient China. In many texts, including texts like the *Zhuangzi* and *Huainanzi*, he who is crazy is also a wise and complete human — a free spirit, so to speak — who follows what is natural without any articulation of artifice. This is clear in a passage from the "Dasheng" 達生 chapter in the *Zhuangzi*, in which the figure of Confucius sees an old man swimming in dangerous waters at the base of a gorge. Thinking that anyone crazy enough to swim there could not be a human and must be a spirit instead, Confucius continues to observe. His thoughts appear to be confirmed when the old man (whom we later find out embraces the Tao): "with unbound hair, proceeded to sing and swim to the bottom of the embankment" 被髮行歌而游於塘下.[19] Real spirit or not, the unbound hair and carefree attitude of this old man helps mark him as someone with superhuman powers.

Other examples of early Chinese writers linking loose hair to natural sprites or ghosts abound in the literature. For instance, a man with unbound hair who appears in a dream turns out to be a divine tortoise.[20] Or an apparition with "unbound hair reaching the ground" 被髮及地 manifests itself in a dream.[21] A few examples from the most fantastical chapters of the *Shanhaijing* even attribute unbound hair to the mythical peoples and creatures living outside the familiar regions.[22] And lastly, the *Shuowen jiezi* at one point explicitly links the hairstyle to "human-like creatures" 如人 who are cannibals and laugh in such a way that their upper lip covers their eyes.[23]

The very act of leaving one's hair unbound, in fact, has special resonance in early Taoist texts, and could even be understood to signal the moment of attainment. We see this in the "Tianzi Fang" 田子方 chapter from the *Zhuangzi*, where the figure of Confucius meets with Lao Dan (i.e., Laozi). In addition to describing Lao Dan's behavioural and affective state of being, the passage first notes that "Lao Dan had just bathed himself and had his hair unbound to dry" 老聃新沐, 方將被髮而乾.[24] Lao Dan is thus physically close to his natural state, and clean, or pure. Notably, it is precisely after the author mentions Laozi's loose hair that the latter is seen in the story to achieve a total state of union with the Tao. This suggests that loose hair may not merely signify union with a higher spiritual power; it may possess talismanic powers in and of itself that aid in the process of self-transformation.

Since in Zhou culture young boys or girls did not gain access to the ritual prerogatives of adults until their capping ceremonies, it stands to reason that prepubescent boys and girls may have worn their hair loose, and that this marker represented innocence and youth as well as social status. There is one instance in the *Shiji* in which a "young boy with unbound hair" 被髮童子 reveals himself to have sage-like abilities regarding the practice of divination.[25] While this passage is reminiscent of depictions of the sages or crazed persons found in texts like the *Laozi*, *Zhuangzi*, and *Huainanzi*, it is noteworthy that the connotations of both youth and extrasensory, sage-like wisdom are combined here. One may argue that merely the figure of the young boy is enough to suggest sagehood, as the primordial *qi* of youth is venerated in Taoist strands of thought. Nonetheless, the element of loose hair enhances such an image, adding an additional layer of meaning. The lad possesses both pristine youth and an unhinged — and hence, unlimited — state of consciousness. One may even argue from other contexts that unbound hair signified the primal and primitive, before the overlays of culture encapsulated by Zhou ritual. This is evident in a passage from the Wenzi, where people who live in an idyllic, primitive past — before humans had been corrupted by culture — "wear their hair unbound".[26]

And lastly, there are certain figures in the historical tradition who are associated with wearing their hair unbound on occasion so as to symbolize the abandonment not just of public decorum, but of responsibility to others as well. We have already mentioned the minister Wu Zixu and how letting his hair down symbolized his shift of allegiance over to the state of Wu (and hence, Wuyue cultural mores). The seventh century BC overlord Duke Huan of Qi, also famously let his hair go unbound at certain times. In two passages from the *Han Feizi*, we hear how the duke let the two famous men under his charge take care of affairs of the state while he "wore his hair unbound and drove around with his wife in a carriage" 被髮而御婦人.[27] Clearly, what is demonstrated here is a transgression that symbolizes the relinquishing of one's official duties and responsibilities. The duke's unbound hair connotes a state of being derelict and lacking any sense of moral obligation to the greater social good. So not only were upright ministers (such as Wu Zixu), paranormal humans, spirits, and idealized primitive peoples depicted in such a way, so were those selfish, immoral men who considered themselves above the law. Many of these layers of meaning were no doubt embedded in the ancient description of the unbound hair of the Wuyue and Hundred Yue peoples.

Sheared Hair (*Duanfa* 斷髮)

The phrase *duanfa*, or "sheared hair", is also a stereotypical marker of Yue identity in ancient texts. The specific phrase, "sheared hair, tattooed body" (*duanfa wenshen* 斷髮文身), appears in Warring States texts such as the *Zhuangzi*, *Zuozhuan*, and *Han Feizi*, as well as some Han texts, to refer to the Yi in the East, or, sometimes, more specifically to the peoples of Wu and Yue in the Jiangsu-Zhejiang-Fujian areas, depending on the text. Before we discuss the reasons why both sheared hair and unbound hair are associated with the ancient Yue peoples, let us first consider the breadth of usage and scope of meaning for *duanfa* in the textual record.

A particularly noteworthy example of sheared hair in association with Yue peoples can be found in the first chapter of the *Zhuangzi*: "A man from the state of Song, who traded in ceremonial caps, went to Yue, but the people of Yue sheared their hair and tattooed their bodies, and had no use for them" 宋人資章甫適諸越, 越人斷髮文身, 無所用之.[28] Given its appearance in an "inner chapter" of the *Zhuangzi*, this mention of the Yue may date to as early as the mid-fourth century BC. Such a period post-dates the rise of the Yue state to hegemonic status over the Central States in the early fifth century BC but may pre-date the conquest of Yue by the state of Chu in 334 BC.[29] The manner in which the author uses the phrase "sheared hair and tattooed bodies" is casual, as though such knowledge was familiar to every educated reader. This suggests that from fairly early in the literary record, the phrase served as a quick shorthand to distinguish Yue peoples from the Zhou through easily identifiable physical markers. Though we cannot know for certain, it seems likely that despite the caricatured usage of such a phrase, there was some factual basis for such a distinction. Visual evidence from the period, which we will discuss shortly, certainly confirms that some people in the southeast engaged in such physical practices, so that it was not just some imagined trope of the savage.

Unlike *pifa*, *duanfa* seems to be used more frequently in association with the Yue peoples. Whereas *pifa* could be used to describe a host of supernatural beings or ethnic groups, "sheared hair" is used mostly in conjunction with "tattooing the body", and is closely linked to the Wuyue or Eastern Yi cultures. For example, a reference in the Han period text *Huainanzi* depicts the mighty Yue king, Goujian, as having cut his hair and tattooed his body:

> 越王勾踐劗髮文身，無皮弁搢笏之服，拘罷拒折之容，然而勝夫差於五湖，南面而霸天下.

> King Goujian of Yue cut his hair and tattooed his body; he did not have leather caps or jade belt ornaments; [he lacked] the postures of bowing and bending. Even so he defeated Fuchai at Five Lakes; facing south he was hegemon of the world.[30]

Since this passage is part of a larger argument for accepting the rituals and customs of various peoples of the world and placing them on par with each other, the author is careful not to proclaim a superior attitude towards King Goujian's appearance. Rather, further down in the same passage, he delimits and relativizes even Huaxia norms by specifying a bounded region where Huaxia rites and customs flourish: in the "states of Zou and Lu" 鄒魯.[31] In this instance, then, having cut hair, while a marker associated with Yue practice, helps the author argue for the equality of customs throughout the lands occupied by the great Han imperium.

Other legends speak of "shearing the hair and tattooing the body" instead of keeping the hair unbound and tattooing the body, as found in the legend of Wu Zixu. The story of the founding of the state of Wu by Wu Taibo 吳太伯, eldest son of Ji Gugong Danfu 姬古公亶甫, the grandfather of King Wen of the Zhou, depicts Taibo and his second brother's move to Wu in terms of their act of "shearing their hair, tattooing their bodies, and putting on the dress of the Yidi peoples" 斷髮文身，為夷狄之服.[32] This description, which dates to the Han, contradicts a passage in the *Zuozhuan* in which Taibo adhered to Zhou rituals while Zhongyong 仲雍, his younger brother and successor, adopted the Wuyue custom of shearing the hair, tattooing the body, and "using the naked body as decoration" 贏以為飾.[33] Regardless of whether Taibo himself engaged in such native practices, it is clear from both stories that the practice of shearing the hair and tattooing one's naked body go together as a physical package denoting Wuyue custom and the lack of Zhou ritual.

In some contexts, sheared hair signifies not only Yue customs and peoples, but also an entirely different religious complex that commands its own logic. Sheared hair and tattooing, some early authors claim, were apotropaic, ritualistic measures of warding off illness or harm. We see such attempts at explaining the practice in relatively late passages dating to the Han, such as the following passage in the *Hanshu*: "Ziyun, the son of Emperor Shaokang by a concubine, was enfeoffed at Guiji. He tattooed his body and sheared his hair so as to ward off harm from flood dragons" 帝少康之庶子云, 封於會稽, 文身斷髮, 以避蛟龍之害.[34] Here, the author justifies the cultural practice of tattooing and shearing the hair in terms of local religious belief, associated with the region of Guiji, around current-day Shaoxing, Zhejiang. Whether the apotropaic justification for such practices is based on fact, we do not know, but it suggests that the authors were going beyond surface appearances to try to explain an alternate world-view linked to a different culture, rather than merely differentiating oneself from the other based on physical appearance alone.

What is interesting about the bulk of references to shearing hair and tattooing the body in the received literature is that, unlike the more general and multivalent signifier of "unbound hair", these references describe an ethnic, and possibly religious, practice that is rather confined to a certain people and region. In addition, the appearances of the term "sheared hair", and the variant, "cut hair" (*zuan fa*), are much fewer than the appearances of "unbound hair" in the received literature.[35] Aside from a single reference each in the *Zuozhuan* and *Zhuangzi*, "sheared hair" occurs in texts that date from the Han period on. And the latter practice is more commonly associated with tattooing. In addition, when sheared hair is combined with tattooing, it provides a ready reference to the Yue, and not some other indication, like being a ghost, achieved human, primitive being, etc.

Recalling the *Zhuangzi* passage above, we note that it was not necessary for Zhuangzi to mention the practice of tattooing to make a point about how the Yue people do not need hats. His gratuitous use of tattooing suggests that when one wished to depict the Yue peoples, one needed only to conjure up the double description of tattooing and shearing one's hair, and one's point would be clear.

Given the real physical differences between sheared hair and unbound hair, why did authors sometimes use "sheared hair" and others use "unbound hair" to describe the Yue? We may be able to explain such a discrepancy by considering that most Huaxia authors of the Warring States and early imperial period may not ever have had first-hand experience with a person from Yue or the Hundred Yue, and that their use of either one of the hairstyle descriptions was simply a matter of picking up on popular clichés of the Yue other. Or perhaps, even if some of these authors had had personal experience with Yue people, they may only have known about one particular branch or subgroup of what might have been accepted as Yue at the time. It is not unthinkable that some Yue groups would have kept their hair unbound while others cut it short. A last explanation may be that Yue hair was both unbound and short. If the Yue had cut their hair only in the front, leaving the back "unbound" and "worn" — like a cape draping over one's shoulders — then it would not be incorrect describing Yue hair in at least two ways.

This leads us to the third type of hairstyle associated with Yue peoples and cultures: the mallet-shaped bun. The fact that this last style is also associated with the Yue almost seems to render the literary record incomprehensible. For one thing, a bun or knot of any sort on the head blatantly contradicts leaving one's hair loose, or unbound. Again, before we ponder the reasons why three seemingly incompatible descriptions of hairstyle are used to typify the Yue, let us at least come to grips with the basic scope of uses and meanings concerning the mallet-shaped bun.

Mallet-Shaped Bun (*Chuijie* 椎髻/魋結)

The mallet-shaped bun, *chuijie* 椎髻 (sometimes written using *chui* 魋 for 椎 and *jie* 結 for 髻), is interesting in that it occurs in spite of the other textual references, discussed above, to the Yue as having sheared or unbound hair.[36] Like the references to sheared hair, mentions of the mallet-shaped bun also appear to have been later, dating from the Han period on. The mallet-shaped hairdo is usually associated with the Yue or Hundred Yue as Southerners, but it is not limited to descriptions of the Yue. As with unbound hair, it could describe foreign peoples of numerous other geographic regions: the Northwest, the far Southwest, and the Shandong coastal areas and beyond, including the Korean peninsula and even tribes in Honshu, Japan.[37] It is worth exploring the spatial range of this description so that we might better gauge its usefulness as an apt description of the Yue peoples.

The first ruler of Chaoxian (a region on the Korean peninsula), Wei Man 衛滿 (Korean, Wiman), is described in both the *Shiji* and *Hanshu* as having, during a period of chaos and revolt, gathered together a force of over one thousand followers who "[adopted] the mallet-shaped bun and clothing of the Man Yi peoples" 魋結蠻夷服 and crossed over the then-Han border of the Yalu River to create a settlement.[38] In the *Nihon shoki*, there are two instances in which the mallet-shaped bun is mentioned to describe local or native customs: the first occurs in a description of a fierce people living in the eastern part of Honshu, dated (probably anachronistically) to Keikō 27:2 or AD 97. In such a location, the "males and females both wore a mallet-shaped buns and tattooed their bodies".[39] Intriguingly, this description fits descriptions of the Yue peoples most precisely, and one wonders whether the *Nihon shoki* was borrowing useful clichés from early Chinese histories to depict its own local natives, or whether there really were fierce peoples on Honshu who adopted some of the same physical habits of the Yue.[40] The second account, dating to Jingū 1:3. or AD 201, a date that covers a historically unverified period of Japanese history, narrates a story of subterfuge by a Yamoto general who was able to convene a so-called "peace parley" of local, rebellious tribes. The mallet-shaped hairstyle figures prominently in this story because the general's troops allegedly hid their bowstrings in their own mallet-shaped buns, while everyone else attended in peace with unstrung bows. The natives were thus tricked and slaughtered.[41] Yet another interesting passage from the *Shiji* tells of a certain refugee from Shandong, Cheng Zheng 程鄭,

who "smelted iron and sold it to the people with mallet-shaped buns" 亦冶鑄, 賈椎髻之民.[42]

Not only are peoples from the Shandong, Korean, and Japanese (Honshu) regions described in early texts as wearing the mallet-shaped hairdo, starting from the Han, this coiffure is sometimes linked explicitly with the Western Di of the northwestern regions. In the following statement appearing in the Han text, *Shuo yuan*, the speaker — a certain Lin Ji 林既 — tells Duke Jing of Qi 齊景公 (d. 490 BC) that famous ministers emerged from peripheral regions, despite their ostensibly backward or uncivilized customs: "In Yue, they tattoo their bodies and cut their hair short, yet the Minister Fan Li and Grandee Zhong came from there. The Western Di fasten their clothing on the left and wear mallet-shaped buns, yet You Yu came from there" 越文身剪髮, 范蠡大夫種出焉; 西戎左衽而椎結, 由余亦出焉.[43] This particular example is confounding because it seems to suggest that the Western Di, and specifically not the Yue, wore mallet-shaped buns. There seems to be a discrepancy in our sources about who might claim the mallet-shaped coiffure.

Since this is the first explicit mention of the Western Di wearing these buns, one might suspect that the author of the *Shuo yuan* passage is merely spouting cultural stereotypes without taking care to link them more accurately to reality. After all, the main purpose of this passage is not to convey vital or strategic information about peoples on the periphery, but to show that good ministers can emerge from any cultural background. However, there may be some truth to the notion that the Di fastened their garments on the left. In a passage from the *Analects*, mentioned above, Prime Minister Guan Zhong, through his victorious exploits against the Di, is said to have saved the Huaxia from having to wear their hair loose and button up on the left.[44] But notice that in the *Analects* passage the Di wear their hair loose, not in the mallet style, as in the *Shuo yuan* passage.

The *Shiji* and *Hanshu* also mention two other regions outside of the South in which the mallet-shaped bun was used: among the Xiongnu in the North, and in a so-called kingdom of Qiongdu 邛都 in the Southwest, just north of the major kingdom of Dian 滇. In this latter location, the people all "wore mallet-shaped buns, engaged in agriculture, and gathered in settlements" 此皆魋結, 耕田, 有邑聚.[45] In addition, an Eastern Han scholar,

Wang Chong, provides a list of places in the South and Southwest where people practise wearing such a coiffure, the content of which is consistent with the fact that so-called "Yue" peoples, among many others, may have sported such styles:

夏禹倮入吳國. 太伯採藥, 斷髮文身. 唐、虞國界, 吳為荒服, 越在九夷, 翦衣關頭, 今皆夏服, 褒衣履舄. 巴、蜀、越嶲、鬱林、日南、遼東, 樂浪, 周時被髮椎髻, 今戴皮弁; 周時重譯, 今吟詩書.⁴⁶

[The Great Yu] of the Xia entered the state of Wu naked. Taibo gathered medicinal herbs, cut his hair, and tattooed his body. At the limits of the world of Emperors [Tang] Yao and [Yu] Shun, the Wu peoples wore uncultivated clothing and the Yue were members of the Nine Yi Tribes, who wore felt garments and closed headgear [helmets?]. Now, they all dress like the Xia [peoples], wearing fine clothing and footwear. In Zhou times, peoples in the following regions *sheared their hair and wore a mallet-shaped bun* [italics mine]: Ba, Shu, Yuexi, Yulin, Rinan, Liaodong, and Yuelang.⁴⁷ Now, they don the leather, conical cap.⁴⁸ During the Zhou, one had to communicate by repeating and translating. Now, they all recite the *Odes* and *Documents*.

This passage is astonishing in more than one way. Not only does Wang Chong's statement link up Southerners and those from the Southwest (including Rinan, an area in what is now north-central Vietnam) with those from the Northeast (Liaodong), but it also connects the practice of "sheared hair" in the same breath with the practice of the "mallet-shaped bun". If Wang Chong is correct, then he helps us partly solve the riddle of the mallet-shaped bun: by Han times, both sheared hair and the mallet-shaped bun were hairstyles associated with the South and Southwestern Yue, Ba, and Shu peoples as well as with the natives inhabiting the Northeastern region of the mainland.

By far the most commonly mentioned story involving the mallet-shaped bun is linked to a familiar figure: King Zhao Tuo of the Southern Yue. The locus classicus for the story about the king's meeting with the Han envoy, Lu Jia, at the beginning of the Han period, appears to be the *Shiji*. In this famous story, Tuo greets his esteemed Han guest wearing the mallet-shaped bun and squatting or sitting in the "dust-pan style".⁴⁹ This story, repeated in texts from Han times on, comes to signify the act of "going native". One may note that passages that mention the mallet-shaped hairstyle generally do not combine such a hairstyle with the practice of tattooing the body (except for the example provided by the *Nihon shoki*, above).

That the mallet-style bun should be implicated in such an act makes sense in light of its ubiquitous proliferation as a descriptive marker of wild, native otherness. This is confirmed in a slightly later story, appearing in the *Lienü zhuan*, about the wife of Liang Hong 梁鴻妻. Liang Hong, a recluse of the Eastern Han period, after having refused numerous marriage proposals from powerful clans, finally chooses to marry a woman who presents herself to him "in coarse clothing, wearing a mallet-shaped bun" 乃更麄衣, 椎髻而前.[50] Even though we may assume that Liang and his wife are of Huaxia descent, the wearing of the mallet-shaped bun on the part of the future wife signals their unified wish to live in the wild as recluses.

Recently, the Chinese scholar, Peng Nian, has demonstrated that the mallet-shaped hairdo was not original to the Yue peoples, but that the ancestors of the Huaxia peoples also sported such a coiffure.[51] If so, then one might note the irony of the fact that, by the time of the Han Empire, this type of hairstyle had not only become uncommon among Huaxia peoples, but it had been transformed into a marker of foreign, primitive status, especially as a "Man Yi", but also as a Northerner or native of the Southwest. Given that the mallet-shaped bun was used to describe Man, Yi, and Di-type peoples, it seems less useful as a defining trait of the Yue, and more useful as a clichéd trope for anyone who has not adopted the refined, civilized ways of the Huaxia and Zhou cultures.

At this point we may question the reason why three seemingly different types of hairstyles were all used as a common shorthand for describing the Yue. Our analysis suggests that early Chinese authors may have mixed-and-matched their cultural stereotypes in an impressionistic way. If they were indeed employing a common trope with the sole purpose of designating "otherness", they would not need to pay heed to ethnographic reality. It is likely that many of our authors referred to the Yue with such an intent. However, given the distinctive nature of the physical marker of tattooing the body, which often accompanied the phrase "sheared hair", I find it likely that such indicators were based on some sort of ethnographic reality. It thus behooves us to consider alternate possibilities for why Central States authors could describe Yue hairstyles so differently.

Another explanation is that Central States authors properly described the alien Yue who were known to them but, by using the term "Yue", they encountered certain problems. No doubt, the ethnonym Yue pointed to a vast diversity of individual cultural and ethnic groups, each with their own practices and histories. As I have argued elsewhere, perhaps the Yue peoples were related linguistically, genetically, or in terms of material culture, but this does not preclude the fact that each subgroup may have had its own practices and religions, as reflected in such markers as hairstyle.[52] Central States authors, by pointing to but a single subgroup's habits as typical of the "Yue", may have thought that they were accurately describing all Yue when in fact they were only speaking about a certain type or subgroup of them. Thus, different authors, writing at different times and potentially denoting substantially different groups of Yue, are likely to have described the Yue in different ways. According to this logic, then, perhaps not all the Yue wore their hair loose; perhaps some of them cut it short, while still others adopted the mallet-shaped bun. Given the large gaps in chronology in our sources, it is also likely that different Yue groups altered their hairstyles at certain points in history, confusing the matter even further.

A recent encounter with an ancient image of a so-called "Yue" person at the Zhejiang Provincial Museum allowed me to realize that Wang Chong's seeming conflation of sheared hair and the mallet-shaped bun may have been correct, and that a single hairstyle may be described in both ways. In Figure 2.1, we see a kneeling man, supposedly from Yue, with tattoos all over his body. From this frontal view, the bangs are neatly cut, parted in the middle, and combed out of the face. Figure 2.2, the view from the side, shows us how the bottom layer of hair is cut short while the rest is pulled back into what seems to be a bun of some sort. In the photographs in Figure 2.3, from the same museum, we see a different Yue figure with tattoos and both sheared hair in the front and back, along with a bun in the centre back. Perhaps these depictions of the Yue are what authors had in mind when they specifically linked the Yue people to "sheared hair and tattooed bodies", as well as "sheared hair and mallet-shaped buns".

FIGURE 2.1
Tattooed, Seated Figure of a Person from Yue (Replica), Front View,
Zhejiang Provincial Museum 浙江省博物館 (Hangzhou, Zhejiang Province)

Source: Photo taken by the author, June 2010.

FIGURE 2.2
Tattooed, Seated Figure of a Person from Yue (Replica), Side View, Zhejiang Provincial Museum 浙江省博物館 (Hangzhou, Zhejiang Province)

Source: Photo taken by the author, June 2010.

FIGURE 2.3
A Picture of a Poster Depicting a Kneeling Yue Person, Zhejiang Provincial Museum 浙江省博物館 (Hangzhou, Zhejiang Province)

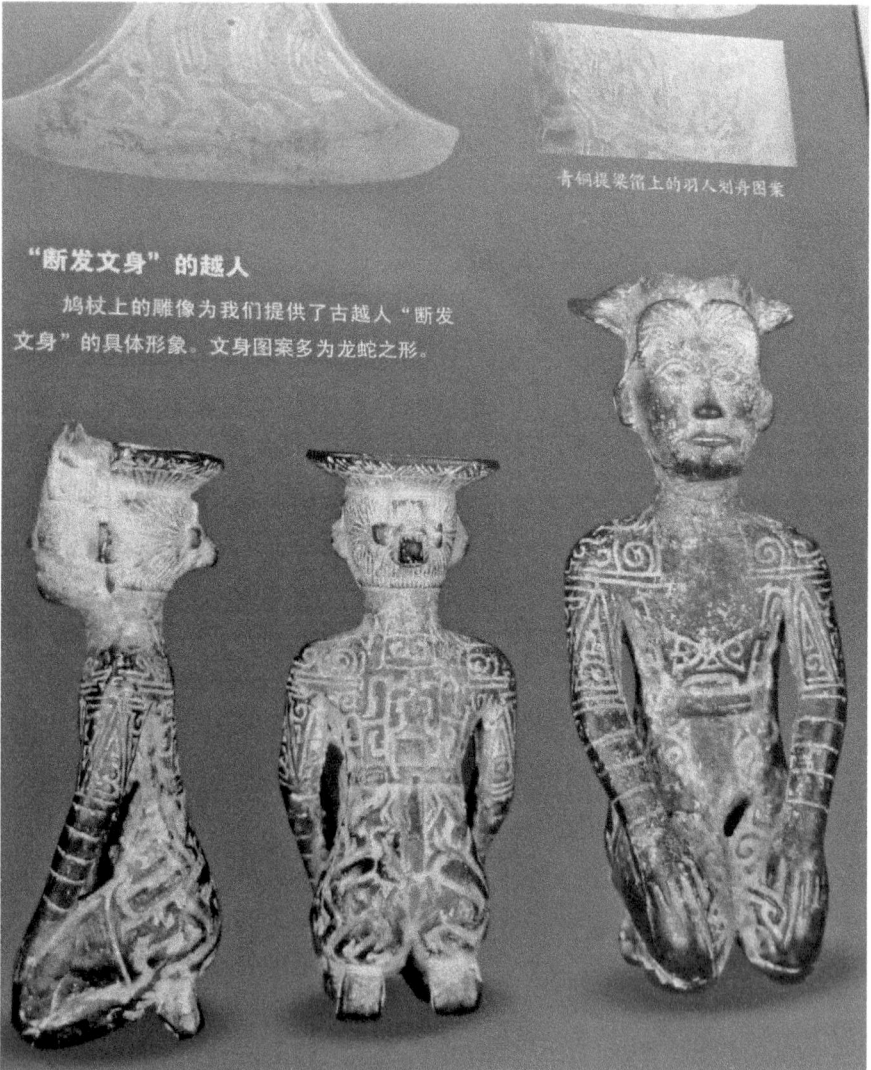

Source: Photo taken by the author, June 2010.

Conclusion

Textual descriptions of the Yue other are often taken at face value as "true", even though they have not been properly or critically vetted and may, in fact, reflect false or incomplete assumptions about the alien other. It is up to textual scholars to help gauge the level of realism, as opposed to rhetoric, fantasy, misinformation, or error, which may inhere in the descriptions of the peripheral other. While certainly every vantage point has its particular biases, there are some perspectives and statements that in fact do a better job at providing a realistic portrayal of the customs, appearances, and ways of the other.

It is also up to textual scholars to explore the broader interpretive contexts in which a given trope appears. In the case of the so-called Yue marker of "loose hair", we learn of the many cultural meanings associated with keeping one's hair unbound, such as the suggestion of numinosity, insanity, youth, purity of the spirit, or proximity to nature or truth. By placing unbound hair into a broader cultural context of meaning, we see how notions of the Yue other might be informed by the above-mentioned values in addition to a sense of alterity, baseness, and that which is uncivilized and primitive.

Some of the hairstyles that are allegedly unique to the Yue turn out not to be so unique at all. The mallet-shaped hairstyle, in particular, seems to have provided authors with a pervasive and easy marker of a person's position as an alien outsider, and therefore it serves nicely as an example of the trope of the savage. Its appearance in the Zhao Tuo story from the *Shiji*, therefore, compels us to reconsider Sima Qian's (or the narrator's) connection to the Yue peoples of the South, shedding doubt upon the veracity of the story that later comes to epitomize what it means for a northerner to have "gone native" in Yue style.

If one takes a sweeping look at the ways in which Sinitic authors describe outsiders throughout Chinese history, one might generally state that as authors came into increased contact with others on the periphery, their descriptions of the other became more precise and accurate, even though biases and rhetorical formulae may still be found. In the specific case of Yue hairstyles examined here, the inconsistencies and stereotypical ways in which the Yue are described all suggest that Central States authors may not have possessed very good or accurate knowledge about the Yue other. Alternatively, it may have been the case that Warring States and early imperial authors possessed accurate information of the other, but that they were still not interested, for some reason, in outlining Yue difference in any detail beyond the simplistic stereotypes concerning hair and tattooing. This latter explanation does not preclude the likelihood that while Central States authors may have been ethnographically accurate in their simplistic descriptions of the Yue, their lack of any kind of deep and sustained encounter with them would have rendered them incapable of penetrating beyond the superficial layers of appearance to understand more minute differences among various subgroups, or the reasons and beliefs that underlay certain practices.

We may therefore safely conclude that the authors — who usually represent the elite culture in the Warring States and early imperial periods — did not possess much substantial knowledge concerning the Yue other. Given the lack of meaningful ethnographic writings on the Yue other, it is likely that cross-cultural encounters and communications between Central States elite and the Yue other were few and far between. We should therefore approach passages that describe the Yue during this period with a critical eye, accepting the likely case that much of what is written contains fantasy and imaginative bias rather than deep knowledge and understanding of the Yue. This does not mean that the literary record is useless, for, as this chapter shows, its lack of depth seems to betray vital information about early Central States and Yue contact. But it does mean that in order to better understand the Yue of this early period, we must try to amass as many types of information as possible (textual, archaeological, linguistic, and genetic), approaching each with a critical stance.

NOTES

1. Mark Lewis, *The Construction of Space in Early China* (Albany: State University of New York Press, 2006), pp. 69–71. See also Alf Hiltebeitel and Barbara Miller, eds., *Hair: Its Power and Meaning in Asian Cultures* (Albany: State University of New York, 1998).
2. Lewis, op. cit., p. 70.
3. For a discussion of nomenclatures for southern peoples associated with the Yue, as well as a brief overview of who may have inhabited the Southlands in

ancient China, see Erica Brindley, "Representations and Uses of Yue 越 Identity Along the Southern Frontier of the Han, ~200–111 B.C.E.", *Early China* 33–34 (2010–11): 1–35.

4. Lothar von Falkenhausen, "The Waning of the Bronze Age", in *The Cambridge History of Early China: From the Origins of Civilization to 221 BC*, edited by Michael Loewe and Edward L. Shaughnessy (Cambridge: Cambridge University Press, 1999), p. 526.

5. See William G. Boltz, "Language and Writing", in Loewe and Shaughnessy, p. 83.

6. See Brindley, pp. 7–13, for more information on this terminology.

7. I am thankful to Gopal Suku for this suggestion. Informal conversation, Columbia University Seminar, 12 May 2012.

8. *Lunyu* 論語 [Analects], 14.17.

9. It is noteworthy that in this passage, the Man — who may very well have been considered to be a type of Yue by some — are not noted for their hairstyle.

10. Sun Xidan 孫希旦, ed., *Liji jijie* 禮記集解 [Collected Explanations of the *Liji*] (Beijing: Zhonghua shuju, 1989), Wangzhi 王制, p. 359.

11. Mark Lewis, *The Flood Myths of Early China* (Albany: State University of New York Press, 2006), p. 89.

12. Wu Zixu (d. ~484 BC) was a noble and famous advisor in the state of Wu who vowed to take vengeance on the state of Chu for wrongly executing his father. His story was immortalized in many different accounts in early Chinese history.

13. *Shuo yuan* 說苑 [Garden of Sayings], Juan 12, Fengshi 奉使.

14. Yang Bojun 楊伯峻, ed., *Mengzi yizhu* [Translation and Commentary to the *Mencius*] (Hong Kong: Zhonghua shuju, Hong Kong branch, 1984), Lilou xia 離婁下, 8.29, p. 199.

15. Lewis, *The Flood Myths of Early China*, p. 89.

16. *Shuo yuan*, Juan 8, Zunxian 尊賢 (also in *Hanshi waizhuan* 韓詩外傳 [Commentary to the Han Version of the Odes], Juan 7, *Dadai Liji* 大戴禮記, Bao fu 保傅 and *Chuci* [Songs of Chu], Xishi 惜誓).

17. *Wuyue chunqiu* 吳越春秋 [The Spring and Autumn Annals of the States of Wu and Yue], 王僚使公自光傳. Contrast this with the depiction in the *Yuejueshu* 越絕書 [Book on the Glory of the Yue] of Wu Zixu going to Wu and "walking barefoot and wearing his hair unbound" 徒跣被髮, 乞於吳市. *Yuejueshu*, Jingping wang neizhuan 荊平王內傳. For Fan Li wearing unbound hair and feigning madness, see *Yuejueshu*, Waizhuan Ji Fanbo 外傳記范伯, and *Yuejueshu*, Pianxu Waizhuan ji 篇敘外傳記.

18. John Makeham, *Balanced Discourses: A Bilingual Edition* (New Haven: Yale University Press, 2002), Yaoshou 夭壽, p. 202.

19. Guo Qingfan 郭慶藩, ed., *Zhuangzi jishi* 莊子集釋 [Collected Interpretations on the *Zhuangzi*] (Taipei: Wanjuan lou, 1993), 19, Dasheng 達生, p. 656.

20. Ibid., 26, Waiwu 外物, p. 933.

21. *Zuozhuan* 左傳 [The Zuo Commentary on the *Spring and Autumn Annals*], Cheng Gong 成公, year 10. Another apparition with unbound hair appears in a story featured in Ai Gong 哀公, year 17.

22. In particular, see *Shanhaijing* 山海經 [Classic of Mountains and Seas], Haiwai xijing 海外西經.

23. *Shuowen jiezi* 說文解字 [Explaining Single-Component Graphs and Analyzing Compound Characters], under the entry for "*qiu*" 叴.

24. Guo Qingfan, 21, *Tianzifang* 田子方, p. 711.

25. Sima Qian 司馬遷, *Shiji* 史記 [Records of the Grand Historian] (Beijing: Zhonghua shuju, 1992), Juan 127, Rizhe liezhuan 日者列傳, p. 3217.

26. *Wenzi* 文子 [The Wenzi], Shangli 上禮. For a detailed account of the received *Wenzi* and the newly excavated version of it, see Paul van Els, "The *Wenzi*: Creation and Manipulation of a Chinese Philosophical Text", PhD dissertation, Leiden University, 2006.

27. *Han Feizi* 韓非子 [The Han Feizi], ed. Wang Xianshen 王先慎; *Han Feizi jijie* 韓非子集解 [Collected Explanations of the *Han Feizi*] (Beijing: Zhonghua shuju, 1998), Nan er 難二, p. 363.

28. Guo Qingfan, 1, Xiaoyao you 逍遙遊, p. 31. A very similar type of anecdote appears in the *Han Feizi*, Shuolin shang 說林上, in which a shoe and hat maker (husband-wife pair) moved to the state of Yue and became poor, since people went barefoot and "wore their hair unbound" (*pifa*). Indeed, nobody had any need for hats or shoes.

29. It is worth noting that even though Yue attains such a status, it never seems to gain acceptance in our sources as one of the "Central States". Indeed, it is unclear which states historically may have formally belonged to such a category, if there was ever a formal way of belonging to such a grouping.

30. Although the exact phrase used here, *zuanfa wenshen* 劗髮文身, differs slightly from what we have been analysing so far, most commentators believe the verb *zuan* 劗 to be but another (perhaps Southern) way of saying "to cut". *Huainan honglie jijie* 淮南鴻烈集解 [Collected Explanations of the *Huainan honglie*], vol. 1, Qisu xun 齊俗訓, 11 (Beijing: Zhonghua publishing, 1989), p. 355. Translation adapted from John S. Major et al., *The Huainanzi: A Guide to the Theory and Practice of Government in Early Han China* (New York: Columbia University Press, 2010), p. 407. Note that the translators of this latter text interpret *zuanfa* 劗髮 as "to shave the head", but I have found no evidence from the commentaries mentioned in the *Hanyü dacidian* 漢語大詞典 [Comprehensive Chinese Dictionary] (Shanghai: Shanghai cishu chubanshe, 1995) that this is the case. Indeed, it also makes more sense with the historical record (all the citations of "sheared hair" in association with Yue) if we imagined short-haired Yue people, rather than bald ones. *Hanyü dacidian*, vol. 2, p. 758.

31. *Huainan honglie jijie*, pp. 355–56. Translation from Major et al., p. 407.

32. *Wuyue chunqiu*, Wu Taibo zhuan 吳太伯傳. The reference to Yidi 夷狄 peoples seems to be a general reference to Yi-barbarians. Since the text dates to the Han period, it is likely that the distinctions between the Yi and Di peoples — originally two distinct groups from two different directions, East and North — were collapsed, and that such a term referred more generally to barbarians.

33. *Zuozhuan*, Ai Gong, year 7, p. 1641.

34. Ban Gu 班固, *Hanshu* 漢書 [History of the Han], Juan 28, Dili zhi xia 地理志下 (Beijing: Zhonghua Publishing, 1995), p. 1669. I am taking *jiaolong* 蛟龍 as a compound referring to one type of dragon, not two. Hugh Clark has pointed out that the reference to *jiao* 蛟 (or *jiaolong*), unlike the *long* 龍 (dragon), was always considered to be maleficent, and that it was usually associated with the far South. At least by later times (Tang and Song), the *jiao* is used in conjunction with the crocodile, so that it may actually have referred to the crocodile in early times as well. Private communication with Hugh Clark, August 2012.

35. The phrase, *zuanfa*, only occurs about twice in the entire pre-Qin and Han corpus: once in the *Huainanzi*, as mentioned here, and once in the *Hanshu*, each with reference to the Yue. The verb, *zuan*, is rare and occurs only four times in total during my search through the pre-Qin and Han corpus. Three of those occurrences are from the *Huainanzi*, where it refers to cutting hair or fur.

36. *Chui* 魋 appears to be a phonetic loan for 椎. It means "bear". *Chui* 椎, on the other hand, refers to a hammer, mallet, or even vertebra. To my mind, none of the translators who use the phrase "mallet-shaped" to describe this hairstyle can confirm with any certainty that the shape is indeed that of a mallet. It may have pointed to braids that resembled the vertebrae or spine of animals. Given our inability to match up this hairstyle with a confirmed pictorial representation, I will use the phrase, "mallet-shaped", as a convenient translation.

37. I am grateful to Jonathan Best for taking an interest in this hairstyle and pointing out various instances in which the phrase "mallet-shaped topknot" was used to describe natives of the Yalu River region and Honshu, Japan. I mention those instances below.

38. Sima Qian, Juan 115, Chaoxian liezhuan 朝鮮列傳, p. 2985, and Ban Gu, Juan 95, Xinanyi yu Chaoxian zhuan 西南夷兩粤朝鮮傳, p. 3863.

39. See *Nihon shoki* 日本書紀 [Chronicles of Japan], 7.297 行 18, in Sakamoto Tarō et al., comp., *Nihon koten bungaku taikei* 日本古典文學大系 [Compendium of Classical Japanese Literature] (Tokyo: Iwanami Shoten, 1965–67), and also William G. Aston, trans., *Nihongi: Chronicles of Japan from the Earliest Times to AD 697*, vol. 1 (London: George Allen and Unwin, 1896), p. 200. I am grateful to Jonathan Best for providing these citations involving Korea and Japan.

40. As Jonathan Best points out, the eighteenth-century scholar Motoori Norinaga was unsettled by the way in which the *Nihon shoki* seemed to borrow descriptive passages from Chinese historical accounts and apply them to things Japanese. I do not know whether this is an instance of considerable borrowing.

41. See *Nihon shoki* 9.347 行 14, and Aston, *Nihongi*, p. 239.

42. Sima Qian, Juan 129, Huozhi liezhuan 貨殖傳, p. 3278.

43. *Shuo yuan*, Juan 11, Shanshuo 善說.

44. *Lunyu*, 14.17.

45. Sima Qian, Juan 116, *Xinanyi liezhuan* 西南夷列傳, p. 2991. For the practice among Xiongnu, see Ban Gu, Juan 54, *Li Guang Su Jian zhuan* 李廣蘇建傳, p. 1458, where the statement reads: "the two people, dressed in the costume of the Hu and wearing mallet-shaped buns" 兩人皆胡服椎結.

46. Huang Hui 黃暉, ed. *Lunheng jiaoshi* 論衡校釋 (Edited Interpretations of the *Lunheng*, or *Critical Essays*, by Wang Chong 王充, Hui guo 恢國 [Restoring the State]), p. 832.

47. All of these locations, with the exception of Liaodong (near the Korean peninsula), are situated in the far southwest of the mainland, including areas in modern-day Vietnam, and areas in Yunnan, Sichuan, Guizhou, and Guangxi provinces.

48. A type of cap worn during Zhou times.

49. *Shi ji*, Li Sheng, Lu Jia Liezhuan 酈生陸賈列傳, p. 2697.

50. *Lienü zhuan jiaozhu* 列女傳校注 [Collected Commentaries on the Collected Life Stories of Women], 梁鴻妻.

51. Peng Nian 彭年, "'*Shu fa chui ji' fei Nanyu zhi su — jian lun shu fa zhi su de qi yuan ji qi ta*" "束髮椎髻" 非南越之俗 — 兼論束髮之俗的起源及其他 [Hair Worn Up in a Bun Was Not the Southern Yue People's Custom], *Zhongyang minzu daxue xuebao* [Journal of the Central University for Nationalities] 中央民族大學學報 6 (2001): 6.

52. See Erica Brindley, "Barbarians or not? Ethnicity and Changing Conceptions of the Ancient Yue (Viet) Peoples (~400–50 B.C.)", *Asia Major* 16, no. 1 (2003): 1–32.

3

SINICIZATION AND BARBARIZATION
Ancient State Formation at the Southern Edge of Sinitic Civilization

Nam C. Kim

Introduction

Past researchers have traditionally viewed ancient Southeast Asia as having been influenced by a virtually unidirectional flow of culture and civilization. Prior to the mid-1960s, many researchers explained the development of large-scale, complex societies (e.g., kingdoms and states) in Southeast Asia by pointing to influence from the more "advanced" civilizations of ancient India and China, citing the transmission of advanced technology and political models by diffusion, migration, or simple military and cultural imposition.[1] Traditional perspectives from the early twentieth century viewed Southeast Asian societies as derivatives of Indian and Chinese counterparts. Intensified archaeological research efforts in recent decades throughout much of the region, however, have increasingly shown these sorts of positions to be untenable, demonstrating a model of unidirectional influence to be overly simplistic. To be sure, communities all over Southeast Asia were in either direct or indirect contact with one another and counterparts in India and China. But the countries of "China", "India", and Vietnam of today did not exist at 2000 BP, and the wider region was home to a kaleidoscope of societies. Modes of interaction and resultant social changes were complex, multilateral, and multidirectional. Societies were engaged in significant forms of interaction that included extensive long-distance trade, the movement of peoples and ideas, and cycles of peaceful relations and warfare.

This situation of complex interactions is evident throughout much of Southeast Asia, and the area of modern-day northern Vietnam is no exception. In this paper, I examine the important cultural frontier that existed between emerging Sinitic and proto-Vietnamese civilizations during the closing centuries BC, focusing specifically on archaeological evidence from the Red River Delta. To reconstruct cultural developments for the area's pre- and proto-history, a combination of textual and archaeological sources are crucial for understanding amorphous cultural boundaries and changing patterns of sociopolitical and economic interactions. During the first centuries BC and AD, the Han Empire began annexing the Red River Delta, as related by historical accounts and other traditions. At the time, a number of important cultural changes were taking place in the adjacent areas of modern-day southern China and northern Vietnam. The foundations for Sinitic and proto-Vietnamese civilizations were being established and much of the formative developments were tied not only to local, cultural trajectories but also to an emergent system of burgeoning maritime and riverine trade. It must be noted, of course, that this frontier area was not home to "Vietnamese" or "Chinese" populations at that time, ethnic identities that were to emerge centuries later and then retrospectively applied.[2] "It is thus only from the time of Đại Việt's political independence in the tenth century that a more definable boundary began to develop that finally resembled something akin to our modern concepts of Chinese and Vietnamese."[3]

Recent archaeological research has complemented our understanding of this crucial, protohistorical period on the eve of Han annexation, revealing a multifaceted picture of interregional interaction combined with local developments, trends that had a mutual impact on various communities of this area. Along the southernmost fringes of an emerging Sinitic world, beyond the mountains and the Lingnan region, the Red River Delta witnessed the florescence of the Cổ Loa 古螺 polity (c.300 BC) centred at the Cổ Loa site, an early example of ancient statehood and urbanism during the closing centuries BC (see Figure 3.1).

FIGURE 3.1

Current Satellite Image of the Cổ Loa Site, with the Three Rampart Enclosures still intact in Various States of Disrepair

Note the location of the 2007–8 Cổ Loa Middle Wall and Ditch Project excavations adjacent to the North Gate of the Middle Wall.

Source: Image adapted from Google Earth.

Though this ancient state emerged without direct imposition of "civilization" from the north, the material evidence does suggest some degree of emulation. Certain elements in the construction process of the city exhibit signs of Sinitic culture, and rulers were likely employing leadership strategies that appropriated ideological symbols and models of authority from the north. These appeals to distant and exotic forms of power were likely important, legitimizing components in the consolidation of centralized power.

Importantly, much like interactions between Sinitic and non-Sinitic societies along frontier areas in the north and west, these frontier relationships were marked by reciprocal influence, not a unidirectional flow of Sinitic "civilization". "Barbarian" others were active agents in selectively co-opting aspects of Sinitic culture, and the appropriation of such elements were tied to local, indigenous political strategies. Accordingly, I also explore the manner in which multidirectional, interregional interactions and cultural contact resulted in tremendous sociopolitical changes in ancient northern Vietnam and in Han society, demonstrating parallel processes of Sinicization and what I would consider its antithesis, namely "barbarization".

At the Edge of Empire

Pre- and Protohistory of the Red River Valley

Located just beyond the southern fringes of an emergent Sinitic imperial power, the Iron Age Đông Sơn Culture communities of the third century BC of the Bắc Bộ region, or what is today northern Vietnam, were part of continuous, local cultural developments with roots extending far back into prehistory.[4] As a crossroads for exchange and migration between developing Sinitic civilization and various Southeast Asian societies to the south, the Bắc Bộ region functioned as a doorway and hub of interaction during the second half of the first millennium BC, leading into the annexation of the area by the Western Han during the first centuries BC and AD. What did the Han encounter as they began to encroach into this region?

For many in Vietnam today, Đông Sơn society is seen as a foundational civilization for proto-Vietnamese cultural identity. Sophisticated forms of metalworking and agricultural intensification were underway during this crucial period, with clear archaeological signs of emergent social stratification, inequality, and social complexity. The Đông Sơn Culture was first recognized on the basis of excavations at the cemetery and settlement of Đông Sơn (in what is today north-central Vietnam), and the culture is renowned for its giant ceremonial bronze drums, which were lavishly decorated with ritual and battle scenes.[5] To date, over one hundred Đông Sơn Culture sites have been identified throughout northern Vietnam. Prehistory in contemporary Vietnam is powerfully present, and images of the tympani from the bronze drums and the decorations they bear are ubiquitous, adorning posters, postcards, advertisements, book covers, and many other everyday items.[6]

An important archaeological settlement for this period is the monumental, urban site of Cổ Loa, located in the Red River plain near modern-day Hanoi. The massive scale and nature of Cổ Loa, whose monumental system of fortification features still dominates the landscape today covering some 500–600 ha of territory, indicates significant complexity and consolidated authority. One example of the Đông Sơn drums was found within the site of Cổ Loa, containing a hoard of bronze farming tools and weapons.[7] As the largest settlement suspected to date to the Đông Sơn period, Cổ Loa has long been the centre of legend and commemoration. Today, a national festival is held at Cổ Loa annually to venerate the site and its semi-legendary history. Cổ Loa has been the subject of tremendous scholarly debate, as historians and archaeologists both in Vietnam and abroad continue to offer speculations and interpretations regarding Cổ Loa's chronology and cultural identity. Were the site's fortifications indigenously constructed, or was a foreign civilization responsible? Specifically, does the construction of the site occur before or after Han conquest? A variety of evidentiary sources have been studied and invoked in proposing interpretations for the massive site.

In reconstructing Cổ Loa's early history, there are three principal sources of information, namely the Vietnamese tradition (which claims to come to some extent from oral histories), Chinese Han textual accounts, and the material record. Until recent decades, historians have relied on descriptions recorded by Vietnamese and Chinese writers to reconstruct the early Iron Age of Vietnam. A major problem with this approach, however, is that these two sources offer somewhat conflicting depictions of cultural development in Bắc Bộ. To complicate the matter, traditional views on the origins of Vietnamese civilization were affected by archaeological work performed by the French and other foreign nationals during the French colonial period.

Overall, the traditional perspective saw a powerful, technologically advanced and numerous Sinitic force descending upon the Red River peoples, more or less swallowing them whole.[8] According to textual accounts, the Han Empire began colonizing the Bắc Bộ region at approximately 111 BC, and Chinese historical records, such as the *Shiji* written by Sima Qian (*c.*145 to 90 BC), are valuable sources for early proto-Vietnamese history, as much of our information on early Vietnam is from the biographies of Chinese officials who served in Vietnam during the period of Chinese colonization and domination.[9] However, and not surprisingly, such Sinocentric texts maintain that agricultural, metallurgical, and political sophistication emerged among the local "barbarians" in Bắc Bộ mainly because of imperial annexation.[10] Viewed from the Han capital, the Đông Sơn people were the most distant of several groups known as the southern barbarians (or "Hundred Yue").[11] These views held that the area of what is now northern Vietnam had a "primitive" level of culture at the time of Chinese annexation with its ascribed date of 111 BC.[12] Partly because of these textual descriptions, some European researchers examining the Đông Sơn bronze drums found during the first half of the twentieth century concluded that they must have dated from the Han colonization period, with casting knowledge being introduced to local, Red River Delta societies by the Han.[13] For instance, the pioneer French Sinologist Henri Maspero offered speculation on early Vietnamese history and in a treatment detailing Han General Ma Yuan's invasion of Bắc Bộ in AD 42–43, Maspero writes that it marked a fundamental milestone in the history of the country, introducing Chinese ideas and social organization, giving the Vietnamese a cohesion and formal structure.[14] Overall, these traditional views deny *in situ* any indigenous cultural development, maintaining that sophistication, in terms of agricultural methods, metallurgical technologies, and governance structures, occurred only after Han colonization.

These Sinocentric views stand in contrast with Vietnamese traditions that indicate considerable social complexity and political centralization in the Bắc Bộ region well before Chinese arrival.[15] More recent research over the past few decades has begun to frame an argument that upon their arrival, the Chinese encountered a stable, structured, productive, populous, and relatively sophisticated society of whose existence they had some knowledge, if not an appreciation.[16] According to what some have argued are Vietnamese oral traditions, ancient kingdoms such as the Văn Lang 文郎 and the Âu Lạc 甌駱 existed during this Đông Sơn period, hinting at the possibility of pre-Han, local complex societies.[17] Cổ Loa purportedly functioned as the capital of the Âu Lạc kingdom during the third century BC.[18] Researchers have long debated the accuracy of these semi-legendary accounts.

Some historians believe that the Đông Sơn civilization rested upon a foundation raised by earlier cultures in northern Vietnam during the preceding millennium and a half, and that the archaeological remains of that culture are echoed by mythological traditions that form the core of Vietnamese identity to this day.[19] The legendary and semi-legendary traditions were recorded in the *Lĩnh Nam chích quái liệt truyện* 嶺南摭怪列傳, the *Đại Việt sử ký toàn thư* 大越史記全書, the *Việt Điện u linh tập* 越甸幽靈集, and the *Việt sử lược* 越史略 during the late medieval period.[20] Overall, these traditions hold that Bắc Bộ was the nucleus of indigenously developed Vietnamese civilization with powerful kingdoms ruling over vast populations before Chinese arrival.[21]

According to these accounts, the Vietnamese Hùng Kings (Hùng vương 雄王) ruled a series of polities known collectively as the Văn Lang Kingdom from approximately 2800–258 BC,[22] although some researchers suggest that if the Văn Lang Kingdom did indeed exist, it more likely commenced much later in time, perhaps near the seventh century BC.[23] In either case, according to Vietnamese traditions, Văn Lang was ruled by a hierarchical government consisting of the Lạc king, the marquises, the under-kings, and the Lạc people.[24] The people worked in the paddy fields and controlled river flooding. The difficulty with the accounts concerning the Văn Lang Kingdom is the absence of unequivocal material remains to substantiate its existence. However, with the polity that ostensibly succeeds the Văn Lang, the situation is quite different. A significant level of political hierarchy and control for the Red River Delta was purportedly inherited by the subsequent Âu Lạc Kingdom.

Keith Taylor suggests the term "Lạc" (meaning "ditch" or "canal") is the earliest recorded name for the Vietnamese or proto-Vietnamese people.[25] It certainly would seem appropriate that the emergence of the Âu Lạc Kingdom coincided with a greater degree of centralized power required to control the waters of the Red River Delta, and it is possible that the Lạc nobility were elite members of Đông Sơn societies in the Red River plain. In addition to flood control, elites of the Đông Sơn era appear to have controlled labour for agricultural intensification and craft production. The evidence for the Đông Sơn phase suggests the existence of a stratified society, perhaps under the rule of a single state centred on Cổ Loa if we are to believe traditional history.[26]

At approximately 258 BC, a man named An Dương Vương 安陽王 (also known as Thục Phán 蜀泮) purportedly overthrew the last of the Hùng Kings of Văn Lang and established the Âu Lạc polity, and our knowledge of this kingdom is based on a mixture of legend and history.[27] An Dương Vương is the first figure in Vietnamese history documented by somewhat reliable historic sources, but most of what we know about his reign has survived in legendary form.[28] Choosing Cổ Loa as his capital, he proceeded to construct a fortified citadel known to history as Cổ Loa Thành 古螺城 ("Old Snail City"), thus named because its walls were laid out in concentric rings reminiscent of a snail shell.[29]

In sum, the Vietnamese traditions hold that, by the third century BC, Cổ Loa already possessed the various fortifications still visible today, including walls, towers, moats and ramparts enclosing approximately 600 ha of territory.[30] This is centuries before the Han fully consolidated their colonial control of the region, which did not occur until the arrival of Han general Ma Yuan to quell the Trưng Sisters' Rebellion in AD 43, thus incorporating local Đông Sơn warrior-aristocrats as an imperial province.[31] Given the conflicting accounts regarding the Âu Lạc and the arrival of Han, it is little wonder that debates about Cổ Loa's founding and construction have gone unresolved.

Compounding the situation are textual records that also chronicle the overthrow of the Âu Lạc Kingdom by Zhao Tuo (known in Vietnamese as Triệu Đà), a former official of the Qin dynasty, who brought the area under the rule of his Southern Yue (Chn., Nanyue; Việt, Nam Việt 南越) Kingdom, while allowing the traditional Lạc aristocracy to remain intact with its royal court at Cổ Loa.[32] The Southern Yue period purportedly occurs during the second century BC and is seen as something of an anti-Han political period[33], although there is evidence to suggest that Southern Yue-Han relations were quite complicated.[34] As mentioned, the Lạc lords would only be fully dispossessed when they were subdued by Han soldiers in AD 43.[35] Though the Vietnamese traditions describe the fall of Âu Lạc to the Southern Yue polity, O'Harrow points out that caution is necessary when considering the validity of these accounts, as there are no solid grounds for accepting that any "Chinese" or "proto-Chinese" polity was actually in control of northern Vietnam during the second or first centuries BC.[36] Currently, conclusive material remains distinctive of the Zhao polity have yet to be found in northern Vietnam.[37]

Potential Challenges and Biases

Without doubt, the traditional sources of information available to reconstruct the early history of Vietnamese culture and civilization within the Red River area are not without potential challenges and biases. First and foremost, we can readily imagine that some degree of imperial and ethnocentric bias colours the textual accounts from Sinitic sources. It is quite common for conquerors to depict their targets of annexation in unflattering terms, thereby justifying various invasions, occupations, and seizures as they occur. On the other side of the coin, the Vietnamese traditions must also be critically examined for several reasons. First, there are appeals to the supernatural or magical qualities indicating that even if there is any historical validity regarding people and events, we are still dealing with the cusp of history. Additionally, much of these narratives were not officially recorded until the thirteenth or fourteenth centuries, and portions may have been based on earlier Chinese texts.[38] Although these narratives can offer clues about the nature of lifeways, cultural practices, and societies during this crucial time period, we have to be cognizant of potential historiographical challenges. As noted by researchers like Haydon Cherry, these texts tell us what later Vietnamese and Chinese scholars thought occurred in this early period in Vietnamese history and cannot be considered primary sources, and the only true sources of information for this period are prehistoric material remains, such as bronze drums, weapons, tools, ornaments, household items, among others.[39] For other scholars, like Liam Kelley, some of the content within the texts as related to the Hung kings may even represent "invented traditions", potentially manufactured in the medieval era as a means for Vietnamese elites to articulate a distinct identity.[40] However, as noted by Taylor, even invented traditions seldom come from acts of pure imagination.[41] To be sure, we have no solid evidence that the societies extant in the Red River plain during the Đông Sơn Culture period were ethnically similar to later Vietnamese-speaking populations in the region during the first and second millennia. Indeed, some researchers propose that the emergence of recognizable "Vietnamese" culture, and language, does not occur until the first few centuries of independence from Sinitic colonial rule, rather than in a distant pre-Sinitic era.[42]

The above-mentioned challenges notwithstanding, we can still use these traditional sources as a starting point, complementing historical analysis with archaeological research in ways that Stephen O'Harrow called for decades ago.[43] Kelley notes that, despite historiographical challenges, the existence of Red River Delta polities in the first millennium BC is supported by the presence of bronze drums and other artifacts.[44] To this I would add archaeological sites and their architectural features, such as Cổ Loa. Although Vietnamese traditions hold that An Dương Vương overthrew the Văn Lang Kingdom, and that his Âu Lạc polity constructed Cổ Loa and its fortifications, this claim may never be fully substantiated. What the material data can do, however, is describe the timing and development process of sociopolitical complexity as exhibited at the Cổ Loa site, thereby either lending support for or refuting existing claims. "Even good ideas need a receptive real-life context to be influential."[45] Archaeological investigations and datasets can help provide a starting point for the resolution of these ongoing debates, and to move our understanding into unchartered areas of inquiry. Given the hazy and sometimes conflicting nature of oral and textual accounts, the material record is vital for furthering our understanding of Cổ Loa's history and social evolution. We can confidently point to the existence of a "Cổ Loa polity", while offering this archaeological case as a starting point to speculate about the foundations of a Vietnamese culture, however tenuous the connection to later Vietnamese/Red River civilization.

O'Harrow points out that the archaeological dating for the structures at Cổ Loa is imperative for understanding this grey area on the outer edges of history.[46] Until recently, the chronology for the society responsible for Cổ Loa's construction was under question. Recent investigations, with findings summarized below, have yielded information that clearly suggests a pre-Han construction chronology.

Recent Archaeological Investigations At Cổ Loa

Today, aerial photographs, satellite imagery, and on-the-ground surveys show that much of Cổ Loa's set of three earthen wall enclosures still remains standing and intact. The settlement was surrounded by at least three ramparts used as defence, these being two outer enclosures ("Outer and Middle Walls") and an inner, rectangular one ("Inner Wall"). Each enclosure was associated with moats and ditches, and the inner enclosure had bastions as well as moats. From surface survey alone, it is difficult to judge if the current dimensions of the enclosures match those from several centuries or several millennia ago. More importantly, without material data it is not possible to establish the identity of the site's builders, and whether or not more than one polity or society was responsible for constructing different portions of the fortification features. Only careful excavation and stratigraphic analysis can furnish the data necessary to make that type of determination, and to ascertain whether or not there may have been multiple phases or efforts of rebuilding, refurbishment, and amplification.

In recent years, a collaborative archaeological project was undertaken by a joint American and Vietnamese team to investigate Cổ Loa.[47] In 2007 and 2008, the Cổ Loa Middle Wall and Ditch Project investigated a portion of an earthen rampart and its ditch to gather cultural and chronological evidence (see Figure 3.2). This constituted the first large-scale, systematic excavation of any of Cổ Loa's monumental fortification features. One of the chief aims of the Cổ Loa Middle Wall and Ditch Project was to provide just such information.

FIGURE 3.2
Photograph of 2007–8 Excavation Location. Excavation Area of 2007–8 Cổ Loa Middle Wall and Ditch Project, Looking Southward

Source: Photo taken by the author.

Regarding the earthen rampart curtains, the Middle and Outer Walls are irregularly shaped enclosures, measuring 6.5 and 8 km in circumference, respectively.[48] The Outer Wall encompasses approximately 500–600 hectares of territory, making Cổ Loa one of the largest, if not the largest, prehistoric settlements in Southeast Asia. I suspect the irregular shapes of the Middle and Outer Walls stem from the natural topography and environment, and that natural hilltops may have been connected in forming the rampart enclosures. This is not all that dissimilar from practices seen elsewhere with other prehistoric Southeast Asian moated settlements on much smaller scales. The Inner Wall is roughly rectangular in shape and measures approximately 1.65 km around its perimeter.[49] In some places, the ramparts stand up to 10 m in height and 25–30 wide at the base.

In the area of excavation at the north gate of the Middle Wall, the rampart's final surviving form was approximately 4.3 m in height and 26 m wide at the base with tiered levels on both exterior faces. The larger part of the earth used to construct the rampart came directly from the ditch at its exterior face, confirmed by stratigraphic analyses and auger core testing.[50] Clearly visible within the rampart's stratigraphy were several construction sequences that employed varied building techniques, including simple piled earth along with forms of stamped earth. Overall, the layers of construction deposits were grouped into three main chronological periods (Period 1: Early, Period 2: Middle, and Period 3: Late) based on major construction episodes, with several phases of building (see Figure 3.3). These major construction events were identified through a combination stratigraphic analysis, *in situ* artifacts, and a suite of radiocarbon and thermoluminescence determinations, with Phase 1 falling within the Early Period, Phases 2–4 corresponding to the Middle Period, and Phase 5 occurring within the Late Period.[51]

Quite unexpectedly, a smaller set of suspected fortification features was discovered buried beneath the rampart, and these are designated as the Early Period, Phase 1, construction. This smaller set of features was interpreted as being constructed by a different, smaller-scale society predating the polity responsible for the larger rampart. The set of features consisted of a small wall of clay, a series of ditches, and an earthen platform with remains of structure sitting atop it. Đông Sơn culture sherds were recovered in association with the features, along with wood

FIGURE 3.3

Phases and Chronological Periods of Construction

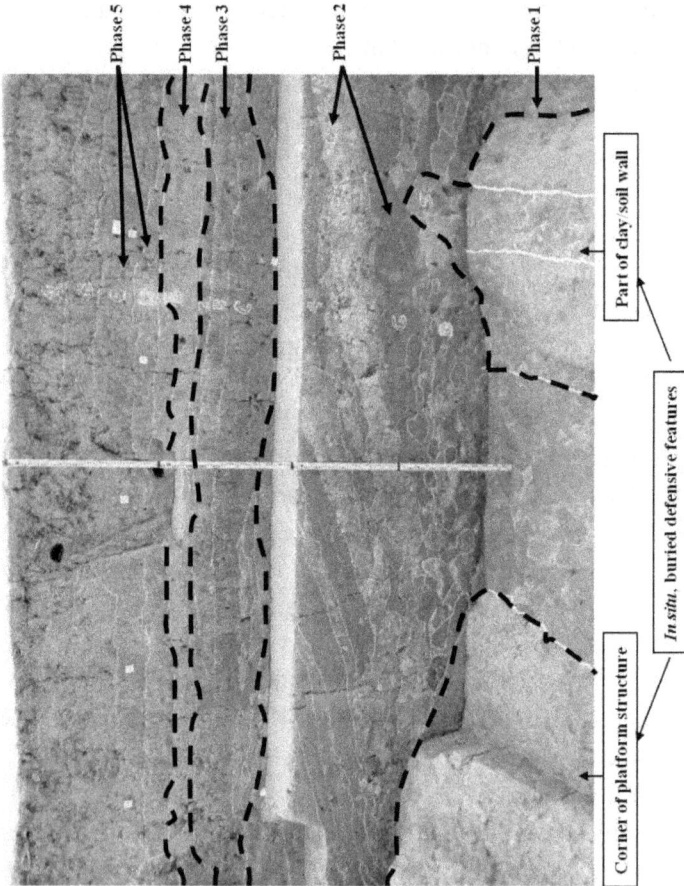

The five phases and three periods of construction seen in the west section:

1. Phase 1, Period 1 features the fourth century BC or later (Early Period);
2. Phase 2 construction of piled earth (Middle Period);
3. Phase 3 construction of thick rammed/stamped earth (Middle Period);
4. Phase 4 construction of earth with roof tiles (Middle Period). Phases 2–4 belong to Period 2 (Middle Period), dated to the third century BC or later. Finally, sequences of thin rammed/stamped earth can be seen above the roof tiles in Phase 5 (Late Period), which may date to the Han or later historical periods.

Source: Photo taken by the author.

charcoal that yielded radiocarbon dates of approximately the fifth to fourth centuries BC.[52]

The monumental earthen rampart and its ditch are part of the Middle and Late Periods, and the Middle Period portion makes up the bulk of the construction. The radiometric and stratigraphic data strongly indicate the majority of the rampart (Middle Period: Phases 2–4) was constructed without significant interruption. Ten wood charcoal samples from Phases 2 through 4 were analysed for radiocarbon dating, offering an approximate range of 300–100 Cal BC for the important Middle Period. There was an absence of any discernible layers of natural deposition or prolonged surficial exposure that would be expected had there been large temporal gaps between phases. Above Phase 4, construction methods and artifacts show that the upper layers of the rampart correspond to the Late Period (Phase 5), and were likely carried out by a different society or political entity as part of a refurbishment episode or set of events.

Rampart construction began with a foundation of soil dug out from the area of the ditch, wherein clumps of soil were dug up, transported, and deposited to create a flat surface. The initial layers of deposition consisted of what appears to be topsoil from rice paddy fields. Significantly, this implies intensified rice farming was well underway within the Cổ Loa area prior to the construction of the rampart. The rampart's construction (Phase 2) probably commenced sometime during the late fourth or early third century BC. Above this foundational layer, additional earthen material was deposited in an organized fashion, resulting in a mounded feature. Most of the artifacts for this Middle Period, consisting of ceramic roof tiles and stones, were recovered from within the Phase 4 sequence at approximately 1 m below the extant rampart surface (see Figure 3.4). These roof tiles and stones are part of the royal or elite-level material remains of the Cổ Loa Culture, similar to the materials found in 2004–5 excavations of the Inner Wall area.[53] Materials related to the Cổ Loa Culture are found only within the expanse of the Cổ Loa site, whereas artifacts of the roughly contemporaneous Đông Sơn culture have been recovered throughout the Bắc Bộ region in various contexts. Because of this key distinction, I refer to the Middle Period (*c*.300–100 BC) as the Cổ Loa Culture Period. Additionally, it is also noteworthy that the roof tiles are stylistically similar to Han period counterparts, a point to which I will return in a later section.

FIGURE 3.4
Photographs of Cổ Loa Roof Tiles Uncovered during Middle Wall Excavation

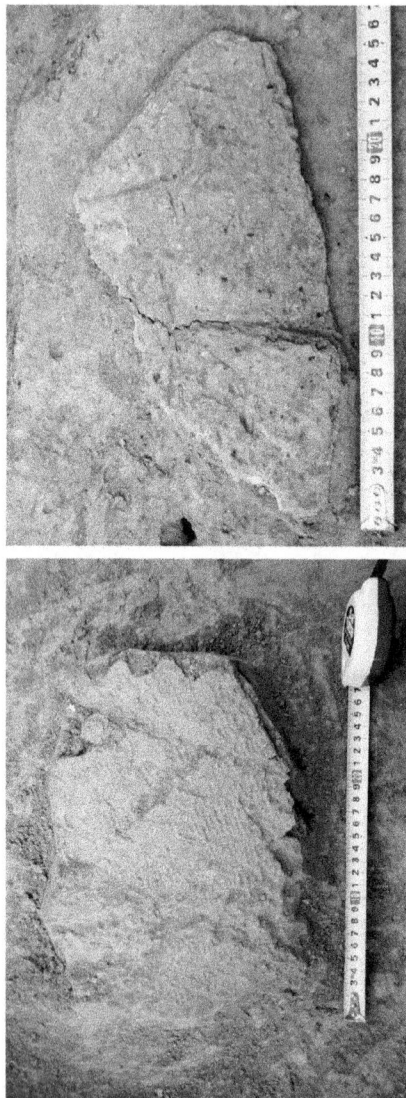

TABLE 3.1
Rampart Construction Chronology, Phases, and Dimensions

Period	Phase	Construction	Max. Height	Width	Date
1 (Early)	1	Clay wall and platform	1 m +	1.8 m	c.500–300 BC
2 (Middle)	2	Dumped earth	2 m	17 m	c.300–100 BC
2 (Middle)	3	Thick stamped earth	2.5 m	24 m	c.300–100 BC
2 (Middle)	4	Dumped earth	3 m	24–25 m	c.300–100 BC
3 (Late)	5	Thin stamped earth	4 m	26 m	Post–100 BC / Historic
3 (Late)	5	Thin stamped earth	4 m	26 m	Second millennium AD?

Several radiocarbon dates secured from wood charcoal samples found with the artifacts within the Phase 4 layer yielded an approximate range of late third century to mid-second century BC (see Table 3.1). Furthermore, thermoluminescence analysis of the roof tiles provided a similar range.[54] Significantly, although excavation was only performed at this one portion of the enclosure system, surveys indicate the roof tiles are located along the entire length of both the Middle and Outer Walls, within the same stratigraphic layer. Surveys at collapsed areas of the ramparts reveal the presence of this artifact class, suggesting a strong possibility that much of the information found at the Middle Wall could be applicable for the entire rampart system. It is clear the majority of the rampart predates Han Chinese colonization. However, there is evidence to suggest affinities and interaction with emergent Chinese civilization, as will be discussed later.

Implications of Excavation Data

For the peripheral areas to the south of incipient Chinese civilization, it was only during the early Eastern Han period that the presence of the Han began to be felt. While it remains unclear the degree to which the Han may have implemented "a new policy of Sinicisation....

with the hope of altering local customs and rendering the native population more amenable to Chinese control",[55] it at least appears that a loosely imposed Han tribute was replaced by more direct efforts to extract resources from the region.[56] An examination of the various Chinese textual accounts and Vietnamese traditions shows nuanced differences in perspective and possible bias, suggesting that not all of the information can be accepted wholesale and uncritically. There are still many questions to be answered regarding the Cổ Loa site. For instance, how accurate are accounts regarding the Southern Yue (or Nam Việt) overthrow of an Âu Lạc Kingdom? I would hesitate to accept the occurrence of such an overthrow as historical fact without further evidence, though it seems reasonable to infer the coexistence of both polities given the evidence for state-level power and complexity in Bắc Bộ. Furthermore, rather than use the moniker of "Âu Lạc", my preference would be to refer to the entity responsible for the construction of Cổ Loa as the "Cổ Loa polity". In addition, given narratives about the Southern Yue or Nam Việt polity, it is possible that a post-Cổ Loa period involving the historical figure of Zhao Tuo was also somehow involved in part of the pre-Han history of the Cổ Loa site. For the time being, though, the archaeological evidence shows continuity of Đông Sơn Culture throughout the region, and no clear signs of the Nanyue or Zhao polity.[57] It is only during the first century BC that a Han Chinese presence becomes archaeologically visible. For instance, at the major Đông Sơn site of Thieu Duong (Thanh Hoa Province), eighteen graves were discovered, of which ten date to the late Western Han (c.50 BC–AD 1) and are larger than Đông Sơn counterparts. Future field investigations are necessary to further elucidate the close of the Cổ Loa period and a connection with the Nanyue polity.

Early Indigenous Urbanism and Political Complexity

Several decades ago, Robert Winzeler commented that the "first evidence of urbanization and state formation in Southeast Asia does not appear before the first centuries of the Christian era, and that which does occur initially is commonly attributed, rightly or wrongly, to outside influence".[58] Smaller and sparser population densities were cited as a possible reason for the absence of significant political development towards statehood, seeing instead small, fragmented, and transient supralocal political entities.[59] Similarly, Paul Wheatley argues that even if valid, the Vietnamese traditions regarding first millennium BC Red River societies refer to chiefdoms and not true states, owing to a lack of urbanism.[60] Collectively, these sorts of perspectives see an absence of local or indigenous trajectories of urbanism and state-like political authority for Southeast Asia in general, and northern Vietnam in particular, prior to the first millennium AD. This general position may have been tenable many decades ago given deficiencies in reliable archaeological data to argue otherwise, but this is no longer the case today.

Early civilization in the Red River Valley has tremendous potential to contribute to the theoretical literature on ancient complexity, state formation, and urban genesis.[61] Pre-Han, local trajectories towards greater levels of complexity were well underway during the first millennium BC in northern Vietnam. I have argued elsewhere that a state-level society had emerged by the third century BC, with tremendous control over resources, wealth, and labor, as materially manifested by the Cổ Loa site.[62]

Cổ Loa is emblematic of an early form of urbanism for mainland Southeast Asia, one marked by monumental constructions of earthworks and hydraulic systems. A major characteristic shared by many of early historic and medieval cities of mainland Southeast Asia is water management, and several sites such as Angkor, Beikthano, and Nakhom Pathom, generally exhibit a concern over water control and a very sophisticated understanding of engineering requirements. This is not surprising given the monsoonal rain patterns, especially in lowland and floodplain areas that result in alternating stretches of high and low precipitation. In Cambodia, the power of the Khmer empire (*c.* eighth to sixteenth centuries AD) was based on expertise in water management,[63] with settlements such as Angkor categorized as "hydraulic" cities.[64] These elaborate systems of water management did not emerge overnight, and their roots can be found in antecedent settlement forms throughout the region. The first millennium BC material record reveals a general pattern of early analogues, designs, and experimentations located in parts of Cambodia, Laos, Myanmar, Thailand, and Vietnam.

In the continuum of developing Southeast Asian urbanism, with sites like Angkor situated closer to a more modern terminus, Cổ Loa's brand of urbanism sits at a transitional mid-point along a historical trajectory from the smaller moated sites of the Iron Age to the large hydraulic cities of the medieval period.[65] For the early Iron Age, Cổ Loa is the largest of a collection of peer settlements within a tradition marked by water management and large-scale earthworks, signalling a trend toward more elaborate forms of urbanism and political complexity that would follow during the early historic period. Some researchers like Miksic see Cổ Loa as an early form of urbanism for Southeast Asia,[66] though more data are still required to further clarify its kind of urbanism.

Of course, more research is necessary to see if analogous forms of moated settlements were also prevalent within parts of first millennium BC southern China. Despite a connection to earlier moated sites in Southeast Asia, we cannot entirely rule out a connection with societies to the north. I would argue that Cổ Loa's form of urbanism was born not only out of a Southeast Asian tradition, but was perhaps influenced by societies within parts of emergent Chinese civilization. In examining incipient urbanism in parts of China, von Falkenhausen notes that the Warring States Period also corresponds to an advanced stage (c.600–221 BC) of urbanism in the core area of the early royal dynasties, namely the Yellow, Huai, and Middle Yangzi River basins and the Shandong peninsula.[67] It is likely that such developments over the mountains to the north could have played a role in affecting lifeways in the Cổ Loa area.

In sum, I argue that the formation of a proto-Vietnamese state was attributable to a combination of both local, internal factors, and external influence. Southeast Asian Neolithic and Metal Age communities did not exist in a vacuum, and the material record clearly shows a tremendous degree of cultural interaction, exchange, and movement throughout the region. The evidence demonstrates that interregional interaction stimulated cultural change, fostering multidirectional influence and emulation, perhaps within some form of a peer polity model.[68] This occurred in conjunction with internal factors and local trends, including agricultural intensification, population growth and nucleation, and the use of leadership strategies related to competition and coercion. At the risk of oversimplification, these variables combined to result in momentous cultural change and growing social differentiation during the Metal Age, as political power, high status, legitimacy and wealth were concentrated into the hands of a select few.

Interregional Interaction and Emulation

The modern national boundaries for China and Vietnam did not exist two to three thousand years ago, and for much of the Neolithic and Metal Age periods, the landscape and geographic terrain would have constituted the only major challenge against the open movement of people, materials, and innovations between regions. Charles Higham argues that the prehistory of each of the two regions should be considered as one, and that despite deeply rooted differences in cultural traditions, there has been for tens of millennia a high degree of unity for the entire area.[69]

Cổ Loa's geographic milieu within the wider Red River plain can provide tremendous insight for cultural development of Imperial China's southern frontier as it was home to a long history of interaction between two cultural worlds. The roots of this interchange are archaeologically visible even earlier than the first millennium BC. Material data clearly show the circulation of people, goods, and ideas between parts of what are now southern/southwestern China and northern Vietnam, particularly along coastal and riverine routes, starting from the late Neolithic (*c.*2500 BC) and intensifying over time.[70] Interregional interaction likely contributed to concurrent and reciprocal processes of increasing sociopolitical complexity in areas that were at the time likely inhabited by a kaleidoscope of cultural groups not distinctly Sinitic or Vietnamese. The flow of bronze-casting technologies and related prestige goods within Yunnan and Bắc Bộ communities, for instance, occurred concomitantly with innovations in agricultural production, growing sophistication in military tactics, population growth, and asymmetries of wealth. Of tremendous significance was the circulation of products and raw materials related to an emergent bronze industry, ultimately connecting these regions to other societies further afield through trade and exchange. Because of its strategic location along the Red River, Bắc Bộ's elites were able to accumulate considerable wealth and political currency through the exchange of bronze prestige goods within an interregional trade network.[71]

Bronze working throughout Southeast Asia appears to have had a significant correlation with the rise of ranked societies, and weapons, vessels and ornaments of metal were probably exchanged between regional elites for purposes of alliance and intermarriage.[72] One class of artifacts that indicates this sort of effect pertains to the renowned bronze drums of the Iron Age, which may have functioned as high-status luxury goods. They have been recovered from scattered localities across Cambodia and Thailand, and down into the Malay portion of the peninsula. These items likely arrived by sea to enter long-established exchange routes along the rivers.[73] By the early Common Era, the massive bronze drums spread rapidly down the length of Indonesia, particularly along the islands of the Sunda Chain and ultimately as far east as the Bird's Head of New Guinea.[74]

There is also evidence to suggest that knowledge of, and contact with, Sinitic forms of leadership and authority may have affected local decisions and leadership strategies, especially during the crucial Đông Sơn period when political consolidation occurs. It is possible that Đông Sơn community elites and aspiring leaders may have utilized a strategy of emulation, one in which appeals were made to exotic and distant forms of political authority.[75] Such exotic forms could have been used to supersede the local and traditional (i.e., Đông Sơn) symbols of authority. Consequently, the Cổ Loa polity and settlement potentially represents an interesting case of hybridity, with Cổ Loa Culture showing affinities with both Southeast Asian and "Chinese" traditions. Overall, the methods and styles of construction at Cổ Loa not only demonstrate continuation of a Southeast Asian tradition, but also signs of a northern influence. This should not be surprising given Cổ Loa's geographic position near the coast and as a sort of hub between nascent Chinese civilization and Southeast Asian communities. The appropriation of material symbols of authority and leadership institutions can be seen in certain forms of evidence.

As mentioned, the Phase 3 construction of the rampart involved a stamped earth technique. This technique bears some resemblance to the *hangtu* 夯土 method of rammed earth construction seen in parts of

Neolithic and Metal Age China. The *hangtu* method was often used to construct walls and building foundations at sites of the Longshan (*c*.3000–1800 BC) and Shang (*c*.1600–1046 BC) cultures.[76] Although the use of stamped earth for construction projects is not unique to China, its presence at Cổ Loa suggests the possibility of emulation. A northern affinity can also be discerned with the Cổ Loa roof tiles, which are stylistically comparable to Han styles of roof tile design, though they are marked by designs unique to the local area. Beyond emulation, some researchers suggest the possibility that local Đông Sơn leaders may have even had access to Sinitic military advisors,[77] though this scenario is currently difficult to demonstrate archaeologically. At the very least, I propose that local, indigenous rulers appropriated symbols and methods of leadership as part of a larger strategy to consolidate power and maintain it, reconstituting them with local cultural and political meanings.

This form of emulation need not be direct, as appeals to distant forms of authority and power may have been part of "down-the-line" imitation where practices and materials were adopted with an understanding of the power they held. Such a phenomenon, for instance, can be seen with the spread of Shang traditions of oracle bone divination throughout East Asia.[78] In this case, a "down-the-line" form of emulation could have seen the use of certain symbols or materials or practices that have come to take on specific meanings, whose original political and cultural contexts may be unfamiliar to the current users. Hence, contact is indirect and may be separated by both space and time.

In addressing Han relations with native Koreans, Hyung Il Pai maintains that a combination of indigenous regional traditions combined with an incoming Han culture to catalyze complexity.[79] The local, political landscape was affected by an increasing demand for Han prestige goods and weapons.[80] Natives on the Korean Peninsula were not passive recipients of incoming Han cultural traditions, but instead played an active role in initiating exchange for their own benefit.[81] Elsewhere, Alice Yao explores the ways in which objects from Han China and the northern Black Sea were used by both nomads and imperial agents in conceptualizing foreign objects through metonymic and metaphoric associations to influence self and group identities.[82]

Bronson notes that models for political regeneration can occur given any contemporary polities (perhaps even belonging to enemies).[83] Perhaps such a model can at least partially explain the emulation seen at Cổ Loa, with appeals being made to Sinitic elements of rulership, authority, and politico-religious ideology. That this occurs towards the end of the Warring States period and not earlier is also interesting, as it suggests that the significant events to the north leading to a unified Qin state may have been known to Đông Sơn leaders. It is possible that the monumental fortification system at Cổ Loa was both inspired by, and erected as a response to, the growing power and potential threat to the north. Elsewhere in the world, there are other examples of distinct societies with clear evidence of shared notions of political ideology and symbolism. In South Asia during the third and second centuries BC, the Mauryan polity was marked by what may have been competitive emulation, a situation in which various societies were not politically linked to the Ganges plain but may have shared social, ritual, or cultural ties.[84] Perhaps the appropriation of Sinitic leadership symbols by Cổ Loa rulers constitutes some form of competitive emulation as well.

Finally, beyond the appropriation of symbols of authority, one might point out the possibility of what I would call "urban emulation". As noted earlier, the use of embankments and moats for controlling water is quite prevalent throughout Southeast Asia. However, the size and scale of the Cổ Loa settlement is unlike any other peer sites within the region. I suspect that the trend toward urban genesis seen in the Red River Delta would have been partly influenced by the trajectory towards more complex forms of urbanism to the north associated with emerging Chinese civilization. What we see at Cổ Loa may reflect this form of hybridity, with authority and power resting on a combination of existing Đông Sơn models and symbols of political authority and foreign elements. Brindley contends that the history of the Yue kingdoms during the Han period is one of Han imperial conquest and incorporation, as well as a gradual, cultural and political encroachment upon local ruling elites and communities in the southern regions.[85] I concur, and would take this assertion a step further. Political elites of the Red River Delta had already begun a process of emulation and appropriation centuries before Han annexation.

Implications for Han Society and Identity — "Barbarization"

In discussing Iron Age colonial interactions of Europe, Tronchetti and van Dommelen argue that colonial practices do not follow predictable pathways where colonial and indigenous cultures are "blended" or replaced.[86] Instead, the dialectic of the colonial encounter altered all parties involved, even if to different degrees. I propose that a roughly analogous development marked interactions between the Đông Sơn and Han worlds. Bắc Bộ's Iron Age archaeological record can illuminate how such cultural and imperial expansion had an impact not only on the indigenous communities of the Bắc Bộ region, but also in a reciprocal manner on Chinese society, both in the frontier areas and also closer to the Han centre. Such bidirectional forms of acculturation can be assessed from clues in the archaeological record textual sources.

Gleaning clues from the textual record of the Han-Tang period in northern Vietnam (*c.*111 BC–AD 938), Churchman states that there is no static dichotomy between ethnic or linguistic concepts of Chinese and Vietnamese, but rather there appears to be more of a fluid distinction between people who were civilized "subjects" and vaguely "barbaric" people who were not completely absorbed into the imperial administrative system.[87] The processes of Sinification or Sinicization are unsatisfactory in that they only describe a one-way process of change from "barbarian" to "Chinese" when the opposite process was also clearly at work.[88]

Archaeologically speaking, the records for areas to the south of the Han heartland make clear that a unidirectional model of influence and emulation, even after the imposition of imperial control, does not accurately reflect reality. For instance, Han tombs in Guangdong have yielded artifacts indicating cultural exchange with areas even further to the south, in parts of Southeast Asia.[89] These cultural materials include models of pile dwellings and ceramic models of boats with a distinct Southeast Asian affinity. Nevertheless, Francis Allard argues that the presence of these exotic materials does not equate with a rejection of Han practices.[90] Rather, the material record of the Lingnan area indicates cultural diversity, one born from a combination of Han imperial culture, local traditions, and influence from the south, all converging to impact lifeways, identities, and cultural patterns.

In northern Vietnam, an emerging Han-Việt class of elites demonstrates a blending of cultural practice and identity as reflected by the material record. As noted by Taylor, this class consisted of Han immigrants who had begun to take on aspects of local life, which included intermarriage with local Vietnamese families. In this sense, after the first or second generation, Han immigrants had effectively begun to be "Vietnamized".[91] The Han tightened control over Bắc Bộ following the Trung Sisters' uprising in AD 43, with the direct imposition of imperial control. According to historical records, Han construction of citadels commenced at this point, and remains can be seen at sites such as Luy Lâu in the Bắc Ninh province.[92] By the second and third centuries AD, Eastern Han cultural elements began to blend with local Đông Sơn practices, and elite Han and Han-Việt graves began to appear, such as the Han-style brick tombs (see Figure 3.5). Đông Sơn artifacts, including drums, continued to be used and adopted into Han-style surroundings, and Han wooden compartment burials first appear in the latter part of the first century AD, later replaced by brick tombs c.AD 100.[93]

Regarding Sinitic perceptions of the indigenous neighbours to the south, Erica Brindley specifically explores the writings of Han authors.[94] Her research asks if the Han considered the Hundred Yue to be different but more-or-less on equal footing, or if they viewed them as sub-humans — as "barbarians" — in relationship to themselves. "Written in Chinese by members of the educated class, these sources hint at an intricate history of ethnic relations in the South, and they speak rather frankly of southern kingdoms and various types of peoples, languages, customs, and origins."[95] As noted by Brindley, the use of the term Yue is a projection of the "other" as it reflects notions of Han self-identity. She points out the likelihood that reference points for the Hundred Yue during the first century AD had already changed dramatically since the late Warring States and early Han eras. By the first century AD, the lands of Yue were thought to cover extremely great distances, suggesting that the category of Yue had become a category for peoples and places situated almost anywhere in the entire southern portion of modern-day China, including northern Vietnam. Further, Sima Qian imparts a more nuanced judgement upon the ethnic other, conveying the sense that, though they might not always demonstrate it, Yue peoples at least had the potential to act in a

FIGURE 3.5

Photograph of a Han Brick Tomb Found in the Bắc Ninh Province of Northern Vietnam

Source: Courtesy of Trinh Hoang Hiep, Vietnam Institute of Archaeology.

civilized manner. Accordingly, the Yue are not demonized barbarians as much as they are generally less civilized. According to Brindley, Sima Qian's presentation of the Yue is more nuanced than suggested by a simple dichotomy of "civilized" versus "barbarian". Though he denigrates the Yue by calling them "southern barbarians", he counterbalances such descriptions by offering evidence for the honour of Yue ancestry and certain of its individual members. Interestingly, Sima Qian recognizes a mythical kinship between Han and Yue peoples in his vision of ethnicity. Overall, it is clear from Brindley's research that the picture is not black and white. Within Han society there were varied perspectives on what constituted "otherness", despite the labels of "Yue" and "barbarian" being applied to various communities.

Archaeological research has shown that frontier regions cannot be seen as passive recipients of core innovations; rather, these areas ought to be reconceptualized as zones of cross-cutting social networks and relationships.[96] Most traditional studies of frontiers have tended to perceive group boundaries as a dichotomist relationship between colonial and indigenous populations, and this perspective does not always accurately reflect complexities of interactions from different temporal and spatial scales.[97] Nuanced approaches at varying scales are vital, not unlike what Brindley's analysis seems to suggest. Her work outlines a changing perspective on the "other" as reflected in Chinese textual accounts.

Why does this shift in perspective towards the "outsider" or "other" happen, with a more complicated and nuanced view emerging at the time of Sima Qian's writings? I suspect one reason for this would be the growing diversity of the imperial realm of the Han. As seen in many cases worldwide, ancient empires tend to encompass a high degree of ethnic and cultural diversity. The cumulative incorporation of others into the folds of Han society necessitated a re-evaluation of barbarians, shifting them from a strictly sub-human category into one of distant kinfolk who could be "civilized" to one degree or another. Moreover, a realization that imperial rule through outright conquest was infeasible for much of the southern peripheral areas may have led to a reappraisal of imperial strategy. Rather than attempting to utterly subjugate the southern barbarians through military force only, it may have appeared far more prudent to absorb them into Han civilization. This in turn would have meant that certain imperial administrators and elites of Han society living in these fringe areas would have had to accept local elites as near equals, taking on elements of local customs and traditions as their own.

Ironically, the Red River plain was actually peripheral to the geographical region where "Yue" or "Southern Yue" was most commonly applied.[98] What might have motivated Han leadership to expand so far to the south, moving into areas that proved difficult to bring into a sphere of political control? Among a number of reasons, I would like to highlight two important possibilities. First, it would seem that certain segments of Han society were motivated by what Mark Lewis refers to as a "cult of exotics".[99] Both nomadic and sedentary peoples, with the latter proving to be less of a military threat, ringed Han China. The motivation to expand into areas like the far south came in part from a desire to obtain exotic and rare goods. Some within the early Han court became interested in southwestern areas of China (i.e., Yunnan) because of reports of possible trade with the far south (i.e., northern Vietnam). To quote Lewis, "The Han obsession with rare objects from distant places originated in the idea that the ruler's power was measured by his ability to attract people and their products to his court."[100] The more exotic a product, the more potent a ruler's power could become. Moreover, Lewis argues that the prestige of the exotic also figured in religion in that points of contact between people and spirits lay at the edges of the earth.[101] It was in these peripheral locales that extraordinary and exotic forms of life and materials were situated. Consequently, from its origins in political and religious life, the cult of exotics spread from Han elite to commoner, with foreign objects permeating every level of society.

A second motivation for expansion into the far southern periphery would have been because expansionary campaigns of this sort clearly identified an "other". Having an "other" in peripheral areas necessitated both physical power and militarized frontiers, in order to maintain a stable centre. Han authors juxtaposed Han identity against the preceding Qin identity, seeing the latter as cruel, coercive, and not unlike the "barbarian" other.[102] Positioning Han identity in contrast with the previous regime was one way to legitimize the new political authority. Over time, Han identity may have required the presence of other forms of the barbarian other in order to promote its own internal cohesion. Thus, movement into the outlying frontiers, including the far south, may have offered a mechanism to do so. Of course, as the exotic lands of the southern barbarians came increasingly under Han control, a clear dichotomy between Han versus "other" became progressively blurred. From this perspective, it seems that Han society was mutually impacted by its interactions with the far south, with degrees of barbarization resulting that were more intense in the Red River Valley and gradually less so towards the north. In this manner, then, the Cổ Loa case can offer insights into how interactions with non-Sinitic populations affected Sinitic societies and their own self-perceptions and self-identification.

Such peripheral relationships, whether with communities of the Xiongnu, the Dian, the Đông Sơn, or native societies on the Korean Peninsula, could have all had an important effect on society and culture in the Central Plain. In a recent cross-regional examination of ancient intercultural exchange, Yao discusses how the Han imperial court interacted with neighbouring societies along silk routes to the west, exploring the ways in which foreign objects "provided a domain from which local peoples attempted to objectify different logics using metaphoric and metonymic frameworks of reasoning".[103] In Yao's argument, the foreign attributes provide the means for an appraisal of existing local values, and are not meaningful simply because they reference concepts about the "other". In that respect, foreign attributes are much more powerful.[104] In sum, I argue that not only should researchers move away from strictly unidirectional models of Sinicization, but perhaps we ought to also consider the ways in which a reverse process of acculturation may have been occurring as well, a "barbarization" of Sinitic elements of identity, and civilization. Ultimately, the complex forms of interactions engendered in these frontier areas are multifaceted, evolving over time in lockstep with changes in regimes and leadership strategies.

Conclusion

By the closing centuries BC, the Bắc Bộ region saw the florescence of an urbanized, state-level society, as manifested at the site of Cổ Loa. Recent field investigations suggest the site was constructed well before

Han annexation, and Cổ Loa can be seen as a forerunner for later forms of urbanism in mainland Southeast Asia. Established by the third century BC, this politically centralized society predates some of its historically known, regional counterparts. Moreover, the case of the Cổ Loa polity generally refutes traditional, unidirectional models explaining the emergence of chiefdoms, kingdoms, statelets, and other forms of complex societies in Southeast Asia that privilege external influences from neighbouring Indian and Chinese civilizations. Essentially, this case indicates that Southeast Asian social complexity was not simply a by-product or derivative of foreign influence. That being said, these traditional models are not entirely unfounded. For instance, northern Vietnam's Neolithic and Metal Age communities did not exist in a vacuum, and the material record clearly shows a tremendous degree of cultural interaction, exchange, and movement throughout the region.

Accordingly, a more accurate assessment of first millennium BC cultural developments in the wider region recognizes a complex process of reciprocal social change, one in which influence was multidirectional and mutual, not unidirectional. For instance, the material data clearly suggest that a peer-polity form of interaction likely contributed to emergent social ranking on both ends of the Red River, with the Dian communities of the Yunnan and the Đông Sơn communities of Bắc Bộ.[105] Hence, when the Imperial Han began to expand into their southernmost fringes, the societies they encountered were not simply passive communities who were recipients of the imposition of civilization. The local societies in various areas of modern-day southern and southwestern China and northern Vietnam were complex societies already interacting with their counterparts throughout the wider region.

For historians and archaeologists alike, relations between Han society and communities along its various southernmost fringes are significant and instructive for understanding the cultural developments and emergent civilizations of two geographically disparate areas within a wider region. Ultimately, much more research is necessary, including ongoing fieldwork at Cổ Loa. I would echo a sentiment offered by O'Harrow decades ago when he explicitly called for greater collaboration between historians and archaeologists examining the issue of Han arrival in northern Vietnam.[106] It would be interesting to see, for instance, if textual or archaeological evidence of Han society can demonstrate changing patterns as correlated with evolving relationships at its periphery. In other words, it would be helpful to know more about archaeologically and historically discernible sociopolitical changes in the Central Plain over the course of the Western and Eastern Han periods as the empire increasingly incorporated the Red River Valley. For the time being, a combination of available philological and archaeological evidence indicates that complementary forms of acculturation resulting from frontier relationships were affecting emergent civilizations, namely forms of Sinicization and barbarization. Further research along this line of inquiry could be productive. Can imperial expansion and changing peripheral relations be tracked and correlated with concomitant internal Han sociopolitical changes in the Central Plain? Can these be further correlated to changing intercultural relationships with other peripheral areas to the north and west?

Future studies would be well served in comparing the ways in which frontier relations might have been similar or different for other edges of the emergent Sinitic civilization. A form of "barbarization" was perhaps occurring along various fringes of emergent Chinese civilization, all throughout the long history of "China", including the northern and northwestern peripheries. It may prove worthwhile to synthesize research from each of these disparate frontier zones, examining cultural change for various communities located in modern-day Mongolia, Korea, Japan, and Vietnam, and the impact that these societies had on Han political and cultural trends. Thus far, it appears that tantalizing clues remain waiting in the ground and in various textual accounts for future research projects to uncover.

NOTES

1. Donn Bayard, "Models, Scenarios, Variables and Supposition: Approaches to the Rise of Social Complexity in Mainland Southeast Asia", in *Early Metallurgy, Trade, and Urban Centres in Thailand and Southeast Asia*, edited by Ian Glover, Pornchai Suchitta, and John Villiers (Bangkok: White Lotus, 1992), p. 13.

2. Michael Churchman, "Before Chinese and Vietnamese in the Red River Plain: The Han–Tang Period", *Chinese Southern Diaspora Studies* 4 (2010): 25–37.
3. Ibid., p. 37.
4. Pham Minh Huyen, "Northern Vietnam from the Neolithic to the Han Period — Part II: The Metal Age in the North of Vietnam", in *Southeast Asia: From Prehistory to History*, edited by Ian Glover and Peter Bellwood (New York: Routledge, 2004), pp. 189–201.
5. Charles Higham, "Mainland Southeast Asia from the Neolithic to the Iron Age", in *Southeast Asia: From Prehistory to History*, edited by Ian Glover and Peter Bellwood (New York: Routledge, 2004), p. 58.
6. Haydon Cherry, "Digging Up the Past: Prehistory and the Weight of the Present in Vietnam", *Journal of Vietnamese Studies* 4 (2009): 84–85.
7. Nguyễn Giang Hải and Nguyễn Văn Hùng, "Nhóm đồ đồng mới phát hiện ở Cổ Loa (Hà Nội)" [Cluster of Bronze Objects Recently Discovered at Cổ Loa (Ha Noi)], *Khảo cổ học* [Archaeology] 47 (1983): 21–32.
8. Stephen O'Harrow, "From Co-loa to the Trung Sisters' Revolt: Vietnam as the Chinese Found It", *Asian Perspectives* 22 (1979): 142.
9. Keith Taylor, *The Birth of Vietnam* (Berkeley: University of California Press, 1983), p. 349.
10. O'Harrow, pp. 143–44.
11. Charles Higham, *The Archaeology of Mainland Southeast Asia* (Cambridge: Cambridge University Press, 1989), p. 193; Higham, "Mainland Southeast Asia", p. 279; Taylor, p. 349.
12. John Tessitore, "View from the East Mountain: An Examination of the Relationship between the Dong Son and Lake Tien Civilizations in the First Millennium BC", *Asian Perspectives* 28 (1989): 31–44.
13. Cherry, pp. 94–96.
14. Henri Maspero, "L'Expedition de Ma Yuan", *Bulletin de l'Ecole Francaise d'Extreme-Orient* 18 (1918): 27–28.
15. Nam Kim, "The Underpinnings of Sociopolitical Complexity and Civilization in the Red River Valley of Metal Age Vietnam", PhD dissertation, University of Illinois at Chicago, 2010; Nguyễn Quang Ngọc and Vũ Văn Quân, *Địa chí Cổ Loa* [Gazetteer of Cổ Loa] (Hanoi: Nha Xuat Ban Hanoi, 2007); O'Harrow; Keith Taylor, "Perceptions of Encounter in *Shui Ching Chu 37*", *Asia Journal* 2 (1995): 29–54; Taylor, *The Birth of Vietnam*; Tatsuro Yamamoto, "Myths Explaining the Vicissitudes of Political Power in Ancient Vietnam", *Acta Asiatica* 18 (1970): 70–94.
16. O'Harrow, p. 142.
17. O'Harrow; Taylor, *The Birth of Vietnam*.
18. John Miksic, "Heterogenetic Cities in Premodern Southeast Asia", *World Archaeology* 32 (2000): 106–20; Tessitore; Paul Wheatley, *Nagara and*

Commandery, Department of Geography Research Paper Nos. 207–8 (Chicago: University of Chicago, 1983), pp. 91–93.

19. Keith Taylor, "An Evaluation of the Chinese Period in Vietnamese History", *The Journal of Asiatic Studies* 23 (1980): 139–64.

20. Taylor, *The Birth of Vietnam*, pp. 303–11. These titles can be translated as the *Arrayed Tales of Collected Oddities from South of the Passes*, the *Complete Book of the Historical Records of Đại Việt*, the *Collection [of Stories] of the Departed Spirits of the Việt Realm*, and the *Outline of Việt History*, respectively.

21. Taylor, *The Birth of Vietnam*, pp. 3–23; Tessitore, p. 36.

22. Nguyễn and Vũ; Tessitore.

23. Peter Bellwood, "Southeast Asia before History", in *The Cambridge History of Southeast Asia*, edited by Nicholas Tarling (Cambridge: Cambridge University Press, 1992), p. 55–136; Taylor, *The Birth of Vietnam*.

24. Nguyen Ba Khoach, "Phung Nguyen", *Asian Perspectives* 23 (1980): 48.

25. Taylor, *The Birth of Vietnam*, pp. 12–13.

26. Bellwood, "Southeast Asia before History", p. 125.

27. Taylor, *The Birth of Vietnam*, p. 20.

28. Ibid., p. 21.

29. Ibid.

30. Charles Higham, *The Bronze Age of Southeast Asia* (Cambridge: Cambridge University Press, 1996); Miksic; Nguyễn and Vũ.

31. Higham, *The Archaeology of Southeast Asia*, pp. 202, 290–91.

32. Francis Allard, "Frontiers and Boundaries: The Han Empire from Its Southern Periphery", in *Archaeology of Asia*, edited by Miriam Stark (Malden: Blackwell Publishing, 2006), pp. 233–54; Taylor, *The Birth of Vietnam*, pp. 23–27.

33. Taylor, *The Birth of Vietnam*, p. 27.

34. Allard, "Frontiers and Boundaries".

35. Taylor, *The Birth of Vietnam*, p. 30.

36. O'Harrow, pp. 146–48.

37. Tong Trung Tin, "Northern Vietnam from the Neolithic to the Han period — Part III: Archaeological Aspects of Han Dynasty Rule in the Early First Millennium AD", in *Southeast Asia: From Prehistory to History*, edited by Ian Glover and Peter Bellwood (New York: Routledge, 2004), p. 202.

38. Taylor, *The Birth of Vietnam*, pp. 349–59.

39. Cherry, p. 130.

40. Liam Kelley, "The Biography of the Hong Bang Clan as a Medieval Vietnamese Invented Tradition", *Journal of Vietnamese Studies* 7, no. 2 (2012): 88 and 122.

41. Keith Taylor, "Comments on 'The Biography of the Hong Bang Clan as a Medieval Vietnamese Invented Tradition' by Liam Kelley", *Journal of Vietnamese Studies* 7, no. 2 (2012): 135.

42. John Phan, "Re-Imagining 'Annam': A New Analysis of Sino–Viet–Muong Linguistic Contact", *Chinese Southern Diaspora Studies* 4 (2010): 23.
43. O'Harrow.
44. Kelley, p. 122.
45. Taylor, "Comments", p. 135.
46. O'Harrow.
47. Kim, "The Underpinnings of Sociopolitical Complexity"; Nam Kim, Lai Van Toi and Trinh Hoang Hiep, "Co Loa: An Investigation of Vietnam's Ancient Capital", *Antiquity* 84 (2010): 1011–27.
48. Nguyễn and Vũ, p. 173.
49. Ibid., p. 173.
50. Kim, "The Underpinnings of Sociopolitical Complexity".
51. Kim et al.
52. Ibid.
53. Kim, "The Underpinnings of Sociopolitical Complexity"; Kim et al; Lại Văn Tới, *Tư liệu Viện Khảo Cổ Học, đợt khai quật năm 2004–2005* [Materials from the Institute of Archaeology, Excavations from 2004–2005], (Hà Nội: Viện Khảo Cổ Học, 2005).
54. Kim, "The Underpinnings of Sociopolitical Complexity".
55. Allard, "Frontiers and Boundaries", p. 238.
56. Higham, *The Archaeology of Southeast Asia*, p. 291.
57. Tong, p. 202.
58. Robert Winzeler, "Ecology, Culture, Social Organization, and State Formation in Southeast Asia", *Current Anthropology* 17 (1976): 623.
59. Ibid., p. 626.
60. Wheatley, p. 367.
61. Miriam Stark, "Early Mainland Southeast Asian Landscapes in the First Millennium AD", *Annual Review of Anthropology* 35 (2006): 407.
62. Kim, "The Underpinnings of Sociopolitical Complexity"; Nam Kim, "Lasting Monuments and Durable Institutions: Labor, Urbanism, and Statehood in Northern Vietnam and Beyond", *Journal of Archeological Research*, vol. 21, no. 1 (March 2013).
63. Elizabeth Moore, "Water-Enclosed Sites: Links between Ban Takhong, Northeast Thailand and Cambodia", in *The Gift of Water: Water Management, Cosmology and the State in South East Asia*, edited by Jonathan Rigg (London: School of Oriental and African Studies, 1992), p. 26.
64. Bernard-Philippe Groslier, "Our Knowledge of Khmer Civilisation: A Reappraisal", *Journal of the Siam Society* 48 (1960): 1–28.
65. See Stark, pp. 417–18.
66. Miksic, p. 109.
67. Lothar von Falkenhausen, "Stages in the Development of 'Cities' in Pre-Imperial China", in *The Ancient City: New Perspectives on Urbanism in the Old and*

New World, edited by Joyce Marcus and Jeremy A. Sabloff (Santa Fe: School for Advanced Research Press, 2008), pp. 211–12.

68. Colin Renfrew, "Introduction: Peer Polity Interaction and Socio-political Change", in *Peer Polity Interaction and Socio-political Change*, edited by Colin Renfrew and John F. Cherry (Cambridge: Cambridge University Press, 1986), pp. 1–18.

69. Charles Higham, "Crossing National Boundaries: Southern China and Southeast Asia in Prehistory", in *Uncovering Southeast Asia's Past: Selected Papers from the 10th International Conference of the European Association of Southeast Asian Archaeologists*, edited by Elizabeth A. Bacus, Ian C. Glover, and Vincent C. Pigott (Singapore: National University of Singapore Press, 2006), pp. 13–14.

70. Kim, "The Underpinnings of Sociopolitical Complexity".

71. Francis Allard, "The Archaeology of Dian: Trends and Tradition", *Antiquity* 73 (1999): 77–85; Pham Minh Huyen, *Văn hóa Đông Sơn: tính thống nhất và đa dạng* [Đông Sơn Culture: Its Unity and Diversity] (Hà Nội: Viện Khảo Cổ Học, Nhà Xuất Bản Khoa Học Xã Hội, 1996); Stark, p. 414.

72. Bellwood, "Southeast Asia before History", p. 116.

73. Berenice Bellina and Ian Glover, "The Archaeology of Early Contact with India and the Mediterranean World, from the Fourth Century BC to the Fourth Century AD", in *Southeast Asia: From Prehistory to History*, edited by Ian Glover and Peter Bellwood (New York: Routledge, 2004), p. 70.

74. Peter Bellwood, "The Origins and Dispersals of Agricultural Communities in Southeast Asia", in *Southeast Asia: From Prehistory to History*, edited by Ian Glover and Peter Bellwood (New York: Routledge, 2004), p. 37.

75. See Erica Brindley, "Barbarians or Not? Ethnicity and Changing Conceptions of the Ancient Yue (Viet) Peoples (~400–50 BC)", *Asia Major* 16, no. 1 (2003): 1–32.

76. K.C. Chang, *Shang Civilization* (New Haven: Yale University Press, 1980), pp. 90–92, 273.

77. Marilynn Larew, "Thuc Phan, Cao Tong, and the Transfer of Military Technology in Third Century BC Viet Nam", *East Asian Science, Technology, and Medicine* 21 (2003): 12–47.

78. Rowan Flad, "Divination and Power: A Multiregional View of the Development of Oracle Bone Divination in Early China", *Current Anthropology* 49 (2008): 403–37.

79. Hyung Il Pai, "Culture Contact and Culture Change: The Korean Peninsula and Its Relations with the Han Dynasty Commandery of Lelang", *World Archaeology* 23 (1992): 306–19.

80. Ibid., p. 315.

81. Ibid., p. 308.

82. Alice Yao, "Sarmatian Mirrors and Han Ingots (100 BC–AD 100): How the Foreign Became Local and Vice Versa", *Cambridge Archaeological Journal* 22, no. 1 (2012): 57–70.

83. Bennet Bronson, "Patterns of Political Regeneration in Southeast and East Asia", in *After Collapse: The Regeneration of Complex Societies*, edited by Glenn M. Schwartz and John J. Nichols (Tucson: University of Arizona Press, 2006), pp. 137–43.

84. Monica Smith, "Networks, Territories, and the Cartography of Ancient States", *Annals of the Association of American Geographers* 95, no. 4 (2005): 843.

85. Brindley.

86. Carlo Tronchetti and Peter van Dommelen, "Entangled Objects and Hybrid Practices: Colonial Contacts and Elite Connections at Monte Prama, Sardinia", *Journal of Mediterranean Archaeology* 18, no. 2 (2005): 203.

87. Churchman, p. 36.

88. Ibid.

89. Allard, "Frontiers and Boundaries", p. 241.

90. Ibid., p. 244.

91. Taylor, "Perceptions of Encounter", pp. 52–53.

92. Tong, p. 203.

93. Masanari Nishimura, "Settlement Patterns on the Red River Plain from the Late Prehistoric Period to the 10th Century AD", *Indo-Pacific Pacific Prehistory Association Bulletin* 25, Taipei Papers, 3 (2005): 102.

94. Brindley.

95. Ibid., p. 1.

96. Kent Lightfoot and Antoinette Martinez, "Frontiers and Boundaries in Archaeological Perspective", *Annual Review of Anthropology* 24 (1995): 471–92.

97. Ibid., p. 488.

98. Churchman, p. 30.

99. Mark Lewis, *The Early Chinese Empires: Qin and Han* (Cambridge, MA: Belknap Press, 2007), p. 151.

100. Ibid., p. 152.

101. Ibid., pp. 154–55.

102. Ibid., pp. 39–40.

103. Yao, "Sarmatian Mirrors and Han Ingots", p. 58.

104. Ibid., p. 68.

105. Kim, "The Underpinnings of Sociopolitical Complexity"; Alice Yao, "Recent Developments in the Archaeology of Southwestern China", *Journal of Archaeological Research* 18 (2010): 203–39.

106. O'Harrow.

4

CLOTHES MAKE THE *MAN*
Body Culture and Ethnic Boundaries on the Lingnan Frontier in the Southern Song

Sean Marsh

Introduction

This chapter examines the ways in which several Southern Song geographies of the Lingnan frontier describe and categorize the various autochthonic peoples of the frontier, what they designated as the most significant boundaries between Chinese and non-Chinese peoples, and where they perceived those boundaries as being transgressed or blurred. Ordering the ethnic landscape of the far south through the act of composing frontier geographies in turn played a significant role in the colonization of the frontier by rendering its inhabitants knowable, and thus legible to other frontier officials and the Song bureaucratic state.[1] For the purposes of this chapter, I define the Lingnan frontier as the two southernmost circuits of the Song Dynasty (Guangnan xilu 廣南西路 and Guangnan donglu 廣南東路), corresponding to the modern Chinese provinces of Guangxi, Guangdong, and Hainan.

In his study of ethnicity during the Tang Dynasty, Marc Abramson argues that the Tang underwent a long-term shift in the criteria that underpinned its ethnic discourse, from an early and high Tang emphasis on bodily difference to a late Tang emphasis on political loyalty and adherence to Chinese cultural values that downplayed physical difference. While Abramson focuses primarily on ethnic discourse related to the northern frontier and Inner Asian peoples, he also briefly mentions Tang images and stereotypes of southern peoples, defined by his sources in physical and bestial ways, as "short, squat, dark and ugly", and "resembling the monkeys native to their region".[2] In contrast to these representations of southern peoples during the Tang Dynasty, Song Dynasty descriptions of the peoples of the southern frontier do not locate the salient ethnic boundaries between Chinese and non-Chinese in their physical bodies, but instead emphasize how frontier people altered, decorated and clothed their bodies in ways distinct from the authors' own sensibilities. This shift from the innate body to performed body culture reflects the changing nature of the ethnically ambiguous population of the frontier in the Song, and is in large part a product of the administrative need for frontier officials to investigate and accurately describe the peoples of the south as they appeared, for practical reasons of governance rather than for cosmological purposes of rule.

While northern regimes had been settling and colonizing the south for a millennium prior, the Song Dynasty marked a decided intensification and expansion of the process. The Nong Zhigao 儂智高 (Viet., Nùng Trí Cao) rebellion in 1052–54 and the Song-Việt wars in 1075–77 revealed the limits of the earlier reliance on "loose reins" borderland proxies to keep the peace, and defined a clear border between the Song and the recently independent state of Đại Việt. As with the hardening of the northern border between Song and Liao in the tenth century, the firming up of the southern border in the eleventh century transformed the relation between the frontier and the dynasty that controlled it.[3] Not long after, the fall of the Northern Song in 1127 forced the Song Dynasty's administrative centre of gravity southwards, along with millions of northern refugees.

The newly relocated imperial court's pressing need to boost tax revenues — having just lost its capital and northern third of its former territory — also encouraged direct administration of the Lingnan frontier, and promoted taxable agriculture and extractive trade. As a result, Guangxi's registered population swelled from 242,109 households in 1081 to 488,655 households in 1163, to 528,220 households in 1224, as demobilized soldiers, war refugees from the north, and land-poor migrants from Guangdong and Fujian flooded into the river valleys and port cities of the far south, and as the state developed an increasing capacity to register the indigenous population.[4] These changes spurred increasing official attention to the complex ethnic world of the southern frontier, intensified the Song state's need to map the territory's inhabitants and their natural resources, and created greater opportunities for ethnic contact. In this context, several Southern Song officials wrote detailed and influential geographies of the far south.[5]

While it was written two centuries earlier than the other sources listed below, the *Taiping huanyu ji* 太平寰宇記, a geographic encyclopedia of China and the known world written by Yue Shi 樂史 in the tenth century, has detailed ethnographic information about peoples and locations covered in the later geographies.[6] Born in Jiangxi, Yue was a court official in the Southern Tang Dynasty who later served in the early Song court, and compiled the massive geography for the Taizong emperor following the Song's unification of the southern kingdoms. As much of the text's ethnographic material is drawn from pre-Song works, it also serves as a useful record of what was known about southern peoples at the beginning of the Northern Song. Fan Chengda 范成大, a prominent official, poet and travel writer of the twelfth century, wrote the *Guihai yuheng zhi* 桂海虞衡志 in 1175 as a record of the Lingnan frontier, gleaned from his experience as the military commissioner in Jingjiang prefecture 靜江府 (present-day Guilin).[7] This work in turn provided much of the foundation for the *Lingwai daida* 嶺外代答 written by minor official Zhou Qufei 周去非, who served under Fan as a district defender in several upland counties outside of Guilin, as well as a Prefectural Instructor in Qinzhou 欽州.[8] On the other side of the passes from Fan and Zhou, Zhu Fu 朱輔, magistrate of Mayuan county 麻園縣 in southern Hunan, wrote the *Ximan congxiao* 溪蠻叢笑, a miscellanea about the strange customs of local upland peoples, in 1195.[9] Finally, while most of the passages in

Zhao Rugua's 趙汝适 late Southern Song geography *Zhufan zhi* 諸蕃志, written in 1225, describes the countries and trade goods of the maritime frontier of the South Seas, there is a detailed entry on the Li 黎 people of Hainan island.[10] While Song geographies of the southern frontier are few in number, they had an outsized influence on subsequent geographies of the region, and one often comes across passages from these texts in later works, both as quotations and unattributed borrowings. As such, they established many tropes of the far south and southern peoples that persist to the present day.

Foreign Bodies

While the innate physical difference of the southern barbarian had long been a trope of ancient Chinese ethnography, several of the Southern Song sources openly question whether there is any essential physical difference between non-Chinese people and Chinese people, and explicitly debunk ancient tales of the strange bodies of the south in order to make this point. One example of this can be found in discussions of the "crossed legs" of people in Jiaozhi 交趾 (Viet., Giao Chỉ), a Tang Dynasty prefecture in the general vicinity of present-day Hanoi that had become the independent state of Đại Việt during the tenth century. In keeping with his general focus on administrative boundaries, Fan Chengda couches his criticisms of the old tales about the crossed legs of Jiaozhi in terms of that territory having recently been part of China:

> The *Jiaozhi ji* 交趾記 [Record of Jiaozhi] said: "The people of Jiaozhi come from Nanding county 南定縣. The bones in their feet have no joints, and there is fur on their bodies. Those who lie down need help to stand." The *Shanhai jing* 山海經 [Classic of Mountains and Seas] also said: "The people of the country of Jiaozhi have crossed shins." Guo Pu 郭璞 said: "Their shins are bent and cross one another, so they are called 'crossed legs.'" The territory of Annan 安南 [Viet., An Nam] today is but the commanderies and counties of Han and Tang. The skeletons of their people are no different from Chinese. Aizhou 愛州 is the true birthplace of the Tang chancellor Jiang Gongfu 姜公輔. How can there still be this talk of crossed shins?[11]

Việt territory had been governed by prior Chinese regimes, and people from that territory had served as high officials. Therefore, Fan reasons, their physical bodies could not be fundamentally different either. In another passage, Fan claims that the emphasis on tattooed foreheads in the *Liji* 禮記 implies that the physical bodies of the Việt, referred to more generically in this passage as Man 蠻 or "Southern Barbarians", were not all that different.[12] Zhou Qufei also debunks old accounts of the strange bodies of the people of Jiaozhi, but does so on the grounds of his own observation:

> The [*Li*]*ji* says: "The [people in the] south are called *Man*. They have tattooed foreheads and crossed feet. There are some who do not cook their food." The *Jiaozhou ji* 交州記 [Record of Jiaozhou] says: "The people of Jiaozhi are from Nanding county. The bones in their legs have no joints, and there is fur on their bodies. Those who lie down need help to stand back up again." I went to Qin[zhou] 欽州, and saw their black teeth and bare feet, those who blacken their clothing are just people. How could I have seen their so-called legs without joints, or those with fur on their bodies? ... How could the people all have no joints in their legs but still help one another up? At the time people were affected by bad *qi*, and thus got this name. It is probably like that.[13]

Like Fan, Zhou couches the differences between Chinese and Việt bodies in terms of cultural practices of bodily modification such as tattooing, blackened teeth, or clothing, and finds the older claims of strange bodies to be preposterous.[14] These passages reflect the tension between the two methods of these officials' "investigation of things": textual classicist knowledge, and personal observation and rational investigation. That tension was at the centre of a larger epistemological debate in *daoxue* 道學 circles during the Southern Song over how best to apprehend the patterns, or *li* 理, inherent in every aspect of existence. While both authors often approach southern customs in terms of seeking out real-life examples of tropes from ancient accounts of the south, when the two come into conflict, they tend to believe their eyes.

Ultimately, these sources do not assert an innate physical difference between Chinese and non-Chinese bodies on the southern frontier. This is not to say that they find bodies of non-Chinese to be exactly the same as Chinese. Rather, they locate the salient ethnic boundaries not in the bodies themselves, but in how these people altered, decorated, and clothed those bodies. It is to these body cultures that we turn next.

Tattoos

Tattoos and scarification are one of the oldest tropes of the ethnic Other in Chinese history, and they are especially associated with the foreign peoples to China's south and east. While texts from the Han or earlier — often quoted by Song ethnographers — tend to make broad sweeping generalizations describing all of the peoples of the south as tattooed, by the early Song Dynasty, these authors began to portray tattoos as a practice of certain southern peoples: the Việt people south of Guangxi, the Liao 獠,[15] especially in the Left and Right Rivers region upriver from Yongzhou 邕州 in the area of what is today Guangxi, and the Li 黎 people on Hainan.[16] Both Fan Chengda and Zhou Qufei quote Han accounts of Man tattoos in their chapters on Jiaozhi.[17] In contrast to his scepticism towards those same sources' fantastical descriptions of Việt bodies, Fan explicitly ties the current Việt practice of tattooing the body to ancient Man customs:

> I made reference to the name of Jiaozhi, its origins are very old. The "Wangzhi" 王制 wrote: "The [people in the] south are called Man, they have tattooed foreheads and crossed legs. There are some who do not cook their food." This probably refers to tattooing the face, to this day it is similar to that.[18]

In one of his passages on Jiaozhi, Zhou Qufei drew a connection between the specific pattern of the Việt tattoos he saw in the border town of Qinzhou and the elaborate patterns on the southern frontier region's famed bronze drums.[19] The Liao people are often identified as being tattooed on both the face and the body, and several Chinese sources use the description "decorated face" (*huamian* 花面) as names for certain Liao tribes.[20] A passage on the Liao in the tenth-century *Taiping guangji* 太平廣記 also suggests that their tattoos derive from the ancient southern custom of tattooing for protection from water creatures, perhaps a reference to the river valleys the Liao tended to settle in.[21]

Tattooing was also related, in the south as elsewhere in China, to slavery and the military.[22] During the Tang Dynasty, Liao people were often brought into the vast Tang slave market as captives of war, or sold into slavery, to the point where the peoples of the south came to be seen by Tang Chinese as slave societies. By the Song, this slavery had come to be seen as barbaric, and while the Song founding emperor had officially abolished the practice of slavery, the sources continue to mention southern peoples branding or tattooing their slaves. Fan Chengda writes of a vast slave trade in Jiaozhi via the tribal prefectures on the border, where Chinese who had been tricked or captured were then tattooed by their new Việt owners.[23] Zhou Qufei also writes of servant girls in the river valleys of Yongzhou (an area identified elsewhere as Liao territory) being tattooed to prevent them from running away.[24] Zhou also describes the Đại Việt army as having the characters "Soldier of the Son of Heaven" (*Tianzi bing* 天子兵) tattooed on their foreheads, presumably to prevent desertion.[25] Unlike the other forms of tattoos discussed earlier, however, these would not necessarily have been seen as ethnic markers, as the practice was widespread in Chinese society as well, as Carrie Reed has shown.[26] Rather, the references to tattoos of slaves and servants signified the persistance of slavery among southern peoples, and as such carried an implication of barbarity.

One contrast to the generally pejorative portrayal of tattoos is the portrayal offered by Fan Chengda and Zhou Qufei of the Li people's practice of tattooing women's faces, which they refer to as "embroidered faces" (*xiumian* 繡面). The phrase has intriguing aesthetic connotations more refined than the usual words for tattoos, most of which imply punitive tattoos or branding. This practice had been noted in earlier ethnographies: the tenth-century *Taiping huanyu ji* entry on Danzhou 儋州 in southern Hainan notes that among the Raw Li (*sheng* Li 生黎), tattoos reflected wealth and status.[27] The same work's passage on Qiongzhou 瓊州, the administrative centre of Hainan, connects Raw Li tattoos to women's bodies specifically, noting that "Women tattoo their necks and hang big hoop earrings from their ears."[28] In the Southern Song, Fan Chengda portrays the delicate facial tattoos as part of a coming-of-age ceremony, and a status symbol denied to servants.[29]

As such, Fan inverts the usual Chinese pattern of tattoos being associated with mean or lower status categories of people, be they slaves, criminals, or soldiers. In a passage that borrows heavily from Fan's account, Zhou Qufei goes a step further by portraying the practice of "embroidered faces" as analogous to his own Chinese society's feminine ideals of beauty, refinement, and chastity:

The Li women of Hainan use embroidered faces as a decoration. It is probably the case that the prettier a Li girl was, in the past they would be stolen away by outsiders. Thus, those Li women who were chaste darkened their faces, and then refined the custom. To this day they revere and imitate this. "Embroidered faces" are like the hairpin ceremony in China. When girls reach the age of maturity, a banquet is held for relatives and old female companions. They apply the needle and brush to make very fine floral or flying moth images, covering the rest with gorgeous faint lines like millet. There are some who have pure white [skin] and the "embroidered" patterns are blue-green. The floral patterns are dazzling, their handiwork is extremely fine. Only slave girls and maidservants are not tattooed. [As for] the maidservants of the river valleys of Yongzhou, [their owners] fear that they will run away, and so tattoo their faces, but this is different from Li women.[30]

Both Fan and Zhou name the "needle and brush" (*zhenbi* 針筆) as tools of the tattooing, which call to mind the embroidery needle and writing brush of the inner quarters of a literati Chinese household.[31] Most striking, though, is how Zhou represents the Li practice of tattooing in such a positive way, especially given how tattoos had served as a trope of southern barbarism for well over a millennium. When viewed in light of the fact that Zhou was a disciple of the twelfth-century *daoxue* figure Zhang Shi 張栻, I suspect that the passage reflects a *daoxue* sensibility, as a proof of the universality of moral principles in all human societies, no matter how superficially different.[32] By finding these very moral principles in the tattooing of a barbarian woman's face, on the southernmost tip of what could be possibly considered China, Zhou demonstrates those principles' universality, humanizing his Li subjects in the process.[33]

Naked Bodies

Nakedness and the relative degree of undress was another way that these sources marked southern ethnic difference. As Chinese officials from the cooler, temperate north ventured into the tropical southern frontier, their cultural assumptions about proper attire, and tropes of the unclothed body as a marker of poverty, impropriety, and barbarity made their way into their depictions of southern peoples. Depictions of total nudity are relatively rare; aside from the supernatural naked forms of *wangliang* 罔兩 demons,[34] the only human example given is of Dan 蜑 children: "When Dan boats moor along the river, throngs of children gather to play on the sand. No matter if it is summer or winter, they wear not a thread on their bodies. Their true kind is like otters."[35] A more enduring trope of southern people's nudity can be found in the spectacle of women bathing in rivers. Both Fan Chengda and Zhou Qufei remark on Li women bathing in rivers. Fan's description combines a voyeuristic attention to detail with a slight nod to Li propriety in depicting how the women use the water to conceal their naked bodies:

> They bathe together in rivers. First they take off their upper clothing and wash themselves, and then wash their feet, gradually raising their skirts to their head, and then letting their bodies sink into the water. After bathing, they then put their skirt on from over their heads, and then emerge from the water.[36]

Zhou merely notes tersely, "They bathe in multitudes in the river."[37]

More often, though, nakedness on the southern frontier was portrayed in relative terms, with authors remarking on bare chests and bare feet, ranking their ethnographic subjects in relation to the degree to which their dress deviated from their own Chinese ideas of propriety. For example, the *Taiping huanyu ji* ordered the three local peoples of Baizhou 白州 in southern Guangxi in relation to degrees of nudity: "Tai 臺 women are somewhat like Chinese, Chai 犲 women are naked from the waist up, Xue 猰 wrap themselves with cloth to the mid-thigh."[38] The *Ximan congxiao* also describes frontier people — in this case, the Gelao 仡佬 — as having naked torsos.[39] Both Zhou and Fan describe both sexes of the Li people of Hainan as being bare-chested, wearing neither jackets nor pants, with both sexes wearing instead a simple wrapped sarong.[40]

Bare feet also served as markers of ethnic difference. As Jacques Gernet has noted, Chinese in the Song, no matter how poor, tended to wear something, even if only hemp sandals, on their feet.[41] While both Fan and Zhou dismiss the ancient trope of crossed-legged southerners as myth, they refer to bare feet repeatedly in their descriptions of the upland tribal peoples of the frontier.[42] In the case of the Yao 傜, Fan attributes their ability to walk barefoot on rough mountain trails to a Yao practice of cauterizing the soles of their feet:

> When [Yao] sons begin to be able to walk, they heat iron and stone and brand the heels and soles of their feet. This makes the "stubborn wood" unfeeling, so that they can tread upon the thorns, thatch, roots and stumps without injury.[43]

Unlike Chinese feet, which presumably needed to be protected by shoes or sandals, Fan believed that Yao feet had been tempered from childhood to be tough and numb. Once again, foreign bodies were not shown as innately different, but were instead made to be different through different body cultures.

Hair

Hair has long been intimately bound up with Chinese ethnic identity, both in the length of hair and how it is braided, tied, and capped. The oldest Chinese accounts of southern peoples mention either unbound hair (*pifa* 披髮) or close-cropped hair (*duanfa* 斷髮) as markers of ethnic difference.[44] Yet in these Song sources, there are no mentions of close-cropped hair, and unbound hair emerges only in a few anecdotes not about people, but about supernatural beings. The first two instances show up in the tenth century *Taiping huanyu ji* passage on Chaozhou 潮州, as mountain spirits "with the form of humans with unbound hair, that run away quickly".[45] The only other time unbound hair comes up is in the twelfth-century *Lingwai daida*, with a group of demonic spirits called *wangliang*: "They had human shadows but without human form. Those that were naked and with unbound hair were numerous beyond count."[46] It is unclear whether these spirits' unbound hair preserves older tropes of non-Chinese southern peoples, or whether it is just being used to signify the strange and supernatural. At any rate, while the oldest tropes about hair and southern people do not appear to be in use by the Song, the manner in which hair was bound remained a very important ethnic boundary.

Nearly every mention of hair in these sources uses the stock phrase *chuiji* 椎髻, which translates literally as "mallet hairstyle". Despite its ubiquity as a marker of ethnic difference, hardly any of these sources actually describe what a mallet hairstyle might look like. One presumes that the "mallet" refers to a topknot or lump of hair bound up on the top of one's head, perhaps bound with a piece of cloth. Wolfram Eberhard suggests that the Yao practice of rolling hair around a small board may be related somehow to what he calls a "dog hairstyle" (which he then links to the Panhu 盤瓠 myth), but it is unclear whether this refers to the same thing as what these Song sources mean by a mallet hairstyle.[47] Several passages do mention the hair being bound by a strap, either of patterned cloth "like a funeral sash", or sometimes white cloth or white paper.[48] The only explicit description of a mallet hairstyle is in the *Ximan congxiao*, in far southern Hunan, very close to the upland Yao counties outside of Guilin. The author describes the hairstyle pejoratively in terms of hygiene, but also in terms of being bare-headed:

> They do not shave foetal hair. When they grow up they do not use combs, and do not wrap their hair in caps. Disheveled, filthy and savage, they have been this way from antiquity, and cannot be transformed. This is what is meant by a "mallet hairstyle."[49]

Intriguingly, Zhu draws attention to the upland peoples' failure to shave their infants' "foetal hair" (*taifa* 胎髮), an ancient Chinese practice that dates back at least to the Warring States. This passage also defines "mallet hairstyle" in terms of the absence of both comb and cap, with an implied contrast to groomed, capped Chinese hairstyles. While Zhu's sentiment about the hygiene of the mallet hairstyle is clear enough, his emphasis on uncovered hair is contradicted by several passages in other texts that describe various southern peoples wearing straw hats and caps in conjunction with their mallet hairstyles.

While mallet hairstyles are by far the most common of the hairstyles mentioned in these sources, the authors recognized that there were differences between the various peoples of the south on this matter. Zhou Qufei distinguishes the Yao mallet hairstyle from the others, describing it as "hanging over their foreheads".[50] Many sources mark the hairstyles of the Li people on Hainan as being different from the standard mallet hairstyle, describing Li men wearing their hair combed up on the top of their head "like women at funerals", and Li women as having "tall chignons" (*gaoji* 高髻) with silver, copper, and tin ornaments and combs decorating the hair, and occasionally chicken tail feathers as well.[51] Only the Dan people are not described in any of the sources as having mallet hairstyles, or any distinct hairstyle at all.

In one sense, the sheer breadth of references to mallet hairstyles across the southern frontier suggests that they may have functioned as a sort of analogue to the braided queue, or *suotou* 索頭 of the northern frontier peoples of Inner Asia. Like the braided queue, the mallet hairstyle was used by twelfth-century Chinese authors to signify the ethnic difference of southern peoples. While mallet hairstyles do not seem to have doubled as an ethnic epithet to the same degree as the steppe braid did during the Song Dynasty, they do seem roughly analogous as ethnic markers.[52] In contrast to the indelible nature of tattoos, hair was a more plastic manner of inscribing culture and ethnic identity upon the physical body, as hair could be unbound and rebound in different ways. In this regard, hair functions somewhat more like clothing, a fluid ethnic marker that can be changed should the occasion call for it.

Clothing

Clothing and fabric have long been central to Chinese ideas of culture and ethnicity, and references to clothing are present in nearly every ethnographic description in these sources. By covering naked bodies, clothing distinguished humans from animals. The manner of clothing in turn distinguished Chinese from other peoples. Clothing linked Song subjects to both the state and to the market through the fabric it was made of, as fabric could serve as a tax in kind, a traded commodity, or a store of wealth. The materials used to make clothing reflected local ecology and climate, as well as the economic mode of production, be it hunter-gatherer, nomadic pastoralist, or settled farmer. Clothing reflected the wearer's ritual order, their class structure, and their gender order. As such, it is not surprising that these sources pay such close attention to it in their ethnographic descriptions. The aspects of clothing that these sources focus on can be divided into three general categories: the raw materials used to make the fabric, the colours and patterns used to dye the fabric, and how the fabric was made into clothing and worn.

Social Fabrics

More than any other aspect, the raw materials used to make cloth reflect the climate and environment of the wearer, and several of the fabrics are made from plants native to the tropical south. The degree to which these raw materials were processed also reflects the technological sophistication of those who harvest and process it. Clothing made from tree bark was associated with those who lived in the most inaccessible, rugged upland terrain, marginal to the riverine lowlands or coastal plains where Song administration and Chinese settlement were most prevalent. To be marginal spatially was to be barbaric in the eyes of Song officials, "raw" (*sheng* 生) in the predominant ethnographic rhetoric of the Song, and this was reflected in these Chinese sources' description of clothing as well. A pair of tenth-century passages on the Raw Li describe them making a woven cloth from tree bark.[53] While the verb used to describe the process, *ji* 績, implies twisting bark fibres into thread like hemp, one wonders whether the bark cloth being described here is related to the pounded bark *tapa* cloth of Papua and the South Pacific, given Hainan's relative proximity. Bark cloth also shows up in a late twelfth-century passage in the *Ximan congxiao* on the Gelao in southern Hunan, who twist mulberry bark to make warp threads to wrap around their waists in a backstrap loom.[54]

Another tropical southern cloth was made from bamboo or banana leaves, which were dried and then boiled in lye to extract fibres for weaving.[55] This fabric is associated in the sources with Man and Liao people in Guangdong's upland and coastal prefectures around Guangzhou,[56] as well as in upland western Guangxi.[57] Unlike the bark cloth, however, this fabric appears to have found a market beyond local barter or subsistence production, as Zhou Qufei notes that finer grades of banana cloth could be valued at several strings of cash per bolt of cloth.[58]

The most common southern fabric that appears in these sources is ramie, which served a role in the south analogous to hemp in the north as the main source of fabric for commoner clothing. Ramie had a long history in the south, and first appeared as a southern tribute item in the *Daode jing*, in the fourth century BCE.[59] Ramie is related to hemp, as a member of the nettle family, but grows predominantly in tropical climates.[60] Its fibres are durable, and the loosely woven fabrics southerners made from it are breathable, qualities that Zhou Qufei noted suited ramie to Guangxi's heat and humidity.[61] Anecdotes of southern people wearing ramie appear across the southern frontier, from a people referred to as "native people" (*turen* 土人), tribal soldiers (*dongding* 洞丁), and valley Man (*dong* Man 峒蠻) in the two rivers region of western Guangxi, to the Yao[62] and Liao living in the upland zone between Guilin and southern Hunan.[63] There appears to have been a sizable market for ramie. Zhou describes Xiangzhou 象州 and Liuzhou 柳州 cloth merchants distributing it "to the four directions",[64] and claims that Han emperor Gaozu esteemed it so much that he put sumptuary restrictions on ramie, forbidding merchants to wear it.[65] By the Song, however, ramie faced no such restrictions, and Zhou claims that the price for fine ramie could be as high as ten strings of cash per bolt.[66] The white caps and bands of cloth used to tie off the mallet hairstyles of the south were also made of ramie.[67]

Cotton, which was later to become very widespread and important in China, was associated in these sources primarily with the Li people of Hainan. Due to the fact that cotton was still an exotic fabric, and largely produced outside of China, there were multiple terms for the same plant and cloth, something that confused Zhou Qufei.[68] Unlike the more widespread fibre crop of ramie, cotton is only mentioned in these sources as being grown in Hainan and the Leizhou peninsula, although Quanzhou merchants are described as running a thriving trans-shipment trade from Hainan, selling Hainanese cotton cloth to points north. Both Fan and Zhou speak very highly of the Li people's woven cotton cloth, and report it being sold in Guilin as multicoloured wall hangings, tablecloths, and bed sheets (but notably not as clothing).[69] As with ramie, the profusion of various grades of cotton cloth discussed in the sources, when combined with their discussion of the long-distance cotton trade,[70] suggests a thriving northern market for southern cotton.

Silk, the prestige fabric par excellence of Chinese civilization, appears to have been relatively rare on the southern frontier, and most of the time it appears in these sources in the forms of silk brocade robes given by the Song government to tribal chieftains as symbols of investiture, often preserved by certain families as heirlooms.[71] There are a few scattered mentions of silk clothing other than this, however: both the Li in Hainan and the Man horse-traders in Yongzhou are described by Fan and Zhou as wrapping their mallet hairstyles with colourful silk,[72] and several decades later, Zhao Rugua shows Li men in Qiongzhou wearing silken sarongs.[73] Only the Việt are shown as being able to produce silk, both as thread for stitching their distinctive snail-shaped bamboo hats,[74] and a coarse silken gauze, which they present as gifts during diplomatic missions to Qinzhou.[75] One reason given for the lack of silk is the paucity of mulberry trees (*sang* 桑) in the south.[76] While some southerners cultivated a similar sort of cocoon-spinning insect on the leaves of the Chinese mulberry (*zhe* 柘),[77] and extracted thread from the cocoon by treating it with lye, the process did not yield the same grade of silk floss, and could only be rubbed together into a lower grade fabric.[78] Another silk substitute mentioned was the "bug silk" (*chongsi* 蟲絲), made by an insect that fed on Chinese sweetgum (*feng* 楓) leaves. The threads were then extracted after being treated with wine vinegar.[79] The Li people acquired silk thread a different way, by cutting apart Chinese or Vietnamese silk, extracting the silk thread, and then weaving it alternating with cotton thread into their own colourful cloth.[80]

These sources' descriptions of southern fabrics define southern difference in two distinct ways. First, they draw attention to the influence of the tropical southern climate, both in the exotic tropical plants that were used to produce them, and in the airy, breathable weaves that southerners preferred. Second, the sources also use southern fabrics as ethnic markers, to distinguish between the different peoples of the frontier, and to rank them relative to the perceived degree of technological or cultural sophistication.

Colours and Dyes

Colour and dyed patterns were another aspect of southern clothing that these texts used as an ethnic marker. Chinese ethnography has long used colour as a way to categorize and distinguish between various groups of non-Chinese peoples, a practice that continues up to the present day. White clothing, especially when worn on the head as a cap or to bind one's mallet hairstyle, caught several authors' attention, because the colour white was associated with mourning dress in northern culture. Zhou Qufei writes,

> Southerners have a hard time obtaining black gauze, so they all use white ramie to make caps. On the street one's eyes are filled with white head cloths. Northerners see this and say, startled, "Southern miasma kills people, nearly every adjoining house is in mourning garb!"[81]

Western Guangxi in particular appears to be associated with white clothing, from the Liao[82] in the two rivers area,[83] to the people of Nanyizhou 南儀州 and Qinzhou just to the east,[84] and further west in the upland frontier with Dali.[85] This region overlaps somewhat with prefectures identified earlier as ones where ramie clothing was common. Fan Chengda claims that a group of Man chieftains wrap their hair with white paper in memory of Zhuge Liang. In so doing, Fan ironically ascribes this strange southern practice to ancient Chinese tutelage.[86]

By contrast, black clothing, especially black caps, appears to be associated with tribal chieftains and higher status individuals, and to a degree with Chinese people. Fan describes tribal chieftains of the streams and valleys in the two rivers area as wearing black caps and white robes in a manner similar to Chinese commoners,[87] "even though they had the titles of prefects or county magistrates".[88] Elite troops of the streams and valleys, called "field households" (*tianzi jia* 田子家) or "shields in front of the cavalry" (*maqian pai* 馬前牌) are also described as wearing black caps.[89] This may have been related to their access to black gauze for caps through their ties to Chinese frontier officials, who often gave Chinese cloth to "loose reins" tribal prefectures as payment to secure their loyalty and the peace. The Việt are also described as wearing dark clothing — Zhou refers to them as "those who blacken their clothing" — with Việt men wearing dark skirts and black robes, and wrapping their heads with fine black silk cloth, and the women wearing black skirts with green robes.[90] Zhou implies that this is similar to Chinese clothing, saying "when you see them on the street, there is no difference from our people, one can only tell by the caps".[91] In southern Hunan, Zhu Fu also suggests that dark clothing is seen as a Chinese ethnic marker, in a passage discussing the murderous enmity that Gelao people had for "dark-clothing people".[92]

The majority of references to coloured clothing in these sources, however, are to brightly coloured or multicoloured clothing. Just as in modern Chinese representations of minority nationalities, or Taiwanese representations of the aboriginal peoples of Taiwan, Song ethnographers used bright-coloured clothing to signify ethnic difference, not only between Chinese and non-Chinese, but also to sort between different groups of peoples on the frontier. In keeping with this approach, these ethnographies tend to associate certain colours of clothing with certain regions of the southern frontier.

The sources associate red clothing with western Guangxi, especially with the forest tribes in the two rivers area that the sources call Liao. The name "red pants" appears in Tang sources in lists of names for Liao tribes quoted in the *Guihai yuheng zhi*[93] and *Lingwai daida*[94] and is used to describe a people called Liaozi 獠子 living along the coast in Qinzhou in the tenth-century *Taiping huanyu ji*.[95] The *Lingwai daida* reports that the native people (*turen* 土人) in the streams and valleys of the two rivers region dye their ramie sackcloth red.[96] Further north, the *Ximan congxiao* also mentions the Gelao people of southern Hunan wearing red skirts.[97]

The peoples of the upland counties of northern Guangxi, by contrast, were defined in the sources by their indigo clothing, often marked with delicate batik patterns. The *Guihai yuheng zhi* describes all of the various southwestern Fan (Xinan Fan 西南蕃) peoples between Yizhou 宜州 and Zangge 牂柯 as wearing blue-patterned cloth,[98] while Zhou Qufei describes Yao people as wearing finely-patterned indigo clothing.[99] The batik patterns of their blue clothing were quite distinctive, and the process of making the fine patterns caught Zhou's attention:

> The Yao dye patterns into cloth with indigo, their patterns are extremely fine. The method is to use two wooden blocks and carve them in fine floral patterns. Then they use the blocks to squeeze the cloth, and melt wax to fill the carvings. Later, they separate the blocks and take out the cloth, and drop it into the indigo. The cloth then takes in the blue dye, and then they boil the cloth to remove the wax. This completes the fine floral patterns, its splendour can be seen. As for this method of dyeing fine patterns, there are none who can compare with the Yao.[100]

Zhu Fu also made mention of batik-patterned indigo cloth in southern Hunan, and claimed that the patterns on the cloth were drawn from motifs on bronze drums.[101] Intriguingly, this connects the Yao and the Việt, whom Zhou Qufei claimed tattooed the same bronze drum patterns on their skin,[102] to the ancient indigenous Yue people who made the southern frontier's famed bronze drums. This may just be a case of Chinese observers trying to connect their observations of local body culture in the present with patterns drawn from the region's antiquity, however.

The brightest and most colourful fabric in these ethnographies was the multicoloured cotton cloth worn by the Li people in Hainan. Every passage on Li clothing mentions the bright colours and the dazzling patterns woven into the cloth that they used to tie their hair, or make hats, robes, skirts, and sarongs. The *Taiping huanyu ji* section on Wan'anzhou 萬安州 in southeastern Hainan describes hats made of "five coloured" cloth (*wuse bu* 五色布), and skirts and robes made of patterned cloth.[103] Fan describes Li tying their hair with crimson and colourful silk, wearing multicoloured hats and short jackets, and wearing skirts edged with multicoloured borders.[104] Zhou Qufei borrows much of Fan's description, describing the patterned cloth Li women wore as skirts as being "multicoloured and brilliant", and other Li cloth as "dazzling".[105]

There seems to have been a significant market for this cloth in Guilin, as both Fan and Zhou mention several different products made from Li cloth: Li sheets with interwoven red and green patterns, which "everyone in Guilin buys for their beds", dazzling multicoloured Li screens, and *anda* cloth (*anda bu* 鞍搭布), which Zhou described as being well suited for using to cover book tables.[106] Notably, all of the instances of Li fabric in Guilin mentioned by these authors use it as decoration, but not as clothing. The same fabric that could mark an ethnic boundary when wrapped around the waist could be appreciated for its aesthetic and exotic qualities, as a deracinated commodity — when taken off the body and hung on a wall, placed on a bed, or draped artfully over a table — without raising questions about the ethnic identity of the consumer. It is not fabric itself, but rather how it was stitched into clothing or wrapped around the body that gave it its power as a boundary.

Wearing Identity

While the fabric may have been made from different raw materials, the dyes might have set them apart from Chinese clothing, and the amount of clothing worn was generally less than north of the passes, the form of the clothing itself was often similar to Chinese dress. Most familiar, of course, were the silk brocade robes, caps, belts, and other elements of official formal dress that the Song government granted to tribal officials. In the early Song, the *Taiping huanyu ji* records a clan in Binzhou 賓州

passing down formal clothing as heirlooms.[107] Later on in the twelfth century, Fan Chengda describes a descendant of a Li chieftain in Hainan wearing Chinese robes given to his grandfather,[108] and Zhou Qufei describes descendants of submitted Li tribal officials "wearing brocade robes and silver belts".[109] Việt formal clothing is also described as being similar to Chinese official dress, with Việt chieftains wearing yellow robes and purple skirts, and commoners wearing black robes with black skirts.[110] The Việt officials that Zhou comes into contact with in Qinzhou also wear a very Chinese form of formal attire:

> When they deliver documents, they wear purple robes and ivory tablets, and hurry to pay respects in a graceful and dignified manner. When emissaries arrive, their civil and military officials all wear purple robes, red leather belts, rhinoceros horn belts but without fish [symbols]. After he brought an elephant as tribute, Li Bangzheng [Viet., Lí Bang Chính 李邦正] again came as an emissary to Qin[zhou], and added a very long and large golden fish [to his belt].[111]

Việt women are also described as wearing Chinese-style clothing, "green, broad-sleeved robes with straight collars, all of which are bound by black skirts".[112]

Aside from official attire, many upland frontier peoples wore tailored clothing that was described by the sources as being analogous to Chinese commoner clothing. The Liao are often defined in Chinese texts by their red pants and white robes,[113] or red pants and coarse cloth jackets.[114] Yao commoners are described by Zhou as "sometimes half-naked, or wearing rags, or patterned cloth robes and pants", while Yao women wear "robes and skirts, resplendent and swirling".[115] Dan people, whose clothing is otherwise barely mentioned at all,[116] are described as wearing rags; as with the Yao, the rags appear to signify poverty rather than a different form of clothing.

By contrast, the sources describe several groups of people on the frontier whose clothing was worn by wrapping cloth around the waist and binding it by knots or folds. In the western uplands, Zhou describes the southwestern Man wearing wool cloth wrapped around the body: "They string a long felt belt through the folded area, and then wear the felt wrapped around their waist, in a spiral manner."[117] Another example of wrapped clothing comes from Zhu Fu in the uplands of southern Hunan, where Zhu ascribes the Gelao people's refusal to adopt tailored pants for fear of supernatural retribution:

> The skirts are sewn together from two pieces, and they pull them up from their feet. They are resplendent and multicoloured, thick and heavy, with the lower section solely using red [cloth]. I suspect it is what Fan [Ye]'s *History* called "*duli* clothing" [*duli yi* 獨力衣].[118] Thus they are naked, but use the skirt in place of pants. Even when they dress for ceremonies they will not discard the skirt. If they did, it would offend the ghosts.[119]

The loop skirt described above, sewn together from several pieces of cloth into a loop, and then wrapped around and tied off, appears to have been very common in the southern coastal lowlands, and shows up in several ethnographic passages.[120] The *Taiping huanyu ji* entries on the customs of Xinzhou 新州 in Guangdong and Wan'anzhou on Hainan both describe a similar sort of loop skirt, called *dulong* 都籠 or *duluo* 都落.[121] The loop skirt is also shown as part of the bridal costume of villagers in Qinzhou, and in several passages on the clothing of Li women in Hainan.[122] The same basic pattern of construction was also used for jackets, sewn together in a loop like the skirts with a hole for the head, in the style of a poncho.[123] In addition to the wrapped loop skirt, there are also several passages that refer to southern peoples on the coast simply wrapping bolts of cloth around their waists. The *Taiping huanyu ji* notes that Xue women in Baizhou, just north of the Leizhou peninsula, "wrap themselves with cloth to the mid-thigh", and both Fan and Zhou describe Li men in Hainan wrapping their waists with patterned cloth.[124] Zhao Rugua's account of Hainan in the late Southern Song shows that while Li men and women had adopted shirts "no different from China", they continued to wrap cloth around their waists, but now the Li men used silk cloth instead of cotton.[125] As with the Gelao refusing to abandon their skirts for fear of divine retribution, this hints at a cultural resistance to abandoning the wrapped cloth for Chinese-style tailored pants or robes, even as Chinese-style clothing was adopted above the belt.

Wrapped clothing may have served to distinguish the peoples of the coast from wearers of tailored clothing further inland, but it also connected them to the other peoples of the maritime frontier of the South Seas, in a vast east-west band of tropical maritime Asia, that extended from the south coast of China all the way to East Africa.

Changing Clothes

One of the interesting things about clothing as an ethnic boundary is that unlike more permanent elements of body culture such as tattoos, one could perform different ethnic identities simply by changing one's clothes. The Song court's long-standing policy of granting silk brocade robes and other symbols of Chinese officialdom to tribal officials was a conscious attempt to transform the people of China's periphery by having their leaders perform that transformation by wearing Chinese clothing. In time, the assumption was that tribal officials' adoption of Chinese-style dress would transform the local populace, "as wind over grass", as the Confucian tradition put it. "Raw" barbarians would become "cooked" (*shu* 熟), "cooked" would become civilized imperial subjects, and the frontier would transform into yet another part of the Chinese ecumene. This civilizing mission was central to the cosmology of imperial rule, and underpinned the very legitimacy of the government and the emperor himself. To rule was to transform, and the frontier was the most productive location for that transformation.

But a few passages about the Cooked Li people in Hainan suggest that rather than a permanent, unidirectional transformation, some people on the frontier were transgressing that boundary in both directions, signified in several sources by the act of changing their clothing. Fan Chengda writes, "The Cooked Li can speak the Han language (*Hanyu* 漢語). They change their clothing and enter the cities and markets. At day's end they sound a horn and gather their groups to return."[126] Zhou Qufei expands on the story, emphasizing the ambiguity of frontier life:

> Li people can halfway speak the Han language. They form groups of tens and hundreds, change their clothing and enter the cities and markets, other people have no way to tell them apart. When the day gets late, sometimes a horn is sounded, then they all gather, one after another, form groups and return. Only then does one begin to know that they were Li.[127]

To not be able to tell who was Chinese and who was Li, and then see the Li emerge at the city gates and reveal themselves *en masse*, destabilized the categories of Chinese and Li, and unnerved Chinese officials stationed on the southern frontier. Making it even more disturbing was the possibility that the Cooked Li weren't even necessarily Li at all. In other passages on the Li people, both Fan and Zhou claim that some who are called Cooked Li were in fact migrants from South China who had gone native. Zhou writes:

> Many of the Cooked Li are traitorous people from Hu[nan], Guang[dong] and Fujian. They are crafty and fierce bringers of calamity. On the surface they pay taxes to officials, but secretly collude with Raw Li into encroaching on Song territory, and waylay travelers and residents.[128]

Zhao Rugua also makes reference to "those of our subjects who have committed crimes" fleeing to Li territory, and both Fan and Zhao mention shipwrecked Fujianese merchants entering Li territory to farm (and presumably, to avoid taxes).[129] While the rhetoric of raw and cooked — and indeed, the very idea of cooking or ripening implicit in that metaphor — positions the cooked as a way station on the road from raw barbarian to civilized Chinese, perhaps "cooked" would be better thought of as a frontier zone of dynamic hybrid ambiguity, populated both by those fleeing China into its frontier periphery as much as those from the periphery becoming acculturated and eventually assimilated into what we call China. All across the Lingnan frontier, at the margins of the Song state's administrative reach, these boundary crossers likely played a significant role in the emergence of regional southern Chinese identities in the late imperial period.

While this other transformation cannot be explained within the unidirectional teleology of Sinification, it was just as much a process of frontier acculturation as Sinification, and it does suggest that some of those Cooked Li who could speak Chinese, and who were so adept at changing their clothing and melting into the market crowds were in fact Chinese migrants or their descendants. When the innate physical body was no longer assumed to be a reliable ethnic boundary, the act of changing clothes enabled some to exist in an ambiguous zone of ethnic multiplicity, performing different roles as needed. When the frontier people being observed and ordered obscure or transgress those boundaries, it frustrates the authors' efforts to categorize, organize, and thus rule the people of the southern frontier. The complex, shifting, and ambiguous nature of the frontier was a constant challenge for those tasked with ordering the frontier into stable categories. Ironically enough, the very process of settling the frontier that these sources were instrumental to was a large part of what blurred those boundaries in the first place.

Conclusion

As we have seen, the Southern Song frontier accounts discussed above devote a significant amount of attention to defining ethnic difference, not only to police the boundary between Chinese and non-Chinese populations, but also to distinguish between various groups of southerners and order them into coherent ethnic categories. In contrast to earlier accounts of the peoples of the south, these texts do not define ethnic difference as an innate physical quality, or uncritically repeat ancient tales of fantastical or monstrous southern bodies. Instead, they tend to frame ethnic difference in terms of body culture, that is to say how the people of the southern frontier altered and clothed (or bared) their bodies, and in so doing, performed their identities. While these sources do sometimes quote earlier passages on southern bodies, they are relatively less reliant on ancient texts than was the case in Tang geographies, and place more weight on ethnographic observation. When the two ways of knowing came into conflict, as we saw in the case of the trope of the "crossed legs" of Jiaozhi, personal observation trumped ancient tropes.

These changes in Song ethnography reflect the transformation of the southern frontier during the eleventh and twelfth centuries from an indirectly governed and thinly garrisoned frontier region to an increasingly settled and directly administered province. This transformation was itself part of a much longer process of southern expansion and colonization that began a millennium before the Southern Song, and which continued well into the late imperial colonization of the internal frontier of the southern uplands, the Yunnan–Guizhou plateau, and Taiwan. Within this *longue durée* of imperial China's "march to the tropics", as Harold Weins has called it, the twelfth century was an important inflection point, especially in terms of how information about the frontier and its inhabitants was gathered, compiled, and constructed into a coherent body of knowledge through the emerging genre of local geographies or gazetteers.

As a consequence of these changes, there was a growing need on the part of frontier officials for accurate information about the myriad peoples of the frontier that they were expected to govern or interact with. Hoary tropes of southern barbarity were decidedly less useful to frontier officials than detailed observations of who the peoples of the south were, how they could be expected to act, and how to distinguish them from other groups. The increasing number of distinct ethnonyms such as Liao, Yao, Dan, or Li — in contrast to generic labels such as *nanman* 南蠻 or *manyi* 蠻夷 — in Southern Song sources reflect this administrative need. While some of the terms such as Liao have their origin in earlier periods, they are used in increasingly specific ways in Song geographies, and are linked to both ethnographic description and distinct territorial regions. As the Song administrative presence intensified and expanded on the frontier, it created a growing demand for a meso-level of ethnic category or type interposed between generic labels such as Southern Man and the dizzying variety of local groups, which were often organized at the village or river valley level. Once new ethnic categories were created and defined, frontier policies and strategies could be formulated to deal with the people they described. The proliferation and definition of ethnic categories on the southern frontier during the Song dynasty was thus a precursor to the steady increase in ethnic categories that Leo Shin has found in Ming-era gazetteers of Guangxi.[130]

As we have seen, these ethnic types were often distinguished visually, in terms of body culture (and especially by clothing). But why body culture, specifically? Since these ethnic categories were being formulated from an outside perspective by Song frontier officials, outwardly visible body culture was an accessible marker for them to use to sort frontier people into ethnic categories. In a manner similar to how the Miao albums or albums of Taiwanese aboriginals that were produced during the Qing dynasty were used, Song frontier officials also periodically painted likenesses of frontier peoples and sent them to administrative offices as references.[131] In Fan Chengda's description of the appearance of the Raw Li, Fan mentions in passing that he based his ethnographic passage upon portraits of submitted Li tribesmen that had been painted by the magistrate of Qiongzhou and sent to the Military Commissioner's Office in Guilin where Fan worked.[132] The images themselves were unfortunately not preserved in these sources, but they would have helped to shape the idea of regular, standard body cultures linked to specific ethnic categories. While the various peoples being depicted and categorized surely had their own understandings and definitions of their own identities, they do not tend to appear in these sources because they were not as accessible or useful to the Song frontier officials who compiled them. Over time, however, the categories imposed by frontier ethnographies were reified through centuries of interaction with the imperial state, until some eventually came to be adopted and internalized by the peoples of the south themselves. Thus, the representation and categorization of clothes — and in a broader sense, body cultures — in Song accounts of the Lingnan frontier did in a sense "make the Man", both in terms of colonial systems of knowledge, and in southern frontier peoples' gradual internalization of those ethnic categories.

NOTES

I would like to thank the Nalanda Srivijaya Centre and the Institute of Southeast Asian Studies for the opportunity to present an earlier version of this chapter at the International Conference on Imperial China and Its Southern Neighbours, and for my fellow presenters for all of their insights and feedback. This chapter is indebted to Wang Ming-ke for the idea of body culture, which grew out of conversations we had at the Institute of History and Philology at Academia Sinica. I am deeply grateful to Beverly Bossler, Nicole Richardson, Elad Alyagon, Wu Yulian, Lin Shan, Chris Tong, Yi Zhou, David Dayton, Doris Duangboudda, and the UC Davis Chinese Studies Association for their many helpful comments, questions, and revisions. Any remaining errors or shortcomings are mine alone.

1. For more on the concept of legibility, see James C. Scott, *The Art of Not Being Governed: An Anarchist History of Upland Southeast Asia* (New Haven: Yale University Press, 2009), chapter three, esp. pp. 73–97.
2. Marc S. Abramson, *Ethnic Identity in Tang China* (Philadelphia: University of Pennsylvania Press, 2008), p. 99.
3. For a discussion of the northern border, see Naomi Standen, *Unbounded Loyalty: Frontier Crossings in Liao China* (Honolulu: University of Hawai'i Press, 2007). For the southern border's transformation in the eleventh century, see James

Anderson, *The Rebel Den of Nùng Trí Cao: Loyalty and Identity Along the Sino–Vietnamese Border* (Seattle: University of Washington Press, 2007).

4. Ruth Mostern, *Dividing the Realm in Order to Govern: The Spatial Organization of the Song State (960–1276 CE)* (Cambridge, MA: Harvard University Press, 2011), p. 249.

5. As such, these officials would have been called "northerners" (*beiren* 北人) in the context of the southern frontier, even if most would be considered southerners in the rest of Song China, hailing predominantly from the developed core of the Lower Yangzi. Fan Chengda was from Suzhou 蘇州, Zhou Qufei was from Wenzhou 溫州, Zhu Fu was from Shuzhou 舒州, and Zhao Rugua was from Taizhou 台州.

6. Yue Shi 樂史, *Taiping huanyu ji* 太平寰宇記 [A Record of the World during the Taiping Era], edited by Wang Wenchu 王文楚 (Beijing: Zhonghua shuju 中華書局, 2007). Hereafter TPHYJ.

7. Fan Chengda 范成大, "Guihai yuheng zhi" 桂海虞衡志 [Treatises of the Supervisor and Guardian of the Cinnamon Sea], in *Fan Chengda biji liucong* 范成大筆記六叢 [A Collection of Six *Biji* by Fan Chengda], edited by Kong Fanli 孔凡禮 (Beijing: Zhonghua shuju 中華書局, 2008), pp. 71–178. Hereafter GHYHZ.

8. Zhou Qufei 周去非, *Lingwai daida jiaozhu* 嶺外代答校注 [Replies from Beyond the Passes, Footnoted], edited by Yang Wuquan 楊武泉 (Beijing: Zhonghua shuju 中華書局, 1999). Hereafter LWDD.

9. Zhu Fu 朱輔, *Ximan congxiao yanjiu* 溪蠻叢笑研究 [Research on a Collection of Laughable Things from the Barbarians of the Streams], edited by Fu Taihao 符太浩 (Guiyang: Guizhou minsu chubanshe 貴州民俗出版社, 2003). Hereafter XMCX.

10. Zhao Rugua 趙如适, *Zhufan zhi jiaoshi* 諸蕃志校釋 [Treatise on the Many Tributaries, Annotated], edited by Yang Bowen 楊博文 (Beijing: Zhonghua shuju 中華書局, 2000). Hereafter ZFZ.

11. GHYHZ, p. 156.

12. Ibid., p. 155. The *Liji* is the *Record of Rites*.

13. LWDD, p. 408.

14. Blackened teeth are explained elsewhere in the *Lingwai daida* as a consequence of chewing betel nut, and not as an innate quality. LWDD, p. 236.

15. The Liao 獠 people of the upland south (sometimes written with the human radical as 僚) should not be confused with the north-eastern Khitan state of Liao 遼, a geopolitical rival of the Northern Song.

16. On the Việt: GHYHZ, pp. 155–56; LWDD, pp. 59, 408. On the Liao: TPHYJ, pp. 3176–77; GHYHZ, p. 145; LWDD, pp. 416 and 419. On the Li: TPHYJ, pp. 3232 and 3234; GHYHZ, pp. 156–57; LWDD, pp. 71 and 419; ZFZ, p. 220. Notably, neither the Yao, Dan, nor "native people" (*turen* 土人) are described as being tattooed in any of my Song-era sources.

17. GHYHZ, pp. 55–56; LWDD, p. 408.

18. GHYHZ, p. 155. The "Wangzhi", or "Royal Regulations", is a chapter in the *Liji*.
19. LWDD, p. 59.
20. TPHYJ, pp. 3176–77; GHYHZ, p. 145; LWDD, p. 416.
21. Li Fang 李昉, *Taiping guangji* 太平廣記 [Vast Records of the Taiping Era] (Beijing: Zhonghua shuju 中華書局, 2008), p. 3976. One ancient Chinese explanation for the southern practice of tattooing the body was that tattooed markings helped protect southern peoples against dangerous water creatures called *jiaolong* 蛟龍 in their wet, perilous riverine environment. Carrie E. Reed, "Tattoo in Early China", *Journal of the American Oriental Society* 120, no. 3 (2000): 361–62.
22. Ibid., pp. 366–70.
23. GHYHZ, p. 153.
24. LWDD, p. 419.
25. Ibid., p. 59.
26. Reed, pp. 366–70.
27. TPHYJ, p. 3232.
28. Ibid., p. 3234.
29. GHYHZ, p. 157. There is a very similar passage on "embroidered faces" on p. 156 as well.
30. LWDD, p. 419.
31. In a different passage on Li tattoos, however, Fan uses the verb "to brand" (*qing* 黥) instead of "to darken" (*nie* 涅). GHYHZ, p. 156. Zhou is more consistent.
32. Zhang Shi was a prominent twelfth-century *daoxue* figure, and a major rival of Zhu Xi within the movement. See Hoyt Tillman, *Confucian Discourse and Chu Hsi's Ascendancy* (Honolulu: University of Hawai'i Press, 1992), esp. chapter two. In addition to studying with Zhang, Zhou also served under him as a prefectural instructor from 1175–78 in Qinzhou, when Zhang was posted to Guilin as Military Commissioner, succeeding Fan Chengda in the post. Yang Wuquan, "Jiaozhu qianyan" 校注前言 [Editor's Preface], LWDD, p. 6; Zhang Shi 張栻, "Qinzhou xueji" 欽州學記 [A Record of Study in Qinzhou], in LWDD, p. 455; Quan Zuwang 全祖望, "Song-Yuan xue'an" 宋元學案 [Survey of Song and Yuan Confucians], in LWDD, pp. 457–58.
33. Mark Abramson discusses this idealization of the foreign by ascribing one's own highest values to them in a Tang context in *Ethnic Identity in Tang China*, p. 12.
34. LWDD, p. 451.
35. Ibid., p. 116.
36. GHYHZ, p. 157.
37. LWDD, p. 71. One sees something similar a century later in Zhou Daguan's fourteenth–century depiction of Cambodian women in the *Zhenla fengtu ji*, which describes expatriate Chinese taking voyeuristic sightseeing excursions to the river for the purpose of watching local women bathe. Zhou Daguan 周達觀, *Zhenla fengtu ji jiaozhu* 真臘風土記校注 [A Record of the Customs of Cambodia,

Annotated], edited by Xia Nai 夏鼐 (Beijing: Zhonghua shuju 中華書局, 2000), p. 179. This itself is echoed, a millennia later, in contemporary Chinese eroticization of ethnic minority peoples in south-west China, e.g., the Yunnan school of ethnic-inspired painting, or the Dai water splashing festival in popular culture. See Dru Gladney, "Representing Nationality in China: Refiguring Majority/Minority Identities", *The Journal of Asian Studies* 53, no. 1 (1994): 92–123; Susan D. Blum, *Portraits of "Primitives": Ordering Human Kinds in the Chinese Nation* (New York: Rowman and Littlefield, 2001), esp. chapter four, "The Fetishized Ethnic Other: The Dai".

38. TPHYJ, p. 3199. Although the character Xue is used here as an ethnonym, it originally appears in the *Shanhai jing* 山海經 [Classic of Mountains and Seas] as a mountain creature with the body of a dog and the face of a human. This has interesting resonances with Song era ethnographic claims that Panhu 盤瓠, a dog, was the ancestor of the south-western upland peoples. *Kangxi zidian* 康熙字典 [Kangxi Dictionary] (Hong Kong: Zhonghua shuju 中華書局, 1958, 2009), p. 642

39. XMCX, p. 93.

40. GHYHZ, p. 157; LWDD, p. 71.

41. Jacques Gernet, *Daily Life in China on the Eve of the Mongol Invasion, 1250–1276* (Stanford: Stanford University Press, 1962), p. 130.

42. TPHYJ, p. 3119; GHYHZ, pp. 141, 146, 147, 149, 156, 160; LWDD, pp. 71, 119.

43. GHYHZ, p. 141.

44. See Erica Brindley, "Layers of Meaning: Hairstyle and Yue Identity in Ancient Chinese Texts" in this volume.

45. TPHYJ, pp. 3035, 3037. Both passages use the exact same words to describe the spirits.

46. LWDD, p. 451.

47. Wolfram Eberhard, *The Local Cultures of South and East China*, translated by Alice Eberhard (Leiden: E.J. Brill, 1968), pp. 49–50.

48. XMCX, p. 119; LWDD, p. 121; GHYHZ, p. 147.

49. XMCX, p. 341.

50. LWDD, p. 119.

51. TPHYJ, p. 3234; GHYHZ, pp. 156–57; LWDD, p. 71; ZFZ, p. 220.

52. There is no southern equivalent of "braided caitiffs", or *suolu* 索虜, for example.

53. TPHYJ, pp. 3233, 3236.

54. XMCX, p. 169. For a description of how a backstrap loom works, see Judith Cameron, "Textile Crafts in the Gulf of Tongking: The Intersection Between Archaeology and History", in *The Tongking Gulf Through History*, edited by Nola Cooke, Li Tana, and James A. Anderson (Philadelphia: University of Pennsylvania Press, 2011), p. 33.

55. LWDD, p. 326. For more on the processing of banana leaves into cloth, see Dieter Kuhn, "Textile Technology: Spinning and Reeling", Part 9 of *Science*

and Civilization in China, Volume 5: Chemistry and Chemical Technology (Cambridge: Cambridge University Press, 1988), pp. 45–52.

56. TPHYJ, pp. 3011, 3035, 3041, 3053, 3057, 3061, 3118.
57. TPHYJ, p. 3190; GHYHZ, p. 137; LWDD, p. 413.
58. LWDD, p. 326.
59. Cameron, p. 35.
60. Francesca Bray, *Science and Civilization in China, Volume 6: Biology and Biological Technology, Part II: Agriculture* (Cambridge, UK: Cambridge University Press, 1984), pp. 535–36.
61. LWDD, pp. 223 and 225.
62. LWDD, p. 223. The passage refers to commoners (*minjian* 民間), but Gu county is identified elsewhere by Zhou as a Yao county.
63. TPHYJ, pp. 3170, 3172, 3191; GHYHZ, pp. 101, 137; LWDD, pp. 223, 413; XMCX, p. 126.
64. LWDD, p. 223.
65. Ibid., p. 223.
66. Ibid., p. 225.
67. Ibid., p. 257.
68. Ibid., p. 228.
69. GHYHZ, pp. 101, 157–58; LWDD, p. 228; ZFZ, p. 228.
70. ZFZ, p. 221.
71. TPHYJ, p. 3157; GHYHZ, p. 160; LWDD, p. 71; ZFZ, p. 221.
72. GHYHZ, pp. 149, 160; LWDD, p. 71.
73. ZFZ, p. 217.
74. LWDD, p. 152.
75. Ibid., p. 226.
76. Ibid., p. 225.
77. *Maclura tricuspidata.* Silkworms could not eat Chinese mulberry leaves, according to Zhu Fu. XMCX, p. 169.
78. LWDD, p. 225; XMCX, p. 111.
79. *Liquidambar formosana.* LWDD, p. 231.
80. GHYHZ, pp. 101 and 157; LWDD, p. 226; ZFZ, p. 220.
81. LWDD, p. 257.
82. One Liao tribe was called "white robes" (*baishan* 白衫). GHYHZ, p. 145.
83. TPHYJ, p. 3171; LWDD, p. 223.
84. TPHYJ, pp. 3115, 3200.
85. GHYHZ, p. 147; LWDD, p. 228.
86. GHYHZ, p. 147.
87. Gernet, p. 128.
88. GHYHZ, p. 138. The implication being that tribal chiefs took on self-aggrandizing, inflated titles, but governed inconsequentially small territories.
89. Ibid., p. 137.

90. GHYHZ, p. 152; LWDD, pp. 59, 60, and 408.

91. LWDD, p. 60. Ironically, the white caps of the Qinzhou people, which Zhou found elsewhere to be somewhat strange, are what allowed him to distinguish them from the black cap-wearing Việt.

92. XMCX, p. 172. Fu Taihao argues in the notes that "dark-clothing people" refers to Chinese.

93. GHYHZ, p. 145.

94. LWDD, p. 416.

95. TPHYJ, p. 3200.

96. LWDD, p. 225.

97. XMCX, p. 93.

98. GHYHZ, p. 146.

99. LWDD, p. 119.

100. Ibid., p. 224.

101. XMCX, p. 131.

102. LWDD, p. 59.

103. TPHYJ, p. 3240.

104. GHYHZ, p. 160. Zhao Rugua later reproduces this passage in the *Zhufan zhi* section on the Li. ZFZ, p. 221.

105. LWDD, p. 71 and 228.

106. GHYHZ, p. 101; LWDD, p. 228; ZFZ, pp. 219–20.

107. TPHYJ, p. 3157.

108. GHYHZ, p. 160. The passage is reproduced with minor changes a century later in ZFZ, p. 221.

109. LWDD, p. 71.

110. Ibid., p. 59.

111. Ibid., p. 60.

112. GHYHZ, p. 152.

113. "Red pants" (*chiku* 赤褲) is listed as one of the Chinese names for Liao tribes. GHYHZ, p. 145.

114. TPHYJ, p. 3200.

115. LWDD, p. 119.

116. The sources define the Dan in terms of where and how the Dan lived — in boats and on water, instead of on dry land — more than by what they wore.

117. LWDD, p. 227.

118. The text referred to in this passage is the *Hou Hanshu* 後漢書 [History of the Latter Han] by Fan Ye 范曄. The word "*duli* clothing" comes from a passage in the *Hou Hanshu* about the clothing of the descendants of Panhu, a mythical canine ancestor of the Man tribes.

119. XMCX, p. 93.

120. The basic form of this kind of loop skirt appears to be roughly similar to the *lao sinh* skirt prevalent in rural Laos today.

121. TPHYJ, pp. 3117 and 3240.
122. GHYHZ, p. 157; LWDD, pp. 71 and 232.
123. TPHYJ, p. 3240.
124. TPHYJ, p. 3199; GHYHZ, pp. 157, 160; LWDD, p. 71.
125. ZFZ, p. 217
126. GHYHZ, p. 157.
127. LWDD, p. 72.
128. LWDD, p. 70. Fan Chengda's passage is very similar. GHYHZ, p. 159.
129. GHYHZ, p. 159; ZFZ, pp. 220–21.
130. Leo K. Shin, *The Making of the Chinese State: Ethnicity and Expansion on the Ming Borderlands* (New York: Cambridge University Press, 2006), pp. 138–83.
131. For more on the Miao albums, see Laura Hostetler, *Qing Colonial Enterprise: Ethnography and Cartography in Early Modern China* (Chicago: University of Chicago Press, 2001), pp. 159–204; For Qing images of Taiwanese aboriginals, see Emma Jinhua Teng, *Taiwan's Imagined Geography: Chinese Colonial Travel Writing and Pictures, 1683–1895* (Cambridge, MA: Harvard University Press, 2004), pp. 149–72.
132. GHYHZ, p. 160.

5

WHAT MAKES A CHINESE GOD? OR, WHAT MAKES A GOD CHINESE?

Hugh R. Clark

Over the course of a thousand years roughly equivalent to the first millennium AD, the Sinitic culture of the Yellow River basin came into contact with the south, the culturally and ethnically divergent lands of the Yangzi River basin and beyond. By the Song Dynasty, which straddles the end of the first and the early second millennia, much of the south had become a full partner in the definition of a new emerging culture. Although this new culture drew heavily on the Sinitic heritage of the Central Lands, it was not simply an extension of the Sinitic world. On the contrary, the new culture that emerged through the course of this millennium, the culture we today call "Chinese", was a hybrid entity, drawing as much on the non-Sinitic models of the south as on the Sinitic heritage of the north.

In this chapter, I intend to show how cultures merged in southern Fujian province to create a hybrid culture. Although there are many avenues through which I could make this case — family structures, economic activities, and cropping come readily to mind — in this chapter, I will focus on religious expression. Across much of China cults devoted to local deities have long been among the most important expressions of culture and local identity. However, whereas deities whose roots lay in the northern culture such as the Queen Mother of the West, Guan Yu, or Zhenwu Xuandi were often identified conceptually either in connection with direction or specific function, those of the south were more often identified as protector deities of designated locales. Although some deities with origins in the south gained broad followings, most cults remained strictly local, sometimes never spreading beyond a single shrine. In the following discussion, I will examine a range of cults that took shape in southern Fujian during the period between the later Tang and Song dynasties in southern Fujian province in an attempt to address two parallel questions: What makes a Chinese god? or What makes a god Chinese?

Cults of the Sinitic Immigration

As the Sinitic immigrants entered the alien lands of southern Fujian through the middle of the first millennium, they encountered the indigenous people. This encounter sometimes led to conflict, and other times unfolded more smoothly. Both outcomes, however, found expression in local cults that survive to the present.

Let us begin with the story of Chen Zheng 陳政 (d. 677) and his son Chen Yuanguang 陳元光 (c.657–711), who pioneered the Sinitic community in modern Zhangzhou 漳州, the region south of the Jin River 晉江 valley defined by the valley of the Jiulong River 九龍江 and the adjacent coastline. Although definitely on the fringe of early Sinitic settlement, the existence of a community was first recognized sometime in the sixth century when Longxi district 龍溪縣 was established.[1] Exactly what transpired in the years that followed is murky, and the surviving narratives, which all come from regional and local gazetteers of the later imperial era, are inconsistent. In fact, should we extrapolate from frontier experience elsewhere at other times, we can imagine that as the community grew, unrest along the settlement frontier had become an ongoing problem, that what had begun in the sixth century as a fairly even competition for resources between indigenes, who had numbers, and early settlers, who had more advanced technology, had gradually swung in favour of the latter as their numbers grew, that the indigenes were forced off the good bottom lands of the lower Jiulong River valley and adjacent regions of the coast, and that violence resulted. It is a reasonable reconstruction, but in fact we do not know.

What we do know is that around the mid-seventh century, the Sinitic community appealed to the Tang court for protection.[2] In 669, Emperor Gaozong (r. 650–684) announced through an imperial edict that the "Liao Man" 獠蠻 were causing a ruckus in the border area between Quanzhou 泉州 and Chaozhou 潮州 and ordered Chen Zheng to proceed at the head of an armed band to "Suian district 綏安縣[3] where the Seven Min [*qi Min* 七閩, i.e., the Sinitic settlements] and Hundred Yue [Baiyue 百粵, the non-Sinitic 'barbarians'] confront each other".[4] Chen Zheng established a self-supporting colony (*tuntian* 屯田) on the coast south of the Jiulong River in the vicinity of modern Yunxiao Village in Zhangzhou 漳州雲霄村.

The colony was plagued by disease, especially malaria, which ultimately forced it to relocate to higher land at Zhangpu 漳浦, nearer the Jiulong River itself and closer to the ultimate site of the Zhangzhou prefectural city. In the face of such challenges, the settlement nevertheless endured. When Chen Zheng died of natural causes in 677, he was succeeded as leader of the outpost by his son Yuanguang. While we can imagine, moreover, that tension with the indigenous communities of the interior continued to plague the colony, nothing is mentioned in the surviving record until 686, when "the Guang[zhou] bandit [Guang *kou* 廣寇] Chen Qian 陳謙 united with the Man barbarian chieftains, Miao Zicheng 苗自成 and Lei Wanxing 雷萬興, and attacked Chaozhou [Guangdong]".[5] None of the three have left any other record, so much of what transpired is unknown. Regardless, it seems certain that "the Guangzhou bandit", Chen Qian, was able to rally the peoples of the mountainous interior for another round of violent resistance to the encroachment of the Sinitic immigrants.

The outbreak focused on Chaozhou: "with light cavalry he attacked and suppressed them."[6] He then petitioned the court to establish a new district between Quanzhou and Zhangzhou. According to late imperial gazetteers, our only source for most of this narrative, this occasioned discussion at court:

Remote places are uncouth and yet to be civilized. We might dispatch a thousand and one officials, but if they do not know the local situation then the people will suffer. Now Yuanguang and his father have tended this land for several years. The barbarians hold them in awe, and the people revere their kindness. If we add "prefect" to his rank so that Yuanguang can run local affairs, then things will not be disordered and the people will not suffer.

Perhaps even more significant, the court luminaries are alleged to have gone on:

[The family of Chen Yuanguang] is to hold the prefectship for succeeding generations [*rengshi shou cishi* 仍世守刺史]... Yuanguang is to recommend appointees for prefectural offices from his administrative assistant [*biejia* 別駕] on down and from country sheriff [*buwei* 簿尉] on up.[7]

Our source for this debate is very late; it does not appear in any of the standard sources of Tang history and may be a later addition to the story. Yet whether the result of a decision at court or a local reality that later worked its way into the historical tradition, it is exactly what transpired. Chen Yuanguang did apparently have complete discretion over local offices. Moreover, except for two brief periods, the Chen family monopolized authority in Zhangzhou from its establishment in 686 until the death of Yuanguang's great-grandson Chen Mo 陳謨 in 819.[8]

Not surprisingly, the establishment of Zhangzhou did not immediately lead to pacification of the local indigenes. Yuanguang himself was a victim of the ongoing unrest, dying in the course of a campaign in 711 said to have been against the sons of "the Man barbarian chieftains" Miao Zicheng and Lei Wanxing.[9] The Zhangzhou–Chaozhou border area, furthermore, was to remain a centre of non-Sinitic culture for many more years. If it took longer to civilize than areas that were more central to Fujian, however, ultimately Zhangzhou, like everywhere else, was brought fully into the sphere of *wen* 文.[10]

Apparently within years of his death, Chen Yuanguang was honoured with a shrine. Initially this was apparently an honorific shrine (*ci* 祠) rather than a god's shrine (*miao* 廟). Later sources tell us that Chen was initially ennobled as the Lord of Yingchuan 穎川侯 and then, because of a series of miracles (*lingyi* 靈異) connected to his spirit, was further granted a succession of titles as the King of Numinous Strategy, Follower of the Right, Reflected Brilliance, and Boundless Succour (Lingzhu shunying zhaolie guangji wang 靈著順應昭烈廣濟王).[11] Writing in the eleventh century, Yu Jing 余京, in his funerary inscription for Chen Tanran 陳坦然 (d. 1032), noted the Shrine to General Chen (Chen jiangjun ci 陳將軍祠) lay to the west of Zhangpu.[12] Roughly contemporaneously, however, Lü Tao 呂璹 (1034 *jinshi*) commemorated the Shrine to Awesome Benevolence (Weihui miao 威惠廟) in a poem of the same name:

> At that time he pacified brigands,
> And was recognized for his extraordinary service.
> Yet his saintliness was not yet recognized,
> His accomplishments as yet unknown.
> The Tang history had no one,
> Who would prepare his biography.
> But there was a shrine on the Zhang River [Zhangpu],
> Which honoured the general.[13]

Like the *ci* shrine mentioned by Yu Jing, the *miao* shrine commemorated in Lü's poem lay just to the west of the Zhangpu district city, as the Shrine to Awesome Benevolence still does today.[14] This reinforces the suggestion that the original shrine was honorific rather than devoted to a god.

In the years that followed, as Xu Xiaowang 徐曉望 has demonstrated, shrines to the cult of Chen Yuanguang spread throughout coastal Zhangzhou as well as to more remote places such as Fengting Village 楓亭村 in Xianyou district 仙游縣.[15] The cult to Chen Yuanguang thrives even today as perhaps the most important cult of the greater Zhangzhou area, where Chen, as the apotheosized King who Settled Zhang [zhou] (Kai Zhang Shengwang 開漳聖王), is the most important regional protector deity.

Another figure who represents the apparent triumph of Sinitic culture, yet in a dramatically different way, is Wu Xing 吳興 from the Putian 莆田 coastal zone. Like so many other coastal zones, that of Putian was not easily available for Sinitic settlement until the extensive marshlands that edged Xinghua Bay 興化灣 were drained. Although there are hints of earlier drainage efforts, drainage really began with construction in the later eighth century of the Yanshou Weir 延壽陂, a complex project involving diversion and retention of the water of the Yanshou Creek 延壽溪 that allowed control of the regular tidal incursion. According to Ouyang Xiu 歐陽修 (1007–72), whose *Xin Tangshu* compiled in the mid-eleventh century has the earliest reference to the project, it brought well over 5,000 acres of "irrigated fields" (*gai tian* 溉田) into production (see Map 5.1).[16] Although Ouyang did not attribute the project to anyone, later materials identify it with Wu Xing.[17]

MAP 5.1

Modern Irrigation Network of the Yanshou Weir (with highlighting)

Source: Image adapted from Google Earth.

Two sources from the Southern Song provide further detail, including the earliest references to Wu Xing himself. One is an inscription compiled sometime after 1235 by Liu Kezhuang 劉克莊 (1187–1269) in commemoration of restoration to the shrine built in Wu's memory:

> [After] I had written commemorative stele for the gods Qian and Li [Qian Li *er shen* 錢李二神],[18] an elder from the "northern coastal plain" [*bei yang*; see explanation in note 30] approached me, saying, "Isn't the shrine of our marquis older than that for Qian and Li? Are not the tombs of his children and descendants only steps away from the shrine, where the herons [make their] display and horses [shake their] manes? The coastal village where my family and I live has never been threatened by drought. Patting our bellies and mindful of the soil we nurture our children and embrace our grandchildren. This is [because of] the meritorious work of Marquis Wu [Wu hou 吳侯]. If we cannot forget the spirits of the mountains and streams, how can I forget him? How can we know so much about the "southern coastal plain" [i.e., Li Hong and Ms. Qian] and so little about that to the north?"
>
> … According to the prefectural gazetteer, the [Yanshou] weir was first built in the Jianzhong 建中 era of the Tang (780–784).[19] Of old, before the weir was built, the tidal flow came as far as Shihua Bridge 使華僑.[20] The Marquis dammed off the seas and blocked the tides; he channeled the streams to irrigate the land, turning saline lands into who knows how many thousands, even tens of thousands, of *qing* 頃 of fertile fields.[21]

For all the valuable information in this inscription, Liu Kezhuang was in fact more interested in the cult to Wu Xing that arose in the following centuries than in his drainage project, and I shall return to his text and the cult below. It is, therefore, a summary of the 1192 Putian district gazetteer (see note 18) that was preserved in the 1499 edition and then transcribed with commentary in the *Putian shuili zhi* compiled in the late nineteenth century that provides the earliest concrete discussion of the weir itself.

> According to the Song gazetteer, the weir was built in the Jianzhong 建中 era of the Tang (780-784), and provided irrigation to over 2,000 *qing* … [The waters coming out of the mountains to the west[22]] combined at Ferry Pond [Du tang 渡塘[23]], from where they flowed into the sea. Wu Xing blocked off the sea to create fields. He constructed the Long Dike and Ferry Pond to block the flow [of the Yanshou Creek] and redirect it to the south and into coastal retaining ponds, from where it provided irrigation to the coastal plain. This is called the Yanshou Weir. . . Both the *Song junzhi* [i.e., Song Prefectural Gazetteer 宋郡志, referring to the 1192 edition] and *Peng zhi*

[i.e., Mr. Peng's Gazetteer 彭志, referring to the 1499 edition] explain that because this was long ago the weir had fallen into ruins and its remains were not to be found.[24]

This basic narrative is echoed in a variety of other late Ming sources, including the *Ba Min tongzhi*, a provincial gazetteer of Fujian with a preface compiled in 1490, an inscription compiled in 1538 to commemorate a restoration project; and the *Minshu*, with a preface compiled in 1631.[25] What we learn is that one Wu Xing oversaw a major project that required the mobilization of a large amount of labour in order to open something on the order of 5,600 acres to cultivation; later extensions increased the drained area more than four-fold to nearly 30,000 acres (or "over 2,000 *qing*"). Before Mr Wu's project, the area that became the Xinghua Plain was a coastal marsh. In the manner of marshlands there may have been some tufts of land that sat high enough to essentially be dry, but nowhere was suitable for the intensive cultivation that was definitive of Sinitic civilization. If men had made use of this, it had been for its fish and shellfish, the very food sources that are identified with the pre-Sinitic indigenous population.

The Yanshou Weir was the first of a series of projects that controlled the flooding and opened the land to the dense settlement and intensive exploitation that had developed even by the eleventh and twelfth centuries. Through a network of dykes and retention ponds, the weir both controlled the waters of the streams flowing from the hills bordering the northern fringe of the Putian flood plain and the main course of the Mulan River and checked the tidal incursions that had rendered much of the plain a marshy, saline wasteland. In recognition of Wu's success, in the centuries between his death in the later eighth century and Liu's mid-thirteenth century inscription he was honoured with an ever more impressive series of posthumous titles conferred by imperial decree. The earliest reference to this sequence of honours is a brief passage in the *Song huiyao*:

> The Shrine to Wu Xing, the God of the Yanshou Creek [Yanshou xi shen Wu Xing ci 延壽溪神吳興祠] is in Putian. In the eleventh month of the third year of the Daguan 大觀 era (1109) the title "Faithful Compliance" [Fuying 孚應] was imperially conferred on the shrine [*miao* 廟]. In the twelfth month of the Shaoxing 紹興 era (1151) the emperor Gaozong granted the title "Courageous and Righteous Lord" [Yiyong hou 義勇侯] [to the god].[26]

Despite its brevity, there is much in this passage. Emperor Huizong, the reigning monarch, was intent on expanding the roster of orthodox deities, both to acknowledge the myriad local cults about which the orthodox imperial hierarchy had little knowledge and to gain better control over popular religious practice. He therefore issued a series of decrees directing local officials to report worthy cults to the court that could then be entered on the roster of approved cults along with the grant of proper titles and shrine names. Although the context is not mentioned in the passage, there can be little doubt that this is precisely what had occurred. But that in turn confirms that by the early twelfth century, a cult had developed around Wu Xing — he was the "God of the Yanshou Creek".[27]

It is not possible to determine exactly when that cult emerged, but the terminology offers some hints. Prior to the imperial grant of 1109, the cult shrine was formally known as a *ci* 祠. In theory, if not always in practice, by the Song, *ci* shrines were established to honour the accomplishments of a secular individual, someone who had in fact lived and accrued exceptional merit. As such they stood in contrast to *miao* 廟 shrines established to honour gods, beings who may have once led a secular existence but who had since transcended secular limits and gained access to the realms of the numinous. Although texts tell us that Wu Xing was honoured with a *ci* shrine soon after his death, the *Song huiyao* is the earliest concrete source to reference this and only proves that such a shrine existed at that time. The crux is that by the late Northern Song, the shrine could still be called a *ci*, yet it honoured a god. The imperial grant recognized this by naming the shrine a *miao*.[28]

If we read between the lines, we can construct a plausible but speculative scenario. At some point following his death, a *ci* shrine was established to honour Wu Xing, the secular magnate who organized construction of the Yanshou project. To the people of the Putian Plain, this was arguably the most important event in their history: Without Wu Xing there would be no Putian Plain. He was exactly the kind of man to whom a *ci* shrine might be devoted. In time, however, practice at the shrine evolved and Wu Xing morphed from the secular man to a god. Through the decades between the first imperial recognition and Liu's inscription, a series of titles had been conferred, beginning with the original grant of a shrine name in 1109. Notably, but not unusually, for this was common, the god himself did not receive an honorific title until 1151.

I have labelled these two cults as products of the Sinitic immigration, which as celebrations of that immigration they undeniably were. It is important to recognize, however, that both were influenced by the culture they encountered; neither was purely, unadulteratedly Sinitic. This is perhaps less obvious in the case of Chen Yuanguang. However, as I suggested above, the apotheosis of secular individuals as local protector deities seems to have been much more a characteristic of southern culture than of the northern culture from which the immigrants arrived. While Chen was commemorated strictly for his role in bringing Sinitic culture to southernmost Fujian, his cult in fact drew on regional patterns of deification rather than those of the culture he represented.

But Chen's background was in fact yet more complex — and more deeply rooted in the traditions and heritage of the south than the official narrative suggests. According to a gazetteer of Jieyang district 揭陽縣, the capitol district of Chaozhou, compiled in 1731,

> [Chen Yuanguang's] grandfather Du 犢 served as sheriff [*cheng* 丞] of Yi'an 義安 [an archaic name for Chaozhou]. Subsequently he moved his family to Jieyang.[29]

As with so much of this cult's early history, we are forced to rely on very late sources. "Grandfather" Du has left no record in orthodox sources including the *Zizhi tongjian* and the Tang histories that are more contemporary to the events. Yet when Yuanguang's father, Chen Zheng, was ordered to occupy the border region, the military title he was given was Adjutant Commander of the Unified Armies of Lingnan (Tong Lingnan xingjun zongguan shi 統嶺南行軍總管事).[30] That is, his command originated in Lingnan, offering some level of support to the suggestion that the Chen had established themselves in the farthest south.

Assuming, therefore, that the link to the farther south is valid, Chen Zheng did not arrive on the borderland directly from the northern heartland, the land of *wen*, but in fact from the adjacent areas of Guangdong.

In a pattern that was long followed on the northern frontier, it appears that from the perspective of the Tang court it was "using barbarians to fight barbarians" (*yiyi fanyi* 以夷反夷). And "barbarians" they were! The village where Chen Zheng initially established himself was "Burned Field Village" (Huotian cun 火田村), an apparent allusion to the slash-and-burn swidden agriculture that was widely practised among the non-Sinitic peoples of the south. That the Chen and those who followed them would draw on the indigenous patterns of the south, therefore, is not surprising.

The local impact on the cult of Wu Xing, in contrast, is overt and central. Following the straightforward and entirely rational account of his project, each and every narrative veers to something dramatically different. Let us look, for instance, at Liu Kezhuang's record of Wu Xing's battle with a *jiao* 蛟:

When the project was complete, a wrathful *jiao* broke the dikes. But [Wu Xing] expelled the evil. His accomplishment stands in history like those of Li Bing and Zhou Chu.[31]

Then Liu adds a poem:

Soon after [he had completed the dikes], beneath the maelstrom
There was a winding, wiggling creature.[32]
The Marquis grabbed his precious knife.
Clenching his empty fist, and
Donating his worthless body,
He plunged into the unfathomable abyss.
The evil that lay within the water was dead,
And the Golden Dike was firm.
I have heard the immortals of ancient times
Must all have done meritorious acts
If they were to ride the wind and rain
And ascend to the Great Source [Shangyuan 上元].
The marvel of Wu Guang's sacrifice,[33]
The injustice of throwing [oneself] in the Xiang,[34]
Or riding on the back of the Great Peng Bird,[35]
How can they compare to submitting to the saliva of a hungry *jiao*?

The fifteenth-century *Bamin tongzhi* was more prosaic — and so perhaps more informative:

Wu Xing grabbed a sword and told the people, "If the water runs blue-green than the demon is dead, but if it runs red, than I am dead." Then he entered the water and battled the demon. Three days later a sword covered in blood washed up on Wu's Blade Beach [Wudao yang 吳刀洋]. Wu and the demon were both dead.[36]

The *jiao*, known also as the *jiaolong* 蛟龍 and a variety of other terms, is well-attested in the literary traditions of the Sinitic world. By one name or another the beast appears in a variety of early texts such as the *Xunzi*, the *Shanhai jing*, the *Shiji*, and the *Chuci*.[37] A commentary on the "Shudu fu" 屬都賦 of Zuo Si 左思 (250–305), a prominent literatus of the Jin Dynasty, refers to the *jiao* as a "water spirit" (*shuishen* 水神), while elsewhere the beast is specifically linked to floods.[38] The *Shuowen jiezi* identified the *jiao* as "a kind of *long*" (*long shu* 龍屬), noting that it can both "swim like a fish and fly".[39] Most importantly, however, the *jiao* was viewed as a destructive beast that savaged river banks and broke dykes, causing catastrophic flooding. As the compilers of the official history of the Liang Dynasty commented in the biography of Kang Xuan 康絢, "It is said by some that the waters of the Yangzi and Huai Rivers are filled with *jiao*, which can summon the wind and rain and lay waste to the embankments. Its nature is wicked (*e* 惡)."[40]

If in Sinitic tradition the *jiao* occurred widely, Tang scholars and poets generally identified it with the far south. The *jiao*, by whatever name, belonged to the alien, the "not-*wen*" — in other words, to the Yue. Moreover, it became distinctly more dangerous: from a beast that harassed, it became a beast that ate people. Liu Zongyuan 柳宗元 (773–819), for example, tells of a demon — a *chi* 螭 in his case, but clearly the same predatory beast known elsewhere as *jiao* and sometimes as *jiaochi* 蛟螭 — that terrorized the people of Yongzhou 邕州 (in what is today Guangxi province), deep in the land of the "loose-reign prefectures" of the Southern Yue:

There was a black *chi* that beat the water. It had destroyed the river bank right up to the city gate. It overturned boats and killed the people, and then went away. The elders lamented, "… It can enter fire and not move. It's a god [*shen* 神]. We have been under its thrall for ten years."[41]

Among Liu's contemporaries there were many who invoked the *jiao* in their poetry, but it was perhaps Han Yu 韓愈 (768–824) who alluded to it as often as anyone. At the height of his career early in the ninth century, Han fell afoul of court politics and suffered the indignity of exile to the far south, which he served in Chaozhou, just to the south of Fujian and fully part of the same pre-Sinitic cultural world of the ancient Yue.[42] He loathed this new and alien world as a land of miasmas and threat, an emotion that comes through with unusual clarity in his poetry. To Han, this was a world filled with the strange and fearsome, and the *jiao* was prominent.

In his poetry, the *jiao* were only one of the many alien phenomena to which his undeserved exile forced Han to adjust. They were a frequent presence that evoked the horror of his life, but they were only threatening by implication. Chaozhou, however, was not the only place where Han found evidence of the *jiao*. Through both his exile and his good friend with Quanzhou native Ouyang Zhan 歐陽詹, he was also familiar with southern Fujian and wrote of *jiao* there as well:

> South of Quanzhou there was a mountain whose peaks stood up vertically. Below was a lake over ten *mou* 畝 around, the depths of which can't be guessed. There was a *jiao e* 蛟鱷 [a term I will have more to say about below] that had caused the people great suffering. If people approached [the lake] by mistake, or if a horse or cow came for a drink, they usually were eaten. The people of Quanzhou had suffered thus for years. For this reason those who lived near the mountain had taken their wives and children elsewhere in order to escape the beast's horror.

Han's tale continues that one night in the fifth year of the Yuanhe 元和 era (810), there was a terrible commotion from within the mountain; it was so great that man and beast all hid in fear. When morning came the intrepid stepped out to see what had happened, and they found the mountain smashed to bits; the detritus had filled the lake, the land was leveled, and all around was the red and black blood of the *jiao e*. On the surrounding rocks, nineteen characters had been inscribed in a style that was ancient and indecipherable; no one could read them — an obvious reference to the nineteen markings that make up the most famous of the Zhangzhou cliff face petroglyphs. But thereafter the people were spared any more of the monster's depredations and the land returned to prosperity.[43]

The key to understanding both Han Yu's passage and Wu Xing's encounter with the *jiao* is Han Yu's term: *jiao e*, or "*jiao* crocodile." The *jiao* was a mythological beast; in its abstraction it was disturbing, alien, frightening, even terrifying, but not real. Yet there was a beast that could be found skulking in the marshes that characterized China's southern coast before they were drained and claimed for agriculture by projects such as that led by Wu Xing, a beast that was terrifyingly real and that also found its way into Han's writing, both in poetry and prose: the crocodile (*e yu* 鱷魚). In fact, the southern coastline was the northern range of the truly terrifying, and man-eating, saltwater crocodile (*Crocodylus porosus*) that has become so famous in recent decades through the modern media of television and the movies.

Han lamented the curse of the crocodile, of which he appears to have been legitimately frightened. Among the most intriguing texts from his exile is the "Offering to the Crocodile", in which he ordered all the beasts to leave Chaozhou after receiving his sacrifice:

In such-and-such a year and date [generally ascribed to the fourth month of 819], Han Yu, the prefect and military commander of Chaozhou, memorialized on helping the people. He had thrown a sheep and a pig into the evil (*e* 惡) waters of the River Tan 潭水 for the crocodiles to eat, and then had addressed them:

"Of old when the ancient kings ruled all the world, they cleared the mountains and marshes, and they wove nets and used halberds in order to chase away noxious pests and vile things. They drove things that harm the people beyond the Four Seas. But the charisma (*de* 德) of their successors was slight, and their influence did not go far. Thus in the lands between the Great River [Da Jiang 大江, i.e., the Yangtze] and the Han River [in modern Hubei] it was disregarded, leading to [the rise of] the Man and Yi peoples, and states such as Chu and Yue. How much more in Chao [zhou], which lies between the southern mountains and the sea, so many myriad miles from the capitol. [Now] crocodiles wallow in the wetness of this place and lay their eggs, and so it has become theirs.

But now the Son of the Heavenly Cosmos [Tianzi 天子], the heir of Tang, is on the throne. His spirit is divine and he embraces the martial. Beyond the Four Seas and within the Six Directions, all are at peace. Should this not also apply to all that is embraced by the traces of Yu, that lies near Yangzhou, that is administered by prefects and magistrates, that proffers tribute as offerings to Tian and Di 天地, to the shrines of the ancestors, to the soil on which the sacrifices to the myriad gods are made?[44]

Han's concluding paragraph is laden with tropes of civilization: the "traces of Yu" (Yu *ji* 禹跡) alludes to the legendary sage king Yu's division of the empire, within which Yangzhou designated all the lands below the Yangzi (or "Great") River; "prefects and magistrates" (*cishi xianling* 刺史縣令) uses Tang terminology to allude to the orthodox agents of the legitimate imperial order mandated by *tian* 天, the ultimate cosmological force, and agents of civilization, or *wen*; Tian and Di, often translated as "Heaven and Earth", the shrines of the ancestors, and the myriad gods are all similarly manifestations of civilization, thus of *wen*. Through these tropes, Han asserted his authority over the beasts, an implicit acknowledgement that they too transcended the merely secular and embraced a numinous power.

As Han Yu argued, once the world of civilization had been free of all such noxious creatures. After the great rulers of the legendary past whose charisma had purged the world, however, lesser rulers whose aura had been so much less allowed the noxious things to return, and this led to "the Man and Yi, to Yue and Chu". In short, the non-Sinitic peoples and their kingdoms were among the noxious things the legendary rulers of the ancient past had purged. As were crocodiles. Man and Yi, Chu and Yue, and crocodiles were one and the same quality of thing. Thus when Han banished the crocodile from the shores of Chaozhou — as we know, from the story of Chen Yuanguang and his father, a place that at least until recently had been emblematic of non-Sinitic culture — he was also banishing the non-Sinitic, not-*wen* cultural remnants. Banishing the crocodile was to assert the primacy of the Sinitic world and *wen* culture.

Wu Xing allegedly had done battle with just such a creature. Crocodiles, like most if not all crocodilians, are notoriously destructive of river banks — and so also of dykes, where they like to wallow. If the legend holds any truth, a crocodile had entered his network of canals and ponds and was causing destruction, and Wu undertook to destroy it — a quest that ended in his own death as well, apparently, as that of the crocodile. By casting the creature as the mythological *jiao*, the legend reframed Wu's battle from the mundane to the clash of civilizations. Wu Xing's cult, therefore, honours him for more than simply leading the first project to claim the Putian marshes for agriculture, the most *wen* of economic activities. Wu Xing is responsible for bringing civilization, or *wen*, itself to Putian.

Hybrid Cults of Sinitic Accommodation

This section will focus on two prominent cults that are closely identified with modern Chinese civilization, both with roots in the Fujian region. I argue that both are hybrid cults with deep roots in the pre-Sinitic indigenous culture. These are the Great Life-Protecting Lord (Baosheng dadi 保生大帝), and the Maternal Ancestress (Mazu 媽祖), best known today as the Cosmic Empress (Tianhou 天后, commonly but misleading translated as Empress of Heaven). Both have attracted the attention of modern scholars. However, overwhelmingly this attention has focused on their "careers" as gods. Because the surviving source base has almost nothing to say about their origins beyond formulaic accounts of their births, neither modern nor traditional scholarship has had much to say about their roots. But that is my focus.

Like the cults of Chen Yuanguang and Wu Xing, both cults are said to be based on historical figures.[45] The Great Life-Protecting Lord is the apotheosized Wu Tao 吳夲.[46] Tradition, which was gaining definition by the mature Southern Song, claimed Wu was born in 979, one year after the assertion of Song authority in the region brought the Five Dynasties/ Ten Kingdoms interregnum to a close. His family lived on the border between Quanzhou and Zhangzhou in an area called Qingjiao 青蕉. The earliest extant text devoted to his cult was compiled in 1209 by Yang Zhi 楊志, a native of Longxi district in Zhangzhou who had earned his *jinshi* degree the year before.[47] Neither Yang nor Zhuang Xia 莊夏, who wrote a companion inscription soon after honouring a second shrine,[48] had anything to say about Wu's origins.

The origins of the Maternal Ancestress are equally ill-defined. Legend says that she was the apotheosized Miss Lin (Lin shi 林氏 or Lin furen 林夫人). She is identified as a native of Meizhou Island 湄州島, off the southern coast of Putian district on the central coast of Fujian, although her actual place of birth may have been on the adjacent mainland, where a shrine to her family and her birth exist today. Just when she may have lived is not clear. Traditions from the later imperial era say she was born in 960, the year the Song dynasty was proclaimed. She is, thus, considered a contemporary of Wu Tao.

More contemporary sources, however, including a controversial text dated 1150 attributed to one Liao Pengfei 廖鵬飛 and preserved in the genealogy of a Li 李 family from outside the Putian district city that would be the earliest firmly dated reference to her if legitimate, are content to point only to the origins of her cult, which they place in the late eleventh century.[49] Liao Pengfei focused on the origins of a shrine in Ninghai 寧海, a small village south of the Putian district city that honoured a trio of deities including "Miss Lin, a native of Meizhou Island". Liao went on, "Formerly, through shamanistic prayers she could foretell a person's ills and fortunes. When she died the people established a shrine in her honour". In 1086 a local fisherman dreamed that a rotten stump that had washed ashore bore the god's spirit, which was subsequently enshrined with two male deities that were already established as the village's protective deities. At about the same time Liao wrote his record, Huang Gongdu 黃公度 (1109–1156), a scholar from Putian district, while referencing the same shrine in a poem, referred to the deity as a "misguided menial female shaman" (*hun wu ao* 混巫嫗) and marvelled at her continued influence.[50]

Both cults, it appears, were well established in local culture by the late eleventh to early twelfth centuries. More importantly to the present inquiry, both claimed to honour individuals who had lived in the later tenth century, just as the Song dynasty was consolidating its authority in the region. And both individuals were honoured for traits that were emblematic of the pre-Sinitic indigenous culture. Wu Tao, for example, is extolled even today for his prowess as a healer, a talent that both Yang Zhi and Zhuang Xia mention. As Zhuang put it:

> He practiced medicine.... Not a day passed that people did not clamour at his door, and without regard to whether they were rich or poor he treated them. People all got what they desired, and near and far he was regarded as a god (*shen* 神).

Yang noted that "far and wide he was called a 'divine healer' (*shen yi* 神醫)" whom "the village elders (*xiang zhi fulao* 鄉之父老) recognized as 'The Perfected Person of Medical Numinosity (*Yiling zhenren* 醫靈真人)'": "After he had died, his numinous distinction grew even more. When

someone was hurt or ill they did not go to the doctors but relied entirely on
the Lord (*hou* 侯)." As his legend subsequently elaborated, it went so far as
to claim that his skill came to the attention of the emperor in Kaifeng, the
far-off imperial capital, who allegedly summoned him to treat his empress
when the latter suffered an unexplained illness. According to the tradition,
Wu Tao cured the empress when no one else could.[51]

Neither Yang Zhi nor Zhuang Xia discuss Wu Tao's medical techniques,
and Barend ter Harar has gone so far as to say he contributed nothing to
Chinese medical tradition.[52] But that ought not be surprising; in fact, one
might say, that is the point. Although Yang and Zhuang avoid the term,
Wu was a local shaman; it bears noting that it was the "village elders",
men — and maybe women — who lived in the same cultural milieu
as he did and who relied on him for their well-being, who praised him
as a "perfected", rather than anybody of higher standing. A similar point
has been made by a range of modern scholars including Zhu Tianshun
朱天順, Xie Chongguang 謝重光, and Zheng Zhenman 鄭振滿.[53] His healing
arts, thus, were not those of the elite medical tradition of orthodox culture;
he drew, instead, on local traditions of healing.

This, in turn, links him to the indigenous, non-Sinitic culture that is
so closely identified with shamanism. Wu Tao came from a peripheral
area — the Zhangzhou/Quanzhou border region — and it has always been
on those peripheries where orthodox influence, be it political, cultural, or
otherwise, has been weakest. We know nothing about his heritage, and so
about his ethnicity. It is certainly possible that in some sense he identified
with the Sinitic immigrants who were entering southern Fujian in growing
numbers. Indeed, he may have descended from Sinitic immigrants through
break-away lines that had settled on the peripheries, a social pattern that
I have attested elsewhere.[54] Regardless, in the peripheral zone where he
lived, indigenous pre-Sinitic cultural patterns were still dominant. It was
in those peripheries where the shamanistic heritage that is so centrally
identified with indigenous southern cultures in the disapproving discourse
of the Central Lands was felt most deeply, where the local people,
themselves of hybrid ethnicity that fused assimilated indigenes with the
de classé break-away lines of Sinitic immigrants, believed most strongly
in the numinous world of spirits, and it is those pre-Sinitic patterns that
we hear echoed most strongly in his legends.

A final legend recounted by Yang Zhi emphasizes Wu Tao's link to the pre-Sinitic heritage. Soon after the Song court had fled the north and settled in Hangzhou, marking the transition from Northern to Southern Song, the Zhangzhou/Quanzhou border area was wracked by bandit violence, a pattern that was widespread across southern Fujian. As Yang wrote, "the people were like scurrying rats, holding their hands in despair and placing their faith blindly in the protection of the deity". The decisive battle, where the bandits were wiped out, was fought on the site of Wu Tao's shrine, which must have been damaged in the process. Subsequently, a local notable urged the construction of a new shrine to honour the deity in recognition of his merit. The new shrine, however, was not built on its old site. As the people celebrated its completion they heard a "loud voice" demanding that the shrine be returned to its original location. On excavating the old site, they found three earthen jars that Wu Tao himself had buried within which a green snake was curled up: "Among those who witnessed this, none failed to feel the aura of the god (*mo bu shensong* 沒不神悚)." In death, Wu Tao and the snake had become one, and the snake was emblematic of the pre-Sinitic culture.

Miss Lin similarly drew on pre-Sinitic traditions. Like Wu Tao she was identified with a culturally marginal periphery — in her case an island. As Lin Guangchao 林光朝 (1114–1178) noted: "There are perhaps a thousand households [on Meizhou], and not one person can read."[55] Although like Wu Tao she was identified as a shaman — in her case explicitly — there is no explicit hint that she was a healer; instead she was said to use "shamanistic prayer" to see into the future. Remarking on the cult that he found so puzzling, Huang Gongdu noted, "In all seasons [her devotees] sang and danced, and brought their children", perhaps alluding to her role as a protector of childbirth that she assumed in later eras. Her most important role, however, was protecting men upon the sea, and here we see a direct link to her natal place, for the men of Meizhou Island were first and foremost fishermen. Perhaps they had gone to Miss Lin in life to ask their fate as they set out on their fishing runs — after all, "she could foretell a person's ills and fortunes". Certainly in the decades following her undated death her reputation for protecting fishermen spread, leading no doubt to her veneration by the fishermen of Ninghai

Village, which lies many miles away on the far side of a complex set of peninsulas and at the mouth of the Mulan River.

Liao Pengfei added a tale that has caused a degree of controversy, alleging that the deity intervened to save from a storm an imperial diplomatic mission crossing the Yellow Sea en route to Korea:

> [In 1123] the Supervising Secretary Lu Yundi 路允迪 led an embassy to Korea. On his way through the Eastern [or Yellow] Sea, he ran into a violent storm. Eight ships collided prow and stern, and seven capsized. It was only on the ship on which Lu Yundi sailed that a goddess [nüshen 女神] appeared at the top of the mast where she turned and moved as though dancing. Immediately after that they made a safe crossing.[56]

The passage is controversial because the official record of the mission, dispatched to Korea when the vassal ruler of the Korean court died, identified a different deity as the intercessor who saved the envoys.[57] However, the Song huiyao adds support to Liao's text: "In Putian district there is the Shrine to the Divine Woman [Shennü ci 神女祠]. In the fifth year of the Xuanhe era of Emperor Huizong [i.e., 1123], the title 'Smooth Crossing' [Shun ji 順濟] was granted [to the shrine]."[58]

Miss Lin was clearly very closely connected to the culture of the coast and to an economy that depended upon the sea. While neither is definitively non-Sinitic, both were central to the lives of the pre-Sinitic indigenes. As with Wu Tao we have no way of identifying Miss Lin's ethnicity: she may have been purely indigenous, or perhaps her heritage was hybridized, and it is certainly possible that she came from a marginal line of Sinitic immigrants. However, in assuming the role of village shaman, she drew on the indigenous legacy that must have still been the dominant cultural pattern on the island where she lived.

Finally, a last question demands to be addressed: When did Wu Tao and Miss Lin live? As I have mentioned above, legend claims that Wu Tao was born in 979 and Miss Lin in 960. While it is possible the legends are correct, these are striking years: 960 is defined as the founding year of the Song dynasty; 979 is the year after the last independent warlord of southern Fujian had accepted Song authority. Both years, in other words, had deep resonance to the Sinitic culture that had consolidated its hegemony among the regional elite in the decades of the tenth-century Five Dynasties/Ten

Kingdoms interregnum. And here is where I believe we see the hybridity that I have suggested defines both cults.

It is impossible, I argue, to know when Wu Tao or Miss Lin may have lived. I would suggest, however, that the dates cited in their respective traditions are most likely later, indeed probably much later, interpolations. Neither, in fact, is attested in the current record before the Ming dynasty, by which time the significance of each date to national or regional history was recognized in a way neither could have been in the tenth century. In short, I argue, there is no reason to accept either date and ample reason to suspect neither is valid.

If we accept that, then is it likely the alleged dates are too early, or too late? Here it is harder to be certain, but the logical conclusion from my argument thus far is that both dates are later than either individual actually lived — if in fact either Wu Tao or Miss Lin ever did really live, itself an issue that can most likely never be resolved. Almost certainly, however, the cults that consolidated into the cults to Wu Tao and Miss Lin during the eleventh century existed in some form at a local level well before. The link between Wu Tao and the snake is strongly suggestive of this; possibly before the deity morphed into the apotheosized Wu Tao among the people of the Zhangzhou/Quanzhou border area it had been manifest as a snake cult.

During the tenth century, however, southern Fujian, like much of South China, experienced a marked influx of refugees from the turmoil that wracked the north. In addition to the demographic transformation this engendered, it also was manifest in a transformation of the regional elite. A limited number of lineages could trace their local roots back to the eighth century, when an earlier wave of immigration driven by the turmoil associated with the An Lushan Rebellion had first introduced a regional elite that professed loyalty to the values of the Sinitic north. These were now joined by a larger wave of immigrants, some of whom were legitimately products of orthodox Sinitic culture and most of whom accepted that culture as the definition of elite culture. Yet this was an overlay on a world that still owed much to its pre-Sinitic heritage. My hypothesis — and indeed it cannot be more than that — is that cults such as Wu Tao and the Maternal Ancestress reflect an emerging synthesis, or hybridization, between these two cultural models.

Finally, is there an answer to the questions posed at the beginning of this chapter? What makes a Chinese god? Or, What makes a god Chinese? Like much of South China, southern Fujian embraced a wide range of local cults. Some among them are clearly drawn from ancient indigenous traditions with little alteration. Others celebrate the supposed triumph of the Sinitic world. Perhaps the most interesting, however, and certainly in terms of later history the most influential, are cults that saw a synthesis between indigenous and Sinitic tradition. What they all have in common is that they are "Chinese".

At one level that seems tautological: of course the gods of China are "Chinese"! But in fact it is more profound. Through the millennium between the fall of the Han Dynasty and the maturation of the Song, a slow-moving but far-reaching transformation evolved within the culture of that part of the world we call "China". The culture of the northern heartland, what I have called "Sinitic", was deeply influenced by the cultures of the nearer and farther south. In the process, a vast array of cults representing a parallel array of influences took shape. Inevitably, however, these cults, be they carry-overs from the pre-Sinitic world, emblems of the Sinitic incursions such as Chen Yuanguang, or cults such as that to the Maternal Ancestress that took shape within the hybridized culture, all had to accommodate to contrasting understandings of the numinous. It is that accommodation that has been my focus, and in that accommodation these cults became emblematic of a new hybridized culture that is "Chinese". A Chinese god is a Chinese god not because its cult is centred in China but because it reflects a new cultural reality that took shape across the millennium, a culture that has for the past millennium consciously defined itself in terms of its Sinitic heritage, but that in fact represents a hybrid culture drawing on multiple influences. And that is the culture we call "Chinese" today.

NOTES

1. Li Jifu 李吉甫, *Yuanhe junxian tuzhi* 元和郡縣圖志 [Maps and Gazetteer of Commanderies and Districts in the Yuanhe Era] (Beijing: Zhonghua shuju, 1983), 29:721 says the district was first established by the Chen 陳 Dynasty (557–89) without specifying a year. The *(Jiading) Qingzhang zhi* (嘉定) 清漳志 [Gazetteer of Qingzhang (in the Jiading Era)] cited by Wikipedia

<http://zh.wikipedia.org/wiki/龍溪> from the *Yongle dadian* 永樂大典 [Yongle Encyclopaedia], says 540, and Wikipedia itself says 507 without attribution but apparently drawing on the same tradition as the *(Qianlong) Fujian tongzhi* (乾隆) 福建通志 [Comprehensive Gazetteer of Fujian (in the Qianglong Reign)], 2:27b.

2. *(Wanli) Zhangzhou fuzhi* (萬里) 漳州府志 [Prefectural Gazetteer of Zhangzhou (in the Wanli Era)], (1573 edition), 12:2a.

3. Suian district, located in the valley of the Zhang River 漳江 where modern Yunxiao district 雲霄縣 is located, was established by the Eastern Jin Dynasty in 413 and abolished in 592. However, the designation seems to have existed more on paper than in fact.

4. "Zhao Chen Zheng zhen gu Suian xian di" 詔陳政鎮故綏安縣地 [Commanding Chen Zheng to Garrison the Lands of Old Suian District], preserved in the *(Jiaqing) Yunxiao tingzhi* (嘉慶) 雲霄廳志 [Subprefecture Gazetteer of Yunxiao (of the Jiaqing Reign)], (1816 ed.), 17:3a; see also <http://pedia.sinica.edu.tw:8057>. The text is not included in the *Tang dazhaoling ji* 唐大詔令集 [Imperial Edicts of the Tang], the official compendium of major court edicts. The *Minshu* 閩書 [Book of Min], compiled by He Qiaoyuan 何喬遠 (Fuzhou: Fujian renmin chubanshe, 1994; henceforth MS), 41:1012, is the earliest source to refer to the dispatch of forces at the emperor's command, but does not cite an edict as such.

5. A composite of MS, 41:1012 and Huang Zhongzhao 黃仲昭, *Ba Min tongzhi* 八閩通志 [Comprehensive Gazetteer of the Eight (Regions of) Min] (Fuzhou: Fujian renmin, 1991; henceforth BMTZ), 1:11–12. While MS provides no date, the BMTZ text dates this incident to the "third year of Sisheng" 嗣聖. However, the Sisheng era lasted for only one month in early 684. Presumably local officials had not received word of the rapid succession of reign changes and stuck to Sisheng; had there been a third year, it would have been 686, so I take that to be the date. An alternative narrative from a later source attributes the unrest to one Liang Gan 梁感, who is said to have been linked somehow to the rebellion of Li Jingye 李敬業 that disturbed the Yangzi valley shortly after the Sui-Tang transition; see *(Qianlong) Fujian tongzhi*, 67:1a–b. On nothing better than closer chronological proximity, albeit still distant, I grant a higher credibility to the earlier texts.

6. MS, 41:1012.

7. *(Wanli) Zhangzhou fuzhi*, 4:2a and MS, 41:1012. Like the imperial edict deploying Chen Zheng, there is no record of this debate in standard and more immediate sources such as Sima Guang's 司馬光 *Zizhi tongjian* 資治通鑑 [Comprehensive Mirror for Aid in Government] or the Tang histories.

8. I have discussed this in depth in "Bridles, Halters, and Hybrids: A Case Study of T'ang Frontier Policy", *T'ang Studies* 6 (1988): 49–68.

9. MS, 41:1012.

10. *Wen* 文, a term used throughout this chapter, is a classical term that embraced all aspects of orthodox civilization as defined by the Sinitic culture of the Yellow River basin. As such, it stood in opposition to any other cultural norm, which by definition was uncivilized, or "not-*wen*". The best English discussion is Peter Bol, *This Culture of Ours: Intellectual Transitions in T'ang and Sung China* (Stanford: Stanford University Press, 1992), along with Bol's exhaustive bibliography.

11. See Du Zhen 杜臻, *Ao Min xunxi shijilüe* 奧閩巡稀視紀略 [A Brief Record of Glimpses from Around Ao and Min], (Electronic Siku quanshu edition [herafter, ESKQS], first published 1684), 4:17b. According to *Song huiyao jiben* 宋會要輯本 [Collected Statutes of the Song], (Taipei: Shijie shuju, 1963 photo reprint of compilation of Xu Song 徐松 [1781–848], published by the Beiping [Beijing] Library, 1936; henceforth SHY), Li 禮, 2:143, this title was not officially awarded to the shrine until 1113, suggesting that it had already emerged in the local culture.

12. Yu Jing 余京, *Wuxi ji* 武溪集 [Collections of Wuxi] (ESKQS ed.), 20:3a–b. SHY, *li*, 20:143 refers to the "Chen Yuanxian ci" 陳元先祠 in Zhangpu. In the eighth year of the Xining 熙寧 era (1075), the god of this shrine was first granted an imperial title as Zhonghui hou 忠應侯.

13. Lü Tao 呂璹, "Weihui miao" 威惠廟, in *Songshi jishi* 宋詩紀事 [Records of Song Poetry], edited by Li E 厲鶚 (ESKQS ed.), 13:31b. Lü may have been motivated to write this poem because he had also recently quelled a bandit uprising in Zhangpu, where he was serving as district magistrate; see the following Song-era work: Wu Zeng 吳曾, *Nenggaizhai manlu* 能改齋漫錄 [Casual Notes from the Nenggai Library] (ESKQS ed.), 18:8a–b.

14. See, for example, "Zhangpu Weihuimiao de minsuxue kaocha" 漳浦威惠廟的民俗學考察 [Examination of the Study of Popular Customs of the Weihui Shrine of Zhangpu] at <http://hi.baidu.com> (accessed 19 July 2012).

15. See Xu Xiaowang 徐晓望, *Fujian minjian xinyang* 福建民间信仰 [Folk Beliefs of Fujian] (Fuzhou: Fujian jiaoyu chubanshe, 1993), pp. 380–82. On shrines in Fengting, see *(Baoyou) Xianxi zhi* (寶祐) 仙溪志 3:18b.

16. Ouyang Xiu 歐陽修, ed., *Xin Tangshu* 新唐書 [New Tang History] (Beijing: Zhonghua shuju, 1975), 41:1065. I have used the *Cambridge History of China* standard area measurements. Ouyang's text states 400 *qing* 頃: 1 *qing* = 100 *mu* 畝 = ca. 14 acres; i.e., a total of ca. 5,600 acres.

17. Later sources claim "over 2000 *qing*" of reclaimed land (see, for example, the 1538 inscription of Zheng Yue quoted below and Chen Maolie 陳懋列, comp., *Putian shuili zhi* 莆田水利志 [Records of Water Conservancy in Putian], (Taipei: Chengwen chubanshe, 1974 reprint of 1875 edition; hereafter PTSLZ), 3:3a, citing the late fifteenth-century Xinghua prefectural gazetteer). This was the result of additions to the network in later centuries.

18. This refers to Ms Qian 錢氏 and Li Hong 李宏, to whom construction of the far-better known Mulan Weir 木蘭陂 is attributed and who are commemorated

in a single shrine. The region irrigated by this project is known as the "southern coastal plain" (*nanyang* 南洋), in contrast to the "northern coastal plain" (*beiyang* 北洋) that is irrigated by the Yanshou Weir. Liu's two inscriptions are in PTSLZ; see 8:26a–28a on Li Hong and 8:28a–30a on Ms Qian.

19. The earliest Putian gazetteer was compiled in 1192 by, among others, Liu Kezhuang's father Liu Mizheng 劉彌正, and this is no doubt Liu Kezhuang's reference. In the omitted text that follows Liu repeats — and accepts — a tradition that the weir had been built as early as the beginning of the eighth century. This is not credible and is rejected in later sources; therefore I omit it.

20. BMTZ, 19:380, notes this about the Shihua Bridge: "It was north of the prefectural city…. It no longer exists." This is consistent with the location of the weir, which is also north of the prefectural city.

21. See Liu Kezhuang 劉克莊, "Yiyong puji Wu hou miao ji" 義勇普濟吳侯廟記 [Record of the Shrine to Marquis Wu, the Just and Brave Benefactor for All], in *Houcun xiansheng daquanji* 後村先生大全集 [The Complete Collected Work of Mr Houcun (Liu Kezhuang)] (Sibu conggan ed.; henceforth HCXS), 92:16b–18b; see also PTSLZ, 8:23a–24a and *Fujian zongjiao beiming huibian: Xinghua fu fence* 福建宗教碑銘彙編: 興化府分冊 [Epigraphic Materials on the History of Religion in Fujian: Xinghua Prefecture Section], edited by Ding Hesheng 丁荷生 (Kenneth Dean) and Zheng Zhenman 鄭振滿 (Fuzhou: Fujian renmin chubanshe, 1996; henceforth Dean and Zheng), pp. 55–56.

22. This is an encapsulation of a long discussion of the several streams that flowed together to form the Yanshou Creek.

23. Also written as 杜塘, perhaps best rendered "Du Family Pond". It is possible that there was a family surnamed Du at this site; Northern Song records do refer to a kin group by this surname. See Hugh R. Clark, *Portrait of a Community: Society, Culture, and the Structures of Kinship in the Mulan River Valley [Fujian] from the Late Tang Through the Song* (Hong Kong: Chinese University Press, 2007), Appendix 2, "Examination Numbers by Surname".

24. PTSLZ, 3:3a–b.

25. BMTZ, 24:493; Zheng Yue 鄭岳, "Wu changguan miao xiusi bei" 吳長官廟修祀碑 [Stele Commemorating the Restoration of the Shrine to Officer Wu], PTSLZ, 8:25a–26a; and MS, 24:577–8.

26. SHY, *li*, 20:148b.

27. BMTZ, 60:410 adds: "In 大觀 3 [1109], because [Wu] Xing had great merit [*dagong* 大功] among the people, and *moreover because when [the people] prayed for rain* they received his beneficence [*hu ying* 獲應], Prefect Zhan Piyuan 詹丕遠 memorialized [and the shrine] was granted its current name" (italics added).

28. It is important to acknowledge that there has never been a hard and fast distinction between *ci* and *miao*. The distinction I am suggesting lay more in theory than practice. For example, the term *shen ci* 神祠, or "god's *ci*", occurs over five

hundred times in the *Song huiyao*, although almost entirely during the Northern Song (based on a search of the digitalized *Song huiyao* at <http://thdl.ntu.edu.tw/L303_SongHuiYao/RetrieveDocs.php>).

29. *(Yongzheng) Jieyang xianzhi* (雍正) 揭陽縣誌 (1731 ed.), 6:1b–2a.

30. This is repeated in every biography of Chen Zheng as well as those of Yuanguang; see also the citation to the alleged 669 edict in note 4.

31. Li Bing 李冰 lived during the Warring States era and saved the state of Shu from a catastrophic flood. Zhou Chu 周處, who lived in the third century AD following the Han Dynasty, battled both a ferocious tiger and a *jiao*, conquering both and rectifying his own wayward habits.

32. The term is *wanyan* 蜿蜒. The double use of the *chong* 虫 ("snake/insect") radical deliberately echoes the character for *jiao*, the wrathful best mentioned in the prose passage.

33. This is a reference to the legend of Wu Guang 務光, to whom Tang 湯, the last of the legendary rulers, was going to give his kingdom. Rather than accept, Wu Guang drowned himself.

34. A reference to the legend of Qu Yuan, the ancient poet who threw himself into the Xiang River in the face of unjust accusations.

35. A reference to the famous tale in the *Zhuangzi* of the Great Peng Bird (*dapeng* 大鵬).

36. BMTZ, b:60:410. See also the parallel comments in GXPT, 3:29a and MS, 24:578.

37. See the definitions in Morohashi Tetsuo 諸橋轍次, *Daikanwa jiten* 大漢和辞典 [Great Chinese-Japanese Dictionary], (Tokyo: Taishugen shoten, 1957–60), vol. 10, p. 10, 467 (#33009), and *Hanyu dacidian* 漢語大詞典 [Great Dictionary of Chinese], edited by Luo Zhufeng 羅竹風 (Shanghai: Hanyu dacidian chubanshe, 1990), vol. 8, p. 893. The texts mentioned here are as follows: *Xunzi* 荀子 [Xunzi], *Shanhai jing* 山海經 [Classic of Mountains and Seas], *Shiji* 史記 [Records of the Grand Historian], and *Chuci* 楚辭 [Songs of Chu].

38. See the definitions and citations in *Daikanwa jiten* and *Hanyu dacidian*, both cited above.

39. For this reference in the *Shuowen jiezi* 說文解字 [Explaining Single-Component Graphs and Analyzing Compound Characters], see <http://www.gg-art.com/imgbook/index_b.php?bookid=53&columns=&stroke=12&page=6>. For further classical references to *jiao* 蛟, see <http://bk.baidu.com/view/285536.htm>.

40. Yao Si 姚思, *Liang shu* 梁書 [History of the Liang] (ESKQS ed.), 18:9a.

41. Liu Zongyuan 柳宗元, "Ligong muming" 李公墓銘 [Tomb Inscription of Lord Li], *Liu hedong ji* 柳河東集 [Collected Works of Liu Zongyuan], (Shanghai: Renmin chubanshe, 1973), 10:154.

42. Today this is the easternmost prefecture in Guangdong, abutting the southern border of Fujian, but in the Tang, Chaozhou, and Quanzhou were both part of one large administrative region.

43. Zhang Du 張讀, *Xuanshi zhi* 宣室志 [Records of the House of Proclamation] (ESKQS ed.), 5:12b–13b. See also *Taiping guangji* 太平廣記 [Extensive Records of the *Taiping (Xingguo)* Era] (ESKQS ed.), 392:1a–2a, the source of the reconstructed *Xuanshi zhi*, including this text.

44. See "E yu wen" 鱷魚文 [Message to Crocodiles], in *Wubaijia zhu Changli wenji* 五百家註昌黎文集 [Collected Works of Han Yu with Annotations by the Wubai jia] (ESKQS ed.), 36:10b–13a. Needless to say, Han's edict was not effective, as Jiang Shaoyu 江少虞 (late Northern Song) complained in his *Shishi leiyuan*: "In the *xianping* 咸平 era [998–1004], when Chen Yaozuo 陳堯佐 served in Chaozhou, the son of Mr Zhang was washing himself on the riverside when he was devoured by a crocodile. Lord Chen observed, 'Formerly Han Yu banished the crocodiles of the Evil Creek (*E xi* 惡溪). That was long ago, but now a crocodile has harmed someone. This cannot be forgiven.'" Chen then denounced the crocodile in the marketplace — which no doubt was very effective! See *Shishi leiyuan* 事實類苑 [The Park of Facts] (ESKQS ed.), 62:11a; the story appears myriad times through the *Siku quanshu*, sometimes with more detail, and other times with less.

45. Xie Chongguang 谢重光 has argued that the transformation (*hua* 化) of historical figures into deities is especially characteristic of popular religion in Fujian; see "Cong Wu Tao de shenhua kan Fujian minjian zongjiao xinyang de tedian" 從吳夲的神化看福建民間宗教信仰的特點 [Special Characteristics of Folk Belief in Fujian from the Perspective of the Deification of Wu Tao], in *Wu Zhenren xueshu yanjiu wenji* 吳真人學術研究文集 [Collected Research on Wu the Perfected], edited by Zhang Guoju 張国擧 et al. (Xiamen: Xiamen daxue chubanshe, 1990), pp. 83–97.

46. Because of his unusual personal name and its close resemblance to *ben* 本, he is often mistakenly referred to as Wu Ben. However that is incorrect. His personal name: Tao, has a *da* 大 over a *shi* 十, rather than a *mu* 木 with a bottom line. Secondary sources on the Great Lord are limited, but see the following essays by Zheng Zhenman 鄭振滿 in *Xiangzu yu guojia: duoyuan shiye zhong de Min Tai chuantong shehui* 鄉族與國家: 多元視野中的閩台傳統社會 [Villagers and Nation: Multiple Perspectives on the Traditional Societies of Fujian and Taiwan], (Beijing: Sanlian shudian, 2009): "Min Tai daojiao yu minjian zhushen chongbai" 閩台道教與民間諸神崇拜 [Taoism in Fujian and Taiwan and Popular Worship of Several Deities], pp. 173–90, and "Wu zhenren xinyang de lishi kaocha" 吳真人信仰的歷史考察 [An Investigation into the History of the Cult of Wu the Perfected], pp. 191–209. See also the collected essays in *Wu Zhenren xueshu yanjiu wenji*, and the following two essays in *Development and Decline of Fukien Province in the 17ᵗʰ and 18ᵗʰ Centuries*, edited by E.B. Vermeer (Leiden: E.J. Brill, 1990): B.J. ter Haar, "The Genesis and Spread of Temple Cults in Fukien", pp. 349–96, especially pp. 366–67, and Kristofer Schipper,

"The Cult of Pao-sheng Ta-ti and Its Spread to Taiwan — A Case Study of *fen-hsiang*", pp. 397–416.

47. Yang Zhi 楊志, "Ciji gong bei" 慈濟宮碑 [Stele Commemorating the Ciji Palace], in *Fujian zongjiao beiming huibian: Quanzhou fu fence* 福建宗教碑銘彙編: 泉州府分冊 [Epigraphical Materials on the History of Religion in Fujian: Quanzhou Prefecture Section], edited by Ding Hesheng 丁荷生 (Kenneth Dean) and Zheng Zhenman 鄭振滿 (Fuzhou: Fujian renmin chubanshe, 2003), vol. 3, pp. 953–54.

48. Zhuang Xia 莊夏, "Baijiao Ciji zugong bei" 白蕉慈濟祖宮碑 [Stele Commemorating the Original Ciji Palace in Baijiao], in *Fujian zongjiao beiming huibian: Quanzhou fu fence*, vol. 3, pp. 954–55. The cult had and still has two "source temples" (*ben miao* 本廟), one on either side of the Quanzhou/Zhangzhou prefectural border. Today this is presented as illustrating a prefectural rivalry. Yang Zhi's inscription commemorated an upgrade to the Zhangzhou shrine, in keeping with his Zhangzhou origins. Zhuang Xia, in turn, who was from the Quanzhou side, wrote to commemorate the Quanzhou shrine. Today, as is easy to see on Google Earth, the Quanzhou Baijiao shrine is significantly larger than its Zhangzhou counterpart.

49. The controversial text is Liao Pengfei 廖鵬飛, "Shengdun zumiao chongjian Shunji miao ji" 聖墩祖廟重建順濟廟記 [Record of the Reconstruction of the Shrine of Smooth Crossing at the Original Shrine of the Holy Mound], in *Baitang Longxi Lishi zongpu* 白塘隴西李氏宗譜 [Genealogy of the Longxi Li family of Baitang] (privately held), reproduced in *Dean and Zheng*, pp. 15–17. I have explained elsewhere why I consider this text legitimate. See Clark, pp. 390–91 [note 114].

The secondary literature on the Maternal Ancestress is vast and much of it is unreliable. I have based my account on Ri Senchô (Li Xianzhang) 李獻璋, *Massô shinkô no kenkyû* 媽祖信仰の研究 [Research on Belief in Mazu], (Tokyo: Taizan bunbutsusha, 1979), and Shu Tenjun (Zhu Tianshun) 朱天順, *Massô to Chûgoku no minken shinkô* 媽祖と中國の民間信仰 [Mazu and Chinese Folk Beliefs], (Tokyo: Heika shuppansha, 1996), plus the secondary sources cited by both authors.

50. Huang Gongdu 黃公度, "Ti Shunji miao" 題順濟廟 [Concerning the Shrine of Smooth Crossing], *Zhijia Weng ji* 知稼翁集 [Collected Works of Huang Gongdu] (ESKQS ed.), 57b.

51. This and other aspects of Wu Tao's elaborated legend have been critically demolished by the modern scholar Zhu Tianshun. See Zhu Tianshun 朱天順, "Baosheng dadi (Wu Tao) chuanshuo fenxi" 保生大帝(吳夲)傳説分析 [Analysis of the Traditions of the Great Life Protecting Lord (Wu Tao)], in *Wu Zhenren xueshu yanjiu wenji*, pp. 71–82.

52. Ter Haar, p. 367.

53. In addition to the essays of Zhu Tianshun and Zheng Zhenman cited above, see Xie Chongguang, "Cong Wu Tao de shenhua kan Fujian minjian zongjiao xinyang de tedian", pp. 83–97, also cited above.

54. See Clark, pp. 92–98.

55. See "Yu Lin Jinzhong" 與林晉仲 [Letter to Lin Jinzhong], in *Aixuan ji* 艾軒集 [Collected Works of Lin Guangchao] (ESKQS ed.), 6:27a–b.

56. I have translated and analysed this passage in *Portrait of a Community*, pp. 205–6, and the following discussion relies on that earlier interpretation.

57. The official account is Xu Jing 徐兢, *Xuanhe fengshi Gaoli tujing* 宣和奉使 高麗圖景 [An Account of the Mission to Gaoli in the Suanhe Era], (Congshu jicheng), *chu*, vol. 3136–9, with excerpted reproduction and translation into Japanese in Ri Senchō, "Massō shiryō hen" 媽祖資料編 [Compilation of Documents on Mazu], appendix to *Massō shinkyō no kenkyū*, p. 3.

58. SHY, *li*, 20:61b. I have argued elsewhere that very likely the ships in the mission were merchant vessels requisitioned by the court with crews from different places. Each crew attributed its salvation to its own local protector deity. See Clark, pp. 205–6.

6

DRAGON BOATS AND SERPENT PROWS
Naval Warfare and the Political Culture of China's Southern Borderlands

Andrew Chittick

It has long been recognized that the southern extent of the major Chinese empires — the region spanning the Yangzi, West, and Red River watersheds — was, in the medieval period (second–tenth centuries AD), still primarily populated by peoples who were not speakers of Chinese languages, and who cannot be considered ethnically Chinese. Early Chinese written records of these peoples are essential to modern attempts to find historical continuity between ancient societies and present-day cultures and peoples, a project highly fraught with the challenge of properly understanding the pseudo-ethnography of early medieval Chinese accounts of "barbarian" peoples.[1] Chinese accounts primarily characterized the distinctiveness of southern peoples in terms of their unusual cultural features, such as tattoos, short haircuts, houses on stilts, and exotic local products. Such descriptive tropes were well established no later than the Han dynasty, and were subsequently re-copied and repeated for many centuries.

Much less attention has been paid to the development in the medieval period of a distinctive southern *political* culture. The political organization of southern regimes was traditionally either summarily denigrated as "primitive" and inherently dysfunctional (if they were dominated by "uncivilized" barbarians) or seen as a pale, flawed reflection of northern imperial culture (when they were dominated by northern immigrants or more Sinicized barbarians). In the larger narrative of Chinese history, even the most impressive southern regimes are seen as falling short of "unification", and are therefore considered not as "empires" but as marginal or partial states that represent a time of "disunion" or "chaos". However, there was nothing particularly "un-united" about the empire based at Jiankang 建康, which persisted for most of the four hundred years from the late Han to the Sui conquest, and which was every bit as viable a political structure as any of its northern competitors, or many subsequent "unified" Chinese dynasties.[2] Its political legacy can be traced forward to the many tenth-century southern kingdoms, and, in more diverse ways, the Đại Việt regime of the Lý and Trần dynasties, the southern Song regime, and even the early Ming dynasty.[3]

The political culture of the Jiankang empire and later southern-based regimes is a complex development to which this short chapter can hardly do justice. Among its distinguishing features, I would tentatively highlight the central role of military patron-client networks; the significance of naval warfare and water-borne trade; the challenges of establishing a stable, primogeniture-based tradition of imperial succession (against alternatives such as fraternal succession); a politico-religious culture in which apotropaic religious rituals played a key role in establishing political legitimacy, especially via Buddhist ritual and institutional frameworks; and a public culture which often emphasized ostentatious display and spectacle entertainments. These traditions are not unique — they are to some extent shared both with northern Chinese regimes and with Southeast Asian regimes — but they have a distinctive expression in the regimes that existed in the medieval period across the area of what is now central and southern China and northern Vietnam that is worth exploring further.

This chapter is not going to attempt to analyse the full range of political expression within this zone. Instead, it will focus on one particular feature of southern political culture that has long been recognized as quintessentially southern, but not usually as "political": the event known in Chinese as *jingdu* 競渡, or "crossing competitions". The intent is to begin to lay some groundwork and point towards some fruitful directions for further study of the distinctive political culture of China's southern borderlands.

Crossing Competitions in the Yangzi Valley

Crossing competitions are first recorded as being held in the central Yangzi region no later than the sixth century AD. They were essentially mock naval battles that mimicked the contested crossing of a river, and involved active physical combat between teams of men rowing longboats. They exemplify a distinctive southern political culture in several important ways: as military practice, as an apotropaic religious ritual, and as public spectacle entertainment.

Southern military engagements relied, to a significant extent, on specialized naval combat, which made them distinct from the cavalry-based specialized units of northern Chinese regimes, or the elephant-based forces of some Southeast Asian regimes. Rowed longboat squadrons were the backbone of river-based naval combat, and they were important in shallow coastal waters as well. Manned by anywhere from thirty to fifty rowers, and running probably about twenty or more meters in length, rowed longboats were the light cavalry of southern warfare: the fastest means of communication, the best means for patrol and reconnaissance, the quickest escape from predicament for commanders, and, in sufficient numbers, effective in rapid attacks involving grappling, boarding, and hand-to-hand combat, as well as occasional incendiary strategies. While large, purpose-built warships and converted merchant vessels were critical for troop transport and occasional large-scale assaults on riverside fortifications, fast longboats were the primary means for engaging in more routine, smaller-scale battles and skirmishes.

This type of warfare first comes into sharp focus in the histories of the medieval Chinese southern dynasties, which detail several naval engagements more thoroughly than any prior historical documents, and which employ a range of terms for boats that had seldom, if ever, been seen previously. These accounts make it quite clear that naval warfare required training, which must have been undertaken on local rivers and lakes adjacent to important southern garrison towns such as Jiangling 江陵 and Xiangyang 襄陽 (both now in Hubei province).[4] These are also the places where the *jingdu* event is first known to have been popular. Accounts of *jingdu* events from the sixth to the ninth centuries clearly show that they were violent and combat-oriented. One Tang official stationed in Hunan noted that their end result was "bloody eyebrows, wounded heads ... overturned boats and broken paddles".[5] Another official in Zhejiang reported that three boatloads of men died in one episode.[6] Several Tang imperial officials wrote accounts that denounced the races as symptomatic of excessive militarism and corrupt morals, and asked for them to be suppressed.

The military element in these events was central to their purpose and execution, but they had important religious elements as well, serving an apotropaic function of dispelling baneful local spirits through the vigorous and threatening action of the oarsmen, and the demon-dispersing decorations of the boats. In medieval China, baneful spirits were conceived of as armies, which could be driven off by a show of virility and force, just as human armies could.[7] This is perhaps the most important reason that crossing competitions were frequently staged on the fifth day of the fifth lunar month, or Duanwu 端午, which in the Chinese calendar is considered the high point of summer and a time when plague demons and other illnesses were believed to be especially rampant. It also coincided with the flood-stage of many southern rivers, rendering the boat competitions particularly dangerous and exciting.[8] A variety of elements of the boat combat appear to have been intended to enhance their apotropaic function: for example, the men on the boat teams would routinely shout in unison as a way of frightening their enemies. Most importantly, they decorated the boats with a profusion of different totemic animals and symbols. Birds of various sorts appear to have predominated — cranes, ducks, geese, and herons — but they also used tigers and dragons.[9]

This leads us to the third point: boat competitions exemplified an ostentatious and often competitive public spectacle culture. The combat element made them a natural spectator sport, enhanced by the opportunities for gambling and the possibility of serious injury or even death.[10] So too did the colourful totemic decorations and the belief that the boat teams were actively scaring off baneful demonic influences from the area. The men of the teams, and the sponsors who organized and underwrote the events, gained prestige and legitimacy by publicly exhibiting their prowess and their role as protectors of the local community; they also gained the gratitude of an entertained and satiated populace.

These local southern traditions did not stay local for long. The Tang imperial court adopted a wide range of local sport and spectacle traditions as entertainment for its emperor and courtiers, including polo, wrestling, and boat competitions. However, the court-sponsored *jingdu* events appear to have been largely private, rather than public spectacles, and lacked any significant link to naval warfare training, which was not an important element of Tang military power after the founding years. The court events did allow for a profusion of poetry, which developed a range of literary associations drawn from the imagery of the *Chu Verses* (*Chuci* 楚辭) and other classically "southern" literary styles. The decoration of the boats was also made more elaborate.

After the Tang declined in the late ninth century, the still-popular local crossing competitions in southern riverside towns gained new military and political significance. The numerous newly-independent southern kingdoms were reliant on naval power for their security and the opportunity to expand their territory against the claims of their neighbours. They were also headed by lower-class military men and their personal patron-client networks, so military prowess, including naval combat, was central to the legitimization of the ruling regime. Thus, unlike the Tang, they aggressively expanded the role of local boat competitions, making them an active part of training and recruitment for their "imperial" navies, and using the public spectacle of combat as a way of showing off their military strength. This occurred in all three major Yangzi valley regimes: Shu, in Sichuan; Chu, in Hunan; and Southern Tang, based at modern Nanjing. In the Southern Tang, for example, the people of every commandery were required to hold crossing competitions, which had been modified to function as a competitive race between two teams, with a silver bowl and a commission in the imperial navy as a prize for the winners.[11] The Southern Tang imperial navy, called the "Rolling Wave troops" (*Lingbo jun* 凌波軍), went on to play a critical role in the defence of Jiankang against the ultimately successful attack by Song forces in 975 AD.

The Song regime, like the Tang, adopted and adapted southern traditions, but they were much more alert to the importance of naval power and used captives from the Yangzi kingdoms to help build their own navy, with which they proceeded to conquer each of the southern kingdoms one by one. As they did so, they shut down the local use of *jingdu* events for naval recruitment, and directed the recruiting system instead towards their own imperial navy. Song Emperor Taizu (r. 960–975) routinely staged *jingdu* events and oversaw them as a part of the review of his naval forces at Jinming Lake (Jinming chi 金明池), an artificial lake west of the capital at Bianjing 汴京, and his brother Emperor Taizong (r. 976–997) initially expanded the practice. Evidence suggests that the practice at the Song court declined after 984, however, with the ebbing of the perceived need for military conquest of southern lands, and it was not actively revived for almost another century. We are fortunate enough to have a fine twelfth-century painting of the Song court's practice of imperial naval review on Jinming Lake, including an imperial dragon ship surrounded by ten racing boats.[12]

Throughout this time, *jingdu* events remained a popular local festival custom in the Yangzi region, and continued to be staged regardless of whether the practice was also employed for Song imperial troop training and review. In fact, there were significant differences between the two traditions. For example, imperial events evolved to be more like a true race, rather than a form of waterborne combat, and employed a prize-marker (*biao* 標) which had to be seized in order to identify a clear winner, a practice clearly in place already in the Southern Tang races described previously. The Song court also staged its events in the late spring, around the time of the Qingming festival, while local races were more often staged at Duanwu, in midsummer. Perhaps most importantly, the longboats for imperial events were decorated to look like dragons, in imitation of the "dragon ship" from which the emperor himself viewed the troops. Eventually, this custom became widespread in local areas as well, crowding out the earlier diversity of decorative animal totems and giving rise to the late imperial tradition of *longzhou jingdu* 龍舟競渡, or "dragon-boat racing".[13] Thus, although the military and political relevance of boat competitions declined in the late imperial period, the Song imperial tradition nonetheless left a considerable imprint on the culture of southern China.

Crossing Competitions in Đại Việt

The practice of using *jingdu* as a way to train naval forces and publicly legitimate the ruling regime was also adopted by the newly established polity of Đại Việt in the Red River Delta, formerly the empire's southernmost region. In the 930s the Ngô 吳 regime had fought off the efforts of the Southern Han regime, based at modern Guangzhou, to re-unify the Lingnan region, but repeated usurpations and civil war characterized the Red River delta until the founding of the regime of Lê Hoàn 黎桓 in 980. Under his regime, we first begin to see the crystallization of what Keith Taylor has called "Lý Dynasty religion", which developed fully during the succeeding, much longer-lived Lý 李 Dynasty (1009–1225).[14] These regimes epitomized several key characteristics of southern-styled political culture: domination by less-educated military elites; reliance on personal leadership and patron-client relations; a relatively weak court bureaucracy; reliance on Mahayana Buddhist institutions for administration; and often-contested succession. Lê Hoàn's legitimacy rested first and foremost on his military prowess, especially his successful defeat of an invasion by Song naval forces at the Battle of the Bạch Đằng river in the spring of AD 981. This was rapidly followed by an effort to develop a supernatural basis for his legitimacy through rituals borrowed from northern Chinese precedents but adapted to local deities. His symbolic plowing of the fields is often mentioned, but equally if not more important was his use of publicly staged crossing competitions.

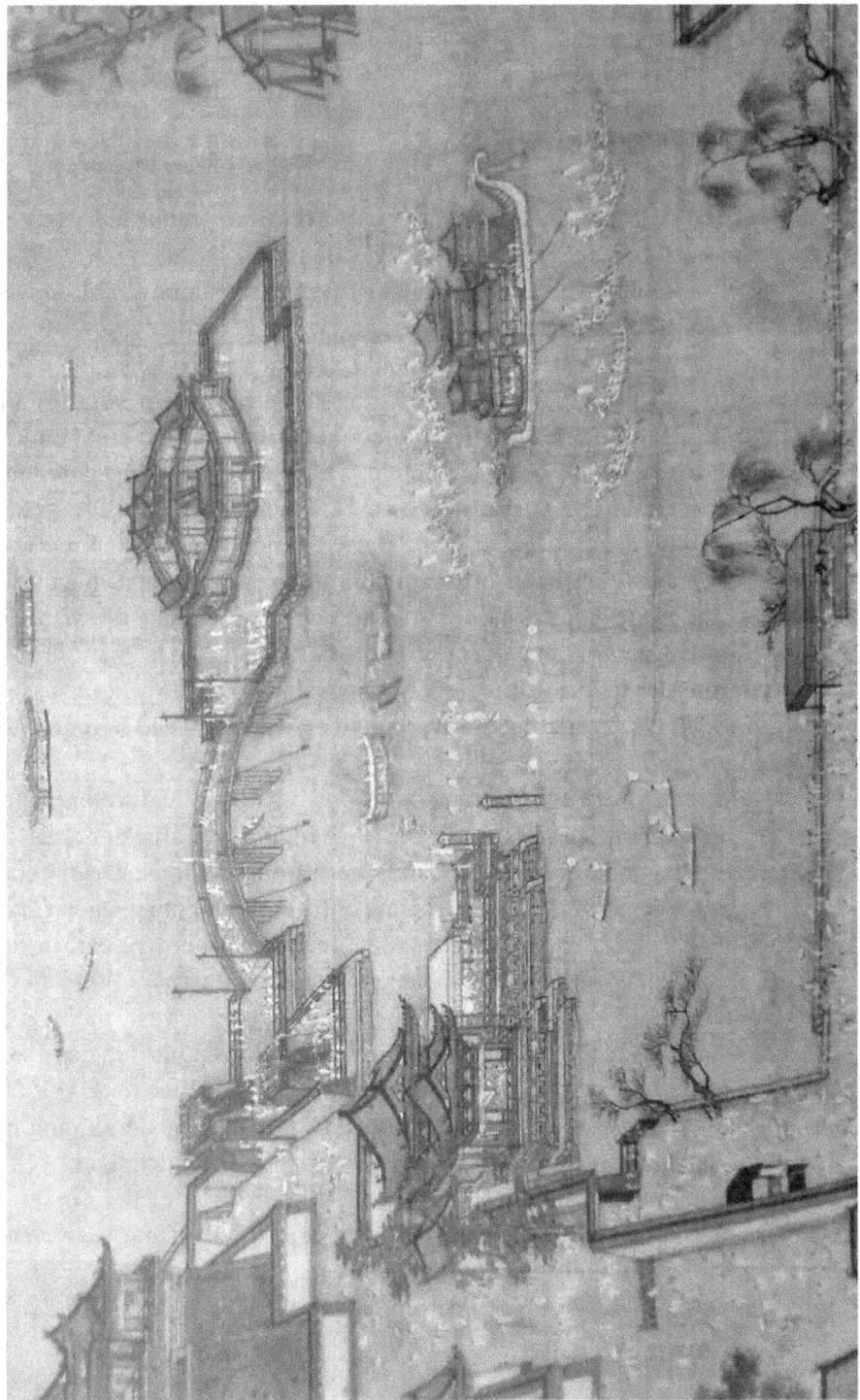

FIGURE 6.1

Zheng Zeduan (Twelfth Century), *Vying for the Prize at Jinming Lake* **(Jinming chi zhengbiao tu 金明池爭標圖) (detail)**

According to the historian Ngô Sĩ Liên 吳士連, crossing competitions were first held on the river by the capital for Lê Hoàn's birthday in the seventh lunar month (early autumn) of 985, and were staged routinely thereafter.[15] The tradition of staging crossing competitions was carried forward by the Lý dynasty; they are recorded early in the reign of the dynastic founder, Lý Công Uẩn 李公蘊 in AD 1013, and noted another twenty times in the Lý dynasty annals.[16] Moreover, boats decorated with totemic animals were a central part of Đại Việt military power. In 1043, when Lý Phật Mã 李佛瑪, Lý Công Uẩn's son and successor, was preparing for a major invasion of the Cham territories to the south, he ordered the building of several hundred warships, all of which were decorated with totemic animals: dragons, phoenixes, fish, snakes, tigers, and parrots are mentioned.[17] It is especially notable that the decorations of these Đại Việt warships retained the very heterogeneous use of many different totemic animals, as had long been the practice in the Yangzi valley. As mentioned previously, areas under Song imperial control increasingly built their racing boats with dragon designs, in order to mimic the imperial ones; in Đại Việt, by comparison, the more diverse earlier decorative practices were retained and adapted to local preferences.[18]

The spectacle of reviewing naval troops may have had a diplomatic purpose as well: to show off the Đại Việt regime's martial prowess to foreigners, most notably the emissaries from Cham regions. The practice was probably begun by the Song regime quite early on; thus, when Cham emissaries arrived at Song Taizu's court in Bianjing on the fourth day of the New Year in spring 961, the emperor staged a review of his naval warfare capabilities only two days later. The following year, the visit of Cham emissaries in the ninth lunar month was followed just ten days later by another naval review.[19] But there is even better evidence for Đại Việt's use of the practice. Of the aforementioned twenty entries mentioning the staging of *jingdu* events by Lý dynasty rulers in the eleventh and twelfth centuries, ten are immediately adjacent to the mention of the arrival of Cham emissaries bearing tribute.[20] The juxtaposition of the two events in the annals is unlikely to be a mere coincidence; instead, it is probable that the emissaries were invited to attend the naval review in order to impress them with the might of Đại Việt's military.

The desire to show off their military prowess may have even compelled the Đại Việt regime to shift the time when the *jingdu* events were held. As previously noted, boat competitions in southern Chinese local traditions were most often held in midsummer, while Song imperial events were staged in late spring, around the time of the Qingming festival. By comparison, all of the crossing competitions in Đại Việt were staged in the fall or winter; the eighth, tenth, and eleventh lunar months account for fifteen of nineteen stagings for which the month is noted. There is no obvious reason for the change in season; one possible motivation, however, is that late fall and winter were the time just following the rainy season when roads became passable and diplomatic missions were most likely to travel.

Developments of this sort in the area we now call Vietnam would commonly be characterized as a "Chinese" influence that was adapted or "localized" in response to indigenous cultural preferences. However, it would make more sense to see boat competitions as a southern borderlands tradition which was adapted by both the northern Song regime and the Đại Việt regime, each for their own purposes. The Song regime had no special claim on these traditions; it borrowed them from the south, and adapted and altered them considerably, in ways which eventually changed how they were practised south of the Yangzi. Only as a result of that alteration did the practice become distinctively "Chinese". By comparison, Đại Việt's use of crossing competitions was in many ways closer to the way the practice had been employed by the other tenth-century southern borderland regimes, as well as to some localized southern traditions which persisted in later centuries.

Influences in Cham and Khmer Regions

This last section will explore the movement of crossing competitions and other military practices yet further south. Repeated interaction by the Cham with the military and courtly traditions of Đại Việt and the Song regime offered an important conduit for the transmission of military, political, and cultural influence in both directions. The Đại Việt practices were probably at least as influential in this regard as were those at the Song court, since Đại Việt was much closer to the Cham geographically, engaged in much more frequent naval warfare with the Cham, and eventually hosted considerably more Cham emissaries than did the Song court.

In the period from 960 through the first decade of the eleventh century, the Cham sent frequent tribute-bearing emissaries to the Song court, while they sent none to Hanoi at all. After the Lý dynasty was established, we begin to have records of regular Cham tribute missions to Đại Việt, while missions to the Song decline in frequency, so that the two are about equal in number. Major Việt campaigns against the Cham in the 1040s and especially in 1069, followed by the Việt defeat of Song forces in AD 1075–76, reversed the pattern further, so that by the late eleventh century Cham tribute missions to Hanoi became an almost annual ritual, whereas very few were sent to the Song court.[21] In total, the Cham are recorded as sending tribute missions to Đại Việt a total of forty-four times in the eleventh and twelfth centuries. As a result, the Đại Việt adaptation of military and court ritual would have been a significant source of influence.

FIGURE 6.2
Cham Embassies to Song and Lý Courts,
Tabulated by Decade

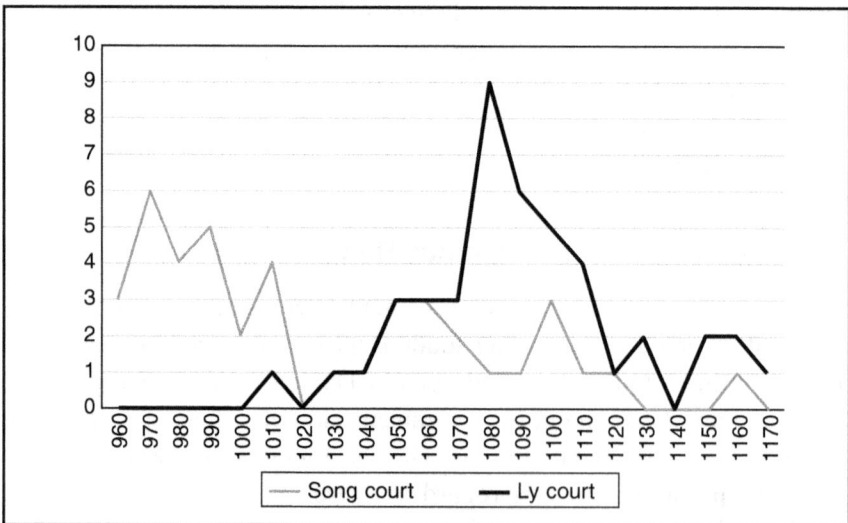

Source: See note 21.

Similar opportunities for military and ritual exchange with Đại Việt pertained for the Khmer regime as well, due both to increasing warfare in the twelfth century, and as a result of tribute visits to the Lý court. Khmer tribute missions were less frequent than those by the Cham, but there were nonetheless seventeen recorded Khmer missions to Hanoi in the eleventh and twelfth centuries. Like the Cham visits, they tended to coincide with the naval review exercises conducted in the late fall and winter.[22] The more significant influence on Khmer ritual practice, however, probably came directly from the Cham themselves. Jayavarman VII (r. 1181–c.1220) spent fifteen years of his youth in Cham territory, and is known to have used Cham allies in addition to Chinese mercenaries in his seizure of the capitol region at Yasodharapura (Angkor) in AD 1177. He subsequently re-asserted Khmer control over a critical central stretch of Cham coastline at Vijaya (modern Qui Nhon, in Vietnam), probably in order to gain a piece of the rich coastal trade routes in the south China sea. As a result, his reign is characterized by especially intensive cultural exchange between the Cham and the Khmers.[23]

There is little doubt that the exchange of tribute and gifts with the Song and especially the Đại Việt court had had a significant impact on Cham military practice. While the Cham sent as tribute all manner of exotic tropical hardwoods, minerals, and animal and vegetable products, the gifts they most sought and most often received from the Song court were horses and military equipment. The latter included crossbows and unspecified "mechanisms", probably ballistae and other complex weaponry.[24] According to Chinese records, these allowed the Cham to substantially upgrade their military capabilities in response to relentless pressure from Đại Việt in the mid-eleventh century.[25] By comparison, the Khmer military is noted as having been relatively primitive. However, the Khmer appear subsequently to have learned from the Cham. Ballistae are not shown in any of the detailed and extensive relief carvings of military events at Angkor Wat, built by the Khmer in the early twelfth century, but they are quite prominent in the carvings of the Bayon and Banteay Chhmar, built under Jayavarman VII a century later. This suggests that the more advanced, northern-influenced Cham military practices were adopted by the Khmer during the relentless Cham-Khmer wars of the late twelfth century.[26]

FIGURE 6.3

Bayon Relief of Two-man Ballistae Mounted on An Elephant

Source: Photo by the author.

A similar pattern is evident with respect to naval warfare. Whereas the Angkor Wat carvings show no evidence of naval warfare capability among the Khmer, the Bayon and Banteay Chhmar carvings offer extensive, detailed images of Cham and Khmer naval warfare. Like the images of ballistae, these suggest a strong kinship to southern Chinese and Đại Việt practices; in fact, the images in these relief carvings are better than any extant early images of boats from south China or Đại Việt. Zhou Daguan's account of Angkor in the late 1200s indicates that Khmer longboats were generally made out of a single hollowed log, unlike those in southern China, which were built up out of finished planks, and the Angkor relief carvings confirm this. However, in other ways the boats match descriptions of longboats in Chinese sources: they are oared by around fifteen men a side, facing backwards, and protected by bulwarks which have been built up from the gunwales. Boats being used for ceremonial purposes, or to carry the commander, are depicted as lacking bulwarks and paddled by men facing forward. The combat boats carry infantrymen down the middle, who engage in grappling, boarding, and hand-to-hand combat with their enemies. Most of the boats are elaborately decorated with one of several kinds of mythical beasts: a makara (a kind of dragon-fish with tusks) carved into the lower prow of the boat, and a garuda (a mythic bird) or naga (a snake) carved at the upper prow and sometimes the tail of the boat. These images are taken from Hindu mythology and are local adaptations of the decorated-boat tradition.[27]

It would be too much of a leap to say that the Khmer and the Cham took the idea of decorating their longboats in this way from Chinese or Đại Việt practices. Chinese sources indicate that boats emblazoned with fish totems were known in Funan as early as the third century AD.[28] On the other hand, the development of naval warfare tactics almost certainly took a significant step forward during this period. The Cham naval attack on Angkor in 1177 is the first known large-scale use of naval warfare in the Khmer domain; it involved launching ships from the Cham coast, running them south along the shallow coastal waters, then up the Mekong delta and into the Tonle Sap. This would have been quite a daring operation, but one the Cham would have been well trained for after decades of coastal and riverine combat with Đại Việt. The prominent use of ornately decorated craft also suggests that the Cham and perhaps

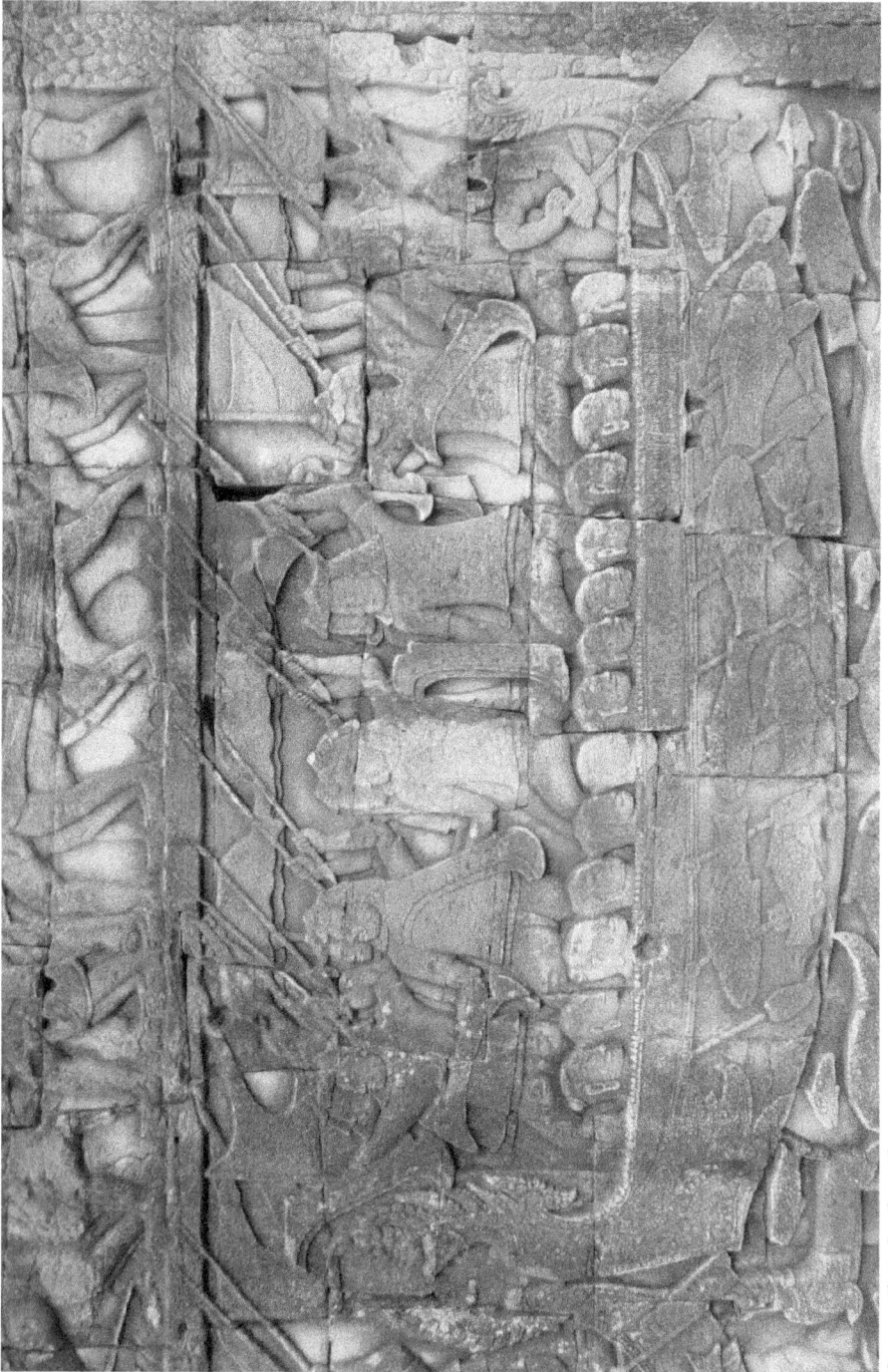

Source: Photo by the author.

FIGURE 6.4
Bayon Relief of Cham War Boat with Carved Prow

the Khmer may have adopted a practice akin to crossing competitions. The Cham, in particular, had close relations, in alliance or in war, with Đại Việt, where crossing competitions were an important element in the regime's naval training and public spectacle displays. The Cham were frequently engaged in naval warfare, and their political culture shows many features akin to other regimes of the south China borderlands (albeit in an especially fractured way), so boat competitions would have been a natural development, which the decorated craft in the Angkor relief carvings tends to corroborate.[29]

Khmer use of crossing competitions or other similar boat spectacles is more doubtful. Zhou Daguan reported that the Khmer regime had a fondness for public spectacles as a means of legitimization, but he does not list boat competitions among these spectacles, though he elsewhere details the construction and use of longboats of a similar type.[30] The Khmer were much less dependent on naval warfare than the southern Chinese, the Việt, or the Cham, so it is possible that they did not adopt the tradition at this time. On the other hand, Jayavarman VII's promotion of a prominently ostentatious, Mahayana Buddhist approach to rulership suggests a strong affinity for contemporary Đại Việt and Cham traditions, within which boat competitions were also a significant element. The large *barays*, or reservoirs, built during his reign would have been very well suited for the practice. Jayavarman VII's successors abolished many of his ritual innovations, including most traces of Mahayana Buddhism, so it is possible that the practice was briefly instituted and then discarded prior to Zhou Daguan's arrival.

In any case, boat racing did eventually become a prominent element in the modern practice of the Khmer "water festival" (Bon Om Touk), which is held in the late autumn/early winter, the time at which the Tonle Sap river reverses direction and begins to flow back into the Mekong. Perhaps coincidentally, this also corresponds to the timing of crossing competitions staged in Lý Dynasty Vietnam. The festival's link with the Tonle Sap river junction with the Mekong suggests that it was a tradition of the Phnom Penh region, thus likely to be a post-Angkor period development at least as far as royal sponsorship goes. Despite this, the origin of the races is now routinely, if perhaps erroneously, ascribed to the famous naval battles of 1177 that are so richly illustrated on the Bayon.[31]

At some point, boat racing spread farther throughout Southeast Asia, though evidence for the specific historical process of this development is slight. No later than the sixteenth and seventeenth centuries, boat competitions and races are known to have been patronized by the Thai and Burmese royal houses. In both cases they followed the Lý Dynasty and later the Khmer practice of staging them in the late autumn or winter, suggesting that their elaborate ritual development and function for naval training, public spectacle, and supernatural efficacy were at least partially inspired by Đại Việt and Khmer royal practices, though they certainly also relied on local boating traditions as well.[32] By this late date, ritualized competitive boat racing had become a widespread phenomenon throughout south China and Southeast Asia, serving as a platform upon which many cultural traditions could be shared and intermingled.

Conclusion

Crossing competitions are one distinctive feature of a military and political culture that was broadly shared among regimes in what is now known as south China and parts of Southeast Asia. Key elements of this political culture can be first identified in the medieval Jiankang empire, especially the fifth-sixth century southern dynasties, and they resurface strongly in the tenth-century Chinese southern kingdoms and the tenth-twelfth century Đại Việt regime. These regimes shared their foundations in a military patron-client network with strong roots in naval combat, low levels of literacy among the military class, and a significant reliance on Buddhist monastic institutions for local and courtly administration. Imagery from Buddhist and local spirit-cult traditions was fused with public spectacles of an overtly military, competitive, and/or violent nature in order to validate the protective function of the court against enemies seen and unseen. Crossing competitions were publicly staged spectacles, intimately tied to naval warfare and to apotropaic functions, which served to legitimate ruling regimes. Thus, they can be seen as exemplifying key elements of southern political culture.

Southern political culture can be contrasted with the developing Neo-Confucian political culture of the Song imperial regime, which did not use Buddhist monks for its educated administrators; was more oriented towards elite, literary approaches to Buddhism (and Taoism) than towards local spirit cults; and emphasized a much less ostentatious, less overtly populist ruling style. Southern political culture at this time is also distinguishable from patterns further to the south and west, in which the personalized, militant, and publicly spectacular approach to rule were quite similar, but Hinduism or Theravada Buddhist traditions and institutions predominated, and the influence of Chinese textual traditions was largely absent. After the late tenth century, in areas that fell under Song imperial control, the symbolic basis of *jingdu* events was channelled into the dragon, the symbol of the northern empire, and their origin myths were increasingly tied, via the legend of Qu Yuan, to classical Chinese poetry, history, and (in modern times) Chinese patriotism and nationalism, even as local practices in south China remained quite diverse in other ways. Further south, in what is now Vietnam and other Southeast Asian states, the diversity of symbols and legends of the pre-Song dynasty *jingdu* tradition is still reflected in the varied local and national traditions of boat competitions.

NOTES

1. Edward Pulleyblank, "The Chinese and Their Neighbors in Prehistoric and Early Historic Times", in *The Origins of Chinese Civilization*, edited by David Keightley (Berkeley, Calif.: University of California Press, 1983); Wang Zhonghan, ed., *Zhongguo minzu shi* [History of China's Nationalities] (Beijing: Zhongguo shehui kexue chubanshe, 1994); Stevan Harrell, ed., *Cultural Encounters on China's Ethnic Frontiers* (Seattle: University of Washington Press, 1995), especially articles by Charles F. McKhann, "The Naxi and the Nationalities Question", pp. 39–62, Stevan Harrell, "The History of the History of the Yi", pp. 63–91, and Ralph Litzinger, "Making Histories: Contending Conceptions of the Yao Past", pp. 117–39.
2. By "Jiankang empire", I am referring to the early medieval regimes with capitals based at Jianye/Jiankang (modern Nanjing), ordinarily referred to as the Three Kingdoms state of Wu, the Eastern Jin, and the four Southern Dynasties of (Liu) Song, southern Qi, Liang, and Chen.
3. Contemporary scholars tend to see the political culture of the early Đại Việt regime as only superficially Chinese, underneath which was a foundation based on essentially "South East Asian" patterns; for examples, see Martin Stuart-Fox, *A Short History of China and Southeast Asia: Tribute, Trade and Influence* (Crows Nest NSW: Allen & Unwin, 2003), pp. 32–34, or Victor Lieberman, *Strange Parallels: Southeast Asia in Global Context, c.800–1830, Volume 1:*

Integration on the Mainland (Cambridge: Cambridge University Press, 2003), p. 355. However, the "Chinese-ness" they compare it to is that of a centralized, bureaucratic hierarchy, recruited by civil service exam, which developed fully only under the Song dynasty. If we compare Lý Dynasty Vietnam instead to the political order of the tenth-century Chinese southern kingdoms (or even the medieval southern dynasties), the resemblance is much stronger; none of these regimes was much like the Song bureaucracy. Rather than concern ourselves with whether early Vietnam was especially "Chinese", or whether the Chinese southern kingdoms were really "South East Asian", it makes more sense to consider all of these regimes as part of a broad continuum of "southern" political culture in which influence flowed in both directions.

4. Andrew Chittick, "The Transformation of Naval Warfare in Early Medieval China: The Role of Light Fast Boats", *Journal of Asian History* 44, no. 2 (2010): 128–50. Jiangling and Xiangyang are mentioned specifically as centres of crossing competitions in *Suishu* 隋書 [History of the Sui], 31.897.

5. Zhang Jianfeng 張建封 (fl. 770s–790s), "Jingdu ge" 競渡歌 [Crossing Competition Song], *Quan Tangshi* 全唐詩 [Complete (Collection of) Tang Poetry], comp. Peng Dingqiu 彭定求 et al. (Shanghai: Shanghai guji chubanshe, 1986), 275.695.

6. Li Rong 李冗 (ninth cent.), *Duyi zhi* 獨異志 [Record of Things Unique], at <http://zh.wikisource.org/zh/獨異志 (accessed 9 June 2012), in supplemental section.

7. Richard Von Glahn, *The Sinister Way: The Divine and the Demonic in Chinese Religious Culture* (Berkeley: University of California Press, 2004).

8. The well-known association of Duanwu with Qu Yuan appears to be a late phenomenon, dateable to no earlier than the sixth century CE; Andrew Chittick, *Patronage and Community in Medieval China: The Xiangyang Garrison, 400–600 CE* (Albany: SUNY Press, 2010), p. 111.

9. Zhang Zhuo 張鷟 (ca. 660–740), *Longjin fengsui pan* 龍筋鳳髓判 [Dragon-Sinews and Phoenix-Marrow Judgements], <http://zh.wikisource.org/zh/龍筋鳳髓判>, juan 2, first of two items from the Directorate of Waterways [水衡監二條].

10. For examples, see Kang Tingzhi 康廷芝 (fl. late 600s), "Dui jingdu duqian pan" 對競渡賭錢判 [In Opposition to Gambling on Crossing Competitions], in *Quan Tangwen* 全唐文 [Complete (Collection of) Tang Prose Literature], comp. Dong Hao 董浩 (1740–818), <zh.wikisource.org/zh/對競渡賭錢判>, juan 260; Yuan Zhen 元稹 (779–831), "Jingzhou" 競舟 [Competing Boats], *Yuanshi changqing ji* 元氏長慶集 [Master Yuan's Collected Writings from the Changqing Era], (Shanghai: Shangwu yinshu guan, 1929 — Sibu congkan edition), 3/3a-b, also *Quan Tangshi*, 398.990.

11. Long Gun 龍袞 (ca. eleventh cent.), *Jiangnan yeshi* 江南野史 [Unofficial History of Jiangnan], in *Quan Song biji* 全宋筆記 [Complete (Collection of)

Song Miscellaneous Writings], comps. Zhu Yi'an 朱易安 et al. (Zhengzhou: Daxiang chubanshe, 2003), series 1, vol. 3, p. 172. See also parallel accounts in Ma Ling 馬令 (fl. early twelfth cent.), *Nan Tangshu* 南唐書 [History of the Southern Tang], in *Wudai shishu huibian* 五代史書彙編 [Compiled of Historical Texts from the Five Dynasties Period], compiled and edited by Fu Xuancong 傅璇琮, Xu Hairong 徐海榮, and Xu Jijun 徐吉軍 (Hangzhou chubanshe, 2004), vol. 9, 5.5294-5; Lu You 陸游 (1125–210), *Nan Tangshu* 南唐書 [History of the Southern Tang], also in *Wudai shishu huibian* 五代史書彙編, vol. 9, 3.5491. For references to Shu and Chu, see Andrew Chittick, "The Song Navy and the Invention of Dragon Boat Racing", *Journal of Song-Yuan Studies* 41 (2011): 12–4.

12. Chittick, "Song Navy", pp. 15–17.
13. Chittick, "Song Navy", pp. 17–26.
14. Keith Taylor, "Authority and Legitimacy in 11th Century Vietnam", in *Southeast Asia in the 9th to 14th Centuries*, edited by David Marr and A.C. Milner (Singapore: Institute of Southeast Asian Studies, 1986), pp. 139–76.
15. Ngô Sĩ Liên, *Đại Việt sử ký toàn thư* 大越史記全書 [Complete Book of the Historical Records of Đại Việt], Kỷ nhà Lê, 17a, online edition by the Vietnamese Nom Preservation Foundation, <http://www.nomna.org/en/nom-project/history-of-greater-vietnam/Fulltext/>.
16. *Việt sử lược* 越史略 [Outline of Việt History], juan 2-3, online edition at Wikisource, <http://zh.wikisource.org/zh/越史略>. These annals are significantly more attentive to listing *jingdu* events than is Ngô Sĩ Liên, who mostly leaves them out.
17. Ngô Sĩ Liên, Kỷ nhà Lý, 33a.
18. Boats decorated with snakes and parrots are not recorded in any southern Chinese source I know of, but the parrot was a favoured bird of Vietnam. See John Guy, "Vietnamese Ceramics and Cultural Identity: Evidence from the Ly and Tran Dynasties", in Marr and Milner, p. 257.
19. Tuo Tuo 脫脫 (1313–55), *Songshi* 宋史 [History of the Song] (Beijing: Zhonghua shuju, 1977), 1.8 and 1.12.
20. *Việt sử lược*, juan 2–3.
21. Tribute missions were determined by seeking references to missions from Zhancheng 占城 in the annals of the *Song shi* and the *Việt sử lược*. These lists are undoubtedly incomplete; more missions are noted in the *Song huiyao* 宋會要 [Important Document of the Song], for example, than in these annals.
22. Tribute missions were determined by finding references to missions from Zhenla 真臘 in the *Việt sử lược*. Though there was also a significant community of Chinese merchants living at Angkor, as well as among the Cham, it is doubtful whether they would have offered an important vector for courtly and military traditions.

23. Anne-Valerie Schweyer, "The Confrontation of the Khmers and Chams in the Bayon Period", in *Bayon: New Perspectives*, edited by Joyce Clark (Bangkok: River Books, 2007), pp. 50–71.

24. Geoff Wade, "Champa in the Song Hui-yao: A Draft Translation", *Asia Research Institute Working Paper Series* 53 (2005): 16.

25. Ibid., p. 19.

26. Michel Jacq-Hergoualc'h, *The Armies of Angkor: Military Structure and Weaponry of the Khmers* (Bangkok: Orchid Press, 2007), pp. 27–35. There is a fine line drawing of the image of a ballistae on an elephant on p. 30.

27. Of course, via Buddhism all of these beasts were known in China as well, including numerous examples in Chinese art from the early medieval period onwards. For example, see J.H. Lindsay, "The Makara in Early Chinese Buddhist Sculpture", *The Journal of the Royal Asiatic Society of Great Britain and Ireland* 3–4 (1951): 134–38. However, there is no evidence that any of these were used as decorations for boats.

28. Li Fang 李昉 (925–96), *Taiping yulan* 太平御覽 [Imperially Reviewed Encyclopedia of the Taiping Era] (Beijing: Zhonghua shuju, 1960), 769.3411, quoting Kang Tai's 康泰 (fl. early third cent.), *Wushi waiguo zhuan* 吳時外國傳 [Accounts of Foreign States in Wu Times]; a shortened version of the account is found in Xiao Zixian 蕭子顯 (489–537), *Nan Qishu* 南齊書 [History of Southern Qi] (Beijing: Zhonghua shuju, 1972), 58.1017.

29. I know of no sources that refer directly to Cham use of *jingdu* practices.

30. Zhou Daguan, *A Record of Cambodia: The Land and Its People*, translated by Peter Harris (Bangkok: Silkworm Books, 2007), pp. 62–63 (festivals and spectacles), p. 78 (boats).

31. See <http://www.tourismcambodia.com/tripplanner/events-in-cambodia/water-and-moon-festival.htm> (accessed 11 May 2012); <http://goseasia.about.com/od/eventsfestivals/a/waterfest.htm> (accessed 11 May 2012).

32. Anthony Reid, *Southeast Asia in the Age of Commerce 1450–1680*, vol. 1, *The Land Below the Winds* (New Haven and London: Yale University Press, 1988), pp. 191–92. Direct cultural exchange with China, either through emissaries or through overseas Chinese, may also have played a part.

7

INVENTING TRADITIONS IN FIFTEENTH-CENTURY VIETNAM

Liam C. Kelley

Introduction

The *Arrayed Tales of Collected Oddities from South of the Passes* (*Lĩnh Nam chích quái liệt truyện* 嶺南摭怪列傳, hereafter, *Arrayed Tales*) is a late-fifteenth century collection of stories from the region of what is today Vietnam. In the late fifteenth century, "Vietnam" was much smaller than it is today, and was centred around the Red River Delta and some of the coastal territory to the delta's immediate south. This Việt "heartland" was ruled over at the time by the Lê Dynasty. Having come to power in AD 1428 after a two-decade Ming Dynasty occupation, the Lê Dynasty inherited this core region and then sought to expand its influence to the west and south. Here the Lê were aided by the fact that they could employ new military technology that had been acquired during the Ming occupation, thereby giving their forces an advantage over those of their neighbours.[1]

It was in this environment of a new and expansionist dynasty that a document resembling the form of the *Arrayed Tales* as we know it today appears to have taken shape. All of the qualifying words in the previous sentence are necessary as we cannot say for certain what the *Arrayed Tales* looked like in the fifteenth century. Having never been published, there are currently some fourteen handwritten copies of the text that are still extant.[2] While most of these manuscripts were likely copied in the nineteenth or early-twentieth centuries, many of them contain a preface by a certain Vũ Quỳnh that claims to date from AD 1492. In his preface, Vũ Quỳnh states that he does not know who wrote the stories, but surmises that "perhaps a draft was composed by pre-eminent scholars during the Lý and Trần (AD 1009–1400), and was then embellished in recent times by gentlemen who were learned and fond of antiquity".[3] Almost three centuries later, the scholar-official Lê Quý Đôn recorded that it was "traditionally held" (*tương truyền* 相傳) that the *Arrayed Tales* was the work of a scholar named Trần Thế Pháp.[4] While Lê Quý Đôn confessed that he did not know who this person was, Vietnamese scholars in the twentieth century argued that this was a scholar who had lived in the fourteenth century.[5]

Thus we are not sure who originally wrote the stories in the *Arrayed Tales* and we cannot be certain what they looked like when Vũ Quỳnh produced an edition of them, nor can we be certain to what extent Vũ Quỳnh himself may have altered their content. Nonetheless, the numerous editions of the text today do largely correspond in content, and from that fact we can surmise that the stories as they exist today are likely similar to the tales Vũ Quỳnh compiled together in 1492.

Related to the question of who exactly wrote these stories is the issue of the degree to which the stories in this collection are creations by members of the scholarly elite or tales that were told by "the folk" and then recorded by someone literate. Vũ Quỳnh indicated that the stories in the *Arrayed Tales* came from "the oral transmissions of the people".[6] However, in the eighteenth century, the eminent scholar-official Lê Quý Đôn noted that the *Arrayed Tales* relied heavily on extant works.[7] In the early twentieth century, French scholars referred to the stories in this text as "legends". Yet at the same time, they pointed to connections between the content of some of these "legends" and information found in other texts.[8] Henri Maspero, for instance, argued that the information in the opening story, "The Tale of the Hong Bang Clan", was based on

material found in earlier Chinese texts, while Édouard Huber found that
the Ramayana was the inspiration for a story called "The Tale of the
Yaksa King".[9]

French scholars thus saw both legends and textual connections in the
Arrayed Tales, however they did not systematically explain how these
elements came together. Starting in the mid-twentieth century, Vietnamese
scholars began a concerted effort to examine the aspects of stories such
as those in the *Arrayed Tales* that they felt must have come from the oral
stories of the folk. In particular, scholars such as Nguyễn Đổng Chi and
Đinh Gia Khánh led a movement in North Vietnam to investigate folk
literature. As part of this effort, they worked hard to define and categorize
what they saw as the many different types of stories that had existed in
the past. In categorizing stories, these scholars did not employ categories
from the past, but instead created new ones, or invested extant terms with
new meanings. These scholars were clearly influenced by Western writings
on folklore, and like their Chinese counterparts who engaged in a similar
enterprise in the twentieth century, their effort to match categories that
originated in the West with the cultural output of "Vietnamese" in the past
proved to be difficult.[10] Nonetheless, this effort succeeded in creating a
new vocabulary and conceptual framework for viewing the stories in the
Arrayed Tales. Hence, some of the categories that they created, such as
thần thoại, *cổ tích*, and *truyền thuyết*, which in their reckoning appear
to roughly correspond with the Western concepts of myth, legend, and
folktale, respectively, are now widely used.

Along with this new terminology, scholars like Nguyễn Đổng Chi
and Đinh Gia Khánh also brought new values into their interpretation
of these old stories. Whereas premodern scholars had often stated that
some of the content in these tales was "absurd" (*hoang đường* 荒唐),
twentieth-century scholars viewed the same stories through a nationalist
prism and believed that they contained something that truly came from
"the people" (*dân gian*), and therefore was valuable. Đinh Gia Khánh
argued, for instance, that certain Vietnamese oral tales could be traced
back to the first millennium BC.[11] In "collecting" (*sưu tầm*) such stories
in a work like the *Arrayed Tales* after they had long existed among the
people, Nguyễn Đổng Chi argued that scholars had not possessed the
right consciousness for properly preserving "folk literature" (*văn học*

dân gian) and that the information they had (even if unwittingly) added to the stories had taken away from the true life of the original tales. And as for the clear cases where we can find the influence of stories from China or India in the *Arrayed Tales*, Nguyễn Đổng Chi stated that these were instances of stories that had entered the region and had completely transformed into "Việt stories" (*truyện Việt*).[12]

In contrast to these efforts to employ modern concepts to categorize old stories and to highlight the "folk", Thomas Engelbert has recently noted an obvious point which scholars have long overlooked, namely that the *Arrayed Tales* was written in the style of a specific historical genre of writing. Engelbert states that it belongs to the *chuanqi* 傳奇 genre; however, in his preface, Vũ Quỳnh likens it to anomaly accounts (*zhiguai* 誌怪) like Gan Bao's fourth-century *Record of Searching for Spirits* (*Soushen ji* 搜神記).[13] While the distinction between *zhiguai* and *chuanqi* tales can be difficult to draw, what they share, particularly the later works in these genres, is a high degree of creativity. And while *zhiguai* tales may have originally recorded some information about phenomena that were supposed to exist, or which the author heard existed, by the time of the Song Dynasty authors were more likely to find their inspiration for *zhiguai* stories in encyclopedic works like the tenth-century *Extensive Records of the Taiping Era* (*Taiping guangji* 太平廣記).

As Lê Quý Đôn noted over two centuries ago, the *Arrayed Tales* was one such work that found a good deal of its inspiration in extant texts. That said, I argue here that there was a logic to the manner in which the stories in the *Arrayed Tales* were crafted. On the one hand, the stories were meant to be didactic. As Vũ Quỳnh pointed out in his preface, the stories in the *Arrayed Tales* all were about "encouraging goodness and punishing evil" (*khuyến thiện trừng ác* 勸善懲惡), a key popular Confucian concept. On the other hand, the subject matter of the stories worked to promote a sense of local identity or sense of place, and it did so in three ways. First, many of the stories were placed in an imagined antiquity, and thereby granted a hallowed history to the region. Second, some of the stories also drew a distinction between the assumed readers of the tales and certain "savages" (*man* 蠻) in the realm. Further, by demonstrating that savage ways were gradually being transformed, the author(s) of the tales reinforced a sense of importance and superiority among the readers of the *Arrayed Tales*.

Finally, a third way in which the stories in the *Arrayed Tales* promoted a local identity or sense of place was by connecting actual geographic sites in the realm to historical tales thereby granting certain places within the realm a greater degree of recognition by the members of the elite.

There are a couple of other points of note that should be made about the *Arrayed Tales*. The first is that it is clea that a large percentage of the historical information that we find in this work is not actually true, and that there is clearly a good deal of information which was simply invented or adapted from extant texts. The second point is that while all of the stories in the *Arrayed Tales* share a similar process of creation, some have endured and become "traditions" and some have not. The question of why some of the stories took root while some did not will be taken up at the end of this chapter. Suffice it to say here that the transformation from an invented tale into a tradition appears to have had more to do with what the elite said about these tales in later centuries than it did about their actual resonance with "the folk". Therefore, this chapter argues that the "traditions" that we find in the *Arrayed Tales* were likely created by the elite and perpetuated by the elite.

The *Arrayed Tales* and History

The *Arrayed Tales* begins with a story called "The Tale of the Hồng Bàng Clan." This tale traces a line of descent from the mythical sage ruler Shen Nong to a purported line of eighteen kings, called the "Hùng kings" (Hùng vương 雄王) who the tale states ruled over the Red River Delta in the first millennium BC before being overthrown by a certain King An Dương (An Dương vương 安陽王). Pronounced "Anyang" in modern Mandarin, this figure appeared in such early Chinese works as the sixth-century *Annotated Classic of Waterways* (*Shuijing zhu* 水經注) where, however, he is recorded as overthrowing a Lạc 駱 king rather than a Hùng king. In the early twentieth century, Henri Maspero began a debate over whether the earliest kings of the region were Lạc kings or Hùng kings. Maspero argued that Hùng was a scribal error for Lạc.[14] By the middle of the century, there were scholars who followed Maspero's scepticism. In the South, Nguyễn Phương and Lê Văn Siêu both published histories that avoided talking about

Hùng kings.[15] Meanwhile, in the North, a series of conferences were held in the late 1960s at which archaeologists and historians "proved" the existence of the Hùng kings.[16] I place proved in scare quotes because this conference was held at the height of the war and, in hindsight, it is easy to find many faults in the scholarship that was presented there. Nonetheless, in the unified Vietnam since 1975, the Hùng kings have not been seriously questioned.

To be fair, while many scholars today would likely admit a degree of myth surrounding the Hùng kings, the idea that they symbolize — that there was a polity in the Red River Delta in the first millennium BC and that memories and stories about it were passed down through the centuries among "the people" — is still widely upheld, and the stories in the *Arrayed Tales* are seen as evidence of this. In fact, there is little if any evidence to support the claim that the stories in the *Arrayed Tales* were transmitted orally before they were written. Further, if they were, it could not have been for long, as there is evidence indicating that people in the Red River Delta did not have a long historical memory.

When medieval Việt scholars wrote the first histories of the Red River Delta region, they structured their histories around the political principle of an "orthodox line of succession" (*chính thống* 正統) from one ruler to another. The fourteenth-century *Outline of Việt History* (*Việt sử lược* 越史略) began this line of succession with Zhao Tuo, a man who was from the area of what is today Hebei Province, but who established his own kingdom in the area of what is today Guangdong Province and declared himself to be an "emperor" in the late third century BC. An envoy from the Han Dynasty subsequently convinced Zhao Tuo to stop using the term "emperor", and his successor therefore appears in Chinese sources and the *Outline of Việt History* as "King Wen" (Wen wang 文王), "king" being an acceptable term for the ruler of a polity that had declared its allegiance to the Han, which is what Zhao Tuo supposedly had done. Meanwhile, the fifteenth-century *Complete Book of the Historical Records of Đại Việt* (*Đại Việt sử ký toàn thư* 大越史記全書) extended the orthodox line of succession back to Shen Nong by incorporating information from the opening story in the *Arrayed Tales*, but like the *Outline of Việt History*, it also indicated that Zhao Tuo's successor took the title of "king".

In the 1980s, Chinese archaeologists unearthed a tomb that they concluded belonged to this "King Wen". Much to their surprise, however, they found in the tomb a seal for "Emperor Wen" (Wen di 文帝), indicating that contrary to what historical sources recorded, Zhao Tuo's successor had continued to employ the title of emperor.[17] The fact that Zhao Tuo had declared himself "emperor" was very important for Việt historians as he was the first person in "the South" recorded to have done so. That their histories do not indicate that his successor did the same, is a good indication that history was not "remembered" in the region before it was written down. Instead, it was created in the centuries after an autonomous polity emerged in the Red River Delta in the tenth century. Much of this creative process was done by compiling information from extant Chinese writings, but some, particularly the history of the Hùng kings and their genealogy that extended back to Shen Nong, was invented. This process of invention, however, was inspired by information in extant Chinese sources.[18]

Actual historical information about the Red River Delta in the first millennium BC, when Vietnamese sources claim the Hùng kings ruled, can be found in the *Record of the Outer Territory of Jiao Region* (*Jiaozhou waiyu ji* 交州外域記), a Chinese work from either the late third or early fourth century AD. This work is no longer extant, but the passage from the work concerning early rulers in the Red River delta is preserved in Li Daoyuan's sixth-century *Annotated Classic of Waterways*, and is as follows:

> The *Record of the Outer Territory of Jiao Region* states that "In the past, before Jiaozhi [Việt, Giao Chỉ 交趾] had commanderies and districts, the land had *lạc* 雒 fields. These fields followed the rising and falling of the floodwaters, and therefore the people who opened these fields for cultivation were called Lạc people. Lạc kings/princes and Lạc marquises were appointed to control the various commanderies and districts. Many of the districts had Lạc generals. The Lạc generals had bronze seals on green ribbons. Later the son of the Thục/Shu 蜀 king led 30,000 troops to attack the Lạc king. The Lạc marquises brought the Lạc generals under submission. The son of the Thục/Shu king thereupon was called King An Dương. Later, King of Southern Yue [Nam Việt/Nanyue 南越] Commissioner Tuo [i.e., Zhao Tuo] raised troops and attacked King An Dương."[19]

This passage was cited in several later Chinese works and was slightly altered with each new appearance. One transformation that eventually took place is that the term *"lạc"* 雒 was replaced by the term *"hùng"* 雄, which closely resembles it, to make *"hùng* fields", "Hùng kings", "Hùng marquises" and "Hùng generals". In the *Arrayed Tales*, "The Tale of the Hồng Bàng Clan" combines both of these terms and refers to the kings as "Hùng kings" but states that they were assisted by "Lạc marquises" and "Lạc generals".[20]

Several of the stories in the *Arrayed Tales* then begin with specific information about events during the time the Hùng kings supposedly ruled. "The Tale of Heavenly King Đồng", for instance, is about a boy who becomes a giant and helps fight an invading Yin Dynasty (i.e., Shang Dynasty) army. It begins,

> Seeing that the All Under Heaven was flourishing, the Hùng king did not perform the ritual of paying homage at court. The Yin king planned to use the pretext of a royal tour of inspection to invade. When the Hùng king heard of this, he summoned his officials and asked them strategies for attacking and defending.[21]

Another story, "The Tale of the Watermelon", which we will discuss in more detail below, begins with similarly detailed information about this early period,

> During the time of the Hùng kings there was an official, Mai [An] Tiêm 枚 [安]暹. He was originally from a foreign kingdom. When he was just seven or eight the king purchased him from a merchant ship as a slave. When he grew up, he was upright in appearance, and could remember and understand many kinds of matters. The king granted him the name, Mai Yển 枚偃, and called him An Tiêm 安暹. [The king] granted him a concubine who gave birth to a boy and girl.[22]

It challenges credulity to believe that information like this could have been transmitted somehow for over fifteen hundred years before being written down in the *Arrayed Tales*. While some of the historical information in this text therefore appears to be pure invention, in other instances, the author(s) transformed historical information in novel ways. We can see this in "The Tale of Nanzhao". In this story, it is claimed that the Kingdom of Nanzhao that came into conflict with the Tang Dynasty in the eighth and ninth centuries, and which was based in the area of what is today Yunnan Province, was ruled and inhabited by descendants of the clan of Zhao Tuo, the man who established a kingdom based in the area of what is today Guangdong Province after the fall of the Qin Dynasty in the late third century BC.[23]

The *Arrayed Tales* also invents historical information about a group of people who are reported to have lived around the end of the second millennium BC called the Việt Thường 越裳. Pronounced Yuechang in modern Chinese, the Việt Thường are mentioned briefly in early works like Wang Chong's first-century AD *Doctrines Evaluated* (*Lunheng* 論衡), where it states briefly that, "During the time of King Cheng [of the Zhou], the Yuechang presented a pheasant."[24] Over time this simple entry was added to and a more elaborate story emerged. In Fan Ye's fifth-century *History of the Later Han* (*Hou Hanshu* 後漢書), for instance, Yuechang is said to be the name of a kingdom to the south of Jiaozhi, an old name for the area of the Red River Delta. The envoys from this kingdom presented a white pheasant to the Zhou, and their message had to be translated three times in order to make sense, so distant was their land from the Zhou capital. Further, King Cheng's assistant, Zhou Gong is recorded to have asked the Yuechang envoys why they came, and their response is that elders in their kingdom said that for years there had been no severe winds or rains, and that this signified that a sage was on the throne in the Middle Kingdom.[25] Finally, in works from the time of the Song Dynasty, we find still more details to this story. In Liu Shu's *Outer Annals of the Comprehensive Mirror for Aid in Government* (*Zizhi tongjian waiji* 資治通鑑外紀), for instance, it is recorded that the Yuechang envoys did not know how to return, so Zhou Gong gave them carriages which pointed towards the direction of the south, and that they travelled in these carriages along the sea by the kingdoms of Funan and Linyi — place names that did not exist during the time of the Zhou Dynasty — until after a year's journey they reached their kingdom.[26]

In a story called "The Tale of the White Pheasant", the *Arrayed Tales* provides this same account of the Yuechang that we find in the *Outer Annals of the Comprehensive Mirror for Aid in Government* almost verbatim. One difference, however, is that the account in the *Arrayed Tales* offers still more novel information to this story. First, there is a comment added that states that when Confucius compiled the *Spring and Autumn Annals* (*Chunqiu* 春秋), he did not include information about the region as it was "in the wilds and was not yet equipped with sufficient civility".[27] The *Arrayed Tales* then concludes this story with a new conversation between Zhou Gong and the Việt Thường/Yuechang envoys. The version of the *Arrayed Tales* that I have consulted cites an "old version" (*cựu bản* 舊本) of the text for this conversation. The conversation is as follows:

> Zhou Gong asked, "Why is it that in Giao Chỉ [i.e., Jiaozhi] people cut their hair short, tattoo their bodies, leave their heads uncovered, walk barefoot and have black teeth?" The Việt Thường clan responded that, "We cut our hair to make it easier to enter the mountain forests. We tattoo our bodies with the designs of the Dragon Lord, so that when we swim in the river, serpents will not violate us. We go barefoot to make it easier to climb trees. We engage in slash-and-burn agriculture and leave our heads uncovered to avoid the heat. We chew betel nut to expel impurities, therefore our teeth are black."[28]

The attributes that are listed here are basically all ones that had appeared in earlier Chinese texts describing people who lived in the south. In Ban Gu's *History of the Former Han* (*Qian Hanshu* 前漢書), for instance, it states of the people in that region that they "tattoo their bodies and cut their hair short so as to avoid being harmed by serpents".[29] Hence, the author(s) of this tale took this information and provided explanations for it. Such an addition of information would seem to suggest a sense of pride in cultural difference; however, as the next section will demonstrate, the author(s) of these stories did not have such a goal in mind. What they did seek to do was to connect the stories in the *Arrayed Tales* to the past. Many of these connections were imagined, but they laid the foundation for the development of these tales into actual traditions by providing them with historical depth.

Othering the Savages

At the same time that the author(s) of the *Arrayed Tales* invented an ancient historical context for many of its stories, he or they also drew a kind of cultural boundary between the assumed readers of these stories and some of the peoples mentioned. In particular, a sense comes through in the *Arrayed Tales* that the life of the present is different from the way things used to be in the past. Further, the way in which the past is described resembles quite closely the lifestyle of peoples whom this and other medieval Vietnamese texts referred to as "savages" (*man* 蠻). We can see this clearly in a passage from "The Tale of the Hồng Bàng Clan", the opening story in the collection, where it makes the following claim about life in antiquity in the kingdom's supposed early years:

> In the early years of the kingdom, the people had insufficient resources for their daily needs. They used tree bark for clothing (other [texts] say for paper), wove reeds into mats, used rice dregs to make wine, made food from sugar palm and windmill palm, salted animals, fish and shrimp, and made salt from ginger root. They engaged in slash-and-burn cultivation. The land was used mainly for sticky rice, which was cooked in bamboo tubes. Houses were built on stilts to avoid being harmed by tigers and wolves. They cut their hair short to make it easier to enter the forests. When a son was born he was laid on banana leaves. When someone died, they would pound on a mortar so that the neighbors would hear and come to help. There was not yet any betel nut. When boys and girls got married, they would start with [the offering of] a packet of salt, and then complete the ceremony with the sacrifice of a buffalo or a goat. Sticky rice would be brought into the room where they would both eat it, and then they would have intercourse.[30]

Many of these practices, such as slash-and-burn cultivation, are ones that elite Việt authors attributed to people of other ethnic groups who lived in remote areas. In the eighteenth century, for instance, Lê Quý Đôn noted that savages who lived in mountainous areas engaged in this form of agriculture.[31] At the same time, there were Chinese who had visited the region prior to the fifteenth century when the *Arrayed Tales* was finalized who had noted that all of the people cut their hair short. A certain Chen Fu made this observation, for instance, in AD 1293.[32] However, these practices subsequently changed among the Việt. As such, in the eighteenth century, Lê Quý Đôn commented on Chen Fu's descriptions of cultural practices in the region by stating that practices like cutting one's hair and tattooing one's body were old customs that the Lê Dynasty had changed.[33]

Hence, it would appear that the *Arrayed Tales* was completed right around a time when some customs had changed, or were changing, and when the Việt elite were in contact with peoples who continued to uphold different customs, some of which were similar to ones the Việt had formerly practiced. What seems to have happened at the time is that these other peoples and their customs then became "the Việt past". We can see this clearly in "The Tale of the Hồng Bàng Clan". That story claims that in the first millennium BC, the Hùng kings had named princesses "*my nương*" 媚娘 and princes "*quan lang*" 官郎. *My nương* comes from the Tai "*mae nang*" where it does indeed refer to a princess.[34] *Quan lang*, meanwhile, is a term which was used for centuries, right up to the twentieth century, to refer to local administrators among non-Việt people like the people we today refer to as the Mường.[35] However, its origins remain unclear. Whatever the case may be, both of these terms belie Sinitic contact, as *nương*, *quan* and *lang* all appear in Chinese with meanings that seem to correspond with the meanings of these terms in these titles. As such, while it is unrealistic to believe that these were actual titles that had existed in antiquity, what they do demonstrate is that some members of the Việt elite in the fifteenth century were engaging in a process of ethnic "othering" in which people who were different from themseves were presented as examples of the Việt past.[36]

While the Sinicized Tai-speaking elite who used terms like "*mae nang*" for their princesses were probably not all that different from their Việt counterparts, commoners undoubtedly were distinct. There was surely a distinction between the Việt elite and the common people who inhabited the villages they hailed from, but the distinction may have been even more stark between the Việt elite and common people of different ethnicities. Obviously it is difficult to say with certainty what ethnic groups existed in the Red River Delta in the fifteenth century, or if ethnicity was used to distinguish people. The one term that does appear in the *Arrayed Tales* to distinguish certain peoples, however, is "savage", and the *Arrayed Tales* clearly gives a sense that the ways of savages were being overtaken by the ways of the Việt elite.

We can see this in two tales about "essences" or "sprites" (*tinh* 精). An essence was a type of supernatural being that often originated in plants and animals. If a plant or animal lived for a particularly long period of time, an essence would develop and would possess the ability to transform itself from one type of object or living thing to another.[37] By the time the *Arrayed Tales* was compiled, essences had long been a feature of the *zhiguai* literary tradition. In the *Arrayed Tales*, the tales about essences appear to have been employed in an effort to create stories about certain place names. At the same time, however, some of these stories contain information about "savages" which give a sense of the cultural differences between the author(s) and assumed readers of the *Arrayed Tales*, and some of the people who inhabited the realm.

One example of this is "The Tale of the Fox Essence". Foxes, fox spirits, and fox essences were a major focus of attention for premodern Chinese writers. The tenth-century encyclopedia, *Extensive Records of the Taiping Era*, for instance, contains nine chapters of fox stories. In keeping with this idea that essences are produced with longevity, this text begins its section on fox stories by explaining that when a fox turns fifty, it can transform into a woman. At one hundred it can transform into a shaman or a man who will engage in intercourse with women. Finally, at one thousand it can become a heavenly fox (*tianhu* 天虎).[38]

The fox essence in the *Arrayed Tales* was one such thousand-year-old fox. It was also white and had nine tails. Like its age, these details were also significant and had their origins in earlier texts. For instance, another tenth-century text, the *Imperially Reviewed Encyclopedia of the Taiping Era* (*Taiping yulan* 太平御覽) contains a story in which such a fox appears. This tale is about a mythical ruler in antiquity, Yu the Great (Da Yu 大禹). At the age of thirty and still unwed, Yu met a woman called the Tushan Maiden. At that time he saw a white fox with nine tails and interpreted this as an auspicious sign for the marriage.[39]

While foxes in Chinese accounts thus did not always play negative roles, the fox essence in the *Arrayed Tales* was of the devious variety. Further, that it was a thousand-year-old white fox with nine tails indicates that elements from extant Chinese sources were mined to fabricate this story. Nonetheless, the work is not entirely fictional, for it begins with a datable historical event. In particular, it recounts how the founder of the Lý Dynasty, Lý Thái Tổ 李太祖, established the name Thăng Long 昇龍 for his new capital. This event reportedly occurred in AD 1010 when Lý Thái Tổ moved his capital from the citadel of Hoa Lư 華閭 to the citadel of Đại La 大羅. While he was still in his boat below Đại La citadel, a golden dragon reportedly appeared in the water. Lý Thái Tổ thereupon decided to change the name of Đại La to Thăng Long which means "rising dragon".[40]

Although the "Tale of the Fox Essence" begins with this historical event, the actual tale of the fox essence's activities that follows is said to have occurred at some unspecified time prior to Lý Thái Tổ's renaming of Đại La as Thăng Long. The significance of this introduction is therefore not to link the tale to an historical period. Instead, Thăng Long is employed merely as a geographical marker. In relaying information about the fox essence, the tale reveals that certain places near Thăng Long have the term "fox" in their names, and the main focus of the tale is to explain the origins of these terms.

As for the actual story of the fox essence, the *Arrayed Tales* records that to the west of Thăng Long was a small stone mountain at the base of which was a cavern where a white fox with nine tails that was over one thousand years old lived. This fox could transform itself in myriad ways. It could become a person or a ghost and would at times move about among the people. One group of people that the fox apparently targeted was a group of savages who lived below Mount Tản Viên and who were known as the "White-Robed Savages" (Bạch Y man 白衣蠻). These people lived in houses made of wood and grass, and they worshipped a spirit that had earlier taught them to cultivate plants and weave textiles, namely the white robes that distinguished this group.[41]

The term "White-Robed Savages" is one which Chinese writers employed from the late Tang through the Song to refer to the Tai peoples who lived along the southwestern frontier of the empire. "White-robed" was later replaced by a homophonous term which means "Hundred Barbarians" 百夷 and this term became more prevalent during the Ming. At times the expression "White Barbarians" 白夷 was also used.[42] As for the area in which these peoples lived, two Song-era works indicate that it extended to the western edges of the Red River Delta. Zhou Qufei's *Replies from Beyond the Passes* (*Lingwai daida* 嶺外代答) states that to the west of Annan, one reaches by land the area of the White-Robed Savages.[43] Meanwhile, Zhao Rugua's *Treatise on the Various Barbarian Lands* (*Zhufan zhi* 諸番志) made the same statement, but referred to Annan by the older term of Jiaozhi.[44]

In the fifteenth century, however, other terms appear to have been used to refer to these peoples. Ngô Sĩ Liên's fifteenth-century *Complete Book of the Historical Records of Đại Việt*, for instance, records that in AD 1207, "mountain savages" (*sơn man* 山蠻) from the area on the western edge of the Red River Delta around Mount Tản Viên plundered, and that in 1226 they fought with neighbouring savages.[45] Meanwhile, a gazetteer created in the early fourteenth century during the Ming occupation refers to the people who lived around Mount Tản Viên as "Liaozi" (Viet., Liêu Tử 僚子), another term that Chinese authors used to refer to non-Han peoples such as the Tai.[46] Hence, regardless of what name was employed, it is clear that Chinese and members of the Việt elite regarded the people who lived on the western edge of the Red River Delta as different.

Continuing with the story, the "Tale of the Fox Essence" records that the fox transformed into a white-robed person and went amongst the savages. It sang songs together with them, and then it seduced savage men and women, after which it hid them in its small stone cavern. Seeing the suffering of these people, Lạc Long Quân 貉龍君, a reference to a mythical figure in the genealogical line between Shen Nong and the Hùng kings, dispatched forces from his underwater palace to draw water upwards and smash the small stone cavern. They also captured and ate the fox. The area where the cavern had once been became a deep reservoir and was called "Fox Corpse Pool" (Hồ Thây Đàm 狐尸潭). A note in the text indicates that this is now West Lake (Tây Hồ 西湖). On the western shore of the lake, the text relates, is an open flat area which people cultivate and which is called "Fox Grotto" (Hồ Động 狐洞). Nearby, on higher ground, is a settlement where people live which is called "Fox Village" (Hồ Thôn 狐村).[47]

The term in Vietnamese for "fox" is "*con cáo*". In all of these place names, the Sinitic term for fox, "*hồ*" (Chn., *hu* 狐), is employed. When Sinitic terms were employed for place names, usually two characters were used, and they normally had a positive connotation, such as the "rising dragon" in Thăng Long, which referred not only to the serpent that Lý Thái Tổ saw in the river, but that had connotations indicating that a new emperor (i.e., Lý Thái Tổ) had come to power. It is therefore unlikely that a body of water was actually called Fox Corpse Pool using Sinitic terms. The term "grotto" (*động* 洞) meanwhile was a term that Chinese originally used to refer to areas in the southwest area of the empire under the autonomous control of non-Han peoples, which can in this sense be translated as "aboriginal settlement". When Chinese wrote the names of aboriginal settlements, they often employed local terms, and therefore the names of such settlements often reflect some non-Chinese language. After an autonomous polity emerged in the Red River Delta in the tenth century AD, the term "aboriginal settlement" continued to be used. For example, Hoa Lư, the area from which Lý Thái Tổ moved his capital, was originally an aboriginal settlement, and this name reflects a non-Sinitic origin.[48] It is therefore unlikely that an aboriginal settlement would have been called Fox Aboriginal Settlement by employing the Sinitic term for fox.

It was perhaps the case that there were two places near Thăng Long called "Hồ Aboriginal Settlement" and "Hồ Village", and that people did not know the meaning of the word "hồ" in these place names. Then there was West Lake (Hồ Tây), which also contains a homophonous character, "hồ", meaning "lake." The author of this tale then appears to have sought a way to link all of these terms together. He did so by creating a story of a fox (hồ) essence, a very common genre of tale in East Asia at that time. This allowed "Hồ Aboriginal Settlement" and "Hồ Village" to gain meaning as "Fox Aboriginal Settlement" and "Fox Village", whereas "Fox Corpse Pool" (Hồ Thây Đàm) was perhaps close enough in pronunciation to "West Lake" as it was expressed in Vietnamese with the adjective following the noun, Hồ Tây, for readers to draw an imagined connection between those two terms. In fact, West Lake had earlier been called "Excessive Rain Pool" (Dâm Đàm 霪潭), so the use of the term "pool" (đàm 潭) here perhaps resonated with knowledgable readers as well.[49]

Hence, in reading this story, members of the medieval Việt elite probably got a laugh out of seeing the ways in which local place names were ingeniously tied together and given specific meanings. At the same time, at a more subconscious level this tale also likely reinforced certain accepted ideas about the distinctions between peoples. The people who could read the *Arrayed Tales* were different from the savages who lived in their midst. Savages were people who lived in aboriginal settlements and who were victimized by forces which the Việt elite, and the powers that they had at their disposal, could bring under control.

Such ideas come through even more clearly in a tale about a tree essence. This tale states that in high antiquity in the area of Phong Châu 峰州, also on the western edge of the Red River Delta, there was a very big tree called "Candana". This tree was said to be more than a thousand fathoms tall, and its leaves provided dense shade over countless thousands of leagues. There was a crane that came to roost on the tree, and that specific area was therefore called "White Crane" (Bạch Hạc 白鶴). Both of these place names, Phong Châu and Bạch Hạc, are recorded in early Chinese sources and are Sinitic terms. Candana (*chiên đàn na*/*zhantanna* 旃檀娜), on the other hand, is the Sanskrit term for sandalwood and was perhaps known to whoever came up with this story from reading Buddhist texts.[50]

This tree, the text relates, passed through many thousands of years. With the passage of time it withered, and transformed into a demon essence (*yêu tinh* 妖精). It changed its form and was ferocious. It could kill living people and animals. The text then relates that King Kinh Dương (Kinh Dương vương 涇陽王), an entirely mythical figure from antiquity who figured in the line of descent between Shen Nong and the Hùng kings, used entertainment to overcome it. This, however, apparently did not last beyond King Kinh Dương's lifetime, for the text states that the demon essence would still appear, transforming unpredictably, and often eat people. The people thereupon set up a shrine, and at the end of every year on the thirtieth day of the twelfth lunar month, they would offer a living person as a sacrifice. The residents were finally at peace, and called this the Fury God (Xương Cuồng thần 猖狂神). The tale then goes on to say that the Hùng kings commanded a certain group called the Bà Lộ Savages (Bà Lộ *man* 婆露蠻) to annually capture and make an offering of a Liêu Tử 僚子 from the mountain plains on the southwestern border near the Mị Hầu Kingdom (Mị Hầu quốc 獼猴國). A note in the text indicates that the area referred to here was the equivalent in the fifteenth century of Diễn Châu Prefecture 演州府 in Nghệ An Province 乂安省, or what is today north-central Vietnam.[51]

Like the rest of the information in the *Arrayed Tales* that purports to describe events in antiquity, this description was invented. First, I have been unable to locate any people named the Bà Lộ Savages. There is mention in the *New History of the Tang* (*Xin Tangshu* 新唐書) of a Bà Lộ

Kingdom (Chn., Polu guo 婆露國), but this was likely located somewhere on Sumatra or in the greater Straits of Malacca region.[52] Further, the Mị Hầu Kingdom likewise appears to be a fabrication. *Mị hầu* (Chn. *mihou* 獼猴) is a term that was sometimes used to translate the Sanskrit "*markata*", a large monkey or ape, and was used in a Buddhist context to describe a mind like a monkey's which was changing and unstable.

One term here that does appear to have a connection to reality is the name of the demon, the Fury God, a name that seems to be related to an important cult in China at that time, the cult of the Five Furies (Wuchang 五猖). Guo Qitao has examined the history of this cult, and although the exact transformations and connections with the past remain somewhat unclear, this cult appears ultimately to have roots in at least the first millennium BC during the period of the Zhou Dynasty. At that time there was an official exorcism that was performed by four officials known as "Fury Men" (Cuồng phu/Kuangfu 狂夫). Among other tasks, these men drove away plagues and pestilences, and their "fury" was essential for the success of that task. This ritual for exorcising pestilence changed over the centuries. By the period of the Song Dynasty, the exorcism rituals had changed, and popular performances, such as the Mulian opera, a Confucianized version of a tale about a Buddhist monk, were incorporated to create events which were both for ritual and entertainment. Further, the four Fury Men no longer officiated at these ceremonies, but instead, a cult emerged around five figures known as the Five Furies.[53]

Guo Qitao has employed the term "fury" to translate two terms — the "*cuồng/kuang*" in Fury Men (Cuồng phu/Kuangfu), and the "*xương/chang*" in Five Furies (Ngũ Xương/Wuchang). Both of these terms are used in this Fury God's name (*xương cuồng/changkuang* 猖狂) in the *Arrayed Tales*, which leads one to suspect that there was some connection between this Chinese cult and what this tale describes. Indeed, the "Tale of the Tree Essence" goes on to describe a ceremony to appease the Fury God that combined entertainment and ritual much as the ceremonies surrounding the Five Furies cult in China did. It states that during the reign of Đinh Tiên Hoàng 丁先皇 (r. AD 968–79) there was a ritual master who arrived from the north by the name of Du Văn Mâu 文俞牟.[54] This man was eighty years old, and he was conversant in the various savage languages. He also practised and transmitted something called the "golden fangs and bronze teeth" (kim nha đồng xỉ 金牙銅齒), which was presumably some magical art.[55] He succeeded in enchanting and killing the Fury God. The way he did this was by putting on a performance of acrobatics, horseback riding tricks, and song and dance to attract the god. An animal was then sacrificed and offered it, and when the god went to eat, Du Văn Mâu (ritually) killed it.[56]

In the gazetteer that the Ming compiled in the early fourteenth century, it is noted that there were certain festivals at which people engaged in activities like pole climbing and wrestling.[57] Whether or not such ritual festivals were inspired by the Five Furies cult is unclear. It may be the case that whoever wrote this tale was inspired by his knowledge of that cult to use a closely related term to name this god. Whatever the case may be, if we step back from the details of this story and view its core information in more general terms, we can see a certain elite view. While there were no Hùng kings in antiquity who had annually ordered Bà Lộ Savages to capture and make an offering of a Liêu Tử, it may well have been the case that the Việt elite looked down upon certain ritual practices by people whom they perceived to be savages, and that they sought to change those practices. Participating as they did in the world of Sinitic culture, there may not have been an actual Du Văn Mâu who came from the North, and the god that was ritually killed may not have actually been a god inspired by the Five Furies cult, but certainly the Việt elite, like their counterparts across the Chinese empire at the time, employed ritual entertainment in an effort to control the common people. As such, I would argue that in a story like "The Tale of the Tree Essence" we can see a situation where the Việt elite were noting their ritual domination over other peoples, and particularly people whom they termed savages.

Appropriating Savage Tales

Mention of savages who sacrifice members of other savage groups to appease an evil spirit, as we see in "The Tale of the Tree Essence", serves to paint a rather unappealing picture of people deemed to be different from the assumed readers of the *Arrayed Tales*. At the same time, the Sinicized terms that the Tai elite employed indicate that there also likely was a significant degree of shared culture between the Việt elite and some of their elite counterparts in other groups. Such people undoubtedly did interact, and it was perhaps through such an interaction that what appears to have originally been a Tai tale was appropriated and transformed into a Việt story in the *Arrayed Tales*, namely "The Tale of Betel Nut".

This tale states that in high antiquity there was a *quan lang* who had two sons, Tân 檳 and Lang 榔.[58] These two boys resembled each other so closely that it was impossible to distinguish who was the elder and who the younger. When they were in their late teens, their parents died and they went to serve a Taoist master who had a daughter named Liên 璉, also in her late teens. They all became fond of each other, but Liên wished to marry the elder of the two brothers. Unable to distinguish between them, Liên devised a plan. She placed a bowl of rice with one pair of chopsticks before them, knowing that whoever was younger would yield to the older, as Confucian mores dictated, and that is precisely what happened.

Liên thereupon married Tân. A while later, feeling unwanted, Lang left and died by a river where he transformed into a tree. Tân went looking for him, and when he arrived at the tree, he died by its trunk and was transformed into a stone. Liên then searched for her husband, and ended up dying as she embraced the stone and then turned into a vine. In their death, however, these three created something essential for wedding ceremonies in the region, as the tree into which Lang had been transformed produced the areca nut, which, combined with the betel leaf of the vine and the lime made from the stone, constituted the mild stimulant that we today refer to as "betel nut". Finally, in the story, it is a Hùng king who discovers how well these three ingredients combine together.[59]

While the technique that Liên employed to determine which was the elder brother relied on Confucian mores, there are elements in this tale that suggest that it originated among people who were different than the Sinicized Việt elite who wrote this story. Reference to the father of Tân and Lang as a *quan lang* indicates that the story was meant to be about someone from one of the "savage" groups. Further, the term used in the tale for "betel leaf" is "*phù lưu*" 芙蕾, a name that does not make sense in Vietnamese or Chinese, but which clearly comes from a Tai language. Today, for instance, the betel leaf is referred to as "*phu*" in Lao and "*phluu*" in Thai.

Given the non-Việt references in the tale, it is interesting to note that there was a Lao version of this same story. In 1971, Pierre-Bernard Lafont published a French translation of a Lao version of this story that he found in an unspecified Lao manuscript that the École française d'Extrême-Orient had obtained in northeastern Laos in 1925. According to Lafont's translation, the Lao story is about Sam Luong, Sam Lan, and Ing Dai. They are three friends, and they study together. Ing Dai is actually a girl, but the other two do not know this. She is also from another village, but is staying in a different village with relatives so that she can go to school. The three are inseparable, and they even sleep on the same bed at times. Then things start to change as Ing Dai's body starts to mature.

At the beginning of the story, they go swimming, and Sam Luong notices that Ing Dai's breasts have gotten larger, but she says that she was bitten by insects the night before, and that they therefore were swollen. Sam Luong, believing this explanation, then invites Ing Dai to go look for girls with him. She agrees, but when they are passing Ing Dai's relatives' house she tells Sam Luong to go ahead, and to come back to the house later. Ing Dai then goes in, changes into a girl's clothes, and starts to blacken her teeth. When Sam Luong comes back, he sees a beautiful young girl blackening her teeth. Not knowing that it is Ing Dai, he asks if he can blacken his teeth together with her. She says yes, and … he leaves early the next morning at the sound of the cock's crow. The two then live a double life. They study together during the day, and then make love at night. Sam Luong still does not realize that his classmate during the day is the same person as the girl he stays with at night.

Ing Dai is then called back to her home. She departs, and leaves a note for Sam Luong in which she reveals her true identity. Sam Luong goes looking for her. When he finds her, the two are very happy and spend the night together. The next morning, Ing Dai's mother finds the two sleeping side by side, and gets angry. She says that she will never give her permission for them to marry.

Sam Luong goes back home, but before he does he talks with Ing Dai. They decide that they would rather die than be apart. Sam Luong then comes up with a plan. He says that he will pretend to die. After he does, he wants Ing Dai to tell her parents that his wish is to be placed in a stone coffin which is big enough to hold two people. Sam Luong leaves, and pretends to get sick on the way back and then "dies". His parents go to cut down a tree to make a coffin, but the axe cannot cut the tree. So they send for Ing Dai to see if she knows if Sam Luong had any final wish. She informs them of what Sam Luong had said, and they make a stone coffin. Then when it is being transported to the cemetery, Ing Dai asks for the people carrying it to stop and open it. When they do, she then gets into the coffin, and somehow it is closed again and the people cannot open it.

The parents of Sam Luong and Ing Dai are sent for, as is the *cao muang* [i.e., the leader of a Tai settlement]. The *cao muang* orders that the best friend of Sam Luong and Ing Dai, Sam Lan, come to answer questions. The coffin is opened and the two are found to be alive. The parents get angry at the trouble the young people have caused and wish them all dead. Magically, all of the three young people die right there on the spot, and then they transform. Sam Lan becomes lime, Ing Dai becomes betel leaf, and Sam Luong becomes an areca nut.[60]

It is remarkable how different these two stories are. The version in the *Arrayed Tales* is very Sinitic. It has a Taoist master, brothers who follow Confucian mores and a proper marriage. The Lao version, in contrast, talks of premarital sex and parents who wish death upon their children for their disobedience. The Lao version is also very detailed. And while there is perhaps no way to say for certain which version came first, it certainly appears that the version in the *Arrayed Tales* is a simplified and Sinicized version of a Tai original, with the references to a *quan lang* and *phù lưu* included for those in the know at the time to understand. Such a view is strengthened by the fact that in the fifteenth century, the Lê Dynasty expanded its control into Tai-speaking areas to the west. Appropriating a story such as this one and transforming it into a tale that fit elite Việt sensibilities might have thus served as a literary manifestation of social and political transformations that were taking place at the time.

Becoming Traditions

It should be apparent by this point that the stories in the *Arrayed Tales* are not accounts that were passed down orally and then recorded by a member, or members, of the elite in the fifteenth century. Instead, it is more likely that these tales were largely created in the fifteenth century and that they represent the world as it was seen at that time by members of the Việt elite. The stories in the *Arrayed Tales* are thus not rooted in antiquity, but were pieced together in the present. In many ways we can see these stories as experimental efforts to craft together tales that would amuse readers. Over time, however, some of these tales did take root, as it were. How and why that happened appears to have depended as much on the elite as their initial creation did. To demonstrate this point we will examine here two stories from the *Arrayed Tales*, one that ultimately became a "Vietnamese tradition" and one that did not.

"The Tale of Watermelon" in many ways appears to be a complete fabrication. In his preface, Vũ Quỳnh states that, "During the summer in Nam Việt there is nothing which people cherish more than watermelon." If this was true in AD 1492, it is difficult to find evidence to support this point. In listing the main fruits in the region in the early fifteenth century, the *General Gazetteer of Jiaozhi* (*Jiaozhi zongzhi* 交阯總志) mentioned fruits such as lychee, longan, coconut, and banana, but not watermelon.[61] Indeed, watermelon was a fruit which was apparently introduced to the Chinese world from areas in Central Asia, from which it gets its name, the "western melon" (*xigua* 西瓜), and was first noted by a Chinese writer in the tenth century.[62] Therefore, if the watermelon was familiar to Vũ Quỳnh in the late fifteenth century, it is unlikely that many of his ancestors had tasted its sweet flavour.

The story that "The Tale of Watermelon" recounts is about an official by the name of Mai An Tiêm who was purportedly employed by one of the Hùng kings. Mai An Tiêm, the story goes, was from a foreign country and had been purchased by the Hùng king when he was a young boy. When Mai An Tiêm grew to become a man, he was entrusted with various duties by the king. In due time he became wealthy and arrogant, and stated that, "Everything here is because of my previous life. It is not because of the beneficence of my master."[63] For this lack of gratitude, the Hùng king exiled Mai An Tiêm to a remote island.

Mai An Tiêm, however, did not fear for the future, stating that "Since Heaven has given me life, it must be able to nourish me. Life and death resides with Heaven. What do I have to worry about?"[64] Indeed, he did not have to worry, for before long a white pheasant flew in from the west and dropped some watermelon seeds which Mai An Tiêm planted, and he then became wealthy by selling the delicious fruit to merchants. Not knowing what this novel fruit was called, Mai An Tiêm named it the "western melon" (*tây qua*/*xigua* 西瓜), since the white pheasant had arrived from the west. The story then concludes by noting that the place where Mai An Tiêm had been exiled was An Tiêm Islet 安暹洲 in Thanh Hóa Province 清化省.[65]

There is much about this story that indicates that it was created in the fifteenth century. First, we can rule out the detailed information about the Hùng king as we do not have evidence that historical information was transmitted from that purported time in the first millennium BC. Second, there is also no evidence that the watermelon had existed in the region prior to the time Vũ Quỳnh compiled this text, and it is certainly the case that the name for the fruit had already been coined by the time that fruit was introduced to the region. Third, one can get a sense of Buddhist traces in this story. We can see this quite clearly when Mai An Tiêm attributes his success to his previous life. When one then considers that the Guanyin of the Southern Seas (Nanhai Guanyin 南海觀音) was accompanied by a white parrot that was sometimes depicted holding prayer beads in its beak, and that there was a popular story about Guanyin called the *Precious Volume of the Watermelon* (*Xigua baojuan* 西瓜寶卷), in which Guanyin, disguised as a mendicant monk, rewards a man for his kindness by giving him watermelon seeds that then make him wealthy, it would seem that the inspiration for this tale might come from various Buddhist sources that were then reworked.[66]

Hence, there seems to be little which actually grounds this story in the life or experiences of the region beyond the presence of trade, and yet this story took root. The nineteenth-century officially-commissioned geography, the *Unified Gazetteer of Đại Nam* (*Đại Nam nhất thống chí* 大南一統志), for instance, cites the *Arrayed Tales* in a section on ancient remains (*cổ tích* 古蹟) in Thanh Hóa Province to give an account of this story in reference to the actual site of An Tiêm Islet.[67] Today this story about Mai An Tiêm is well known.

This contrasts with another story in the *Arrayed Tales*, "The Tale of the Fish Essence", which does contain an actual historical event at its core, and yet this story was dismissed in the nineteenth century, and today is not well known. The core of this tale concerns a historical event whereby someone sought to clear an area along the coast of some boulders in order to facilitate the passage of ships. The one historical figure who is known to have done this was the Tang Dynasty administrator Gao Pian 高駢. According to the *Complete Book of the Historical Records of Đại Việt*, which in turn relied on information that had already been recorded in works like the *History of the Tang* (*Tangshu* 唐書), in AD 867, while touring the coastal areas between what is today northern Vietnam and Guangdong Province in China, Gao Pian saw that in the waterways along the sea coast there were many boulders just below the surface that caused boats to capsize, thereby disrupting transport. He thereupon ordered two of his subordinates to direct their troops to open up a channel. They were able to clear an area of all but a couple of large boulders, which they could not get to budge. In the end though, a sudden storm arose and thunderbolts shattered the boulders to pieces. Afterwards, the area which had been cleared was called "Heaven's Awe Harbor" (Thiên Uy Cảng 天威港).[68] An inscription was subsequently carved to commemorate this event. In it, the harbour is referred to as "Heaven's Awe Passage" (Thiên Uy Kính 天威徑).[69]

The "Tale of the Fish Essence" in the *Arrayed Tales* does not mention this harbour or passage. Instead, it mentions a place called "Buddha-Molded Harbor" (Phật Đào Cảng 佛陶港), and a place nearby called White Dragon-Tail (Bạch Long Vĩ 白龍尾), which is referred to as a mountain in the text. While neither of these place names is mentioned in the *Complete Book of the Historical Records of Đại Việt*, both are mentioned in other works. Both of the place names, for instance, appear in the early-fourteenth-century *General Gazetteer of Jiaozhi*. That text states that there was a White Dragon-Tail Mountain that had steep cliffs and that its "tail" stuck out into the sea. This text also records that there was a tradition that in the past an "extraordinary person" (*dị nhan* 異人) wanted to bore through some of the stones along the coast to facilitate transportation between Jiao and Guang, that is, between the area of what is today northern Vietnam and Guangdong Province in China. However, he was unable to do so and had to give up. The part which had been completed was then called "Buddha-Molded Water Passage" (Phật Đào Kinh 佛陶涇). This was located in Vạn Ninh District 萬寧縣 in Hoa Châu 華州.[70] It is difficult to determine where exactly this was, as the Ming employed different names for administrative units in the region. However, the *Map of the Hồng Đức Era* (*Hồng Đức bản đồ* 洪德版圖), a map that purports to represent the realm as it looked in the fifteenth century, indicates that there was a place called White Dragon-Tale along the northern coast.[71]

So while the name for the passage which Gao Pian cleared appears to have changed over time, the information recorded in the *General Gazetteer of Jiaozhi* about an "extraordinary person" who sought to clear the coast indicates that some kind of memory of Gao Pian's historical endeavour was still maintained in the early fourteenth century. It was perhaps based on this information that "The Tale of the Fish Essence" was created. The actual tale begins in a rather disjointed manner by talking about three separate supernatural beings. It first talks about a fish-serpent essence, which the text says was also called a fish essence, that lived in the Eastern Sea, had many legs like a centipede, and could transform itself in myriad ways. The potency of this essence was unfathomable, and when it moved it created tremors like a storm. It was also able to eat people, and people feared it. The text then essentially begins the story again by talking about a separate supernatural being. It states that in distant antiquity there was a fish which was similar in form to a human. It roamed along the shore of the Eastern Sea, and transformed into a person and could speak. It gradually grew, and produced many boys and girls who ate fish, shrimp, and oysters. Finally, following this passage, the text mentions a third supernatural being. It records that there was also an egg-person who was born on an island in the sea and who specialized in catching fish as his occupation. It later transformed into a human, and traded with savages for salt, rice, clothing, knives, and axes. It often moved about in the Eastern Sea.[72]

The text then turns to the main content of its tale about the fish essence. It states that there was a place called Fish Essence Crag (Ngư Tinh Nham 魚精岩) where jagged stones stuck out along the sea coast. Below it was a cavern where the fish essence lived. The fish essence would harm people who passed in their boats. People wanted to open a different passage along the coast by boring through some stones, but this was too difficult. Then one night, some immortals bore the stones away to make a harbour for the benefit of travellers. When they had done so, the fish essence transformed into a white chicken and called out from above. The group of immortals heard this and suspecting that it was morning, they all ascended into the Heavens. The text then says that to this day, it is still called "Buddha-Molded Harbor".[73]

It is not clear what the name "Buddha-Molded Harbor" has to do with this story. However, the text goes on to mention *yaksas* (dạ xoa 夜叉), a kind of evil being common to all of the main Indian religious traditions, including Buddhism. In particular, the "Tale of the Fish Essence" goes on to state that the Dragon Lord, a reference to the mythical figure in the genealogical line between Shen Nong and the Hùng kings, Lạc Long Quân, pitied the people and ordered the *yaksas* of the water realm to prevent spirits from creating large waves. The Dragon Lord then enticed the fish essence to the surface of the water by pretending to prepare to throw a human in the water for the fish essence to eat. When it did, the Dragon Lord cut off its tail. He then peeled the skin off it and spread it on a mountain, which the text states is now called White Dragon Tail. The head of the fish essence, meanwhile, flowed out to sea and transformed into a dog. The text becomes a bit unclear at this point, but it appears that the Dragon Lord threw stones into the sea to prevent the dog from returning, and that he also beheaded it. The stones and head then transformed into something called Dog Head Mountain (Cẩu Đầu Sơn 狗頭山), most likely an island.

While this story does not mention Gao Pian, it is clear that the historical information about, or memory of, his exploits are the inspiration for this tale. The compilers of the nineteenth-century official history, the *Imperially*

Commissioned Itemized Summaries of the Comprehensive Mirror of Việt History, likewise believed that Gao Pian's historical exploits were what this tale recounts. However, they argued that this historical episode had not taken place within the bounds of their kingdom. In examining the primary source for this story, the *History of the Tang*, and then consulting the *Unified Gazetteer of the Great Qing* (*Da Qing yitong zhi* 大清一統志), these men concluded that the coastal area which Gao Pian had ordered cleared had been to the north of the bounds of the Việt realm.[74] Their conclusion contradicts what Ming officials recorded in the early fourteenth century in the *General Gazetteer of Jiaozhi*. Nonetheless, today this story is not well known.

Conclusion

In noting that nineteenth-century scholars cited the *Arrayed Tales* to include information in an official geography about "The Tale of Watermelon" and that they dismissed "The Tale of the Fish Essence" as a local story, I am not arguing that it was these writings alone that determined what stories today are considered "traditions". My argument, however, is that traditions are largely invented and perpetuated by the elite, rather than created and preserved by the folk. The opinions of nineteenth-century scholars were one of several elite interventions that have served to create what is today perceived as "Vietnamese tradition". The more significant and influential intervention was that of twentieth-century scholars who promoted and exalted folk literature.

What the *Arrayed Tales* demonstrates, however, is that the stories that become traditions are elite creations. That said, this does not mean that they are not important. To the contrary, in this chapter I think we can see that the stories in the *Arrayed Tales* are very important in the way that they demonstrate how the elite in the fifteenth century thought about the world they inhabited. In demonstrating cultural superiority over savages and inventing an antiquity for their land, the men who created the stories in the *Arrayed Tales* were, perhaps unconsciously at the time, inventing a form of Việt identity as well. That enterprise ultimately proved to be very important indeed.

NOTES

1. For more on the transfer of military technology and the expansion of the Lê, see Sun Laichen, "Chinese Gunpowder Technology and Đại Việt, *c*.1390–1497", in *Việt Nam: Borderless Histories*, edited by Nhung Tuyet Tran and Anthony Reid (Madison: University of Wisconsin Press, 2006), pp. 72–120; and Li Tana, "The Ming Factor and the Emergence of the Việt in the 15th Century", in *Southeast Asia in the Fifteenth Century: The China Factor*, edited by Geoff Wade and Sun Laichen (Singapore: National University of Singapore Press, 2010), pp. 83–103.

2. For basic information about the *Arrayed Tales*, see Trần Nghĩa, ed., *Tổng tập tiểu thuyết chữ Hán Việt Nam* [Collection of Vietnamese Novels in Classical Chinese], Tập I (Hà Nội: Thế Giới, 1997), pp. 145–52; Keith Weller Taylor, *The Birth of Vietnam* (Berkeley: University of California Press, 1983), pp. 354–57; and Émile Gaspardone, "Bibliographie Annamite", *Bulletin de l'École Française d'Extrême-Orient* 34 (1934): 128–30.

3. Vũ Quỳnh 武瓊, comp., *Lĩnh Nam chích quái liệt truyện* 嶺南摭怪列傳 [Arrayed Tales of Selected Oddities from South of the Passes], (orig., 1492), Manuscript A. 1200, 1/8a.

4. Lê Quý Đôn 黎貴惇, *Kiến văn tiểu lục* 見聞小錄 [Jottings about Things Seen and Heard] (1777), Manuscript A. 32, 4/3b.

5. Trần Văn Giáp, *Tìm hiểu kho sách Hán Nôm* [Investigating the Treasury of Books in Han and Nom], Tập II (Hà Nội: Khoa Học Xã Hội, 1990), p. 192.

6. Vũ Quỳnh, 1/7b.

7. Lê Quý Đôn, 4/3b.

8. Emile Gaspardone, "Bibliographie Annamite" [Annamite Bibliography], *Bulletin de l'Ecole française d'Extrême-Orient* 34 (1934): 128–29.

9. Henri Maspero, "Etudes d'histoire d'Annam. IV. Le Royaume de Văn-lang" [Studies of the History of Annam. IV. The Kingdom of Văn-lang], *Bulletin de l'École française d'Extrême-Orient* 18 (1918): 1–10; and Édouard Huber, "Etudes indochinoises" [Indochinese Studies], *Bulletin de l'Ecole française d'Extrême-Orient* 5 (1905): 168.

10. Unfortunately, a detailed history of the development of folklore and folk literature studies in Vietnam, one that traces the intellectual origins of this movement, has yet to be written. For China, see Chang-tai Hung, *Going to the People: Chinese Intellectuals and Folk Literature, 1918–1937* (Cambridge: Council on East Asian Studies, Harvard University, 1985).

11. Dinh Gia Khánh, "Vai trò chủ đạo của văn học dân gian" [The Leading Role of Folk Literature], *Văn hóa* [Culture] 3, no. 10 (1970): 6.

12. Nguyễn Đồng Chi, *Kho tàng truyện cổ tích Việt Nam* [The Treasury of Legendary Stories of Vietnam] (Hà Nội: Viện Văn Học, 1993), pp. 123–24.

13. Thomas Engelbert, "Mythic History: Representations of the Vietnamese Past in the Collection 'Lĩnh Nam chích quái'", in *Southeast Asian Historiography Unravelling the Myths: Essays in Honour of Barend Jan Terwiel*, edited by Volker Grabowsky (Bangkok: River Books, 2011), p. 272.

14. Maspero, pp. 7–9.

15. Nguyễn Phương, *Việt Nam thời khai sinh* [Vietnam at the Time of Its Birth] (Huế: Phòng Nghiên Cứu Sử, Viện Đại Học Huế, 1965); and Lê Văn Siêu, *Việt Nam văn minh sử* [History of Vietnamese Civilization] (Sài Gòn: Trung Tâm Học Liệu, 1972).

16. Four volumes were published containing papers from these conferences. Each volume was entitled, *Hùng vương dựng nước* [The Hùng Kings Establish the Nation].

17. Erica Brindley, "Representing and Uses of Yue 越 Identity Along the Southern Frontier of the Han, ~200–111 B.C.E.", *Early China* 33–4 (2010–11): 1–35.

18. For more on this, see Liam C. Kelley, "The Biography of the Hồng Bang Clan as a Medieval Vietnamese Invented Tradition", *Journal of Vietnamese Studies* 7, no. 2 (2012): 87–130.

19. Li Daoyuan 酈道元, comp., *Shuijing zhu* [Annotated Classic of Waterways 水經注], (ca. 515–24), 37/7a-b. There is one term in this passage, *vương/wang*, which can be translated as either "king" or "prince".

20. Vũ Quỳnh, 1/8a.

21. Ibid., 1/19a.

22. Ibid., 1/30a.

23. Ibid., 2/16b–2/19a.

24. Wang Chong 王充, *Lunheng* 論衡 [Doctrines Evaluated], (Electronic Siku quanshu edition, hereafter ESKQS, orig., first cent. AD), 19/11b.

25. Fan Ye 范曄, *Hou Hanshu* 後漢書 [History of the Later Han], (ESKQS, orig., AD 445), 116/liezhuan 76/7a.

26. Liu Shu 劉恕, *Zizhi tongjian waiji* 資治通鑑外紀 [Outer Annals of the Comprehensive Mirror for Aid in Government], (ESKQS, orig., eleventh cent. AD), 3/15a.

27. Vũ Quỳnh, 1/32a–32b.

28. Ibid., 1/32b.

29. Ban Gu 班固, *Qian Hanshu* 前漢書 [History of the Former Han], (ESKQS, orig., 92), 28 xia/48a.

30. Vũ Quỳnh, 1/16a–1/16b.

31. Lê Quý Đôn, 6/43a.

32. Chen Fu 陳孚, *Annan ji shi* 安南即事 [Present Matters in Annan], (1293 AD), in Gu Sili 顧嗣立, *Yuan shixuan erji* 元詩選二集 [The Second Collection of Yuan Poetry], (ESKQS, orig., 1702 C.E.), 6/53b.

33. Ibid., 2/38a.

34. See Ma Duanlin 馬端臨, *Wenxian tongkao* 文献通考 [Comprehensive Examination of Documents], (ESKQS, orig., 1224 C.E.), 330/11a.
35. Keith Taylor, "On Being Muonged", *Asian Ethnicity* 2, no. 1 (2001): 31.
36. For more on this, see Liam C. Kelley, "Tai Words and the Place of the Tai in the Vietnamese Past", *Journal of the Siam Society* 101 (2013): 55–84.
37. Robert Ford Campany, *Strange Writing: Anomaly Accounts in Early Medieval China* (Albany: State University of New York Press, 1996), p. 252.
38. Li Fang 李昉 et al., comps., *Taiping guangji* 太平廣記 [Extensive Records of the Taiping era], (ESKQS, orig., AD 978), 447/1b. See also Rania Huntington, *Alien Kind: Foxes and Late Imperial Chinese Narrative* (Cambridge: Harvard University Asia Center, 2003), p. 1. The first chapter of this monograph provides a good introduction to the fox story genre.
39. Li Fang 李昉 et al., comps., *Taiping yulan* 太平御覽 [Imperially Reviewed Encyclopedia of the Taiping Era], (ESKQS, orig., AD 984), 447/1b.
40. Vũ Quỳnh, 1/18a; Ngô Sĩ Liên, *Đại Việt sử ký toàn thư* 大越史記全書 [Complete Book of the Historical Records of Đại Việt], (AD 1697 ed., orig. comp. AD 1479), Manuscript A. 3, Bản Kỷ 2/3a.
41. Vũ Quỳnh, 1/18a–18b.
42. For a more detailed discussion of these terms, see Geoff Wade, "The Bai-Yi Zhuan: A Chinese Account of a Tai Society in the 14th Century", paper presented at the 14th Conference of the International Association of Historians of Asia, Chulalongkorn University, Bangkok, 20–24 May 1996, pp. 3–4.
43. Zhou Qufei 周去非, *Lingwai daidai* 嶺外代答 [Replies from Beyond the Passes], (ESKQS, orig., AD 1178), 2/1b.
44. Zhao Rugua 趙汝适, *Zhufan zhi* 諸番志 [Treatise on the Various Barbarian Lands], (ESKQS, orig., 1225 AD), Shang/1a.
45. Ngô Sĩ Liên, Bản Kỷ 4/25a and 5/1b.
46. See Léonard Aurousseau, ed., *Ngan-nam tche yuan* [*Annan zhiyuan* 安南志原] (Hanoi: École Française d'Extrême-Orient, 1923), pp. 212–13. The gazetteer which was compiled during the Ming occupation was known as the *General Gazetteer of Jiaozhi* [*Jiaozhi zongzhi* 交阯總志]. It was at some point combined together with a short work by a sixteenth-century Chinese scholar called the *Treatise on Annan* [*Annan zhi* 安南志] which contained an "original preface" [*yuanxu* 原序]. This entire manuscript somehow came to be referred to as the *Annan zhiyuan* 安南志原, a title which does not make sense. It appears that "*Treatise on Annan*" was combined with "original" from "original preface" to create this incomprehensible title. In 1992, Zhang Xiumin identified the core of this text as the *General Gazetteer of Jiaozhi*. See Zhang Xiumin 張秀民, *Zhong Yue guanxishi lunwenji* 中越關係史論文集 [Collected Essays on the History of Sino–Vietnamese Relations] (Taibei: Wenshizhe chubanshe, 1992), pp. 139–44. See also Li Tana, p. 98.

47. Vũ Quỳnh, 1/18b–19a.
48. For reference to Hoa Lư as a grotto, see Phan Thanh Giản 潘清簡 et al., *Khâm định Việt sử thong giám cương mục* 欽定越史通鑿綱目 [Imperially Commissioned Itemized Summaries of the Comprehensive Mirror of Việt History] (AD 1881), A. 2674, Tiền Biên 5/24b.
49. For a reference to West Lake as Excessive Rain Pool, see Ngô Sĩ Liên, Bản Kỷ 2/35b.
50. The text actually just has *chiên đàn/zhantan* 旃檀. I have taken the liberty to use the entire Sanskrit term. Vũ Quỳnh, 1/25b.
51. Ibid., 1/26b–1/25a.
52. Ouyang Xiu 歐陽修, Song Qi 宋祁 et al., *Xin Tangshu* 新唐書 [New History of the Tang], (ESKQS, orig., AD 1043–60), 43 xia/38a.
53. See Guo Qitao, *Exorcism and Money: The Symbolic World of the Five-Fury Spirits in Late Imperial China* (Berkeley: Institute of East Asian Studies, University of California, Berkeley, 2003), pp. 21–39, and for the Mulian opera, see his *Ritual Opera and Mercantile Lineage: The Confucian Transformation of Popular Culture in Late Imperial Huizhou* (Stanford: Stanford University Press, 2005).
54. The text I am using actually has Du Văn Tường 文俞祥. However, other versions and modern translations have Du Văn Mâu. "North" here means what we would today call "China".
55. Another Chinese term which was used from the Tang through the Yuan periods to refer to some Tai peoples was Golden Teeth [Jinchi 金齒]. Perhaps the name of this mysterious art was meant to call to mind "savages" like the Tai. For more on this term for Tai peoples, see Christian Daniels, "The Formation of Tai Polities between the 13th and 16th Centuries: The Role of Technological Transfer", *Memoirs of the Research Department of the Toyo Bunko* 58 (2000): 69–70.
56. Vũ Quỳnh, 1/26a–1/27a.
57. Aurousseau, p. 102.
58. These two characters together constitute the common Chinese term for "betel nut" [*binlang* 檳榔].
59. Vũ Quỳnh, 1/27b–1/28b.
60. Pierre-Bernard Lafont, "Contes P'u Tai" [Tai Tales], *Bulletin de la Société des Études Indochinoises* 46, no. 1 (1971): 12–17.
61. Aurousseau, pp. 75–76.
62. Berthold Laufer, *Sino–Iranica: Chinese Contributions to the History of Civilization in Ancient Iran, with Special Reference to the History of Cultivated Plants and Products* (Chicago: Field Museum of Natural History, 1919), p. 438.
63. Vũ Quỳnh, 1/30b.
64. Ibid.

65. Ibid., 1/31a-b.
66. Marsha Wiedner, ed., *Latter Days of the Law: Images of Chinese Buddhism, 850–1850* (Lawrence: Spencer Museum of Art, University of Kansas; Honolulu: University of Hawaii Press, 1994), pp. 163–66 and 168, and Chün-fang Yü, *Kuan-Yin: The Chinese Transformation of Avalokitesvara* (New York: Columbia University Press, 2000), p. 436.
67. Cao Xuân Dục 高春育 et al., *Đại Nam nhất thống chí* 大南一統志 [Unified Gazetteer of Đại Nam] (Tokyo: Indoshina Kenkyukai, 1941, orig. comp. nineteenth cent.), 16/48b.
68. Ngô Sĩ Liên, Ngoại Kỷ 5/15a–16a.
69. Phan Văn Các and Claudine Salmon, eds., *Épigraphie en chinois du Việt Nam* [Epigraphy in Chinese of Vietnam] (Paris and Hà Nội: École française d'Extrême-Orient and Viện Nghiên Cứu Hán Nôm, 1998), pp. 33–35.
70. Aurousseau, pp. 35 and 46.
71. Bửu Cầm et al., eds., *Hồng Đức bản đồ* 洪德版圖 [Map of the Hồng Đức Era] (Sài Gòn: Bộ Quốc Gia Giáo Dục, 1962, orig., 1490 C.E.), pp. 50–51.
72. Vũ Quỳnh, 1/16b–17a.
73. Ibid., 1/17a–17b.
74. Phan Thanh Giản et al., Tiền Biên 5/12a.

8

EPIDEMICS, TRADE, AND LOCAL WORSHIP IN VIETNAM, LEIZHOU PENINSULA, AND HAINAN ISLAND

Li Tana

Vietnam is geographically very close to the Leizhou Peninsula and to Hainan Island, and the human connections between these sites go back thousands of years. But what is the history and nature of these connections?

We note that the Leizhou Peninsula and Hainan Island do not share land borders with Vietnam, as Guangxi and Yunnan provinces do, for example, and that they do not share Vietnam's strong economical development, so we may ask whether these entities were loosely or closely connected with the Red River Delta. We know rather little about the matter largely because trade in this region was primarily carried out by peddlers rather than by big merchants, and it therefore was rarely recorded. As a result, among all the Chinese peripheries, the connections between Vietnam and the Leizhou Peninsula and Hainan have been the least known.

Archaeological findings, however, suggest long and deep connections between the various coasts of this region. For example, among all the coasts of Guangdong, bronze drums are found most numerously in the

Leizhou Peninsula.[1] Together with the bronze drums found in Guangxi and on Hainan Island, this makes the Leizhou Peninsula stand out for its evident connections with Vietnam, and it highlights the unity of the Gulf of Tongking as one region from the time of antiquity. Local gazetteers of Hainan and Leizhou also record official connections between these coasts. A search of the biographies of scholars recorded in these local gazetteers indicates a striking phenomenon: the scholars of Leizhou and Hainan provided the majority of lower officers during the twenty years of Ming occupation of Vietnam (AD 1407–28).[2]

This fact might be the tip of an iceberg. What connected the different peoples on these disconnected coasts still largely remains a mystery. This paper attempts to offer insights into these connections. It starts by examining epidemic data of the seventeenth and eighteenth centuries in this region, then moves on to look at the trade within, and the local worship shared throughout, the region. These data seem to suggest a rather surprising frequency and intensity of contacts among the peoples in this region. As such, this paper tries to shed some new light onto this shadowy corner of the South China Sea.[3]

Epidemics from Hainan and the Leizhou Peninsula

For much of the period before the nineteenth century, Hainan and the Leizhou Peninsula experienced many epidemics simultaneously with Vietnam. We do not know what specific disease caused these epidemics, but the frequency with which they occurred simultaneously in these areas in particular is striking, if we put the data side by side.

Examples are not lacking, but here I will concentrate on one epidemic between 1680 and 1683.[4] Hainan and Vietnam shared a drought and epidemic at the same time. As in Tongking, in 1681 there was a severe drought in Hainan.[5] No rain was recorded between the fifth lunar month of 1681 and the second lunar month of 1682, and rice prices reached as high as two taels of silver per litre. In 1682, a famine occurred and with it a grave epidemic. "Bodies covered the roads", the local gazetteer recorded.[6]

What is interesting is that along the entire coast of Guangdong and Guangxi, this epidemic of 1682 had only one parallel, and that place seems to have been the origin of the epidemic on Hainan.[7] The Wuchuan 吳川 district on the Leizhou Peninsula across the Qiongzhou Straits 瓊州海峽 recorded epidemics first in 1680, when this area was said to have been ravaged by pirates.[8] These pirates were none other than the pirates led by Yang Yandi 楊彥迪 (Viet., Dương Ngạn Dịch).[9] The sources describe the circumstance that the Yang group attacked Haikou with over one hundred junks, which would have involved around a thousand fighters. This group, which must have been infected by the epidemic in Wuchuan district when they attacked Hainan in 1680, captured over 3,000 hostages from Chengmai 澄邁, Gan'en 感恩, and Changhua 昌化 districts for ransom from their families.[10] When the Qing army sailed across the Qiongzhou Strait 瓊州海峽 and defeated the Yang group in the third lunar month of 1681, these hostages were sent back to their homes. This would have helped the virus to spread further inland on this island. Most of the districts where the hostages had been released were struck by the epidemic in the spring of 1682.[11]

When the Yan Yandi group was comprehensively defeated in the third lunar month of 1682, it appeared in the Gulf of Tongking. The English East India Company's factory in Phố Hiến 舖憲 reported on 9 March 1682 that,

> This day we had news of 200 China junks or better … being near Batsha which did extremely perplex the King and Court, there being a fresh plat [sic] at that instant discovered, to which he thought they were confederate: it proves however that their business was only to aske for helly [sic] tymber, they being bound to Siam; but the wind being contrary, they were forced to put in Batsha in the hope of procuring provisions; in which however they were disappointed and were obliged to go away without obtaining any except what they took by force.[12]

Tongking was suffering a particularly widespread famine at this time: the main harvest at the end of 1681 failed, leaving it, from the month of March with no rice to last till the harvest of the new rice in May. The famine was so severe that the Trịnh Lord asked the Dutch to bring rice from Java, but no ship arrived until June by which time many people had died of starvation.[13] The Yang group lurked in the Gulf of Tongking area for another month or so, according to the same English East India Company's factory in Phố Hiến on 24 April 1682:

The China junks before mentioned were 206 in number, they were cruising about to go to a place where they may procure rice, they having forsake Batsha, and the Allchor, called by the Tonqueeners the Shy Dinh providence, and intended in 5 or 6 days more to depart out of these ports. These 206 junks or vessels have but little in them but men with weapons and other provisions for war, with their wives and children which boarded with them, they being all forced to fly their country to save their lives, or other ways the Tartar have dispatched them off at once.[14]

The epidemic that struck the Leizhou Peninsula in 1680 and 1681 and Hainan Island in 1682 landed at Tongking at this point. According to a Chinese junk's report to the officers in Nagasaki on 29 June 1682,

… as the country has been plagued by epidemic, the numbers of the deaths from illness and starvation have mounted beyond count. We purchased yellow raw silk 小黄糸. We purchased it last year [AD 1681] but it was actually produced the year before last [AD 1680]. Since last year, so many people have died of illness and starvation everywhere that there was no one to harvest silkworms. No raw silk was produced during the last and this year. It is a tragic situation for the people of Tongking.[15]

This information filled a gap in the Vietnamese chronicle, the *Đại Việt sử ký toàn thư*, which failed to record the drought of 1681. This piece of information, however, does not make it entirely clear whether the epidemic occurred in Tongking in 1681 or in 1682, but this was remedied by an English record which stated that in March 1682, severe famine occurred in nearly all the villages of Kinh Bắc and Sơn Tây and left more than two-thirds of the weavers dead as well as "the poor people that used to wind the silk from the silkworms".[16] Although this record indicated that there was a big famine in March 1682, it did not mention anything about the epidemic. This indicates further that the epidemic was predominantly brought by the Yang Yandi group after March 1682.

The epidemic, in other words, struck an already famine-stricken Tongking. The silk harvest of 1682 was lost, and by 1684 silk production still had not recovered. Ship No. 227 that arrived at Nagasaki on August 1684 stated that,

Since the year before last, Tonking has been stricken by a serious famine in which widespread epidemics have killed a third of the entire population in Tonking. Last year, yellow raw silk that was produced everywhere was not available throughout the country. Two ships, including ours and Lin

Yuteng's, were unable to come to Nagasaki and hence remained there. This
year [1683–84] we hoped to procure newly-harvested raw silk and travel to
Nagasaki, but again Tonking experienced a bad year and produced no raw silk.[17]
We obtained only half the amount of raw silk that we used to procure here.[18]

This information confirms the casualty rate from the epidemic given by
Samuel Baron, who said that the famine in 1682 "swept away two-thirds
of the inhabitants".[19] From the *Kai-hentai* we find that people blamed the
poisonous air of the epidemic for the poor silk harvest: "Tonking suffered
from a great famine and terrible epidemics all over the country. The people
perished everywhere. About a half [of the people] died … probably due
to the environment polluted by the pandemic; silkworms did not grow
and even the mulberry trees, on which silkworms feed, failed in the past
few years."[20]

Although Vietnamese sources recorded that the Chinese pirate groups
of Yang Yandi and Chen Shangchuan 陳上川 arrived in Cochinchina in
1679, all other sources — English, French, Japanese, and Chinese —
agreed that the bulk of the groups arrived later. Chen Jinghe points out
that Yan Yandi's group most probably arrived in the Mekong Delta in
two groups: one in December 1682 and the other in May 1683.[21] This
means that between April 1682 and May 1683, they must have roamed
along the coast of Cochinchina for several months to a year. This was long
enough to spread the virus to Cochinchina. In 1683, a big epidemic was
recorded in the capital and the northern part of Cochinchina. The main
Nguyễn Dynasty chronicle recorded this rare occurrence and reported that
"many soldiers and ordinary people died".[22]

Were the Yang group suffering from the epidemic themselves? The
answer is most probably "yes". When the Yang group was defeated
in February 1682 and fled to Cochinchina, their fleet was recorded as
numbering 206 junks by the English East India Company's factory in Pho
Hien on in April 1682, as we saw above.[23] However, when they arrived in
Quảng Nam, in the centre of present-day Vietnam, the number of junks was
little more than fifty (Vietnamese source), or just over seventy, according
to the Japanese *Kai hentai*.[24]

What happened to Yang's junks between the time the journey started
in March 1682 with 206 junks and the time it ended a few months later
when the fleet reached Quảng Nam and the Mekong Delta? Chen Jinghe

has asked this question and quotes Adhémard Leclère's *Histoire du Cambodge*, which gives the explanation that they met a typhoon at sea so that some of the junks were lost and others were scattered. This could partly explain the missing junks, but when a fleet loses about two-thirds of its number of ships in a typhoon, some other factors might also be at work. Since the epidemic was recorded as a severe and violent one, it is difficult not to suspect that some of Yang's pirate troops were infected, or more accurately that they themselves were carriers of the virus.

The Vietnamese gave a different story of the setback that befell the Yang group, caused not by epidemic but by some beautiful Vietnamese women. This was all planned by a minister of the Lê court, Vũ Duy Chí 武惟志:

> At the time there were over 100 sea junks from China that came to Hồng Đàm of our country. [The court] ordered him to attack them. He came up with the plot of employing beautiful women. He fetched over 300 prostitutes and singing girls (*hoa nương* and *đào nương*) and sent them in small boats to the enemy junks. He had told everyone to take a red handkerchief. When entertaining the enemies they should wet their handkerchiefs and drip water into [enemies'] gun barrels. After this they should leave in the small boats they came in. On the following day, Vũ arranged his navy in a row and started shooting the enemy fleet. The enemies rushed to their guns to shoot back but none of them could do so. They sailed away, and our army won the battle in a big way.[25]

The liaisons between the over 300 northern Vietnamese girls and Chinese pirates would have provided a direct channel for the transmission of the epidemic to the Tongking society.

Further evidence of correlations between northern Vietnam and Hainan Island can be found in the eighteenth century records of the two regions. Hải Thượng Lãn Ông 海上懶翁 (Nguyễn Hữu Trác 黎有晫, 1724–91) was the best known and most celebrated doctor in Vietnamese history. The reason that he decided to become a doctor, according to his own account, was that his only son died in a smallpox epidemic in 1758 when he was five. Lãn Ông believed that the boy was incorrectly treated by the doctors in his village. He was so heartbroken that he isolated himself from the world for fifteen years to learn medicine, with a focus on curing smallpox. On this he built his reputation and became a famous doctor.[26]

Lãn Ông's son contracted smallpox in March 1758. At the same time an epidemic was spreading in Lingao 臨高 on Hainan and Lianjiang 廉江 on the Leizhou Peninsula.[27] Since the overlap between northern and central Vietnam with Hainan and the Leizhou Peninsula is strikingly frequent, there is perhaps good reason to speculate that the epidemic that occurred in this year in the latter region was also smallpox. In fact, once we put the occurrences in Vietnam into the context of this regional background, we can see that there was an epidemic throughout the region between 1756 and 1765. Table 8.1 shows the overlapping reports on the epidemics in the region between 1680 and 1762. The first peak of such overlap occurred in 1680–83, followed by the second in 1756–59.

The data on the Tongking–Hainan–Leizhou Peninsula connections discussed above throw some light onto this corner of the shadowy world of the greater South China Sea. To the local peoples, the sea passages between the three coasts — northern Vietnam, the Leizhou Peninsula, and Hainan Island — were more like, to quote Roderich Ptak, "country roads used for regional transportation" rather than international waters.[28] Dr Gutzluf reported a rather large-scale and quite regular rice trade carried out in the region in the nineteenth century, but it could be that this could go back hundreds of years, with greater and lesser activity over that time. He states that northern Vietnam's

> … principal trade exists with the various emporiums of Haenan: the junks are very small that start from thence to Tunkin and Hué, as well as Faifo; they exchange home produce and export a great deal of rice: their number is never under 200, some of which make three voyages per annum, principally to Tunkin; the adjacent districts of Kwangtung likewise carry on a small coasting trade.[29]

"The adjacent districts of Kwangtung" that Gutzluf refers to here would have been the Leizhou Peninsula. This regional trade provides further context to the Chinese-Vietnamese piracy during the Tây Son period, as studied by Dian Murray and Robert Antony. Murray reported that, between 1805 and 1809, the pirates obtained iron, cannons and ammunition from their agents in Haikang 海康, Wuchuan 吳川, and Hainan.[30] All of these names appear frequently on our table above, and presumably they suffered the same epidemic as Vietnam in the same time frame.

TABLE 8.1
Epidemics in Northern Vietnam, Western Guangdong, Hainan, and Guangzhou 1680–1762[1]

	Vietnam		Western Sea area				Hainan Island					Canton area	
	Cochin china	Bac Thanh	Gao zhou	Lian jiang	Feng kai	Wu chuan	Lin gao	Qiong shan	Cheng mai Dan, Dong fang	Wen chang	Guang zhou	San shui
1680						1	1					
1681							1					
1682		1					1	1	1	1		
1683	1		1									
1756							1					
1757			1				1					
1758		1		1			1					1
1759					1			1			1	
1760				1								
1762		1										

Note: [1] For 1758 in Vietnam, see Hải Thượng Lãn Ông, quyển 1, p. 2. For 1762, see Phan Thanh Giản, vol. 8, p. 3720. For 1756, see Lingao xianzhi 臨高縣誌 [Gazetteer of Lingao District], juan 3. For the rest of the districts, see Lai and Li, pp. 77–219.

Source: The sea passages that appear in *The Tongking Gulf: Country Roads for Regional Transportation.*

This area also had a long history of human trafficking, and the main direction was from the Leizhou-Hainan area to Đại Việt. Only a few stories of human trafficking in the South China Sea area survive, but they seem to focus on the Gulf of Tongking area. In 1449, it was reported that "four men and women from the Xuwen 徐聞 district had been captured and sold to Annam. They have recently come back by sea."[31] In the 1460s, a Hainan ship with thirteen men on board ran ashore on the coast of Đại Việt on its way to Qinzhou 欽州. The Thăng Long court sent most of them to *đồn điền* 屯田 (land reclamation) but made the youngest one into a eunuch who spent about a quarter century as a palace attendant.[32] Also during the reign of Lê Thánh Tông 黎聖宗 (1460–97), it was reported in 1472 that a man from Nanhai District "ran off course" to Đại Việt and was sent to its army. He said upon "escaping" back to China that there had been over a hundred Chinese men held in Đại Việt who were either sent to the army or made into eunuchs.[33] This practice of selling people of the Leizhou and Hainan area to Đại Việt could be traced even further back, and it seemed the practice was systematic. In 1320, "the poor people of Hainan captured the local children and sold them to Annam as servants. The king [of Annam] heard about this, he ordered that the human traffickers be taken into custody, the sold children traced and sent back."[34] As the thirteenth-century source *Lingwai daida* 嶺外代答 reported: "The people in Jiaozhi have the advantage of [accessing] gold thus tend to buy our people [in Guangxi] as slaves."[35]

Were so many ships "off course" as they claimed? John Whitmore suggests that they were most probably carrying out regular trade within the region. It is interesting that records of contacts are relatively dense in the fifteenth century, suggesting that the Gulf of Tongking maritime system was still very much alive and active, and that the Leizhou Peninsula and Hainan Island played an active role in the Gulf of Tongking region.

Thunder God and Stone Dog

Two distinctive local deities, the Thunder God and the Stone Dog, were worshipped by the peoples of this region. These two seemed to have been related to each other: many stone dogs collected by the Leizhou Museum exhibit carved patterns of cloud and thunder, both emblems regarded as the guardians of the local people and both connected to rituals of praying for rain.[36] Leizhou (which literally means the "prefecture with much thunder") was so named because people believed that they had more thunderstorms in the area than in other places. Because thunder usually brings the rain, they worship the Thunder God. Thunder was also believed to have suppressive power over typhoons.[37]

There is still a huge temple devoted to the deity in Leizhou. Temples for the Thunder God are also found in Hainan Island's Dingan, Chengmai, Wenchang, and Lingshui districts, place names that appear repeatedly in the sources in contexts that reveal relations with Vietnam.[38] Not surprisingly the Thunder God is also worshipped by some people as *thành hoàng* 城隍 (a local deity or spirit) in northern and central Vietnamese villages. The location of these villages is very interesting: they are mostly situated in the eastern part of the Red River delta along the ancient sea-river route, but not on the new coast made by the alluvial plain, as Map 8.1 shows.[39]

MAP 8.1
Districts Worshipping the Thunder God in Northern and Central Vietnam

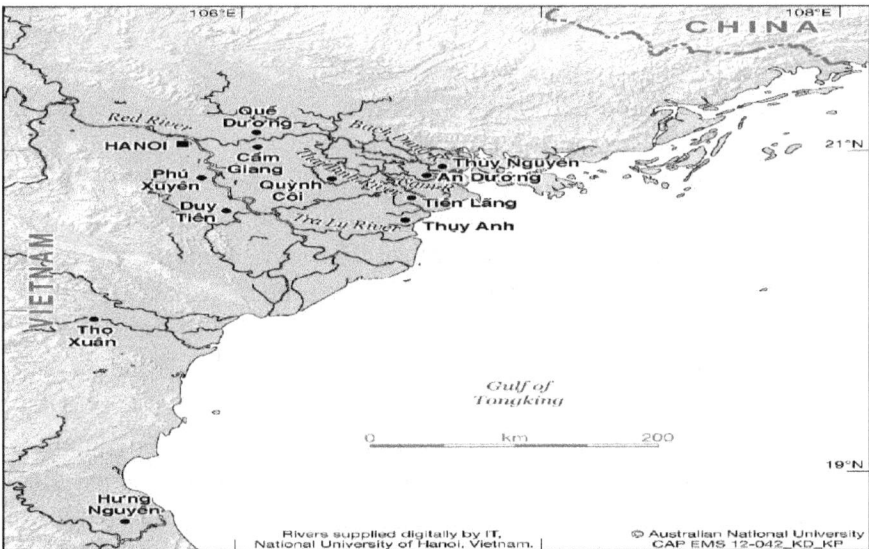

Why was the God of Thunder revered specifically at these locations? Before the fifteenth century, the main waterway connecting Đại Việt's capital and the Chinese coast was the Bạch Đằng River (i.e., it was the main stream of the Red River, in contrast to the present main stream running between Nam Định and Thái Bình).[40] These villages are more or less located right along the main traffic route of the day, in the heart of the Tongking Gulf trading zone. The human traffic discussed above would have followed this waterway up to Đại Việt's capital, Thăng Long.

The celebrated Vietnamese ceramic-producing area, Chu Đậu, is situated right in the heart of this traffic lane. A Hong Kong scholar has compared the Chu Đậu ceramics with those from the Haikang kiln (in Leizhou) and has concluded that they were correlated. The brown painted wares of Vietnamese ceramics of the late thirteenth to fifteenth centuries show a very similar style to the painted pieces from the Nanhai and Haikang kilns. A distinctive type of bowl that has its outside wall glazed in brown but possesses a white interior is found both in Vietnamese ceramics and in those from Haikang.[41]

Routes Bypassing Guangxi, and the Fujian Connection

On examining the repeatedly appearing place names of the Leizhou peninsula in connection with their relations with Vietnam, one main observation emerges: they are all located at the eastern side of the Leizhou Peninsula rather than on the western side, i.e., in the Gulf of Tongking. The parallel epidemics in Vietnam, Hainan, and the Leizhou Peninsula discussed above were rarely shared by Guangxi. This is puzzling. Since Guangxi is situated midway between Vietnam and the Leizhou Peninsula, there should have been more interactions with both locations, not fewer.

To solve this puzzle I have examined the Chinese maritime routes to Vân Đồn 雲屯, the major port of Đại Việt, recorded by sixteenth-century Chinese merchants. These merchants were most often from Fujian, so their departure point was Dadan Island 大擔島 in Fujian. To go towards Vân Đồn, junks would sail all the way west and arrive at the port near Guangzhou. An intriguing thing happened here: instead of continuing to sail west down to the Qiongzhou Straits and arrive at Vân Đồn, which is not far from the other side of the Qiongzhou Straits, the merchants sailed down to the south, rounded the entire island of Hainan, then sailed up to the Tongking Gulf, and finally arrivef at Vân Đồn.[42] This would almost double the length of the journey from less than four days and nights to more than six days and nights. This was also the route taken by Guangdong junks visiting Vân Đồn. The *Annan tuzhi* 安南圖誌, an early seventeenth-century book compiled by a Guangdong senior military officer, Deng Zhong, records that those going from Guangdong to Vietnam took the same route, and thus eliminated only the Fujian section.[43] This same route was recorded in a late seventeenth-century book, the *Dongxi yangkao* 東西洋考, as well.[44] All of these routes (basically the same one) would come around Hainan Island and up to the Gulf of Tongking rather than pass through the Qiongzhou Straits. This route is clearly marked on military maps made in the early eighteenth century, as Map 8.2 shows.

MAP 8.2
Sea Routes to the Eastern Sea and the Southern Sea, by
Shi Shibiao, made between 1712 and 1721[45]

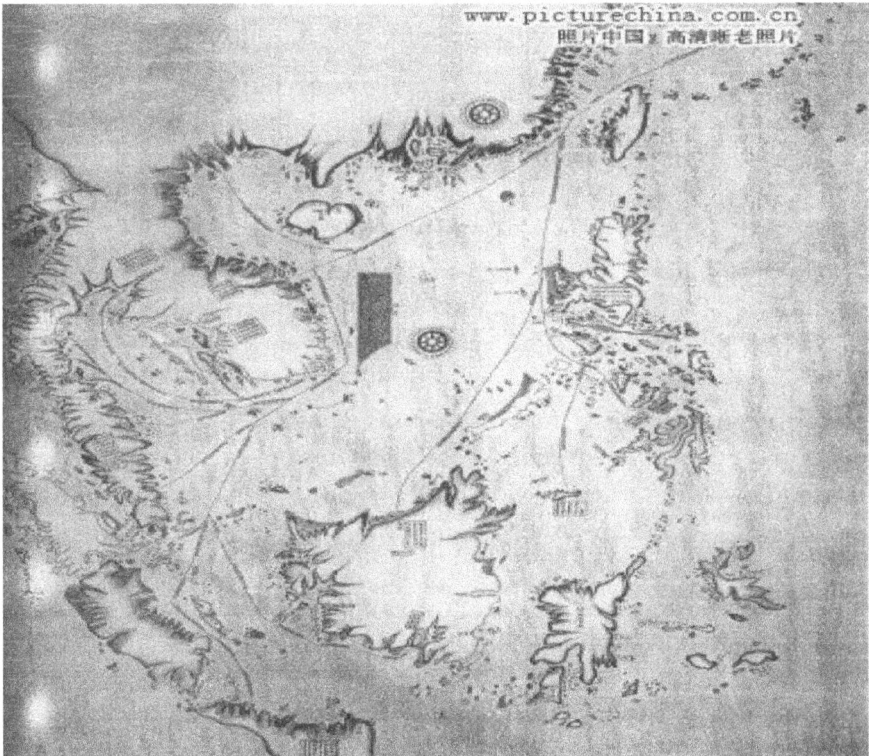

Scientists point out that the strong tidal currents of the Tongking Gulf are located in the Qiongzhou Strait and near the southwestern coast of Hainan Island.[46] These two locations appear to have been carefully avoided by the maritime travellers mentioned above. An eighteenth-century Chinese book gives more reasons why these locations were to be feared and avoided. Its author says that, in sailing from the Dianbai 電白 district of Guangdong south to the Xuwen district of the western Leizhou Penisula, there were "numerous submerged rocks and hidden sand bars, so many that one cannot list all of them. [This is why] no one dares to enter this route [or strait] unless the sailors know the route extremely well". Along the western coast of Hainan Island there were equally many hidden sand bars. This same text notes that, "it is really exceedingly difficult and dangerous to sail this route."[47]

All of the maritime routes of different periods mentioned above are recorded by the Fujianese. It is important to mention that although the region of Leizhou Peninsula and Hainan Island were administrated by Guangdong, the coastal areas are predominantly occupied by the southern Hokkien-dialect speakers, as shown in Map 8.3 on the Leizhou dialects. These Hokkien-dialect speakers were pioneers in Chinese maritime activities. Before they headed to, and settled down in, Southeast Asia in large numbers, the Leizhou Peninsula, Hainan, northern and central Vietnam would have been where they chose to make their livelihood. Two existing family genealogies in northern Vietnam each records that their ancestors came from Fujian in the twelfth and sixteenth centuries, respectively,[48] and Vietnam's main chronicle clearly records that the royal family that founded Vietnam's Trần Dynasty (1225–1400) was from Fujian.

We also know that there were close links between the Muslim merchants in Quanzhou, Hainan, and Champa.[49] This route around Hainan Island to Đại Việt's major port, Vân Đồn, might also have been established there because it had been the route most familiar to the Cham merchants who engaged in trade with Hainan and Đại Việt. This means that while the coastal and regional dimension was important, perhaps it is equally important in understanding the historical connections between the three to include the Fujian and Muslim links via Champa, at least until the early sixteenth century.

MAP 8.3
Map of Leizhou Dialects[50]

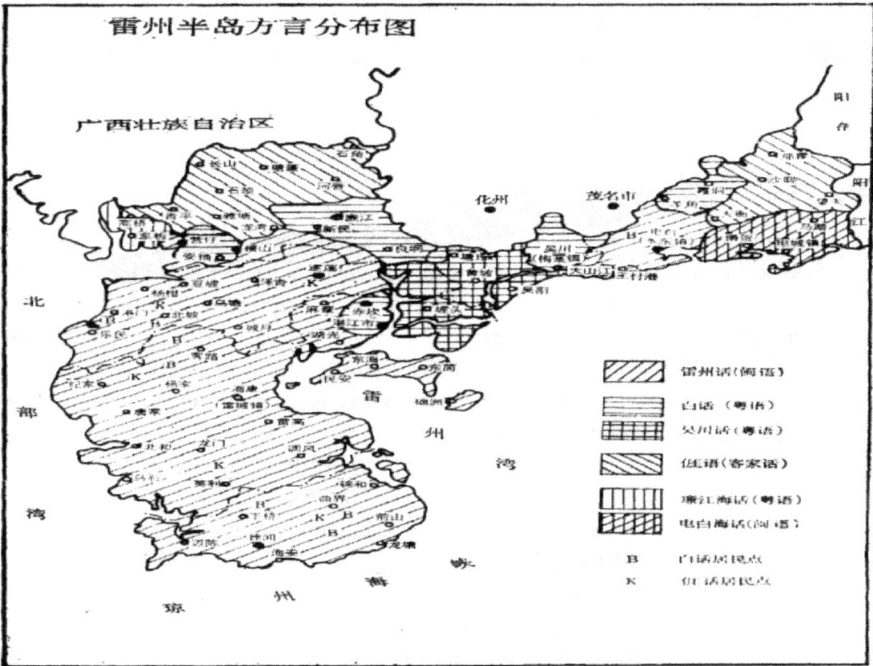

In this chapter I have tried to conduct a preliminary survey of the interconnections between northern Vietnam, Hainan Island, and the Leizhou Peninsula in the last ten centuries. These interconnections are shown in trade, human trafficking, piracy, and importantly, epidemics. These connections are so deep and go back so far in the history of this region that waters between them should be properly regarded as country roads rather than international waters. It is interesting to note in this context that when, in 1899, the French forced the Qing government to "lease" them a port on the Chinese coast, they chose Zhanjiang 湛江 on Leizhou Peninsula, which they called Kwang-chou-wan (Guangzhou wan 廣州灣), or Guangzhou Bay, as their concession port. This completed the French control of the entire Gulf of Tongking. To get into the Chinese interior they used three major routes. Strikingly, all of these routes are familiar and all have appeared repeatedly in this chapter.[51]

Although the name of Kwang-chou-wan was somewhat misleading since this region is about 400 km away from Guangzhou, the French did seem to have an insight in seeing the natural connections between the Leizhou Peninsula with their colony of Tongking, which they had acquired only six years before.

NOTES

1. *Guangdong difangzhi* 廣东地方志 (Local Gazetteer of Guangdong) 4 (2009): 54.
2. See the names of Chinese served as officers in Vietnam during the Ming occupation of the early fifteenth century in a gazetteer of Hainan in *Riben cang Zhongguo hanjian difangzhi congkan*: [Wanli] *Qiongzhou phu zhi* 日本藏中國罕見地方誌叢刊: [萬歷] 瓊州府誌 [Collection of Rare Chinese Local Gazetteers Held in Japan: (Wanli Era) Gazetteer of Qiongzhou Prefecture] (Beijing: Shumu wenxian chubanshe, 1990), vol. 1, pp. 441–72.
3. Robert J. Antony, "Introduction: The Shadowy World of the Greater China Seas", in *Elusive Pirates, Pervasive Smugglers: Violence and Clandestine Trade in the Greater China Seas*, edited by Robert J. Antony (Hong Kong: Hong Kong University Press, 2010), p. 7.
4. One previous example was in 1597. There was a drought in the Qiongshan district, Hainan, followed by a big epidemic. In the following spring when a drought occurred in northern Vietnam, an epidemic also broke out. 1597: 瓊山春大疫旱饑. Lai Wen 賴文 and Li Yongchen 李永宸, *Lingnan wenyi shi* 嶺南瘟疫史 [A History of Epidemics in the Lingnan Area], (Guangzhou: Guangdong renmin chubanshe, 2004), p. 117; 1598: 3 月旱疫. Phan Thanh Giản 潘清簡 et al., *Khâm định Việt sử thong giám cương mục* 欽定越史通鑒綱目 [Imperially Commissioned Itemized Summaries of the Comprehensive Mirror of Việt History], (Taibei: Guoli zhongyang tushuguan, 1969, orig. comp., 1881), vol. 8, p. 3744.
5. Iioka Naoko, "The Trading Environment and the Failure of Tongking's Mid-Seventeenth-Century Commercial Resurgence", in *Tongking Gulf Through History*, edited by Nola Cooke, Li Tana, and James A. Anderson (Philadelphia: University of Pennsylvania Press, 2011), p. 127.
6. 康熙 20 年, 春二月, 海寇楊二, 謝昌攻海口城, 據之, 郡城戒嚴. 三月順德總兵官蔡璋, 虎門副將張諭自省城統水師渡瓊, 賊大半解散, 餘黨遁入黎, 盤踞數月始平. 秋 7 月啟明星晝見, 地震, 瓊澄文儋臨感各州縣旱饑, 自 5 月不雨至明年 2 月, 斗米銀二兩. 壬戌 21 年 (1682) 春二月, 饑, 大疫作. 瓊山、文昌、儋州、感恩各州縣饑疫並行, 死者載道. *(Daoguang) Qiongzhou fuzhi* (道光) 瓊州府志 [Gazetteer of Qiongzhou Prefecture (in the Daoguang Era)], juan 42.
7. Lai and Li list all of the recorded epidemics in Guangdong and Guangxi by district. No epidemic was recorded in any of the districts other than Wuchuan and on Hainan Island for the 1681–82 period discussed in this chapter.

8. 康熙 19 年夏 4 月, 疫 … 是時吳川為海寇所擾, 荒殘已極 … 康熙 20 年辛酉 … 又疫, 疫更烈, 邑人多死, 戶絕者幾半. *(Guangxu) Wuchuan xianzhi* (光緒) 吳川縣誌 [Gazetteer of Wuchuan District (in the Guangxu Era)], juan 10, jishu shilue 紀述事略.

9. *Qiongzhou fuzhi*, juan 31 and 42; Chen Jinghe 陳荊和, "Qingchu Zheng Chenggong canbu zhi yizhi Nanqi (shang)" 清初鄭成功殘部之移殖南圻(上) [Migration of Zheng Chenggong's Remnant Troops to Cochinchina (Part 1)], *Xinya xuebao* 新亞學報 (New Asia Journal) 5, no. 1 (1960): 445.

10. *Guangdong tongzhi* 廣東通志 [Gazetteer of Guangdong], juan 261/8A-8B; *Qiongzhou fuzhi*, juan 31 and 42.

11. Chen, pp. 444–46.

12. "Abstracts of the Tonquin Factory Journal Register from 1681 December 15 to 1682 July 28", Books Record from India, no. 210–41, quoted from Chen, pp. 446–47. For the Vietnamese version of this statement, see Hoàng Anh Tuấn, *Tư liệu các công ty Đông Ấn Hà Lan va Anh về Kẻ Chợ — Đàng Ngoài* [Materials of the Dutch and English East India Companies on Hanoi and Tongking], (Hà Nội: Nhà xuất bản Hà Nội, 2010), p. 372.

13. Hoàng, p. 224.

14. Chen, p. 447.

15. Naoko Iioka, "The Junk Trade from Southeast Asia: Translation from Tosen Fusetsu-gaki for Vietnam" (unpublished manuscript).

16. The provinces were actually spelled "Shuback" and "Shuta", which probably comes from the terms "Xứ Bắc" and "Xứ Tây", meaning the "Northern Region" and "Western Region", respectively. In this chapter I am using the more familiar terms of Kinh Bắc and Sơn Tây for these areas. Anthony Farrington, "English East India Company Documents Relating to Pho Hien and Tonkin", in *Pho Hien: The Centre of International Commerce in the XVIIth–XVIIIth Centuries* (Hà Nội: Thế Giới, 1994), p. 158.

17. There was a heavy flood in 1684 that seriously damaged both rice and silk production. Hoàng, p. 229.

18. Iioka, "The Junk Trade from Southeast Asia".

19. Iioka, "The Trading Environment and the Failure of Tongking's Mid-Seventeenth-Century Commercial Resurgence", p. 127.

20. *Kai hentai* 華夷變態 (Transformation from Hua to Barbarian), juan 8, the statements of ship no. 4, 27 August 1684.

21. Chen, pp. 453–54.

22. 順化疫作軍民死者甚眾. *Đại Nam thực lục tiền biên* 大南實錄前編 [Chronicle of Greater Vietnam, Premier Compilation], vol. 5, p. 84.

23. "Abstracts of the Tonquin Factory Journal Register from 1681 December 15 to 1682 July 28", Books Record from India, no. 210–41, quoted from Chen, pp. 446–47; Niu Junkai and Li Qingxin, "Chinese 'Political Pirates' in the Seventeenth-Century Gulf of Tongking", in Cooke, Li, and Anderson, p. 139.

24. *Đại Nam thực lục tiền biên*, vol. 5, p. 82; *Kai hentai*, juan 8, the statements of no. 5 Siam ship, 1 June 1683; no. 19 Siam ship, 17 July 1683.

25. 時有北國人駕海舟百餘艘來我國之洪潭, 命公進討. 公用出女子計, 覓花娘、桃娘約三百餘, 放下賊艘, 托為弄月醉花之狀, 密教各把紅巾一幅, 浸以水, 乘夜索艘間銃口, 取濕巾水滴入, 仍各依朝從小船回去. 次日陳船, 排開. 賊倉忙取銃應之, 射不發, 揚帆遁去, 官軍大捷. See the *Nam Thiên trân dị tập* 南天珍異集 [Collected Preciosities from the Southern Heavens], in *Yuenan Hanwen xiaoshuo jicheng* 越南漢文小說集成 [Collection of Vietnamese Stories Written in Classical Chinese], edited by Sun Xun 孫遜, Zheng Kemeng (Trịnh Khắc Mạnh) 鄭克孟, and Chen Yiyuan 陳益源 (Shanghai: Guji chubanshe, 2010], vol. 10, p. 149.

    Another Vietnamese work said that the junks were led by Deng Yao, an anti-Qing pirate leader active in the Gulf of Tongking in the 1650s. Deng was reportedly killed in 1661. If so, the event recorded here would have happened about twenty years earlier. But since Deng Yao had been the leader of the Yang Yandi group, and this group had been active in the Gulf for three to four decades, the group might have been known as the Deng Yao group in Vietnam even after he had died. See *Công dư tiệp ký* 公餘捷記 [Quick Notes Made at Leisure], manuscript number R.229, p. 8.

26. Hải Thượng Lãn Ông 海上懶翁, *Mộng trung giác đậu* 夢中覺痘 [Confused Attempts at Diagnosing Smallpox], quyển 1, p. 2.

27. 三水、臨高疫; 廉江春夏大疫. Lai and Li, p. 82.

28. Roderich Ptak, "Some Glosses on the Sea Straits of Asia: Geography, Functions, Typology", *Crossroads: Studies on the History of Exchange Relations in the East Asian World* 1/2 (2010): n.p.

29. Dr Gutzlaff, "Geography of the Cochin-Chinese Empire", *Journal of the Royal Geographic Society of London* 19 (1849): 125–26.

30. Dian Murray, "Piracy and China's Maritime Transition, 1750–1850", in *Maritime China in Transition, 1750–1850*, edited by Wang Gungwu and Ng Chin-keong (Wiesbaden: Harrassowitz Verlag, 2004), p. 53; Robert J. Antony, "Piracy and the Shadow Economy in the South China Sea, 1780–1810", in *Elusive Pirates, Pervasive Smugglers*, edited by Robert Antony (Hong Kong: Hong Kong University Press, 2010), p. 110. Another example was in May 1807, when a typhoon overturned a pirate ship near Swatow, and ninety-one men and women were captured by the Qing army. Most of them were from the Western Sea (from the Leizhou Peninsula to the coast of northern Vietnam) area. 5.11日汕頭放雞洋海面颶風海盜船沉沒清軍捕得 "男婦 91 名籍茂名石城吳川合浦遂溪陽江欽州番禺". *Ming Qing shiliao* 明清史料庚編 [Archival material of the Ming and Qing dynasties], (Beijing: Zhonghua shuju, 1987), Vol. G, 3 ben, p. 225.

31. 正月乙未: 廣東雷州府徐聞縣男婦 4 人為人掠賣于安南國, 至是挈家泛海來歸. *Ming Yingzong shilu* 明英宗實錄 [Veritable Records of Ming Yingzong], juan 174.

32. John Whitmore, "Van Don, the Mac Cap, and the Jiaozhi Ocean System", in Cooke, Li, and Anderson, eds., p. 109; *Ming Xiaozong shilu* 明孝宗實錄 [Veritable Records of Ming Xiaozong], juan 153.

33. *Ming Xianzong shilu* 明憲宗實錄 [Veritable Records of Ming Xianzong], juan 106.

34. Lê Trắc 黎崱, *An Nam chí lược* 安南志略 [Summary Treatise on An Nam], (Beijing: Zhonghua shuju, 1995), p. 382.

35. Zhou Qufei 周去非, *Lingwai daida* [Replies from Beyond the Passes], [compiled in 1178; Beijing: Zhonghua shuju, 1998], Shengjin 生金 (Raw Gold), p. 270.

36. Liu Lan 劉嵐 and Li Xiongfei 李雄飛, "Leizhou shigou chongbai bianqian yu minzu geju zhi guanxi" 雷州石狗崇拜變遷與民族格局之關係 [Changes in the Worship of Stone Dogs in Guangxi and Its Connection to the Ethnic Situation], *Guangxi shehui kexue* 廣西社會科學 [Guangxi Social Sciences] 8 (2008): 146. For stone dogs in Leizhou, see the huge collections of the Leizhou Museum, and for stone dogs in Vietnam, see Viện khoa học xã hội Việt Nam and Viện Khảo cổ học, *Hoàng thành Thăng Long: Thăng Long Imperial Citadel* (Hanoi: The Culture Information Publishing House, 2006), p. 16, although it was wrongly identified as a lion. For a more recently identified stone dog, see Nguyễn Thị Bích Hồng, Nguyễn Xuân Cao, "Nhóm hiện vật phát hiện ở Mỹ Trung (Nam Định)" [Assemblage Discovered in Mỹ Trung (Nam Định)], *Những phát hiện mới về khảo cổ học năm 2009* [New Discoveries of Archaeology in 2009], (Hanoi: Nhà xuất bản Khoa học xã hội, 2011), p. 507.

37. 南海秋夏, 間或雲物慘然, 則其暈如虹, 長六七尺. 比候則颶風必發, 故呼為颶母. 忽見有震雷, 則颶風不能作矣. 舟人常以為候, 豫為備之. Liu Xun 劉恂, *Lingbiao luyi* 嶺表錄異 [Record of Strange things in Lingbiao], juan 1, <http://zh.wikisource.org/wiki/%E5%B6%BA%E8%A1%A8%E9%8C%84%E7%95%B0/%E5%8D%B701>.

38. 瓊州府: 雷廟在西廂下田村 ... 祈禱災疫多應; 澄邁: 雷廟(在)縣東五裡 ...; 文昌: 火雷廟在縣南街; 陵水: 火雷祠在北西. *(Wanli) Qiongzhou fu zhi* (萬曆) 瓊州府志 [Gazetteer of Qiongzhou Prefecture (in the Wanli Era)], (Beijing: Shumu wenxian chubanshe, 1990), pp. 107–9.

39. It is interesting that nine out of the eleven *thần tích* 神蹟, or "spirit records", for the Thunder God were complied in the sixteenth century, but the two in Thái Bình Province were compiled in the 1730s–40s. For examples of villages that worshiped the God of Thunder in northern Vietnam, see Liu Chunyin 劉春銀, Lin Qingzhang 林慶彰, and Trần Nghĩa 陳義, eds., *Di sản Hán-Nôm Việt Nam: Thư mục đề yếu bổ di* 越南漢喃文獻目錄提要補遺 [The Sino–Nom Heritage of Vietnam: Additions to the Catalogue and Abstracts] (Taipei: Academic Sinica, 2004), item 0213, p. 68; item 261, p. 82; item 0387, p. 121; item 0504, p. 152; item 0550, p. 164; item 0579, p. 172; item 0680, p. 197; item 0693, p. 200; item 0701, p. 202; item 0925, p. 256; and item 0966, p. 267.

40. Đào Duy Anh, *Đất nước Việt Nam qua các đời* [Country of Vietnam Throughout the Ages], (Hanoi: Khoa học, 1964), p. 37.

41. Yang Shaoxiang 楊少祥, "Guangdong ciqi yu guoneiwai ciyaoqi de guanxi" 廣東瓷器與國內外瓷瑤器的關係 [Guangdong Ceramics and Their Relationship with Other Chinese and Foreign Ceramic Wares], in *Guangdong chutu Wudai zhi Qing wenwu* 廣東出土五代至清文物 [Archaeological Finds from the Five Dynasties to the Qing Period in Guangdong], (Guangzhou: Guangdong sheng bowuguan; Hong Kong: Xianggang Zhongwen daxue wenwuguan, 1989), pp. 172–73.

42. Dadan (Fujian) to Jiaozhi: 7 geng to Nanao — 23 geng to Dong Jiang — 5 geng to Wuzhu — 3 geng to Qizhou Ocean — 5 geng to Limu Mountain in Hainan — 15 geng to Haibao mountain — 5 geng to Jijiao gate (Vân Đồn). 63 geng — about six days and nights. See "Zhinan zhengfa" 指南正法 [True Technique for Navigation] and "Da dan wang Jiaozhi" 大擔往交趾 [Dadan to Jiaozhi], in Da Xiang 向達, comp. and annotate, *Liang zhong haidao zhenjing* 兩種海道針經 [Two Types of Navigation Guides of Sea Routes], (Beijing: Zhonghua shuju, 1982), p. 167.

43. Deng Zhong 鄧鐘, *Annan tuzhi* 安南圖志 [Treatise and Maps of Annan], (Beijing: Guoli Beiping tushuguan shanben congshu, 1937), pp. 30–31.

44. Zhang Xie 張燮, *Dong-Xiyang kao* 東西洋考 [A Study of Eastern and Western Oceans] (Beijing: Zhonghua shuji, 1981), pp. 171–72.

45. *Dongyang Nanyang haidao tu* 東洋南洋海道圖 [Map of the Sea Route between the Eastern and Southern Oceans], created by Shi Shipiao 施世驃 while he was serving as Fujian provincial naval commander (1712–21), <http://www.world10k.com/blog/?p=2108>.

46. Jianyu Y. Hu, Hiroshi Kawamura, and Danling L. Tang, "Tidal Front Around the Hainan Island, Northwest of the South China Sea", *Journal of Geophysical Research* 108, issue C11 (2003): 3342.

47. 自放雞而南，至於海安，中懸州，暗礁暗沙，難以悉載，非深諳者，莫敢內行.... 海南 "西路沿海，惟澄邁之馬嫋港，儋州之新英港，昌化之新潮港，感恩之北黎港，可以灣泊船隻，其餘港汊雖多，不能寄舶. 而延海沉沙，行舟實為艱險". Chen Lunjiong 陳倫炯, *Haiguo wenjian lu* 海國聞見錄 [Record of Things Seen and Heard in Countries Overseas], (Zhengzhou: Zhongzhou guji chubanshe, 1985), pp. 24–25.

48. 先祖福建漳州府龍溪縣山后社人, *Thẩm gia thế phả* 沈家世譜 [Genealogy of the Thẩm Family], (Hanoi: Han-Nom Institute manuscript A. 758); 先祖北國福建長樂人, *Đặng thị tộc phả* 鄧氏族譜 [Genealogy of the Đặng Clan], (Hanoi: Han-Nom Institute manuscript A. 2951). See also Niu Junkai 牛軍凱, "Shi lun fengshui wenhua zai Yuenan de chuanbo yu fengshuishu de Yuenan hua" 試論風水文化在越南的傳播與風水術的越南化 [An Initial Discussion of the Transmission of the Culture of Geomancy in Vietnam and of the Vietnamese Transformation of Geomantic Techniques], *Dongnanya yanjiu* 東南亞南亞研究 (Southeast Asian Research) 1.

49. Geoff Wade, "Early Muslim Expansion in South-East Asia, Eighth to Fifteenth Centuries", in *The New Cambridge History of Islam*, Vol. 3: *The Eastern Islamic World, Eleventh to Eighteenth Centuries*, edited by David Morgan and Anthony Reid (Cambridge: Cambridge University Press, 2010), pp. 366–408.

50. Zhang Zhenxing 張振興, "Guangdong sheng Leizhou bandao de fangyan fenbu" 廣東省雷州半島的方言分布 [Distribution of Dialects on the Leizhou Peninsula in Guangdong Province], *Fangyan* 方言 (Dialects) 3 (1986): 205.

51. The three routes were from Wuchuan to Gaozhou in the Western Guangdong; from Suixi to Haikang on the Leizhou Peninsula; and from Suixi and Lianjiang to Guangxi's Qinzhou, Lianzhou, and Yulin. See Ma Muchi 馬木池, ed., *Beihai Zhentai hao shangye wanglai wenshu* 北海貞泰號 商業往來文書 [Commercial Correspondence of the Zhentai Firm of Beihai], (Hong Kong: Huanan yanjiu chubanshe, 2003), p. xxi.

9

SOUTHEAST ASIAN PRIMARY PRODUCTS AND THEIR IMPACT ON CHINESE MATERIAL CULTURE IN THE TENTH TO SEVENTEENTH CENTURIES

Derek Heng

Introduction

The economic interaction between Southeast Asia and China is well known and fairly well documented. The basic premise is that China's possession of technological knowledge and capabilities enabled it to produce manufactured products that were often not matched outside of its economy. At the same time, its geographical predisposition and its limited flora and fauna resources caused it to look abroad for primary resources for its material needs. One of the key sources of such materials was Southeast Asia. The region was a major supplier of raw materials and natural products to China from as early as the mid-first millennium, although this role took off strongly only from the late tenth century onwards. A wide range of high and low unit-value products, including select and bulk volume items, were imported by China during the eleventh through the second millennium AD.

In considering the issue of material cultural influences between China and the societies of Southeast Asia, the basic assumptions have hitherto been one of transfer from a more sophisticated culture to a less sophisticated other. The premise is based primarily on technological know-how, artisanal or aesthetic finesses, or iconographic complexities that embody specific representations. The notion that there may have been gaps in the recipient society that were thus filled in the process of transfer, including economic and sometimes social gaps, have been argued to be the structural context within which such material cultural influences have occurred across Asia. The developments in the ceramics traditions of such Southeast Asian societies as Vietnam and Thailand in the fifteenth and sixteenth centuries, and the development of the silk industry of Vietnam, are prime examples of such arguments.[1]

However, if we were to reimagine the flows of material cultural influences, we might gain a different perspective on the flow of the transfer processes. Material cultural construction, for instance, does not begin only at the point of manufacturing, or the value-added stage in which human knowledge application is the key ingredient, but at the stage of raw material availability and acquisition. The raw materials determine the nature of the final product, with the influence, of course, of the means by which the materials are manipulated.

The variability of outcome may not be confined only to physical manifestations such as form or motif, but also include such social aspects as usage within existing functionalities of key articles, such as religious consumables in the performance of rituals, precepts of ingredient usage in medicinal practices, and aesthetic appreciation in connoisseurship. Within such consumption behaviours, new products for new or existing uses may be introduced. In addition, the propagation of new and existing products, uses and functions may be effected across a wider spectrum of society than had previously been the case, with key products and finished items morphing from being confined solely to the elite, to becoming common and widespread.

All of these have an impact on our perspective of the endurance of these material cultural influences and changes. Often, the assumption is that an influence is effective only when the changes are lasting or permanent. In reality, important influences could be more limited in terms of their historical time periods. This should not discount their significance, because such influences no doubt do play a role in shaping the material culture of societies over the *longue durée*. In other words, what may be observable are series of changes that, when taken together, demonstrate the perpetual ability of a foreign society or region to influence the consumption behaviours of another.

This chapter seeks to illustrate the viability of the above discussion by examining the impact that importation of camphor, lakawood, and construction timbers into China had on Chinese material culture, not just in the physical sense, but also in terms of the construction of knowledge pertaining and relating to these products, and how such changes in turn had permanent effects on Chinese perceptions of hallmark aspects of their material culture.

Camphor

Camphor was an important Southeast Asian aromatic that was imported into China from the Tang period onwards.[2] Camphor products were derived from two main plant sources. *Dryoblanops aromatica*, or Barus camphor, found in Sumatra, Borneo, and on the Malay Peninsula in Tregganu, Pahang, Johor, and Selangor,[3] was traded as a resin and often compared to frankincense, a resinous aromatic from the Middle East. The other is *Blumea balsamifera*, which was traded to and within China in the form of oil and powder, and is from Nepal, Island Southeast Asia, and the Philippines.[4] While the former was confined to the Malay Peninsula, the Malacca Straits region, and Borneo, the latter could be found in not just the Indian subcontinent and Southeast Asia, but also in the subtropical regions of coastal China, including Zhejiang, Jiangsu, Fujian, Guangdong, and Hainan Island. Another important point to note is that while the camphor obtained from the former region was harvested solely through the slashing (and therefore killing) of the trees, the camphor obtained from the latter (i.e., coastal China) had to be extracted through a distillation process. In other words, Barus camphor was a gathered primary product, whereas camphor oil and powder was a manufactured item.

Up until the late eleventh century, Barus camphor was the type of camphor that was shipped to China. It first entered China during the Sui Dynasty (589–618), when the resin was presented as tribute to the Sui court. It is important to note that up until the Tang period, camphor was not noted as an ingredient in Chinese medicinal encyclopedias, including the *Nanfang caomu zhuang* 南方草木狀 (306) by Ji Han 嵇含. This suggests that camphor, even that which could be derived from plants that existed in coastal South China, and which later in the nineteenth and twentieth centuries became the predominant type being manufactured in China,[5] was not known to the Chinese until the early seventh century.

Very quickly, by the mid-seventh century, the product became a tribute item that was presented to the Tang court by diplomatic missions arriving in China. While the Chinese clearly developed an instant desire for this product, its import remained fairly limited both in terms of the means by which it entered China and the quantity that was made available. While polities in Southeast Asia and India then began presenting camphor as part of their tribute to China, the quantities were extremely limited. While no information is available for the Tang period, figures from the first four decades of the Song period indicate a very limited import trade. Champa's missions were noted to have presented between thirty taels and ten katis of camphor per mission, with white camphor being the predominant type presented.[6] Boni, a polity most likely located on the north coast of Borneo, presented a total of 400 taels of camphor of three different grades, along with five camphor planks (timber), in 977.[7] Java presented five katis of camphor in 992.[8]

The camphor trade with China paled in significance to other aromatic resins, such as frankincense, of which quantities presented to the Song court during the same period numbered several hundred to several thousand katis per mission. In addition, other important trading partners, including those from the Malacca Straits region, such as Srivijaya, were not making camphor available as part of their trans-shipment activities to China. After 1011, the presentation of camphor was discontinued by all of China's trading partners in their diplomatic missions to the Song court.

The reason for the discontinuation of presentation of camphor to the Song court are not known. The missions between 1011 and 1070, when camphor reappeared on the list of tribute items presented to the Song court, were bringing products that would have been classified as both high and low value items within China's maritime trade context. It is likely that the product might not have gained significant credibility in terms of its usage at the level of society to which it had hitherto been channelled, that is, the upper echelons of Song society. Indeed, while Chinese official texts note camphor as an increasingly frequently occurring tribute item from the South Seas, its use in the Chinese context, up until the late eleventh century, was confined only to a handful of medical handbooks, of which the *Yinhai jingwei* 銀海精微, for example, suggested its use as an ingredient in the concocting of an eye wash.[9]

The widespread use of camphor appears to have begun only in the late eleventh century. Medical guidebooks published from the late eleventh century onwards recommend camphor as an ingredient for a greater number of uses. These include topical and oral applications for the expelling of "wind" in children,[10] as a treatment for food poisoning,[11] and for the manufacture of specific types of incense. It is important to note that these medical guides date from the early twelfth century onwards, suggesting that the increasingly widespread use of camphor for medicinal purposes, and in particular for the purposes that continued in Chinese medical practice over the next centuries, was developed only from the late eleventh century onwards. It is in the *Xiangpu* 香譜 (*c*.1094) that the first detailed description of the different types of resinous camphor appears in the Chinese corpus.[12] This is followed by the *Chenshi xiangpu* 陳氏香譜 by Chen Jing 陳敬,[13] dated to the Southern Song, in which camphor features as the first detailed ingredient of a compilation of recipes for the production of incense. This is followed by the *Zhufan zhi* 諸蕃志 by Zhau Rugua 趙汝适 (*c*.1225).[14]

The more widespread usage of camphor amongst the Chinese had been preceded, from 1070 onwards, by the return of camphor as a tribute item, first by the Arab and Cham missions to China, and from 1078 by the Srivijayan missions. The more widespread practice, which included kingdoms from the Indian subcontinent, was likely an indication of the increasing use of camphor in China by the second half of the eleventh century. I have argued elsewhere that the first half of the eleventh century witnessed the increasing integration of the Chinese domestic trade networks with the maritime networks arriving at the South Chinese ports, with domestic trade in foreign products gradually liberalized into the hands of Chinese private traders, and international trade relegated to the ports, handled by the Superintendencies of Mercantile Shipping, rather than by the Ministry of Rites at the imperial capital.[15] It is likely that these developments caused such foreign products as camphor to be available to a wider market in China, than to be confined to the imperial centre, as had been the case up until the late tenth century. The increased accessibility of camphor to the wider Chinese market would have enabled the product to be experimented upon in various ways, and for its medicinal properties to be married into the Chinese medicinal repertoire. Indeed, the preface to the *Chenshi xiangpu* notes that many of the aromatic and medicinal ingredients were sourced from the South Seas and foreign lands,[16] suggesting that the availability of raw materials from abroad, via maritime trade channels, had become one of the most important means by which Chinese material culture in the medical and homeopathic fields, as well as ritual purposes, was being developed.

By the late eleventh century, resinous camphor was not the only type made available to the Chinese market. During the Shenzhong Yuanfeng period (1078–85), Srivijaya presented camphor oil as a tribute item to the Song court.[17] The increase in maritime trade activity also saw the number of types of camphor products imported into China increase through the course of the twelfth century. The list of foreign products that were being assessed during the reforming of the regulations governing the sale of products conducted by the Mercantile Shipping Superintendencies in 1133 records seven types of camphor products, namely: grain camphor, *lusu* 鹿速 camphor, red and green camphor, timber with camphor paste, bundled camphor, and camphor oil.[18] By 1141, eleven camphor products were imported into China, namely: matured camphor, plum-blossom camphor, grain camphor, pale white camphor, oily camphor, pale red camphor, *lusu* camphor, camphor paste, bundled camphor, *zhang* 獐 or roe camphor (possibly alluding to the physical form of this type of camphor), and camphor oil. By the mid-twelfth century, the trade in camphor was well-established in China and had become very vibrant. This product was not only shipped to China as tribute to the Song court, but was also shipped to the Chinese ports by traders operating outside of state-sponsored trade.

The value band of camphor products had also expanded to encompass both the low and high value product categories established in 1141. All the camphor products noted in 1141, with the exception of *zhang* camphor and camphor oil, were classified as high value products, although they differed significantly in terms of their potency, as may be noted in the *Xiangpu*, suggesting that their unit prices may have varied significantly as well.[19] The availability of low value camphor-derived products such as oils suggests that while camphor remained chiefly a high value product, its consumption base in the Chinese market appears to have expanded from being select in the late tenth and eleventh centuries, to including sections of the Chinese market that could afford the low-value camphor products by the mid-twelfth century.

The appearance of camphor oil, first introduced by Srivijaya to the Song court in 1090s, suggests that new types of camphor products, obtained through manufacturing processes and derived from other plants, were successfully being introduced to the Chinese market by Southeast Asian traders. While there is no textual information regarding the way in which the oil traded during the Song period was derived, it is likely that it was distilled from the *Blumea balsamifera*. It is likely, given the absence of mention of camphor oil as a tribute item presented by any of China's trading partners other than Srivijaya, that this product was introduced to the Chinese market by traders from the Malay region. More importantly, this was a low value product, which suggests that the usage of camphor by the Chinese had spread, by the twelfth century, to include those at the lower economic levels of society.

The widespread use of camphor as reflected in the detailed knowledge of it in China, including both the various types of camphor products and their market value, reflects the familiarity that Chinese consumers and Chinese and foreign traders had with camphor by the mid-twelfth century. By the late twelfth century, a proliferation of Chinese records noting the sources of camphor imported by China becomes available, reflecting the increasing level of Chinese commercial activities in Southeast Asia by this time. The *Yunlu manchao* 雲麓漫鈔 (*c.*1206) notes that Srivijaya, Xintiao 新條 (Sunda?), Kampar, and Borneo were key exporters of camphor to Quanzhou during the early thirteenth century.[20] Similarly, the *Zhufan zhi* notes that Borneo, Barus, Srivijaya-Jambi, Tambralingga, Langkasuka, and

Java were key exporters of camphor to China. Interestingly, small pieces of resin (*naozi* 腦子) were the type of camphor traded by the Chinese during this time.

This pattern continued into the fourteenth century. The *Daoyi zhilue* 島夷誌略 (1349) by Wang Dayuan 汪大淵 notes that camphor grains, camphor strips, and camphor pieces were made available from the northeastern ports of the Malay Peninsula and Sumatra, such as Samudra, Jambi, Tambralingga, Pahang, Trengganu and Srokam, and Borneo.[21] The minute pieces appear to have been sought after primarily due to the way in which camphor was used in medicinal concoctions in China, which typically required quantities purchasable at one cash value. It may in fact be possible to argue that the inherently small size of the camphor resin affected the quantity of the resin used in any typical concoctions in the Chinese medicinal guides.

The camphor supplied to China, at least up until the fifteenth century, appears to have been obtained solely from the *Dryoblanops aromatica*. While the camphor tree of subtropical China, or more accurately, the *zhang* 樟 tree (a term used to designate a type of flora of the family *Lauracceae* from as early as the Warring States period, and which by the mid-first millennium was used to designate the camphor tree of subtropical coastal China), whose geographical distribution included the subtropical zone of coastal China and its outlying islands, was already known for its aromatic qualities since the late first millennium BC, its use had been confined almost entirely to carpentry and construction.[22] While the trade in camphor oil appears to have disappeared by the early thirteenth century, the introduction of the oil in the late eleventh century appears to have sparked off the development of camphor oil production in China. The appearance of camphor distillates suggests that Chinese manufacturers may have begun to pick up the manufacturing process for oil-based camphor from China's foreign trading partners by this time.

These developments appear to have been accompanied by a corresponding decline in China's import trade in camphor from the second-half of the thirteenth century. The Quanzhou wreck (*c.*1270s), which had returned from the Malacca Straits region, one of the few key regions from which resinous camphor could be sourced, did not carry any camphor as part of its cargo. This is in contrast to the large quantities of Malacca Straits region aromatic woods recovered from the wreck's hull. This suggests that Chinese traders were no longer heavily involved in the camphor trade by the end of the thirteenth century. By the fourteenth century, the camphor trade had become even more limited. Only three types of camphor products were imported by the Chinese during this time, as opposed to eleven types in the mid-twelfth century. In addition, the hitherto key purveyors of camphor, such as Champa, Java, and Srivijaya, were no longer noted to have exported the resin to China. Instead, the suppliers were small port-cities located along the Malacca Straits and northeast Malay Peninsula.

Foreign camphor, which had not been known to the Chinese market until the seventh century, and which had only become a critical ingredient in Chinese medicine by the late eleventh century, appears to have begun to face competition from a substitute product that was possibly produced in China itself. This trend may have been further exacerbated by the maritime ban in the mid-fifteenth to sixteenth centuries under the Ming dynasty. Under such circumstances, local sources of camphor-like products had to be found, and this was done successfully with the *cinnamomum camphora*, which is found in Taiwan and parts of the subtropical regions of China. Indeed, the Chinese were so successful in producing camphor from this plant through the distillation process that it became a product of economic contention between the Japanese and the United States in the nineteenth century.[23] The trade and use of the original resinous camphor of the *dryolabanops aromatica*, however, appears to have all but declined by the late Ming period, as is attested to in the customs lists from the *Dong-Xiyang kao* 東西洋考 (1618).[24]

Lakawood

Lakawood was a Southeast Asian product that had a fundamental impact on Chinese material culture. Unlike camphor, lakawood was not necessarily a new product previously unknown to the Chinese market. As early as the mid-first millennium AD, Ji Han, in the *Nanfang xaomu zhuang*, noted that *ziteng* 紫藤 ("purple vine" [incense]) was used both as a preservative in wine and, when smoked, became an incense wood used for the summoning of spirits.[25] Li Hui-Lin has identified this Chinese variety, which flourished in the provinces of Guangdong and Guangxi until the twelfth century, as *Acronychia Pedunculata* and *A. Laurifolia.*[26] Nonetheless, by the tenth century, foreign sources of lakawood had already begun to be known to the Chinese. Widely available in the Malay Peninsula, Sumatra and the coastal regions of Mainland Southeast Asia, Southeast Asian lakawood, obtained from the scented heartwood and root wood of the *Dalbergia parviflora,*[27] was imported into China by the late tenth century. It was first noted during the Song period in 982 as one of the thirty-seven foreign products in common use to be permitted to be freely traded by the Chinese,[28] suggesting that Chinese knowledge of this Southeast Asian aromatic wood was already fairly well-developed by this time. Similarities in characteristics between the varieties in China and Southeast Asia most likely enabled the latter variety to be accepted easily by the Chinese market.

Familiarity in the Chinese market of its key characteristics, its form and colour, and its aromatic qualities, enabled lakawood to be a product around which knowledge development and exploitation, in the form of the introduction and production of other products through name association, occurred over the course of the tenth to fifteenth centuries.

Lakawood was never a product exported to China via state-level exchange, as it was not recorded as a product presented by any tribute mission to the Song court. The export of lakawood to China was thus carried out outside of state purview. From the outset, lakawood incense was consistently regarded as a low value product. It was classified as a "coarse" category product in the 1141 exercise carried out by the Mercantile Shipping Superintendencies to standardize the classification of foreign products for customs purposes.[29] This continued to be the case in the early thirteenth century. The *Zhufan zhi* notes that this product was very cheap and used by both the rich and poor.[30]

The wide availability of Southeast Asian lakawood to all economic strata of Chinese society enabled this product to become widely adopted and consumed by the Chinese. The rapid acceptance of lakawood incense appears to have stemmed from its similarities with the native *ziteng.* The *Zhufan zhi* notes that lakawood was similar in appearance and aroma to "purple vine incense" (*ziteng xiang* 紫藤香)."[31] Lakawood was thus regarded as a suitable substitute for what was originally a

Chinese product. Even the Song period name for lakawood incense —
jiangzhenxiang 降真香 or "truth bearing incense" — indicates that the
product was not named after its appearance, but rather after its functional
purpose,[32] most likely the result of its role as a substitute product very
early on in its introduction into the Chinese market.

Interestingly, up until the twelfth century, Southeast Asian lakawood
and Chinese *ziteng* incense were still clearly distinguished from each
other. The 1141 list of foreign products submitted by the Mercantile
Shipping Superintendency, for example, mentions lakawood and *ziteng*
incense as separate products. This official position would have reflected
the treatment of this product by both the traders and consumers of the
Chinese market in the mid-twelfth century.

However, by the early thirteenth century, the two names were
already used interchangeably, as is noted in the *Zhufan zhi*.[33] In other
words, there was now essentially only one product, even if they may
have been obtained from different sources. More importantly, while
Guangdong and Guangxi may have continued to be sources from which
ziteng was obtained during this time, Southeast Asia, and the Malay
Peninsula and Sumatra in particular, had become the key sources of
lakawood to the Chinese market. Product substitution, which had
not yet occurred in 1141, had, by the early thirteenth century, clearly
taken place.

The sources of lakawood sent to China also broadened significantly
over the course of the thirteenth and fourteenth centuries. While Srivijaya,
given its role as a key trading partner of China, was most likely the
source of the best quality of lakawood through the twelfth century,
by the early thirteenth century, given that more ports in the Malacca
Straits and northeast Malay Peninsula had begun to participate directly
in the trade with China, and as the commercial activities of Chinese
traders in Southeast Asia increased, the number of sources from which
lakawood could be obtained increased as well. The *Zhufan zhi* notes
that Shepo (Java), Srivijaya-Jambi, Borneo, Folo'an (Kuala Berang), and
Tambralingga exported lakawood to China.

In addition, lakawood also appears to have gained in status amongst
the Chinese by the early thirteenth century. In 1228, the *Baoqing siming
zhi* 寶慶四明志 notes that lakawood was to have levied upon it customs

duties as a fine quality product.[34] While the polities that maintained these ports no doubt continued to ship lakawood to China, towards the end of the Song period, Chinese traders played a critical role in this trade, most likely overtaking the Malacca Straits region traders in this respect. This can be seen from the large quantity of lakawood recovered from the Quanzhou wreck, indicating that Chinese traders, of both large and small scale, were heavily involved in the lakawood trade by the 1270s.[35] The quantity of lakawood, which was amongst the largest in terms of all the plant aromatics recovered from the wreck, suggests that the trade in lakawood had come to dominate the maritime trade that the Chinese conducted in the Malay region.

By the fourteenth century, Chinese knowledge of the sources of lakawood incense in Island Southeast Asia was at the port level, rather than in terms of polities or trading partners in the region, as had been the case in the early thirteenth century. The *Daoyi zhilue* by Wang Dayuan records eight ports as the sources of lakawood incense by this time — Tambralingga, Kelantan, Srivijaya-Jambi, Tamiang, Samudra, Lambri, Tanjongpura, and Malilu, all of which were located in the Malay region. The Chinese possessed detailed knowledge of the respective quality of the lakawood made available. Whereas in the early thirteenth century, Srivijaya was the source of the best lakawood, by the mid-fourteenth century, Lambri was known as the source of the best lakawood, while Jambi, the former capital of Srivijaya, exported only lakawood incense of middle quality.[36] The products of the other ports were either of coarse or undocumented quality.

In thinking of the key issues that this paper is attempting to address — materiality and culture — Southeast Asian lakawood appears to have been a product that caused the Chinese to develop an increased level of knowledge of the sources from which it could be obtained. The detailed quality grading suggests that there was sufficient variation in unit price, dependent on the quality of the product in question, and also that there was sufficiently high demand for it across a broad spectrum of the economic hierarchy in China. In and of itself, this development in the level of knowledge of a product would have amply demonstrated the importance that lakawood played in affecting the nature of material culture in China, at least from the perspective of knowledge generation. However, the impact of lakawood on Chinese material culture went beyond that. By the fourteenth century, lakawood was noted in Chinese texts, and the *Daoyi zhilue* in particular, through two terms — *jiangzhenxiang* 降真香 and *jiangzhen* 降真. Both product names had specific sources identified with them, and more importantly, both products had comprehensive quality grades assigned to them as well. In other words, they were regarded as two distinct, even if nonetheless related, products that served specific, and most likely distinct, purposes in the Chinese market.

Indeed, this distinction had already appeared by the early thirteenth century, in the *Zhufan zhi*, which noted that Sujidan (Kediri, Java) exported *jiangzhen*, while six other ports in Southeast Asia were noted to have exported *jiangzhenxiang*. Given the trajectory of development in the use of this product name, the early thirteenth century may be a point in time during which a divergence of uses of imported lakawood was beginning to occur.

This divergence in use is hinted at in the *Zhufan zhi*. In the entry on dragon's blood, an aromatic resin of Middle Eastern origin (*Dracaena schizantha* and *D. cinnabari*),[37] the author Zhao Rugua notes that an imitation dragon's blood, which was purple in colour, was produced using the sap of the lakawood.[38] Presumably, the sap was mixed with other types of resins to produce something that looked similar to real dragon's blood. The *Zhufan zhi* also notes that imitation dragon's blood was being made available for export by Srivijaya.[39] The absence of any effort to pass off the imitation as the real product suggests that a new product, possibly a substitute for real dragon's blood, was being made available to the Chinese consumers.

At first glance, one might assume that this was an effort by Srivijaya to introduce a manufactured product into the Chinese market by riding on the demand for an existing one. However, I have argued elsewhere that Srivijaya's tribute items presented to the Song court during the second-half of the twelfth century, up until its last mission in 1178, mirrored the larger maritime trade in products that were already well established staples and in high demand in China during that time.[40] If Srivijaya was indeed the production point of imitation dragon's blood, it was more likely introduced into the Chinese market by Chinese traders, who were becoming increasingly aware of the array of products that could be obtained in Island Southeast Asia. It also suggests that products made available in Island Southeast Asia were being introduced by the Chinese themselves as product substitutes for other items that may have been either too expensive for the general market to afford, or that the substitute products were so affordable that they came to replace the genuine products themselves.

This import of imitation dragon's blood may have continued into the fourteenth century. The *Dade nanhai zhi* 大德南海志 (*c*.1306) by Chen Dazhen 陳大震, a geographical gazetteer of Guangzhou, records sixty-nine products imported through the port-city. Of these only nine were ones that had to be sourced from the Middle East. The dragon's blood, noted in the text, may have been a mix of both real and imitation varieties.

The other key point concerning imitation dragon's blood was colour. For imitation dragon's blood, colour, and not odour, was the key purpose for using lakawood sap in the production process. This postulation presents an interesting dilemma. While *jiangzhenxiang*, in the context of the *Zhufan zhi*, is used to denote "lakawood" (*Dalbergia parviflora*), this plant is not known to have been used as a source of dye in Southeast Asia. Instead, other such lianas as the *Emblica officinalis* were known to have been used by the Javanese and possibly people in the Malacca Straits region as a source of red dye. Javanese texts make mention of the usage of a material known as "*laka*". Javanese inscriptions dating from the tenth century onwards contain the word "*manglaka*", which means "processor of lakawood dye". In other words, "laka" occurs regularly in Old Javanese literature as a term for a red dyestuff in the textile industry.[41] Given that "*jiangzhenxiang*" had become a generic name used for vine-type purplish-red aromatic strips by the early thirteenth century, it is possible that many in China may not have been aware that two different types of products, albeit with fairly similar visual qualities, were being referred to here.

This possible confusion, along with the fact that Kediri was noted in the *Zhufan zhi* to have been the only source of *jiangzhen*, suggests that the dyestuff as denoted by the term "*jiangzhen*" may have only been recently introduced into the Chinese market. Its use in China, however, appears to have been different from that in its place of origin. Whereas *"laka"* was used only as a textile dye in Island Southeast Asia, its use in China was clearly associated with lakawood, or more specifically, the aromatic qualities of lakawood. The production of imitation resins from the Middle East may have been a Chinese manufacturing effort, even if similar products were being made available in the Malacca Straits. By the mid-fourteenth century, however, Chinese demand for this product, whatever its purposes and uses, had grown sufficiently large to warrant traders such as Wang Dayuan in providing a full classification of the qualities and sources of the product in Island Southeast Asia. This demand appears to have continued into the fifteenth century. The "Mao Kun map" (Mao Kun tu 茅坤圖), part of the *Wubei zhi* 武備志 (*c*.1621) and based on information obtained from the Zhenghe voyages, show *jiangzhen* and *jiangzhenxiang* produced between the Kelantan and Patani rivers.[42]

By all accounts, both lakawood and *jiangzhen* became products that were highly sought after by the Chinese in the fourteenth and fifteenth centuries. By the early Ming period, the status of lakawood had been elevated to that of a tribute item. According to the *Yingyai shenglan* 瀛涯勝覽, a 1433 record of the voyages of the Ming admiral Zhenghe conducted in the first three decades of the fifteenth century, ports along the northeastern coast of Sumatra as well as Siam were dispatching lakawood as tribute to the Ming court.[43] Its new status as a tribute item, an ascendency that was evident by the early thirteenth century, suggests that it had become an important trade product in Southeast Asia's trade with China. This suggests that lakawood was regarded as a high value product by the early fifteenth century. In turn, this development would have likely further boosted the status of *jiangzhen* as an ingredient with aromatic affiliations.

Furniture Timber

Timber and other related products used in the manufacture of furniture constituted an important category of trade items from Island Southeast Asia that had a significant impact on the material culture of the Chinese. While much of the textual and art historical materials available presently on the subject are predominantly from the Ming period onwards, the basis of what is termed classical Chinese furniture no doubt had much earlier precedents, including such aspects as the raw materials, sensorial qualities including sight and scent, intangible qualities such as association with certain types of items that would in turn confer intrinsic and unquantifiable value, and taxonomy by association including the use of certain key terms as identifying markers.

From the outset, furniture timber that was highly valued possessed two key characteristics — it possessed characteristics that associated it with wood aromatics imported through the South Seas trade, and its colour revolved around the purplish-red palette. This can be seen in one of the earliest mentions of imported construction timber, found in the *Bencao shiyi* 本草拾遺 by Chen Cangqi 陳藏器 (Tang period). In a note on *hualu* 花櫚 timber from Annam and Hainan Island, the author notes that *hualu* resembles *zitan* 紫檀 or purple sandalwood (presumably *peterocarpus indicus or peterocarpus santalinus*[44]), even though this plant has nothing to do with sandalwood incense (*santalum album*) but is somewhat redder.[45] These basic tenets do not appear to have changed at all over the course of the next millennium. The fifteenth century text *Gegu Yaolun* 格古要論 by Cao Zhao 曹昭 (1462), for example, notes that huali 花梨 timber, found in the southern foreign lands, is purplish red and has a fragrance very much resembling that of lakawood.[46] It is possible that the visual attribute of lakawood, its purplish-red colour, was also included in this association. Given that none of the timbers sourced from indigenous Chinese flora possessed any of these qualities, the question of how these qualities came to characterize furniture woods during the zenith of furniture connoisseurship needs to be addressed.

As early as the tenth century, the Chinese were aware of foreign timbers that could be sourced from Southeast Asia. However, the types and quantities imported were very limited. Up until the eleventh century, the primary woods imported by China were ebony, and sappanwood, as mentioned in a 976 memorial on the occasion of the establishment of the Mercantile Shipping Superintendency at Guangzhou.[47] However, through the course of the eleventh century, much larger quantities appear to have been shipped to China, including ten thousand katis of sappanwood dispatched by Ligor (Dengliumei 登流眉) in 1001,[48] and fifty-five thousand

and thirty katis of ebony by Champa in 1053.[49] Of these two wood-based commodities, only ebony was clearly used in craftwork. Sappanwood was most likely used as a dyestuff.

By the mid-twelfth century, however, a number of products directly related to furniture construction began to be imported into China. According to an 1133 memorial in the *Song huiyao* 宋會要, timber with musk-like scent (or muskwood), timber coated with camphor paste and rattan were recorded as coarse goods by the Mercantile Shipping Superintendency.[50] Similarly, in an 1141 memorial containing a comprehensive list of commodities imported into China by sea, muskwood, sappanwood, and three types of rattan were noted as coarse products.[51] Muskwood was recorded in the *Zhufan zhi* as being used in Quanzhou for the construction of articles that were being manufactured with the South Chinese construction timber, *huali* timber.

Two key points may be noted for the nascent trade in timber. Association with incense woods known during that time appears to have been an important factor in the desirability of these newly introduced timbers. Thus, muskwood and timbers coated with camphor paste were initially introduced and demanded by the Chinese, presumably because the association with known aromatics allowed them to be readily accepted by the Chinese market. Aromatic timbers were clearly preferred and prized over those that did not possess this quality. According to the *Zhufan zhi*, in the entry on muskwood, those that underwent humification and therefore had an odour similar to musk were regarded as of higher quality, while those that did not undergo the humification process, and therefore had a sour smell when cut, were considered of lower quality.[52]

It could be argued that the maritime trade liberalization of the late eleventh century, which opened the way for the development of large volume shipping by the Chinese and the consequent shift from high to low value commodities trade, spurred the development of a trade in construction timber and building materials. Presumably, the availability of freight capacity, coupled with the projection of Chinese consumption patterns and tastes into foreign sources of products, enabled the trade in timber to take off in a significant way. Scented timbers had been known to the Chinese since the tenth century, given that camphor planks (or planks scented with camphor), were presented to the Song court as early as the late tenth century. Rattan, possessing similar characteristics as bamboo and widely available in coastal south China, was already in use in Chinese furniture construction since the mid-first millennium AD.[53] What the Southeast Asians provided for China was alternative types of this material, as well as the availability of the Chinese-preferred colour palettes that included red, purple, and white. By the early thirteenth century, the *Baoqing siming* notes that, apart from muskwood and white rattan, Champa was now exporting a new timber product — sandalwood timber (*tanmu* 檀木) — to China through Guangzhou.[54]

By the early fourteenth century, the number of timber products imported by China had increased significantly, as may be seen from the *Dade nanhai zhi*. Under the designation of "aromatics", the Chinese were by this time importing muskwood, black incense, sandalwood, and three new aromatic woods (*xiangmu* 香木) named *dapai* 打拍, *anba* 暗八, and *rong* 沉. In addition, a new designation — timber — had now appeared in the literature on maritime trade. Under this trade designation, sappanwood, gharuwood timber, ebony, and red-purple timber was now imported.[55] In total, five new timber products were now imported via Guangzhou, and timber products were now viewed as a category of products in their own right. In addition, under the designation "miscellaneous", purple rattan, rattan stalks, and rattan staff were products imported into China.[56]

The broadening of the range of timber products coming into China continued through the course of the fourteenth century. The importance of the timber trade to Chinese merchants was evident from the preface of the *Daoyi zhilue*, which mentions aromatic woods as one of five products of importance in the South Seas trade.[57] The same text also notes that Chinese traders appear to have been interested in a number of such products, including *dapai* incense, *luozhen* incense, camphor planks, sappanwood, ebony, sandalwood timber, muskwood, timbers with fine patterns (wood grain), and white rattan. In addition, *jialan* wood, or eggplant wood, presumably so named for its purple appearance, was now made available by Champa and Bingtonglong (Philippines).[58]

A key pattern that was emerging by the early thirteenth century, and continued to be apparent through the course of the fourteenth century, was evident in the geographical sources of the construction materials made available to the Chinese. Timbers were primarily the export products of Mainland Southeast Asian polities, initially such well-known ones as Zhenla (Khmer Cambodia) and Champa (present-day south-central Vietnam) in the early thirteenth century, and came to include minor ports in the Philippines and the northeastern tracts of the Malay Peninsula by the fourteenth century. Rattan, on the other hand, was primarily sourced from the Malacca Straits region, with the best quality rattan exported by Sumatran coastal polities such as Jambi, Palembang, and Lambri through the thirteenth and fourteenth centuries.[59]

Chinese trade in Southeast Asian furniture construction materials continued well into the seventeenth century. The *Suma Oriental* by Tome Pires notes that the Chinese arriving at Malacca annually were purchasing infinite quantities of the black wood (tropical hardwoods of a reddish brown to purplish red hue) from Singapore Island.[60] The *Dong Xiyang kao*, which contains a list of import tariffs imposed on products imported into China from abroad, includes sandalwood incense (tanxiang 檀香, *satalum album*) that was used for construction, ebony not used for construction (which implies that there were also ebony pieces used for construction), rattan seats, decorated seats, and *zitan* (purple sandalwood timber).[61] It is important to note that the dating of this list coincides with the height of furniture connoisseurship in Ming China — the Jiajing and Wanli reigns (1521–1620).

Interestingly, most of the timber varieties that had featured fairly prominently during the thirteenth and fourteenth centuries, with the exception of muskwood, ebony, and sappanwood, seem to have disappeared from the Chinese customs lists by the early seventeenth century. In particular, red-purple timber is distinctly missing. Instead, *zitan*, *huali* and *jichi* 雞翅 were the only timbers whose descriptions resemble the timbers that were imported into China in earlier centuries. Indeed, the *Gegu yaolun* notes that *huali* timber was sourced from the foreign lands of the South.[62] It is likely that many of the Southeast Asian timbers that possess a purplish-red hue, including such examples as *jialan* wood, red-purple timber, and sandalwood timber, were now imported under the trade names of *zitan, huali*, and *jichi*. The distinguishing feature of *zitan* was its scent, the denseness of its wood, the fineness of its grain, and its rarity. *Huali* was distinguished by being reddish in hue and possessing a pleasant scent, while *jichi* had a purplish-brown hue and an absence of any aromatic scent, and was marked by a wood grain that resembled a chicken's feathers.[63] Of the hardwoods recognized by Chinese furniture connoisseurs by the late Ming period, none of these timber types were explicitly noted to have been sourced solely within China's boundaries. Indeed, the fact that the southern coastal ports, and Guangzhou in particular, were the key locations from which these timbers could be acquired suggests that foreign sources south of China continued to play an important role in supplying China with these construction timbers well into the seventeenth century.[64]

Southeast Asia thus provided, over the course of the tenth century, a wide range of construction timbers that eventually provided the sensorial repertoire upon which Chinese furniture connoisseurship was eventually developed. More importantly, the key characteristics that identified Southeast Asian timbers from the eleventh century onwards became the characteristics of the most highly prized furniture timbers by the late Ming dynasty.

Conclusion

The above case studies provide us with a means by which several observations on the material cultural influences of Southeast Asia on China during the tenth to the sixteenth centuries may be noted. To begin with, these products were not necessarily new items previously unknown in China. Categories and types similar to those mentioned above had already been known to the Chinese since fairly early on in the first millennium AD, and their uses were fairly widespread and well established. Aromatic resins, for example, were known to the Chinese firstly from locally sourced plants, and by the early first millennium AD, from the Middle East via the land and maritime silk routes. For instance, lakawood, an aromatic liana native to the subtropical zone of South China, was already known and widely used by the fourth century AD. Finally, timber and furniture building were already extremely well-established artisanal crafts and materials by the early Han Dynasty. At the point at which the foreign products detailed in this chapter were introduced into the Chinese market, they did not make, nor were they perceived by the Chinese as having made, new contributions to the nature of material cultural life. They were, in fact, substitute products.

It is when these introduced products began to morph within the context of the recipient society after some time that the actual influence on Chinese material culture occurred. These products began to take on new uses. Over time, they acquired a new, elevated, status that previous products, including those for which they initially served as substitutes, never enjoyed. They became part of the lexicon and even rubric of characterization in the discourses of specific genres of Chinese material creation, production, consumption, and appreciation. Indeed, they became so indispensible within the categories of material culture that they had become part of, that when their supplies were threatened, local substitutes, sourced and produced from locally available materials, were developed. In other words, these imported products were able to invert the processual stages of material cultural influence to their favour, and in the process subvert their original role and status as *substitute* products to eventually being that of a *substituted* product.

The present chapter has tried to engage a number of questions pertaining to the fundamental importance of material cultural influences across regions and societies. Influences of this nature have often been thought of in terms of technological transfers, and/or the transference of such visible manifestations as forms and motifs. Art history's fixation on such physical and visible manifestations of influence masks more important underlying dynamics, and that is that such manifestations often serve no perceivable function in the recipient society or culture, perhaps other than as possible status distinguishing indicators, or that they reflect changes in the social demographics of the recipients' society that come under these influences. Herein, propagation of change may be understood to have been made by the originating society, for members of the originating society establishing themselves in the recipient society.

What this chapter has tried to achieve is to suggest that material cultural influence can be seen to be taking place at the resource and materials level. Foreign societies and regions could affect the material culture of recipient societies consciously or otherwise. The key to understanding this paradigm would be through the explication of the changes in the knowledge creation that underpin the very nature and characteristics of the recipient societies' material cultural practices.

NOTES

1. For a detailed study of the development of the Vietnamese silk trade in the early modern era, see Naoko Iioka, "Literati Entrepreneur: Wei Zhiyan in the Tonkin-Nagasaki Silk Trade", PhD dissertation, National University of Singapore, 2009; for a discussion of the development of Mainland Southeast Asian high-fired ceramics, see Roxanna Maude Brown, *The Ming Gap and Shipwreck Ceramics in Southeast Asia: Towards a Chronology of Thai Trade Ware* (Bangkok: Siam Society, 2009).

2. Lin Tianwei 林天蔚, *Songdai xiangyao maoyi shigao* 宋代香藥貿易史稿 [Draft History of the Trade in Aromatics and Pharmaceuticals during the Song Period], (Hongkong: Zhongguo xueshe, 1959), p. 28.

3. I.H. Burkill, *A Dictionary of the Economic Products of the Malay Peninsula* (Oxford: Oxford University Press, 1935), p. 862.

4. Burkill, pp. 334–39 and 862–67; Janice Stargardt, "Behind the Shadows: Archaeological Data on Two-Way Sea Trade between Quanzhou and Satingpra, South Thailand, 10th–14th Century", in *The Emporium of the World: Maritime Quanzhou, 1000–1400*, edited by Angela Schottenhammer (Leiden: Brill, 2001), pp. 309–94. For a detailed study of the historical uses of these two types of camphor in Southeast Asia, see R.A. Donkin, *Dragon's Brain Perfume: A Historical Geography of Camphor* (Leiden: Brill, 1999).

5. Walter A. Durham, Jr., "The Japanese Camphor Monopoly: Its History and Relation to the Future of Japan", *Pacific Affairs* 5, no. 9 (1932): 797–801.

6. Grace Wong, *A Commentary on the Tributary Trade between China and Southeast Asia, and the Place of Porcelain in this Trade during the Period of the Song Dynasty in China* (Singapore: Southeast Asian Ceramics Society, Transaction 7, 1979).

7. Ibid., p. 13.

8. Ibid., p. 15.

9. See Song Simiao's 孫思邈 tenth-century *Yinhai jingwei* 銀海精微 [Essential Subtleties of the Silver Sea], (Electronic Siku Quanshu edition, hereafter ESKQS), 1/41a–41b.

10. Anon., *Xiao'er weisheng zongwei lunfang* 小兒衛生總微論方 [Discussions and Prescriptions for General and Detailed Matters Concerning Children's Health] (ESKQS), 1/17b–18a.

11. Chen Shiwen 陳師文, *Taiping huimin heqi jufang* 太平惠民和劑局方指南 [Guide to the Formulary of the Taiping Welfare Dispensary Bureau] (ESKQS), 10/55a.
12. Hong Chu 洪芻, *Xiangpu* 香譜 [Manual of Aromatics] (ESKQS), 1/1a–1b.
13. Chen Jing 陳敬, *Chenshi xiangpu* 陳氏香譜 [Master Chen's Manual of Aromatics] (ESKQS), 1/2b–4b.
14. Chen Jiarong 陳佳榮 and Qian Jiang 錢江, *Zhufan zhi zhubu* 諸蕃志注補 [Annotated and Supplemented Treatise on the Various Barbarians] (Hongkong: Hongkong University Press, 2000), p. 313.
15. Derek Heng, *Sino–Malay Trade and Diplomacy from the Tenth Through the Fourteenth Centuries* (Athens: Ohio University Press, 2009), p. 42.
16. Chen Jing, 1/1b.
17. Ma Duanlin 馬端臨, *Wenxian tongkao* 文獻通考 [Comprehensive Examination of Documents and Institutions], 332/29a.
18. Wang Yunhai 王雲海, *Songhuiyao jigao kaojiao* 宋會要輯稿考校 [Examined and Collated Draft Recovered Edition of the Collection of Important Documents from the Song] (Shanghai: Shanghai guji chubanshe, 1986), Zhiguan 職官 (henceforth SHY ZG), 44/17b–19b.
19. Ibid., 44/21a–23a.
20. Zhao Yanwei 趙彥衛, *Yunlu manchao* 雲麓漫鈔 [Random Records from Yunlu] (ESKQS), 5/19b.
21. Su Jiqing 穌繼慶, *Daoyi zhilue jiaoshi* 島夷志略校釋 [Brief Account of Island Barbarians, Collated and Explained], (Beijing: Zhonghua shuju, 1981), pp. 79, 93, 96, 102, 141, 148, and 240.
22. Donkin, pp. 61–64.
23. Durham.
24. Zhang Xie 張燮, *Dong-Xiyang kao* 東西洋考 [Examination of the Eastern and Western Oceans], (Beijing: Zhonghua shuju, 1981), pp. 141–46.
25. Li Hui-Lin, *Nan-Fang Ts'ao Mu Chuang: A Fourth Century Flora of Southeast Asia* (Hong Kong: The Chinese University Press, 1979), p. 103.
26. Ibid.
27. Lakawood is still used as incense today in the Malacca Straits region. For details on the description, habitat, and distribution of the *Dalbergia parviflora*, refer to Henry N. Ridley, *The Flora of the Malay Peninsula*, Vol. 1 (London: L. Reeve & Co., 1922), p. 589.
28. SHY ZG, 44/2a-b.
29. Ibid., 44/21a–23a.
30. Chen and Qian, p. 368.
31. Ibid.
32. For a more detailed discussion of the product name, see Derek Heng Thiam Soon, "The Trade in Lakawood Products between South China and the Malay World from the Twelfth to Fifteenth Centuries AD", *Journal of Southeast Asian Studies* 32, no. 2 (2001): 133–50.

33. Chen and Qian, p. 368.

34. Luo Jun 羅濬, *Baoqing siming zhi* 寶慶四明志 [Gazetteer of Siming from the Baoqing Era] (ESKQS), 6/11a.

35. For a discussion of the lakawood incense cargo recovered from the Quanzhou wreck, see Nanjing Yaoxueyuan 南京藥學院 [Nanjing Pharmaceutical College] et al., "Quanzhouwan chutu songdai muzhao haichuan changnei jiangxiang de xiangwei jianding" 泉州灣出土宋代木造海船艙內降香的顯微鑒定 [Microscopic Identification of the Lakawood in the Holds of Wooden Seafaring Ships from the Song Salvaged from Quanzhou Bay], *Haojiaoshi yanjiu* 海交史研究 5 (1983): 115–16.

36. Su, p. 141.

37. Paul Wheatley, "Geographical Notes on Some Commodities Involved in Sung Maritime Trade", *Journal of the Malayan Branch of the Royal Asiatic Society* 32, no. 2 (1959): 109.

38. Chen and Qian, p. 325.

39. Ibid., p. 46.

40. Wang Yunhai, Fanyi 藩夷, 7/55b–56a.

41. Jan Wisseman-Christie, "Texts and Textiles in 'Medieval' Java", *Bulletin de l'École française d'Extrême-Orient* 80, no. 1 (1993): 206–7.

42. Heng, "The Trade in Lakawood", p. 144.

43. J.V.C. Mills, *Ying-yai Sheng-lan, "The Overall Survey of the Ocean's Shores" (1433)* (Cambridge: Hakluyt Society, 1970), pp. 122 and 124.

44. Chen Rong 陳嶸, *Zhongguo shumu fenlei xue* 中國樹木分類學 [Study of the Classification of Chinese Woods], 2nd rev. ed. (Shanghai: Science and Technology Press, 1959), p. 539.

45. Wang Shixiang, *Classic Chinese Furniture — Ming and Early Qing Dynasties* (San Francisco: China Books and Periodicals Inc., 1986), p. 17.

46. Cao Zhao 曹昭, *Gegu yaolun* 格古要論 [Essential Criteria for Investigating Antiquities] (ESKQS), 3/9b.

47. SHY ZG, 44/1a-b.

48. Wong, p. 12.

49. Wong, p. 8.

50. SHY ZG, 44/21a–23a.

51. SHY ZG, 44/21a–23a.

52. Chen and Qian, p. 370.

53. Wang, p. 14.

54. Luo, 6/11a.

55. Chen Dazhen, 7/17b–18a.

56. Ibid., 7:18b.

57. Su, p. 1.

58. Ibid., pp. 55 and 59.

59. Ibid., pp. 141, 187 and 261.

60. Armando Cortesao, *The Suma Oriental of Tomè Pires and The Book of Francisco Rodrigues*, Vols. I and II (London: The Hakluyt Society, 1944), p. 123.

61. Zhang, p. 141

62. Cao, 3/11b.

63. Wang, p. 17.

64. Qu Dajun 屈大均, *Guangdong xinyu* 廣東新語 [New Anecdotes of Guangdong] (Taipei: Xuesheng Shuju, 1968, facsimile of 1700 ed.), 25/48a–50b.

10

NEW EVIDENCE ON THE HISTORY OF SINO–ARABIC RELATIONS: A Study of Yang Liangyao's Embassy to the Abbasid Caliphate

Rong Xinjiang

Translated by Rebecca Fu and Gianni Wan

Professor Zhang Guangda 張廣達 briefly explained the main points of Sino–Arabic relations in his article "Ocean Ships Arrived at Mecca, Silk Roads Led to Arabia: A Review of the History of Connections between China and the Arab World". Notably, he pointed out in the article that in AD 750, Abū'l 'Abbās (r. 750–754, recorded in the Tang histories as Abu Luoba 阿蒲·羅拔) overthrew the Umayyad Caliphate and established the Abbasid Caliphate (750–1258, in Tang histories Heiyi Dashi 黑衣大食 "Black-robed Tazi"), whose political centre was gradually moved to the east. Although it lost the western frontier to the Umayyad Dynasty, the Abbasid Caliphate firmly governed the eastern part of the Islamic world, created a brilliant Arabic civilization, and, with China's Tang, Song, and Mongol Yuan dynasties, founded the golden age of Sino–Arabic relations. The first Abbasid caliph, Abū'l 'Abbās, moved the capital in Umayyad times from Damascus to al-Kūfah, in the mid-Euphrates Valley (present-day Meshed-Ali). Then his successor, al-al-Manṣūr (r. 754–775), built a new capital at Baghdad in the mid-Tigris Valley and called it Dār al-Salam, "Peace Capital". One of his intentions in doing so was to promote trade with countries to the east, such as China. In his *Ta'rīkh al-rusul wa'l mulūk* (The History of the Prophets and Kings), al-Ṭabarī stated: "This place [Baghdad] is an excellent headquarters. In addition, the Tigris is here. That will allow us to contact countries as far away as China, and will bring us all that can be provided by the ocean."[1] Professor Zhang also notes: "During the Tang dynasty, two Chinese men crossed the Indian Ocean and left us their names. One is Daxi Hongtong 達奚弘通; the other is Du Huan 杜環."[2]

Now we can add the name of Yang Liangyao 楊良瑤, a eunuch who served as an envoy to the Abbasid Caliphate at the beginning of the Zhenyuan 貞元 era (785–805). "The Stele of Yang Liangyao", erected to record Yang's life and deeds, sheds fresh light on the study of Sino–Arabic relations during the Tang Dynasty (618–907). Despite its brevity, the account provides precious evidence for our research. Due to limited materials, the exploration of Sino–Arabic relations has in the past been far from sufficient. Basing itself on previous studies, the present chapter examines in detail the cause and result, the concrete details, and the route of Yang's embassy. It will hopefully bring us new knowledge of the relations between Tang Dynasty China and the Abbasid Caliphate.

"The Stele of Yang Liangyao" and the Account of the Envoy

"The Stele of Yang Liangyao" was excavated in 1984 at Xiaohuyang 小戶楊 village in the Yunyang 雲陽 District of Jingyang 涇陽 County, Shaanxi Province. Later it was moved to and preserved in the Museum of Jingyang County. In 2005, Zhang Shimin 張世民, who works in the Xianyang Municipal Office of Gazetteers, published an article, "Yang Liangyao: The Envoy of China Who First Voyaged to the Western Ocean" (mentioned below as "the Zhang article"). He transcribed the entire inscription of the stele, in addition to analysing and commenting on many points in the epitaph.[3] He proved such a thorough and excellent resource that I wish to acknowledge that the present study greatly relies on Zhang's generosity. Thus I must first show my respect to his brilliant work.

Thanks to the assistance of Professor Zhang Jianlin 張建林, of the Shaanxi Provincial Institute of Archaeological Research, I was able to gain access to the Museum of Jingyang County and finally to see the original stele, on 29 March 2012. After having a rubbing made, I recorded its characteristics and revised the inscription. The stele measures 85 cm at the head and 190 cm at the body in height, 94 cm at the upper part and 102 cm at the lower in length, and 23 cm at the upper and 27 cm at the lower in width. It was marked in the creeping weed pattern on both sides, and carved in the centre with ornaments depicting flowers and birds.

Yang Liangyao was never recorded in any extant histories and biographies. His reappearance from a long-neglected and dusty corner of history is only because of the excavation of the Stele of Yang Liangyao. According to the inscription, Yang was from the Yang clan of Hongnong 弘農. His great-grandfather had been a meritorious statesman of the Tang Dynasty, a general of the imperial army who helped Emperor Xuanzong (r. 713–756) eliminate the clique of Empress Dowager Wei. In the Zhide 至德 era (756–757) of Emperor Suzong (r. 765–762), Yang Liangyao entered the palace and became a eunuch. In the Yongtai 永泰 era (765–766) of Emperor Daizong (r. 762–779), because of his merit in quashing the rebellion led by Tashilijizhang 塌實力繼章,[4] the leader of the Langshan 狼山 clan, he was appointed Acting Work Supervisor of the Office of Female Services of the Palace Domestic Service 行內侍省掖庭局監作. In the sixth year of the Dali 大曆 era (771), he received the additional titles, Gentleman for Court Discussion 朝議郎 and Assistant of Palace Gates Service 宮闈局丞. Later he also became an envoy to Annan. In the ninth year (774), he went to Guangzhou as an envoy, where he encountered the rebellion of Geshu Huang 哥舒晃. He was detained by the rebel but was not to be swayed by threats. In the twelfth year (777), the rebellion was suppressed, and Yang Liangyao was appointed Director of Palace Gates Service 宮闈令 for his merit. At the beginning of the Xingyuan era (784) of Emperor Dezong, at the time Zhu Ci 朱泚 (742–784) revolted, Yang Liangyao served as envoy to the Xirong 西戎 (Tibet), asking the Tibetan troops to assist, and he returned with the Tibetan troops. After the insurrection was pacified, he was appointed Executive Assistant of the Palace Domestic Service 內侍省內給事. In the sixth month of the same year, he received, in addition, the title Grand Master for Closing Court 朝散大夫. In the first year of the Zhenyuan era (785), he served as an envoy to the Abbasid Caliphate, and he successfully completed that mission. In the sixth month of the fourth year (788), his title was changed to Grand Master of the Palace 中大夫. In the seventh month, Yang Liangyao was titled Baron of Founding the State of Hongnong District 弘農縣開國男, with a fiefdom of three hundred households. In the twelfth year (796), the title Superior Master of the Palace 太中大夫 was given to him, and he also kept all the other titles. In the fifteenth year, he was commissioned to deal with the rebellion in the Huaixi 淮西 region and to superintend the troops of the Metropolitan Eastern Imperial Capital 東都畿 and Ru Prefecture 汝州. By means of pacification, Yang Liangyao stopped this crisis. In the first year of the Yongzhen 永貞 era (805), he returned to Chang'an and received an audience with Emperor Shunzong (r. 805). In the fifth month of the same year, he was assigned a concurrent commission to control the affairs of the Three Troops of the Right 僻仗使. In his later life, Yang Liangyao "converted to Buddhism, built pagodas and temples, copied Buddhist canons, donated money and purchased lands, offered charity and helped patients". On the twenty-second day of the seventh month of the first year of the Yuanhe 元和 era (806), he died at the age of seventy-one in his private house in Fuxing 輔興 Ward in Chang'an. A survey of the life of Yang Liangyao as a eunuch shows that his main merits arose in serving as envoy to lands in all directions and in resolving very difficult situations. Several of these masions were very important, among which the most fascinating one was the embassy to the Abbasid Caliphate.

About Yang Liangyao's embassy to the Abbasid Caliphate, the stele records:

貞元初, 既清寇難, 天下乂安, 四海無波, 九譯入覲. 昔使絕域, 西漢難其選; 今通區外, 皇上思其人. 比才類能, 非公莫可. 以貞元元年四月, 賜緋魚袋, 充聘國使於黑衣大食, 備判官、內傔, 受國信、詔書. 奉命遂行, 不畏厥遠. 屆乎南海, 舍陸登舟. 邈爾無憚險之容, 懍然有必濟之色. 義激左右, 忠感鬼

神. 公於是剪髮祭波, 指日誓眾. 遂得陽侯斂浪, 屏翳調風. 掛帆淩汗漫之空,
舉棹乘顥灝之氣. 黑夜則神燈表路, 白晝乃仙獸前驅. 星霜再周, 經過萬國.
播皇風於異俗, 被聲教於無垠. 往返如期, 成命不墜. 斯又我公杖忠信之明効
也. 四年六月, 轉中大夫. 七月, 封弘農縣開國男, 食邑三百戶.

In the beginning of the Zhenyuan era, after the removal of the calamity
caused by the enemy, all under heaven became peaceful and tranquil; no
wave was there in the four seas; foreign countries had audiences. Formerly
for dispatching a mission to the remote places, the Western Han court had to
make a difficult choice; now, for communicating with foreign countries, the
emperor thought at once of the right person. After comparing the ability of
men, only Mr. Yang could be seen to be qualified. In the fourth month of the
first year of the Zhenyuan era (785), the red official robe and fish-shaped tally
were bestowed upon him, and he assumed the position of state ambassador
to the Abbasid Caliphate. He was accompanied by administrative assistants
and domestic retainers, and he took along imperial letters and edicts. The
embassy departed immediately after receiving the imperial order, despite
the long distance. When the embassy reached Nanhai, they went on board.
Although the destination was remote, Mr. Yang's expression showed him to
be fearless of the danger; his solemn manner showed that he was confident
of success. His righteousness encouraged the attendants; his loyalty moved
ghosts and spirits. At that time he cut his hair and offered it to the sea, saluting
the sun and making vows to the masses. Thereupon Yanghou (god of waves)
calmed the waves; Pingyi (god of winds) attenuated the winds. The sail rose
high into the vast sky; the oar drove with great strength. At night the divine
light showed the route; in the day the celestial beast guided the navigation.
When the star and the frost had cycled twice, the envoy had passed thousands
of countries. The imperial tradition was made known to all according to the
alien custom; the manner of the embassy conveyed its prestige to all. The travel
there and back was completed on schedule, and the mission was accomplished.
This is the evident effect of Mr. Yang's loyalty and faithfulness. In the sixth
month of the fourth year (788), he was promoted to Grand Master of the
Palace, and in the seventh month, the title Baron of Founding the State of
Hongnong District was conferred upon him, with a fiefdom of three hundred
households.

I examined the original inscription and the rubbing, and below I explain
several points of character transcription:

1) "九譯", the Zhang article mistook as "九澤".
2) "備判官、內傔, 受國信、詔書" — in the Zhang article the
   punctuation is "備判官內, 傔受國信詔書". It appears that he did

not understand the meaning here. When the Tang court sent an envoy, an Administrative Assistant 判官 and Retainer 傔人 had to accompany him. "內傔" perhaps refers to the eunuchs from the Palace Domestic Service 內侍省, because the position of envoy had been assumed by a eunuch.

3) "厥" in "不畏厥遠" is a Tang popular form, but the Zhang article mistook it to be "乎."

4) "邈爾", the Zhang article mistook as "退邇".

5) "往" in "往返如期", the Zhang article mistook as "德".

Because the stele is very large, the inscriptions cannot be conveniently read. In addition, the inscription is written in the running script, and several characters are almost in cursive script, thus it is not easy to conduct the textual research, which makes such small mistakes entirely understandable.

According to this inscription, the Tang Dynasty dispatched the eunuch Yang Liangyao as envoy to the Abbasid Caliphate in the fourth month of 785. Yang Liangyao and his retinue brought the imperial letter and edict for this voyage with them, arriving at Nanhai (namely Canton) and then setting out on shipboard from there. After a long journey at sea, they finally reached the Abbasid Caliphate. By the sixth month of 788, the embassy had returned to Chang'an.

Although Zhang Shimin has described and explained the embassy of Yang Liangyao, there are still several issues that should be examined more deeply. Below is a detailed discussion.

The Background and Reason for Dispatching the Envoy

Nothing remarkable between the Tang and the Abbasid happened prior to 785. Why did the Tang court dispatch an official diplomatic corps to undertake a long voyage to the Abbasid Caliphate? It is probable that the reason arose from the conflicts between the Tang and Tibet.

In the fourteenth year of the Tianbao 天寶 era (755), the An Lushan Rebellion broke out in the Tang Empire. Consequently, the main martial forces of the Tang once deployed in the upper Yellow River valley and the Western Regions were moved to the Central Plains. The Tibetans took advantage of this and attacked northwards from the Tibetan plateau, encroaching on the Tang dominion. From 764 to 776, the Tibetans occupied several prefectures: Liangzhou 涼州, Ganzhou 甘州, Suzhou 肅州, Guazhou 瓜州, etc., and besieged the prefecture Shazhou 沙州, but did not attack the latter. This is attributed to the improvement of Sino–Tibetan relations for a time: in the first month of the fourth year of the Jianzhong 建中 era (783), the Tang and the Tibetans met at Qingshui 清水 to form an alliance and delimit a boundary line, and they subsequently coexisted peacefully.

In the tenth month of the same year, the Jingyuan 涇原 mutiny broke out in Chang'an. Zhu Ci usurped the throne in Chang'an, and Emperor Dezong fled to Fengtian 奉天. In the first month of the first year of the Xingyuan 興元 era (784), the Tang court hastily dispatched the Director of the Palace Library 秘書監, Cui Hanheng 崔漢衡, as an envoy to Tibet to ask for its military assistance in quashing Zhu Ci's rebellion, at the expense of the territorial sovereignty of Anxi 安西 and Beiting 北庭. The subject of this article, Yang Liangyao, served in the retinue of the Cui Hanheng envoy. The stele states:

興元初, 天未悔禍, 蛇豕橫途. 皇上軫念於蒼生, 臣下未遑於定策. 公乃感激出涕, 請使西戎; 乞師而旋, 遮寇以進.[5]

At the beginning of the Xingyuan era, Heaven had not removed the disaster, and snakes and boars ran amok everywhere. The emperor sorrowfully thought of the people, and the subjects had not yet enacted a strategy. Mr. Yang then was moved to tears of gratitude, and requested to serve as envoy to the western barbarians [Tibetans]. He solicited them for military assistance and returned, and the [Tibetan] troops obstructed the advance of the rebellious army.

In the fourth month of 784, the Tibetan troops were dispatched, and in the fifth month they assisted the Tang army to defeat Zhu Ci; probably because of the hot weather, they then immediately retreated. The Tibetans' martial support prevented a catastrophe for the Tang court, and the stele gave the credit to the hero:

覆武功之群盜, 清盩厔之前途; 風雲奔從而遂多, 山川指程而無擁. 興元既得以軷蹕, 渭橋因得以立功. 再造寰區, 不改舊物, 翳我公乞師之力也.[6]

[The army] eliminated the bandits of Wugong and cleared the road to Zhouzhi; the wind and clouds rushed after them and expanded [the armed forces];

mountains and rivers directed the way, and cleared any obstacles. In the Xingyuan era the emperor would rest along this route, and Mr. Yang made an offering at the bridge on the Wei River. The restoration of this world to the way it was and the preservation of this scene, is solely due to Yang's gaining the needed military assistance.

As a result, Yang Liangyao was promoted and awarded titles of honour:

其年二月, 遷內侍省內給事. 六月, 加朝散大夫. 此例驟遷, 蓋賞勞矣.

In the second month of the same year [784], he was promoted to Executive Assistant of the Palace Domestic Service; in the sixth month, the title Grand Master for Closing Court was added. Such a rapid promotion was the reward for his contribution.

In the seventh year, Emperor Dezong returned to Chang'an from Fengtian. The Tibetan envoy came to ask for the lands in Anxi and Beiting. The trusted advisor Li Mi 李泌 had this opinion:

安西、北庭, 人性驍悍, 控制西域五十七國, 及十姓突厥, 又分吐蕃之勢, 使不能並兵東侵, 奈何拱手與之, 且兩鎮之人, 勢孤地遠, 盡忠竭力, 為國家固守近二十年, 誠可哀憐. 一旦棄之以與戎狄, 彼其心必深怨中國, 他日從吐蕃入寇, 如報私讎矣. 況日者吐蕃觀望不進, 陰持兩端, 大掠武功, 受賂而去, 何功之有![7]

The people in Anxi and Beiting are valiant. They control the fifty-seven states in the Western Region, and the ten clans of the Turks. They also diffuse the energy of the Tibetans and make them concentrate on the eastward invasion. How can we surrender this land to the Tibetans? Moreover, despite their isolated situation and remote location, the people in the two garrisons have been loyal to China and defended it for more than twenty years, and we should really be compassionate to them. If we abandoned them to the Tibetans, they would certainly deeply resent China. Some day they would invade us along with the Tibetans, just like a person taking a private revenge. In addition, the Tibetan army has been two-faced, waiting and watching the situation, then plundering heavily and leaving with bribes. What merit do they have?

Emperor Dezong eventually refused to cede the two places, and, as a result, the Sino–Tibetan relationship broke up. The Tibetans "let their military forces trample on the crops, and plundered the people living on the frontiers". By the eighth month of the second year of the Zhenyuan era 貞元

(786), the Tibetan force had invaded Jing 涇 (present-day Zhenyuan 鎮原),
Long 隴 (present-day Longxian 隴縣), Bin 邠 (present-day Binxian 彬縣),
and Ning 寧 (present-day Ningxian 寧縣). Their rangers penetrated deeply
into Haozhi 好畤 (now the northwest of Qianxian 乾縣), the environs of
the imperial capital. Emperor Dezong ordered Hun Zhen 渾瑊 and others
commanding troops stationed in Xianyang 咸陽 to prepare for battle. In the
ninth month, the Tibetan army attacked Haozhi, and Chang'an proclaimed
martial law.[8]

It was only in the fourth month of 785, when the Sino–Tibetan
relationship had broken down, and before the Tibetan invasion, that Yang
Liangyao was sent as an envoy to the Abbasid Caliphate. The purpose
of his embassy was probably not only to ensure that "The imperial
tradition was made known to all according to the alien custom; the manner
of the envoy conveyed its prestige to all", as stated in the stele, but also
to ally with the Abbasids and request that they join in combating the
Tibetan Empire.

Among the Tang sources, it is widely attested that a significant policy
was proposed by Li Mi, the chancellor of Emperor Dezong, as is recorded
in the memorials of the Uighur envoy in the ninth month of 787:

既而回紇可汗遣使上表稱兒及臣, 凡泌所與約五事, 一皆聽命. 上大喜,
謂泌曰: "回紇何畏服卿如此!" 對曰: "此乃陛下威靈, 臣何力焉!"上曰:
"回紇則既和矣, 所以招雲南、大食、天竺奈何?" 對曰: "回紇和, 則吐
蕃已不敢輕犯塞矣. 次招雲南, 則是斷吐蕃之右臂也. 雲南自漢代以來臣
屬中國, 楊國忠無故擾之使叛, 臣於吐蕃, 苦於吐蕃賦役重, 未嘗一日不
思復為唐臣也. 大食在西域為最強, 自蔥嶺盡西海, 地幾半天下, 與天竺
皆慕中國, 代與吐蕃為仇, 臣故知其可招也."[9]

Subsequently, the Uighur Khan dispatched an envoy and sent up a memorial,
proclaiming himself to be the son and subject. He also stated that he would
obey the command of Li Mi on the five affairs that previously had been agreed
upon. The emperor was greatly delighted, and asked Li Mi: "How is that the
Uighurs are so obedient to you?" Li Mi answered: "This is the great power
of Your Majesty, not of mine!" The emperor said: "Since the Uighurs are
peaceful, how shall we ally with Yunnan, the Arabs and India?" Li Mi replied:
"Now that the Uighurs have made peace with us, the Tibetans dare not think
that they can easily invade the northern frontier. Then we will make peace and
ally with Yunnan. This is like cutting off the right arm of the Tibetans. Since
the Han Dynasty, Yunnan has been subordinate to China, yet Yang Guozhong

harassed it for no reason, so the country rebelled and became a vassal of Tibet. Now it suffers the heavy taxes and corvée of Tibet, and always wants to return to the Chinese dominance. The Arabs are the strongest country in the Western Regions, with its territory from the Pamirs to the West Sea, covering almost the half of All Under Heaven. Both the Arabs and India revere China, and they have been hostile to Tibet for generations. Therefore I observe that we can make peace and ally with them."

Although the passage above was composed more than two years after the envoy of Yang Liangyao, Li Mi, as the trusted advisor of Emperor Dezong, suggested the idea of refusing to cede lands to the Tibetans, as well as the plan of forming an alliance with the Uighurs, Nanzhao, the Abbasids, and India against the Tibetans. This opinion, recorded in the third year of the Zhenyuan era, might have been a strategy that had already matured. Since the Tibetan invasion was a result of the Tang's breach of the treaty, Li Mi must have conceived of the countermove against the Tibetans by the date of the breach. Therefore, a reasonable surmise is that the embassy conducted by Yang Liangyao was intended to put into practice the alliance strategy that had been considered by Li Mi and Emperor Dezong in the first year of the Zhenyuan era.

The reason the Tang court established in Chang'an thought of the remote Abbasid Caliphate is related to the situation in Central Asia, in which the Arabs and the Tibetans were struggling with each other. According to Arabic chronicles, by the time of the establishment of the Abbasid Caliphate in 750, Sogdiana and Tokharistan in Central Asia had been in the dominion of the Arabs. Although the Battle of Talas in 751 took place between the Tang and the Arabs, the subsequent An-Shi Rebellion weakened the forces of the Tang in its western frontier. So the Arab troops could advance eastwards and directly face the Tibetans who occupied the Baltistan–Gilgit region. In or shortly after the year 768, the Arab forces conquered Kashmir, and in 769 they invaded Kabul, and this undoubtedly touched the interests of the Tibetan Empire. A battle of the two forces west of the Pamirs seemed to be inevitable.[10] In the second year of the Zhenyuan era, when Yang Liangyao was still on his journey to West Asia, Han Huang advised the emperor:

吐蕃盜有河湟, 為日已久. 大曆已前, 中國多難, 所以肆其侵軼. 臣聞其近歲已來, 兵眾寖弱, 西逼大食之強, 北病回紇之眾, 東有南詔之防.[11]

It has been a long time since the Tibetans occupied the Hehuang region. Before the Dali era, there were internal calamities in China, and therefore we had to leave the invasion unchecked. I have heard that in recent years, the Tibetan forces have been weakened, with the threat of the strong Arabs to the west, the problem of the numerous Uighurs to the north, and the defence of Nanzhao to the east.

Also in the Dashi 大食 entry of the *Tang Huiyao* (Institutional History of the Tang), we read:

貞元二年, 與吐蕃為勁敵, 蕃兵大半西禦大食, 故鮮為邊患, 其力不足也.[12]

In the second year of the Zhenyuan era (786), [the Arabs] were the formidable adversaries of the Tibetans. The Tibetan troops were mostly occupied defending their western frontier against the Arabs. So they rarely bothered our frontier, for they did not have enough forces.

Both sources indicate that even before Li Mi proposed his plan, the Tang had known that the Arab army could attack the Tibetans from the west and weaken their forces, so that the Tibetan harassment of the Tang would decrease significantly. Given the date at which the Arabs and the Tibetans had begun to fight, it is reasonable to conjecture that the strategy of allying with the Arabs and requesting they attack the Tibetans was completely probable, and even that it worked.[13]

Why Yang Liangyao Chose the Sea Route

According to the inscription:

奉命遂行, 不畏厥遠. 屆乎南海, 舍陸登舟.

The embassy departed immediately after receiving the imperial order, despite the long distance they would have to go. After the embassy reached Nanhai, they went on board.

Here Nanhai refers to Guangzhou (Canton). The administration seat of Guangzhou was in Nanhai County. In the first year of the Tianbao era (742), Guangzhou was renamed Nanhai Prefecture. In the first year of the Qianyuan 乾元 era (758), it was again named Guangzhou.[14] In 785, although the formal name was Guangzhou, Nanhai was still an alias used especially in literature. The Yang Liangyao embassy departed from

Guangzhou, and went to the Abbasid capital, Baghdad, via the sea route.
Why did Yang Liangyao choose the sea route?

As stated above, by the fourth month of 785, when Yang Liangyao's
trip began, the Sino–Tibetan relationship had already been disrupted. A
strong Tibetan cavalry spanned the region northwest of Chang'an. The
most convenient passageway west from Chang'an, the Hexi Corridor,
was controlled by the Tibetans. If the envoy went north to the Uighur
khanate, and then turned westwards along the Silk Road north and
south of the Tengri Tagh 天山, it would risk encountering the Tibetans
or being robbed by local tribes, though this way had not been blocked.
Moreover, the Yang envoy was responsible for an explicit political and
military purpose. In the imperial edict they carried must have been
written the strategy of allying with the Arabs against the Tibetans. If
the edict fell into the hands of the Tibetan army or pro-Tibetan tribes,
the envoy would be killed, and the mission of the court would not be
accomplished.

In contrast, if they chose the sea route from Guangzhou, though they
would be "passing thousands of countries", there would not be any hostile
nation. Thus the envoy would travel safely, and the tokens and the imperial
edict would be delivered with ease. The only difficulty, however, was
overcoming, not the obstacles made by men, but the separation imposed
by nature — by sailing across the ocean.

The best starting point to reach the Caliphate via the sea route was
Guangzhou. Guangzhou was an important port for the overseas trade in
the Tang Dynasty, and it was also one of the starting points of the maritime
Silk Road. As late as the second year of the Kaiyuan 開元 era (714), the
Tang government had established the administrative infrastructure
for overseas trade — the Maritime Trade Bureau 市舶司, which was
administered by the Maritime Trade Commissioner 市舶使. As is recorded
below:

開元二年 ... 市舶使右威衛中郎將周慶立、波斯僧及烈等, 廣造奇器異
巧以進.[15]

In the second year of the Kaiyuan era (714) ... the Maritime Trade
Commissioner and Commandant of the Right Awesome Guard, Zhou Qingli,
the Persian monk Jilie, etc., produced numerous strange implements and
presented them to the court.

This indicates that Guangzhou was the port where strange implements from overseas entered China.

Guangzhou was also a place where ocean-going ships were concentrated. In 748, when the famous monk Jianzhen 鑒真 was in Guangzhou, he saw at the port "in the river there are innumerable ships from India, Persia and Kunlun (Southeast Asia). All ships carry aromatic drugs and jewelry piled up into mountains. The lengths of these ships were six to seven *zhang*. Many kinds of people from Ceylon, Arabia, the Gutang country 骨唐國,[16] the White barbarians, and the Red barbarians come into contact and dwell here."[17] So if people of that time prepared to undertake an ocean-going journey, they could select form many kinds of ships. As a formal envoy of the Tang Empire, Yang Liangyao probably selected ships of the Tang style. The prologue of J. Sauvaget's *Relation de la Chine et de l'Inde* states: "The merchants of the Persian Gulf sailed on the big Chinese ships, and finished their first couple of journeys across the South China Sea."[18] The date of their voyage might have been close to that of the Yang embassy's travel. Kuwabara Jitsuzō also acclaimed the Chinese ships: "Although the Arab ships were light and speedy, they were fragile in structure and small in shape, so that their ability to resist the stormy waves was not great."[19] Thus the large ships made in China would have been the first choice of the Yang envoy.

It is also probable that one reason the envoy chose Guangzhou as his starting point was because of his previous experience as an envoy to Guangzhou. As is stated on the stele:

復命至於廣府, 會叛軍煞將, 凶徒阻兵, 哥舒晃因縱狼心, 將邀王命, 承公以劍, 求表上聞. 公山立巍然, 不可奪志. 事解歸闕, 時望翕然. 至十二年, 遷宮闈令.

[Yang Liangyao] received the order to visit Guangzhou, and encountered rebellious troops killing generals, and bandits hindering the imperial army. With his audacious ambition, Geshu Huang wanted to take credit from the emperor, so he coerced Mr. Yang with a sword, and asked for an appointment to a position from the court. However, Mr. Yang, with a lofty manner, flatly rejected this. After the incident was resolved, Mr. Yang returned to the palace and was extolled for the reputation he had gained. In the twelfth year (777) he was promoted to Director of Palace Gates Service.

The passage above mentions a former trip by Yang Liangyao to Guangzhou in the eighth year of the Dali 大曆 era (773), during which time the Prefectural Governor 刺史 of Xunzhou 循州 (the administrative seat at Haifeng 海豐, present-day Haifeng Xian, Guangdong Province), Geshu Huang 哥舒晃, revolted and killed the Prefectural Governor of Guangzhou and Military Commissioner of Lingnan 嶺南節度使 Lü Chongfen 呂崇賁. From the inscription, it appears that Geshu Huang wanted Yang Liangyao to ask the Tang court to grant him the position of Military Commissioner. Yang Liangyao resolutely refused, however. Later, in the eleventh month of 775, the Surveillance Commissioner of Jiangxi, Lu Sigong 路嗣恭, captured Guangzhou and decapitated Geshu Huang, and the rebellion was suppressed. Subsequently, when Yang Liangyao returned to the capital, he attained a high reputation and was promoted to be Director of the Palace Gates Service in 777:

(路) 嗣恭初平嶺南, 獻琉璃盤, 徑九寸, 朕 (代宗) 以為至寶.[20]

Just after [Lu] Cigong's victory in Lingnan, he presented a glass plate of nine *cun* in diameter; We [Emperor Daizong] treated it as a precious treasure.

This glass plate was probably carried by Yang Liangyao to the court. It must have been a precious artwork from overseas.

When the Yang embassy arrived at Guangzhou in 785, Du You 杜佑 was the prefectural governor of Guangzhou and Military Commissioner of Lingnan. Du You moved to serve at Guangzhou in the third month of the first year of the Xingyuan 興元 era (784). He "then repaired buildings, constructed broad ways. Therefore the etiquette and custom became abundant, and the calamity of fire ceased automatically. Gold from the South and ivory were imported by maritime trade." The city began to have a new outlook. The overseas trade was developed, and valuable goods were imported. Du You also "conducted its beneficial profits and promoted it with trust and honesty. Myriads of ships came continuously, and a hundred kinds of goods were exported."[21] Guangzhou in the Du You administration enjoyed a peaceful and developed status, able to provide the Yang embassy with sufficient supplies and with suitable social circumstances.

Another reason Yang Liangyao might have chosen Guangzhou as his port of departure may have been to profit from the knowledge of the Caliphate and the sea route that could be provided by Du Huan 杜環, the nephew of Du You. We know that Du Huan followed the Military Commissioner of the Four Garrisons at Anxi 安西四鎮節度使, Gao Xianzhi 高仙芝, marched westwards to Chach (present-day Tashkent), and was defeated at Talas. After becoming a captive, Du Huan was able to depart for the core region of the Arab world (present-day Iraq), and stayed at al-Kūfah, then the capital of the Abbasid Caliphate, and other Arab cities for about ten years. In the first year of the Baoying 寶應 era (762), Du Huan was able to get passage with a commercial ship and returned to Guangzhou via the sea route. Du Huan's itinerary *Jingxing ji* 經行記 (Record of Travels) has been lost, but fragments of this work are preserved in volumes 192 and 193 of the *Bianfang dian* 邊防典 (Institutional Records on Frontier Defence) section of the *Tongdian* 通典 (Comprehensive Institutional Records) composed by his uncle Du You.[22] Therefore it is conceivable that the *Jingxing ji* portion in Du You's work was the best guide for the Yang embassy. Not only was the destination of the embassy the region travelled by Du Huan, but he also knew about the sea route, as selected by Yang Liangyao. According to the *Tongdian*, Du Huan landed at Guangzhou. We do not know whether Du Huan was still in Guangzhou in 785, but there is such a possibility. At least, Yang Liangyao would have been able to look at the *Jingxing ji* found in Du You's work, which was the best guide for his embassy to Baghdad.

In addition, since the Yang embassy would "pass thousands of countries", they would need to prepare many gifts to be bestowed at these foreign lands. The Tang empire had set up the Maritime Trade Supervisory at Guangzhou, and it often appointed eunuchs as maritime trade commissioners. Their abundant properties could provide material support for the Yang embassy, which could utilize the eunuch bureaucratic system to prepare the gifts, and this arrangement would save transport from the distant capital, Chang'an. This fact might also have been one of the reasons the Tang court chose Guangzhou as the port of departure of the Yang embassy.

The Sacrificial Ceremony at Nanhai

Taking the sea route meant that the Yang embassy would have had to face tempestuous waves. Yang Liangyao originated from Hongnong 弘農 in Henan. Because his great-grandfather was a meritorious general of the Tang court, upon whom was bestowed a villa in Yunyang 雲陽, Yang Liangyao was a native of the capital. Therefore we may state that he was an inhabitant of the interior unfamiliar with the sea. Before his embassy to the Abbasid Caliphate, Yang Liangyao had been to Annan 安南 (the administrative seat at Jiaozhi 交趾, present-day Hanoi, Vietnam) and Guangzhou. He must therefore have had experience of inshore navigation. But the Arab empire was remote, and the ocean route was accompanied by much risk and various dangerous elements. How did Yang plan to face the turbulent waves that lay ahead?

The inscription on the stele reads:

邈爾無憚險之容, 凜然有必濟之色. 義激左右, 忠感鬼神. 公於是剪髮祭波, 指日誓眾. 遂得陽侯斂浪, 屏翳調風.

Although the destination was remote, Mr. Yang's expression showed him to be fearless of the danger; his solemn manner showed that he was confident of success. His righteousness encouraged the attendants; his loyalty moved ghosts and spirits. At that time he cut his hair and offered it to the sea, saluting the sun and vowing to the masses. Therefore Yanghou (god of waves) gentled the waves; Pingyi (god of winds) attuned the winds. The sail rose high into the vast sky; the oar drove with great strength.

While this inscription contains much flowery language, the core information reveals that the ancients must have held a solemn sacrificial ceremony at the edge of the ocean, to beg for the help of Heaven, the ghosts, and the spirits.

Where, then, was the ceremony held? The most likely place is the Nanhai Temple 南海祠/南海廟 in Guangzhou.

The Nanhai Temple was established in the fourteenth year of the Kaihuang era (594) of the Sui Dynasty. It was situated at Guangzhou (present-day Miaotou Cun in Huangpu District), Nanhai District, Nanhai Defence Command. The Tang Dynasty inherited the Sui institution, which had made the sacrificial ceremony to the deity of Nanhai a component of the national sacrifice system, one of the so-called "Mountains, Garrisons, Seas, and Rivers" 嶽鎮海瀆, and therefore a sacrifice of a moderate size. In the tenth year of the Tianbao era (751), the deity of Nanhai was given the title "Guangli Wang" 廣利王 (Profit Expanding King). Local administrators were required to make a sacrifice to the deity once a year, and for this precise reason envoys were sent to Guangzhou to make offerings to the deity, who was not only an object of the official sacrifice, but also an idol that was worshipped by local businessmen and fishermen. The ocean-going embassy must certainly have worshipped the deity of Nanhai.[23] So the site of the sacrificial ceremony for the Yang embassy must have been the Nanhai Temple. The content of their prayers must simply have been to ask to be taken under the protection of the deity of Nanhai.

During the Tang Dynasty, the Nanhai Temple must have been at the bank of the Zhujiang River, and thus the Yang embassy probably left the land and went on board immediately after the sacrificial ceremony.

The Timeline of the Embassy

As noted in the carving on the stele, the Yang embassy experienced:

星霜再周, 經過萬國. 播皇風於異俗, 被聲教於無垠. 往返如期, 成命不墜.

When the star and the frost had cycled twice, the envoy had passed thousands of countries. The imperial tradition was made known to all according to the alien custom; the manner of the embassy conveyed its prestige to all. The travel there and back was completed on schedule, and the mission was accomplished.

The "star" here means the constellations that revolve one cycle per year; while the "frost" refers to the eighteenth solar term *Xiangjiang* 霜降 ["Frost's Descent"]. Therefore the first phrase here means the envoy lasted at least two years from the fourth month of 785.[24] Since, in the sixth month of 788, Yang Liangyao was promoted 中大夫, the envoy probably returned to Chang'an in the sixth month of 787. Thus, the journey may have lasted three years.

We can also surmise from the situation that the envoy must have utilized the monsoon winds. Utilizing the guide book of the Arabian sailors, James K. Chin 錢江 of Jinan University analysed the situation of voyages via the Indian Ocean and the South China Sea, and pointed out that it took eighteen months for a round trip of an Arab commercial ship from the Persian Gulf to Guangzhou. The voyage from China to the Persian Gulf involved: departure from Guangzhou in October to December, sailing to the Straits of Malacca by the northeast monsoon, crossing the Bay of Bengal in January, reaching the Arabian Peninsula in February or March, and arriving at the port of Muscat in April by the southeastern monsoon. The voyage from the Persian Gulf to China entailed: departure from the Persian Gulf in September or October, passing the Indian Ocean by the northeastern monsoon, arriving at the Malabar Coast of India in November or December and at the Malay Peninsula in January where they waited for the monsoon, and finally arriving at Guangzhou when there was no typhoon in the South China Sea.[25]

In view of the above, we can calculate and reconstruct the itinerary of Yang Liangyao's embassy as follows:

The fourth month of the first year of the Zhenyuan era begins with May thirteenth, 785, and ends on June twelfth. Therefore, calculated in the Gregorian calendar, Yang Liangyao departed from Chang'an in June 785 and arrived at Guangzhou in August of the same year. After a sojourn, the envoy left Guangzhou on board in October and arrived at the port of Muscat in April 786 and in Baghdad in May. After a stay of several months in the Abbasid Caliphate, the envoy departed from the Persian Gulf in September 786, arrived at Guangzhou in May 787, and returned to Chang'an in July 787 (approximately the fifth to the sixth months of the third year of the Zhenyuan era). According to the inscription, if he was promoted in the sixth month of the fourth year of the Zhenyuan era (788) because of the embassy, it is more probable that he stayed in the Abbasid Caliphate for about one year, since the most reasonable explanation was that the Tang court granted him promotion just after he had returned home.

Yang Liangyao's Route

The stele summarized the route of the Yang embassy very briefly:

掛帆淩汗漫之空, 舉棹乘灝淼之氣. 黑夜則神燈表路, 白晝乃仙獸前驅.
星霜再周, 經過萬國.

The sail rose high into the vast sky; the oar drove with great strength. At
night the divine light showed the route; in the day the celestial beast guided
the navigation. When the star and the frost had cycled twice, the envoy had
passed thousands of countries.

Most of the passage above is formulaic, without substantial content.
What then was the actual route the embassy took?

We can, fortunately, see the route from Guangzhou to Baghdad
detailed in the *Huanghua sida ji* 皇華四達記 (Record of Embassies to
the Four Directions), composed by Jia Dan 賈耽 preserved in the *Xin
Tangshu, dili zhi* 新唐書·地理志 (New History of the Tang, "Treatise on
Geography"):[26]

Departing from Guangzhou to the southeast by sea, after a voyage of 200 *li*,
we arrived at Tunmen Mountain 屯門山 [now the northwest coast of the
Kowloon Peninsula)], then with a fair wind we voyaged westward, and after
two days we arrived at Jiuzhoushi 九州石 [now the Qizhou Archipelago
七洲列島 northeast of the Hainan Island/Taya Archipelago]. Then we sailed
south to Xiangshi 象石 [present-day Dazhou Island 大洲島, southeast of
Hainan Island/Tinhosa Island]. Then we sailed for three days to Mount
Zhanbulao 占不勞山 [Culao Cham, now one of Vietnam's Cham Islands];
this mountain was in the sea, 200 *li* east from the Huanwang state 環王國
[or Champa, in present-day central Vietnam]. After a two-day sail we
arrived at Lingshan 陵山 [the Sa Hoi Cape of Vietnam]. After another day,
we reached the Mendu state 門毒國 [Qui Nhon, Vietnam)], after another day
to the Guda state 古笪國 [present-day Nha Trang, Vietnam], and after half
a day to Bentuolang Islet 奔陀浪洲 [Panduranga, present-day Phan Rang,
Vietnam)]. After a two-day sailing we arrived at Juntunong Mount 軍突弄山
[now Poulo Condore island in Vietnam]. We then voyaged for five days and
arrived at the Straits [present-day Malacca Straits], which the barbarians
there called *Zhi* 質 [Bahasa Melayu, *selat*]; the width of the Strait is 100 *li*.
On the north[eastern] bank there is the Luoyue state 羅越國 [the southern
tip of the Malay Peninsula]; on the south[west] bank there is the Foshi state
佛逝國 [southeast part of the island of Sumatra]. From the Foshi state we

navigated four or five days to the east, and arrived at the Heling state 訶陵國 [Java], which is the largest state among the southern islets. Then we left the Straits to the west, and after a voyage of three days we arrived at the Gegesengzhi state 葛葛僧祇國 (now Brouwers Archipelago in the southern part of the Straits of Malacca], an islet located on the northwest corner of the Foshi state. The people of the Gegesengdi state were mostly pirates, and the passengers feared them. The Geluo state 箇羅國 is located to the north[east] of its bank [now Kedah on the Malay Peninsula]. [North]west of the Geluo state is the Geguluo state 哥谷羅國 [Qaqola/Kakula, now the Kra Isthmus of the Malay Peninsula]. We departed the Gegesengzhi state and sailed four to five days, and arrived at Shengdeng islet 勝鄧洲 [now Deli in northeastern Sumatra], and then navigated westwards for five days, arriving at the Polu state 婆露國 [Baros Island, northwest of Sumatra]. Then we sailed six days, to the Qielan islet 伽藍洲 [now Nicobar Archipelago of India] of the Po state 婆國 [Cola]. After a four-day navigation to the north,[27] we arrived at the Shizi state 師子國 [present-day Sri Lanka], the northern bank of which is 100 *li* from the coast of southern India. After another four-day journey to the west, we passed the southernmost point of southern India, the Molai state 沒來國 [present day Malabar, India]. We turned northwest, passed tens of small states, and arrived at the western coastline of India. Then we navigated for two days to the northwest, and arrived at the Bayu 拔颺國 state [present day Broach on the western bank of India]. After another journey of ten days, passing five small states at the west frontier of India, we arrived at the Tiyu state 提颺國 [Diul, present-day Diudul on the Kathiawar Peninsula, India]. The Milantai River 彌蘭太河 [Nahr Mihran, the Arabic name of the Indus River], also named Xintou River 新頭河 [now the Indus River] comes from the Bokun state 渤昆國 in the north [probably Greater Bolü 大勃律, present-day Baltistan, northwest of Kashmir], flows on the north of the Tiyu state and then into the sea. Then, after a westward navigation of twenty days from the Tiyu state, passing more than twenty small states, we arrived at the Tiluoluhe state 提羅盧和國 [Djerrarah, present-day Abadan, Iran], also named the Luoheyi state 羅和異國 [Larwi]. The people of this state built ornamental columns in the sea, and placed a torch on these at night, so that the sailors would not lose their way. After a voyage for one day to the west, we arrived at the Wula state 烏剌國 [now al-Ubullah, Iran], where the Fulila River [the Euphrates] flows into the sea. We transferred to small boats and sailed upstream for two days, and arrived at the Moluo State 末羅國 [now Basra, Iraq], an important city of the Arabs. Then we traveled a thousand *li* by land, and finally arrived at the capital of King Maomen 茂門 [Amīr al-Mu'minīn], the city of Fuda 縛達城 [Baghdad].

Note that Jia Dan was director of the Ministry of Works 工部尚書 in 784. In the second month of 785, Jia Dan and the vice director of the Ministry of Works 工部侍郎, Liu Taizhen 劉太真, were dispatched to inspect Luoyang, Henan, and Hebei, respectively. In the sixth month, he began to hold a concurrent post as Censor-in-Chief, Regent, and Chief Defence Commissioner of the Metropolitan Area of the Eastern Imperial Capital 御史大夫東都留守判東都尚書事東都畿汝州都防禦使. In the ninth year of the Zhenyuan era (793), Jia Dan went to the royal court, and was promoted to Chief Administrator of the Right 右僕射 and Joint Manager of Affairs of the Secretariat–Chancellery 同中書門下平章事, that is, the prime minister. In the tenth month of 801, Jia Dan presented the *Hainei Huayi tu* 海內華夷圖 (Map of Chinese and Barbarian Territories in the World) and the forty-volume *Gujin junguo xiandao Siyi shu* 古今郡國縣道四夷述 (Exposition on the Four Barbarians in the Commanderies, Principalities, Districts and Circuits from Past to Present), and stated:

> 去興元元年伏奉進止，令臣修撰國圖．旋即充使魏州汴州，出鎮東洛東都．間以眾務，不遂專門，續用久虧，憂愧彌切．近乃力衰朽，竭思慮，殫所聞見，叢於丹青．謹令工人畫《海內華夷圖》一軸 ⋯ 並撰《古今郡國縣道四夷述》四十卷。

> In the first year of the Xingyuan era [784], [I] received the imperial edict that ordered me to compile an atlas of our country. Immediately I was ordered to inspect Weizhou and Bianzhou from where I was garrisoned at the eastern capital, Luoyang. With many of the services asked, I could not succeed. It is still not well done, and my shame and sorrow is keen. Recently, my strength and energy have diminished, [because] I have racked my wits and exhausted my knowledge, and so I have gathered [what I have] into the painting. I hereby order the painters to prepare a scroll of the *Hainei Huayi tu*. . . and compose the forty-volume *Gujin junguo xiandao Siyi shu.*

As stated in the *Xin Tangshu, dili zhi*, "the Prime Minister in the Zhenyuan era, Jia Dan, analysed most minutely the distance between localities. He recorded the itinerary of those who departed from the frontier to the foreign lands in their entirety, as well as those of the foreigners, translated at the Court for Dependencies 鴻臚." This indicates that, as early as 784, Jia Dan began to collect materials. He visited the Tang envoys "who departed from the frontier to the foreign lands", and also interviewed foreigners through interpreters, finishing his work in 801. At the same time, he and Yang Liangyao were both in Chang'an, and as the itinerary of Yang Liangyao would have been the most direct and the most authentic, Jia Dan must have used it.[28] Therefore, we might venture to surmise that the above record by Jia Dan was the route of the fleet led by Yang Liangyao. In Jia Dan's work, the port of departure was Guangzhou, and the destination was Baghdad; Yang Liangyao was certainly the envoy from Guangzhou to the new capital of the Abbasid Caliphate. Also, the Yang embassy was the event that came most shortly before the compilation of Jia Dan's work. It is noteworthy that the description in which "The people of this state built ornamental columns in the sea, and placed a torch on these at night, so that the sailors would not lose their way" in Jia Dan's work exactly tallies with "at night the divine light showed the route" in the inscription. Both were first-hand experiences of Yang Liangyao, were even his personal statements. Since it is from the standard extant texts, we may assume that the description by Jia Dan comes from the official report from the Yang embassy,[29] and possibly contains the personal narration of Yang Liangyao.

The latter half of Volume 100 of the *Tang huiyao* comes from the *Gujin junguo xiandao Siyi shu* by Jia Dan. This account was considered one of the earliest and most precise Chinese records concerning the Arab world, the other being the report of Du Huan.[30] Now we can see that the latest exact information might well have been derived from Yang Liangyao's report.

The route from Baghdad or the Persian Gulf to Guangzhou is also preserved in Arab-Persian geographical works, and it corroborates our knowledge of the route of the Yang embassy from another perspective. For instance, in the first volume of the Arab historical work *Kitāb 'Ahbār al-Sīn wa' l-Hind*, the route from the Persian Gulf to Guangzhou as well as the information about the seas and islands, as reported by Sulaymān al-Tājir and other merchants, is preserved in detail.[31] The *Kitāb al-Masālik wa 'l-Mamālik* by Ibn Khurdādhbih also recounts the sea route from Basra to Guangzhou from the latter half of the ninth century to the beginning of the tenth, with meticulous accounts of locations and precise distances.[32] On these sources, there have been comprehensive studies,[33] so I will not discuss the details here.

The Achievement and Influence of the Yang Embassy

Regarding the achievement of the Yang Liangyao embassy, it is stated concisely on the stele:

播皇風於異俗, 被聲教與無垠. 往返如期, 成命不墜.

The imperial tradition was made known to [all who follow] alien customs; the manner of the embassy conveyed its prestige to all. The travel there and back was completed on schedule, and the mission was accomplished.

Since the author of the inscription did not describe the purpose of the Yang embassy, it is natural that the result would not have been mentioned. Instead, only these exaggerated statements were included: "The imperial tradition was made known to [all who follow] alien customs; the manner of the embassy conveyed its prestige to all."

In fact, the Yang embassy probably achieved its intended purpose. The aforementioned rivalry of the Arabs and the Tibetans in northwest India in the late 860s would not have ended quickly. According to the *Dashi zhuan* 大食傳 (Account of Dashi) in the *Jiu Tangshu* 舊唐書 (Old History of the Tang), "in the mid-Zhenyuan era, the Tibetan troops mostly defended the Arabs to the west" — this appears to be the actual circumstance. The situation was aggravated in the late Zhenyuan era. If this is the case, it is quite probable that the Arabs were aroused by the Tang embassy, specifically the diplomatic efforts of Yang Liangyao.

From the perspective of the history of Sino–foreign relations, the Yang embassy to the Abbasid Caliphate via the sea route greatly promoted East–West cultural interchange. It appears that from the beginning of the Zhenyuan era, the maritime Silk Road gradually began to thrive. Wang Qianxiu 王虔休 said in his *Jin Lingnanwang Guan Shiboshiyuan Tubiao* 進嶺南王館市舶使院圖表 that "[in the Zhenyuan era,] the lords and chiefs of foreign countries admired the decency of the empire;

their great ships came in succession, doubling the ordinary number"
諸蕃君長, 遠慕皇風, 寶舶薦臻, 倍於恒數, "they traveled across the
difficult way and navigated the sea, coming to China year after year"
梯山航海, 歲來中國.³⁴ At the end of the Zhenyuan era, "every year the
foreign countries came and traded. Precious pearls, tortoise shells,
extraordinary fragrances, and rhinoceros horns, all came by ship from
overseas" 蕃國歲來互市, 奇珠、瑇瑁、異香、文犀, 皆浮海舶以來.³⁵ Plenty
of products were continuously transported to the shores of northeastern
China.

In the middle and later Tang Dynasty, imported products via the
maritime Silk Road gradually increased and were unearthed at many
places in Guangzhou and the northeastern region. Some of these were
also carried to the capital Chang'an, where the treasures of All Under
Heaven were gathered. Here we cite only one example, the eighteen
pieces of Islamic glassware buried in the late Tang Dynasty, which
were discovered in 1987 at the underground palace of the Famen Temple
法門寺, Fufeng 扶風 District, Shaanxi Province. This glassware include
a beaker vase with a relief design, a blue glass vase with a silk-
coloured surface, an enamel dish with a floral design of poppies, a
blue glass plate in a flower-cluster design with carved cross-like lines,
a blue glass plate with eight arching wave-like lines and with a carved
flower-cluster design painted in gold), a blue plate with a carved flower
cluster design (with four flowers painted in gold), a blue glass plate
with eight carved arches and a flower-cluster design painted in gold, an
incised Mihrab on a net-patterned azure glass plate and so on; all of these
are pieces of intact Islamic glassware. They do not look like items that
usually arrived via the land route to the Central Plains, but seemed to
have come from the sea route. According to the research of an expert
on Islamic cultural relics, Ma Wenkuan 馬文寬, the provenance of
these glassware is Iraq,³⁶ i.e., the Abbasid Caliphate, which I believe to
tally with the historical background. We can further suppose that these
cultural relics were originally collected or used at the royal court in
Chang'an. Among these pieces of glassware, it is not impossible that
there were items of tribute brought by Yang Liangyao from the Abbasid
Caliphate.

NOTES

The present chapter was originally a paper submitted to the International Conference on "Land and Maritime Communication and World Civilizations" at Sun Yat-Sen University on 4–5 December 2011. The author wishes to thank Professor Wang Zijin 王子今 at Renmin University, Mr Liu Yunhui 劉雲輝, Deputy Director of the Shaanxi Bureau of Cultural Relics, Professor Zhang Jianlin 張建林, Deputy President of the Shaanxi Institute of Archaeological Research, and Mr Zhao Liguang 趙力光, Curator of Xi'an Beilin Museum, for their assistance to his investigation of the Yang Liangyao stele. The author also thanks the rubbing worker Mr Geng 耿 of Beilin Museum, and acknowledges the warmly appreciated help of his students Luo Shuai 羅帥, Zheng Yanyan 鄭燕燕, Chen Chunxiao 陳春曉, and Guo Guikun 郭桂坤.

1. Al-Ṭabarī, *Ta'rīkh al-rusul wa'l mulūk* (Annals), vol. 3, edited by M.J. de Goeje (Leiden, 1879–1901, reprinted 1964–65, p. 272. The summary above is derived from Zhang Guangda 張廣達, "Haibo lai Tianfang, Silu tong Dashi — Zhongguo yu Alabo shijie de lishi lianxi yu huigu" 海舶來天方, 絲路通大食 — 中國與阿拉伯世界的歷史聯繫的回顧 [Ocean Ships Arrived at Mecca, Silk Roads Led to Arabia: A Review of the Historical Connections Between China and the Arab World], originally collected in the *Zhongwai wenhua jiaoliushi* 中外文化交流史 [History of Sino–Foreign Cultural Exchanges], edited by Zhou Yiliang 周一良 (Zhengzhou: Henan renmin chubanshe, 1987). Here the article is cited from Zhang Guangda, *Wenben, tuxiang yu wenhua jiaoliu* 文本、圖像與文化交流 [Texts, Images and Cultural Exchange], (Nanning: Guangxi shifan daxue chubanshe, 2008), pp. 139–40.
2. Zhang, *Wenben*, pp. 144–45.
3. Published in the *Xianyang shifan xueyuan xuebao* 咸陽師範學院學報 [Bulletin of Xianyang Normal College], 20, no. 3 (2005): 4–8. Before this article, Mr Zhang also published an introductory article "Zhongguo gudai zuizao xia Xiyang de waijiao shijie Yang Liangyao" 中國古代最早下西洋的外交使節楊良瑤 [The Earliest Chinese Diplomat to Undertake an Expedition to the West Ocean], in the *Tangshi luncong* 唐史論叢 [Symposium on Tang History], vol. 7 (Xi'an: Shaanxi shifan daxue chubanshe, 1998), pp. 351–56. In light of Mr Zhang's article in the *Tangshi luncong*, Zhou Weizhou 周偉洲 also briefly introduced the deeds of Yang Liangyao in his "Tangchao yu Nanhai zhuguo tonggong guanxi yanjiu" 唐朝與南海諸國通貢關係研究 [A Study of the Tributary Relationship Between the Tang Dynasty and the Countries in the Nanhai], in *Zhonguoshi yanjiu* 中國史研究 [Journal of Chinese Historical Studies], 3 (2002): 72–73. The same content is seen in Zhou Weizhou 周偉洲, *Chang'an yu Nanhai zhuguo* 長安與南海諸國 [Chang'an and the Countries in the Nanhai] (series on the ancient capital Chang'an) (Xi'an: Xi'an chubanshe, 2003), pp. 157–59.

4. This name is definitely a transcription of a non-Chinese name. However, since this person cannot be seen in any other extant source, all that we can do here is to leave the transliteration as it is in this chapter.

5. *Wei* 未 in 天未悔禍 was copied by the Zhang article as *bu* 不; *zhe* 遮 in 遮寇以進 was copied as *sui* 邃. Here the transcription is corrected according to the original inscription.

6. *Qing* 清 in 清盤屋之前途 was copied by the Zhang article as *qing* 請, here corrected according to the original text.

7. Sima Guang 司馬光, *Zizhi Tongjian* 資治通鑑 [Comprehensive Mirror for Aid in Government], (Beijing: Zhonghua shuju, 1956), vol. 231, p. 7442.

8. Sima, *Zizhi Tongjian*, vol. 231, pp. 7470, 7472.

9. Sima, *Zizhi Tongjian*, vol. 233, p. 7505.

10. Regarding the relationship among the Tang Dynasty, the Tibetan Empire, and the Arabic Empire, see Zhang Riming 張日銘, *Tangdai Zhongguo yu Dashi Musilin* 唐代中國與大食穆斯林 [Tang China and the Muslims of Arabia], (Xining: Ningxia renmin chubanshe, 2002), pp. 93–101; Wang Xiaofu 王小甫, *Tang Tubo Dashi zhengzhi guanxi shi* 唐吐蕃大食政治關係史 [A History of Political Relations among the Tang, the Tibetans, and the Arabs], (Beijing: Beijing daxue chubanshe, 1992), pp. 206–14.

11. Liu Xu 劉昫, *Jiu Tangshu* 舊唐書 [Old History of the Tang], vol. 129, Han Huang zhuan 韓滉傳 [Biography of Han Huang] (Beijing: Zhonghua shuju, 1975), p. 3602.

12. *Tang Huiyao* 唐會要 [Important Documents of the Tang], vol. 100 (Shanghai: Shanghai guji chubanshe, 1992), p. 2127.

13. Zhang Shimin held that the Yang Liangyao embassy was intended to fulfil the policy of Li Mi, but his article did not take into account that the time of the diplomatic mission was before the proposal of Li Mi.

14. *Yuanhe junxian tuzhi* 元和郡縣圖志 [Maps and Gazetteers of the Commanderies and Counties in the Yuanhe Era], vol. 34, Lingnan Dao 嶺南道 [Lingnan Circuit], the entry on Guangzhou [Beijing: Zhonghua shuju, 1983], pp. 885–87.

15. Wang Qinruo 王欽若 et al., eds., *Songben Cefu yuangui* 宋本冊府元龜 [Song Version of the Outstanding Models from the Storehouse of Literature] (Beijing: Zhonghua shuju, 1989), p. 1490. See also Liu, *Xuanzong ji* 玄宗紀 [Annals of Xuanzong], vol. 8, p. 174.

16. According to the *Yiqiejing yinyi* 一切經音義 [Sound and Meaning of All Scriptures], vol. 81, Gutang was a barbarian tribe in the archipelagos south of China. See Chen Jiarong 陳佳榮 et al., *Gudai Nanhai diming huishi* 古代南海地名匯釋 [A Collective Interpretation of Place Names in the Ancient Nanhai], (Beijing: Zhonghua shuju, 1986), p. 590.

17. Zhenren Yuankai 真人元開 (Ōmi Mifune 淡海三船), *Tang Daheshang dongzheng zhuan* 唐大和上東征傳 [Account of the Grand Monk of the Tang's March to the East], (Beijing: Zhonghua shuju, 2000), p. 74.

18. Anonymous, *Zhongguo Yindu wenjian lu* 中國印度聞見錄 [A Record of Things Seen and Heard in China and India], translated by Mu Genlai 穆根來, Wen Jiang 汶江, and Huang Zhuohan 黃倬漢 (Beijing: Zhonghua shuju, 1983), prologue, XXV.

19. Kuwabara Jitsuzō 桑原騭藏, *Zhongguo Alabo haishang jiaotongshi* 中國阿拉伯海上交通史 [The History of Maritime Communications Between China and Arabia], translated by Feng You 馮攸 (Beijing: Shangwu yinshuguan, 1934), p. 119.

20. Sima, *Zizhi Tongjian*, vol. 225, p. 7253.

21. Quan Deyu 權德輿, "Dugong Huainan Yiai beiming bing xu" 杜公淮南遺愛碑銘并序 [Master Gong of Huainan's Benevolently Bequeathed Epitaph and Preface], *Quan Tangwen* 全唐文 [Complete Tang Writings], vol. 496 (Beijing: Zhonghua shuju, 1983), p. 5056. About the achievements of Du You at Guangzhou, see Guo Feng 郭鋒, *Du You ping zhuan* 杜佑評傳 [A Critical Biography of Du You], (Nanjing: Nanjing daxue chubanshe, 2004), pp. 101–8.

22. Du You 杜佑, *Tongdian* 通典 [Comprehensive Institutional Records], vol. 191, *Bianfang dian* 邊防典 [Institutional Records on Frontier Defence], juan 7 and related sections (Beijing: Zhonghua shuju, 1995), p. 5199. Zhang Yichun 張一純 composed *Jingxing ji jianzhu* 經行記箋注 [Record of Travels, Annotated], which was combined with Huichao's 慧超 *Wang Wu Tianzhuguo Zhuan* 往五天竺國傳 [Record of the Itinerary to the Five Indian Countries] and published by Zhonghua shuju in 2000.

23. See Wang Yuanlin 王元林, *Guojia jisi yu Haishang Silu yiji — Guangzhou Nanhai shenmiao yanjiu* 國家祭祀與海上絲路遺跡 —— 廣州南海神廟研究 [The Historical Remains of the State Sacrifice and the Maritime Silk Road: A Study of the Nanhai Temple in Guangzhou], (Beijing: Zhonghua shuju, 2006), pp. 49–97.

24. Kuwabara, pp. 109–11. In this book, Kuwabara conducted a special investigation of the dates of navigation between Arabia and China, and his study indicates that a round trip in the Tang Dynasty normally took more than two years.

25. Qian Jiang (James K. Chin) 錢江, "Gudai Bosiwan de hanghai huodong yu maoyi gangbu" 古代波斯灣的航海活動與貿易港埠 [Navigational Activities and Trading Ports in the Ancient Persian Gulf], *Haijiaoshi yanjiu* 海交史研究 [Studies on Maritime Communications] 2 (2010): 12. On the eastward navigation of the Arab-Persian sailors who took advantage of the monsoons, see also J.W. Meri, ed., *Medieval Islamic Civilization: An Encyclopedia* (New York and London: Routledge, 2006), pp. 556–57, 816–18.

26. There have been a great many research articles written about this passage, and the analyses are different from one another. Here we adopt only one textual method, selecting a useful one and following it in our detailed discussions. See the works below: Gabriel Ferrand, *Ancient Voyages to Condor Island and the China Sea* [昆侖及南海古代航行考], translated by Feng Chengjun

馮承鈞 (Beijing: Zhonghua shuju, 2002); Paul Pelliot, *Deux itineraires de Chine en Inde à la fin du VIII e Siecle* [交廣印度兩道考], translated by Feng Chengjun (Beijing: Zhonghua shuju, 2003); Feng Chengjun, *Zhongguo Nanyang Jiaotongshi* 中國南洋交通史 [A History of the Communications between China and the Nanhai Region], with an introduction by Xie Fang 謝方 (Shanghai: Shanghai Guji Press, 2005), pp. 31–33; Han Zhenhua 韓振華, "Dibashiji Yindu Bosi hanghai kao" 第八世紀印度波斯航海考 [A Study of Indian and Persian Navigation in the Eighth Century], in *Zhongwaiguanxi lishi yanjiu* 中外關係歷史研究 [Studies on the History of Sino–Foreign Relations], (Hong Kong: Xianggang daxue Yazhou yanjiu zhongxin, 1999), pp. 353–62; Chen Jiarong (Chan Kai-Wing) 陳佳榮, *Zhongwai jiaotongshi* 中外交通史 [A History of the Communications Between China and Foreign Countries], (Hong Kong: Xuejin shudian, 1987); Su Jiqing (Su Chi-ch'ing) 蘇繼卿, *Nanhai gouchen lu* 南海鉤沉錄 [A Collection about the Nanhai], (Taipei: Shangwu yinshuguan, 1989), pp. 373–78; Liu Yingsheng 劉迎勝, *Silu wenhua: Haishang juan* 絲路文化·海上卷 [The Silk Road Culture: The Sea Route], (Hangzhou: Zhejiang renmin chubanshe, 1995); Zhang *Wenben*, pp. 133–80; Chen Yan 陳炎, *Haishang Sichouzhilu yu wenhua jiaoliu (zengdingben)* 海上絲綢之路與文化交流 （增訂本） [The Maritime Silk Road and Cultural Exchange (Revised Version)], (Beijing: Beijing daxue chubanshe, 2002); Lin Meicun 林梅村, *Sichouzhilu kaogu shiwu jiang* 絲綢之路考古十五講 [Fifteen Lectures on Silk Road Archaeology], (Beijing: Beijing daxue chubanshe, 2006); Liu Yingsheng, *Hailu yu lulu — zhonggu shidai dongxi jiaoliu yanjiu* 海路與陸路 — 中古時代東西交流研究 [The Sea Route and the Land Route: Studies on the East-West Exchange in Medieval Times] (Beijing: Beijing daxue chubanshe, 2011), pp. 202–7.

27. Paul Pelliot held that the "north" 北 here is an error and should be "ten" 十 or "twenty" 廿, thus the voyage from the Qielan Islet to Sri Lanka would have lasted fourteen to twenty-four days. See Pelliot, p. 281.

28. Jia Dan and Yang Liangyao must have had a very close relationship. In the fifteenth year of the Zhenyuan era (779), Wu Shaocheng 吳少誠 rebelled at Huaixi 淮西. According to the inscription of the stele, Yang Liangyao's strategy was to offer amnesty and enlistment, which was eventually accepted by Emperor Dezong. The chronicles document that the strategy of appeasement was proposed by Jia Dan, and was accepted by Dezong. Yang and Jia are in agreement on this event, indicating that they must have communicated with each other.

29. The Zhang article held that "the route from Nanhai to Baghdad as depicted by Jia Dan possibly came from the navigation report by Yang Liangyao as an envoy to the Abbasid Caliphate", which was very insightful.

30. Zhang, *Wenben*, p. 145.

31. J. Sauvaget, *Relation de la Chine et de l'Inde* [中國印度見聞錄], translated by Mu Genlai et al. (Beijing: Zhonghua shuju, 1983), pp. 3–10.

32. Ibn Khurdādhbih, *Kitāb al-Masālik wa'l-Mamālik* [道里邦國志], translated and commented on by Song Xian 宋峴 (Beijing: Zhonghua shuju, 1991), pp. 63–74.

33. G.F. Hourani, *Arab Seafaring in the Indian Ocean in Ancient and Early Medieval Times* (Princeton: Princeton University Press, 1995), pp. 61–79; Ma Jianchun 馬建春, "Tangchao yu Dashi de haishang jiaotong" 唐朝與大食的海上交通 [The Maritime Communications Between China and Arabia], in his *Dashi, Xiyu yu gudai Zhongguo* 大食、西域與古代中國 [Arabia, the Western Region and Ancient China], (Shanghai: Shanghai guji chubanshe, 2008), pp. 3–24.

34. *Wenyuan Yinghua* 文苑英華 (Blossoms and Flowers from the Garden of Literature), vol. 613.

35. Li Ao 李翺, Proofreader, Director of the Ministry of Rites, Duke of the Eastern Sea, Account of Conduct 檢校禮部尚書東海公, *Wenyuan Yinghua*, vol. 976.

36. Abdullah Ma Wenkuan 阿卜杜拉·馬文寬, *Yisilan shijie wenwu zai Zhongguo de faxian yu yanjiu* 伊斯蘭世界文物在中國的發現與研究 [The Discovery of and Research on the Islamic Cultural Relics Found in China], (Beijing: Religion and Culture Press, 2006), pp. 1–26.

11

THE PEACOCK'S GALLBLADDER
An Example of Tibetan Influence in
Late Imperial China

Rebecca Shuang Fu and Xiang Wan

In the past decades, we have witnessed academic articles and monographs published at an astonishing rate on the cultural interactions between Tibet and China. These studies have tended to focus on the religious ideas and practices influencing the elite class, namely the Tibetan Buddhism that interested the rulers of the Yuan, Ming, and Qing dynasties. Tibetan influence on the popular culture of the Chinese has been largely ignored. This is partly because the Tibetans have never been rulers of the East Asian Heartland. Moreover, for geographic and historical reasons, Tibet was — until the 1950s — a mystical and hermetically enclosed society in the Chinese imagination. It has consequently been believed that Tibetan culture could not have any direct or lasting effect on Chinese society during the imperial period.

This study aims to challenge these assumptions, and to rethink Sino-Tibetan cultural communications from a different perspective. We begin with a survey of the surviving textual records on the usage of the peacock's gallbladder and the image of the peacock, revealing several clues for further exploration. Following these clues, we close in on the origin of the peacock's gallbladder as a lethal poison in the Tibetan culture of medicine and pharmacy. We examine the introduction of Tibetan medicine to China under the Mongol rule, and its tremendous impact on the Mongol elites in the second section of this paper, and focus on the medicinal usage of the peacock's gallbladder recorded in two major works of Tibetan materia medica, namely the *rGyud-bZhi* and the *Shel gong shel phreng*, in the third section. Lastly, we discuss the possible Buddhist influence on the reception of the peacock in Tibetan tradition.

The Peacock's Gallbladder and the Peacock in the Chinese Tradition

A pharmacologist would point out that the "peacock's gallbladder", at least as a poison, simply does not exist: like the gallbladders of many other birds, it is in no sense toxic. Why, then, did this story, so at odds with any kind of fact, survive?

What is the peacock's gallbladder? Can we associate the poisonous mythical "peacock's gallbladder" with the actual gallbladder of a peacock? Alternatively, is the item in question something possessing a fancy name but actually having nothing to do with the peacock? An examination of the history of the myth, especially regarding the cultures that have accepted it, may help answer these questions.

The modern *locus classicus* of this myth is Guo Moruo's 郭沫若 (1892–1978) famous historical play entitled *The Peacock's Gallbladder* (1942). It takes place in Yunnan 雲南, the territory of the former Dali 大理 Kingdom (937–1254), in the late Yuan (1275–1368). In this story, the Prince of Liang 梁王 marries off his beautiful daughter, Princess Agai 阿蓋 to Duan Gong 段功, the governor of Dali, as a reward for his support in quelling a rebellion. Later, Liang asks Agai to poison her husband with a peacock's gallbladder, so that he can seize Duan's power. Agai rejects her father's order but keeps the poison. Duan is nevertheless assassinated by the Prince, and, as a result, Princess Agai commits suicide by swallowing the peacock's gallbladder originally intended for her husband.[1] It is, unsurprisingly, impossible to prove the authenticity of this story, though the figures involved, and background have, as it appears, some sort of basis in history.

The myth of the peacock's gallbladder, the lethal poison in the story, was not invented by Guo but was actually borrowed from pre-existing historical records. The earliest identification of this object as a poison dates to the Ming (1368–1644). In literary collections such as *Yaoshan tang waiji* 堯山堂外紀 (Unofficial Records from the Hall of Yaoshan), *Yanjiao jiwen* 炎徼紀聞 (Notes of What is Heard in the Torrid Frontier), *Dian zaiji* 滇載記 (Notes Written down in Dian), and Feng Menglong's 馮夢龍 (1574–1646) *Qing shi* 情史 (History of Love), the legend of the peacock's gallbladder was repeatedly invoked.[2] This anecdote was also recorded in the *Xin Yuan shi* 新元史 (New History of the Yuan), compiled in 1920.[3] Meanwhile, there were some other sources from the Ming onwards, claiming this toxicity. For example, *Yangyi zhai shihua* 養一齋詩話 (Notes on Poetry from Yangyi Studio), a Qing dynasty literary collection, records two lines by the famous Ming littérateur Wang Shizhen 王世貞 (1526–90), which read, "Although the peacock is venomous, [the beauty of] the lines and patterns [of its feathers] cannot be concealed" (孔雀雖有毒, 不能掩文章).[4] Also, the compiler of the *Qingbai leichao* 清稗類鈔 (Classified Records of the Trivia of the Qing) Xu Ke 徐珂 (1869–1928), documented the idea that the blood of the peacock was severely poisonous. A similar record can also be seen in the *Mao yuan* 貓苑 (Cat Garden) by Huang Han 黃漢 (fl. 1851–61).

A parallel to this literary tradition is the medical tradition represented by the *Bencao gangmu* 本草綱目 (Compendium of Materia Medica) compiled by Li Shizhen 李時珍 (1518–93), in which the blood, dried flesh, and dung of the peacock are listed as medicines. In the forty-ninth volume of the *Bencao gangmu*, however, it claims that the blood, gallbladder, and tail feathers of the peacock are all poisonous.[5] The source of this passage is from the *Ji Yue jiji* 冀越集記 (Collected Notes from Ji to Yue) by Xiong Taigu 熊太古 (fl. 1335) in the Yuan dynasty, who speculated that the peacock's toxicity came from its intercourse with the snake, a widespread idea.[6]

The peacock's gallbladder, as a single item, is rarely found in the pre-Yuan sources. One text addressing this object is a short passage from the *Mohe sengqi lü* 摩訶僧祇律 (*Mahāsāṃghika-vinaya*; Disciplines of the Great Sangha), which was translated in the Eastern Jin dynasty (317–420) by the Indian monk Buddhabhadra 佛陀跋陀羅 (359–429) and the Chinese monk Faxian 法顯 (337–422). This passage indicates that the peacock's gallbladder could be used together with verdigris as dyes for tattooing.[7] This usage is also invoked in *Youyang zazu* 酉陽雜俎 (Miscellany from Youyang), an encyclopedic collection compiled by Duan Chengshi 段成式 (803–863) in the Tang (618–907).[8] However, since the peacock's gallbladder was thought to be a dye for tattooing, we may surmise that it was at that point considered harmless.

Now we can answer the first question raised at the beginning of this section. In the materials listed above, the peacock's gallbladder was associated with the measure words "*ju* 具" and "*fu* 付", both of which are used for small solids, like a gallbladder; and some records suggest that the peacock's gallbladder was something soaked in alcohol. It seems to have been drunk in the same way as the snake's gallbladder, which is to say, processed into a medicinal liquor. Furthermore, *Bencao gangmu* explicitly associates the "peacock's gallbladder" with the peacock bird. These evidence make it very clear that the "*kongque dan*" under discussion should be understood in its literal meaning, which is an internal organ of the peacock bird.

The emergence of the peacock's gallbladder as a poison was sudden, completely overturning the image and high value placed on the peacock in the Chinese tradition. Contrary to the claim that "the peacock is venomous", ever since the sources in the Han dynasty, the peacock had not been associated with toxicity, but rather viewed as an agent of *detoxification*. It is believed, according to extant materials, that this species of bird was introduced to China through the Silk Road during the Han (206 BC–AD 220).[9] The mention of these birds can be easily found in *Han shu* 漢書 (History of the Western Han), *Xu Han shu* 續漢書 (A Sequel to the History of the Western Han), and *Han ji* 漢紀 (Annals of the Han). According to Edward H. Schafer, these "peacocks" in Han chronicles were all from the west of China, probably originating in Kashmir, Anxi 安息 (Parthia) or Tiaozhi 條支 (Antiochia), and all of them were Indian peafowls (*Pavo cristatus*). Later on, along with the territorial expansion of the Chinese empire, peacocks began to be imported to China from its southern neighbours. It is not until the Three Kingdoms period (220–265) that the green peafowls (*Pavo muticus*) of Indochina were known to the Chinese. It is recorded in both *Sanguo zhi* 三國志 (Record of the Three Kingdoms) and *Jin shu* 晉書 (History of the Jin) that the State of Wu once dispatched an envoy to Jiaozhi 交阯 (present-day northern Vietnam) and imported three thousand peacocks from there.[10] However, for most Chinese during that time, this exotic species was still not easily accessible and consequently sparked plenty of imagination. For example, in the famous long poem "Kongque dongnan fei" 孔雀東南飛 (Peacocks Flying to the Southeast), which is believed to have been composed between the third and the sixth centuries,[11] the peacock is depicted as extremely loyal to its mate. It says, in this poem, that the male and female peacocks pair off and fly around together, as mandarin ducks normally behave. This account does not agree with the actual habits of this bird, who definitely has more than one mate in its life and usually flies alone. This contrary-to-fact description reveals that the Chinese of that period did not know much about this exotic species.

Later, during the Tang, the peacock became one of the major tributes to the imperial court from Luozhou 羅州 (present-day Huazhou 化州 in Guangdong province). At that time, the peacock was named *Yue niao* 越鳥 (bird of Yue) and *nan ke* 南客 (visitor from the south), both indicating its exotic provenance.[12] Documents compiled in the early Northern Song (960–1127), such as the *Taiping yulan* 太平御覽 (Imperially Reviewed Encyclopedia of the Taiping Era) and the *Taiping guangji* 太平廣記 (Extensive Gleanings of the Taiping Era), both recount a queer custom of people in southern lands, as well as the marvellous effects of the peacock. It says that the people in Jiaozhi hunted peacocks for food and were especially fond of what we might think of as "peacock jerky". They also raised domestic peacocks, whom they used as bait to capture wild ones. On another occasion in the *Taiping guangji*, it mentions that the peacock in the mountainous areas of Luozhou was hunted and consumed by the locals, and that "… it tastes like the meat of goose and can antidote various poisons. If one eats its flesh, his disease, which may not be cured by any other medicine, will be cured. Its blood and head can also be used to treat severe poisoning."[13] This is one of the earliest account in extant Chinese sources stating that the peacock is edible, and also the first associating this bird with medicinal use. However, in the Chinese tradition, no one, in fact, would have dared to hunt or eat these birds symbolizing power and wealth, and which were exclusively owned by the imperial house and the ruling elite.

Another way that ancient Chinese knew about the peacock was through the voluminous Buddhist works translated into Chinese beginning in the end of the Eastern Han dynasty (25–220). The image of the peacock was usually associated with medical practices and detoxifying ceremonies. According to the *Xiuxing benqi jing* 修行本起經 (*Cārya–nidāna*; Sutra of the Buddha's Origins; also written *Suxing benqi jing* 宿行本起經), which was translated by Zhu Dali 竺大力 and Kang Mengxiang 康孟詳 during late Eastern Han, the peacocks do not fear venomous snakes at all and even eat them.[14] In the Three Kingdoms period, the famous translator-monk Kang Senghui 康僧會 (d. 280) introduced the divine power of the Peacock King to the Chinese. In the *Liuduji jing* 六度集經 (*Ṣaṭ-pāramitā-saṃgraha*; Sutra on the Collection of the Six Perfections) and the *Jiu Zapiyu jing* 舊雜譬喻經 (The Old Sutra on Various Metaphors), which were translated during his stay in Wu, a story, which became widely known in later times, is repeatedly mentioned: in one of his former lives, the Bodhisattva was a Peacock King, who always showed mercy for people. His flesh could be used as medicine, and even water touched by him could heal the sick immediately. In the *Kongque wang zhou jing* 孔雀王咒經 (*Mahāmāyūrīvidyārājñī*; Sutra on the Peacock King's Incantations), which was translated during the Liang dynasty (502–557), and also its Tang dynasty translated version, there is a story telling how the Buddha taught his followers to detoxify snake poison via the power of the Peacock King (or the Peacock Queen in the Tang dynasty version). In addition to these Chinese Buddhist texts, records on the curing effects of peacock feathers can also be found in the canonical works of the Japanese Shingon Buddhist school.[15]

To summarize, then, in the Chinese tradition, the peacock was an exotic tribute for the imperial court from southern neighbouring states. Because of its special living conditions, it was not well known by the Chinese people until modern times, and to this day has not been widely bred in northern China. In surviving Chinese sources, this bird has always been depicted as a mysterious exotic species. Except for viewing by the elite, its only use seems to have been its highly decorative feathers. In addition to this function, in the documents from overseas and the frontiers (mainly Chinese Buddhist literature), we see that the peacock was used as a medication for healing patients, detoxifying poisonous substances, and even driving out evil spirits.

It is clear, then, that neither the peacock itself, nor any part of its body was thought of as poisonous. Why was the peacock's gallbladder later singled out as a poisonous item? Why did the reception of this bird's gallbladder as a deadly poison originate from the Yuan dynasty? Was the Mongol background of the Prince of Liang, mentioned in the legend of the peacock's gallbladder, relevant to the history of its reception? The above examination of surviving textual records provides a clue to solve these puzzles — in Chinese reception, both the image of the peacock and this bird's gallbladder have always been associated with exotic cultures and intercultural communications; thus, we must cast our eyes at civilizations who had social, commercial, and cultural contacts and exchanges with imperial China, especially its southern and western neighbours, familiar with the peacock, from whom and through whom the peacock was introduced to China.

The Introduction of Tibetan Medicine and Pharmacology into the Mongol Imperial Court

As we have seen, the idea of the peacock's gallbladder as a poison penetrated into Chinese culture during the Yuan dynasty, a period generally seen as "one of great cultural vitality".[16] During the Mongol conquest, elements of vibrant, multifaceted, and cosmopolitan civilizations are introduced to China on such an unprecedented scale that it becomes difficult to define the exact origin/origins of the peacock's poisonous gallbladder. Nevertheless, it seems that the search can be greatly simplified for the following reasons:

First, the usage of the peacock's gallbladder as either poison or medicine, which has been kept on record, directs our search at the development and change in the practice of medicine and pharmacology under Mongol rule;

Second, the notorious policy of racial segregation during the Yuan, as well as the well-documented history of the conquered Chinese still tenaciously clinging to their own traditions, rules out the possibility that the target which we are looking for lies in native Chinese civilization.

Lastly, the story of "The Peacock's Gallbladder" which we have discussed in the previous part is the earliest depiction of this item as acutely toxic, and the Mongol prince thereby becomes the first poisoner who employs its toxin on record. This leads to the conjecture that the peacock's gallbladder may have been a poison known to the Mongol elites. However, if this is true, given the late development of Mongolian medicine and the fact that the peacock was not a common bird to the northern-grassland-origin Mongols, where, then, did the Mongol elite learn about this item?

Now, all of the clues point to the Tibetan civilization, which exerted a remarkable impact on the Mongol elites in medical and pharmaceutical sciences. It has been well accepted that Tibetan Buddhism had a great influence on the Mongol elites. Most non-Chinese rulers soon became more or less Sinicized after they conquered China; the Mongols, in contrast, differing from any other non-Chinese conqueror, were instead, to some extent, "Tibetanized". The Mongol imperial house was converted to Tibetan Buddhism at the beginning of the Yuan dynasty, with the majority of the elites following them. From 1270, when Kublai Khan (r. 1260–94) appointed the Tibetan monk 'Phags-pa (1235–80) as the "Imperial Advisor", till the collapse of the empire, fourteen eminent Tibetan monks had been granted this title.[17] Under the influences of these Tibetan "Imperial Advisors", Tantric Buddhism, as well as other Tibetan cultural elements, permeated every facet of the life of the Mongol elite. A striking example is the adoption of the 'Phags-pa script system, which was invented by the first Imperial Advisor 'Phags-pa.[18] It is under these circumstances that Tibetan medicine began to impact the life of Mongol elites. As Walther Hessig discusses, it seems that Tibetan medicine and Tantric sorcery were considered by the Mongol elites to be far more efficient in medical practice than the Mongol shamans' prayers.[19] It has long been acknowledged that the Tibetan Buddhist leaders converted the Mongol conquerors primarily through "the influence of Tibetan medicine and the powerful effects of Tantric magic".[20] According to extant materials, the first follower of Tibetan Buddhism among the Mongol elites is Godan Khan (1206–51), a grandson of Genghis Khan (d. 1227).

In 1240, Godan dispatched an army to Tibet, and soon afterwards wrote a letter to summon the great master Sa-skya paṇḍita (1182–51),[21] who went north without delay with his nephew 'Phags-pa, and arrived at Liangzhou 涼州, where he met Godan in 1246. Godan was deeply impressed by Sa-skya paṇḍita, not only because of his charisma and mastery of Buddhist canons, but also because he had successfully cured his disease. This event is recorded in both the Mongolian history *Erdeniin Tobchi* (The Origin of the Mongols; *Menggu yuanliu* 蒙古源流) and the famous Tibetan history *Bod-kyi deb-ther dpyid-kyi rgyal-mo'i glu-dbyang* (Records of Tibetan Kings and Officials; *Xizang wangchen ji* 西藏王臣記), which were both compiled in the seventeenth century. It mentions in the *Erdeniin Tobchi* that, "In the Dingwei year when Sa-skya paṇḍita was sixty-six years old, he met the Khan (Godan). Then he moulded a statue of the Simhanada Avalokiteshvara (or Bodhisattva Avalokiteshvara of the Lion's Roar), and performed for the Khan the Abhisheka, a Buddhist prayer ceremony, because of which, the Khan immediately recovered, and all became delighted."[22] This event is recounted with several plot variances in the *Bod-kyi deb-ther dpyid-kyi rgyal-mo'i glu-dbyang*. This version of story exaggerates the leechcraft of Sa-skya paṇḍita by claiming that he not only cured Prince Godan, but also successfully exerted his magic healing power on a Mongol emperor in the imperial capital of Yuan.[23]

Curing patients during the process of preaching seems to have been a tradition among the monks of the Sakya Buddhist school, many accounts of whose medicinal practices in the Mongol court can be found on record. For example, it says that Dam-pa (1230–1303), also an Imperial Advisor, during his stay at Chaozhou 潮州, cured the severe illness of a Mongol general's wife by attaching his prayer beads onto her body. He also cured the Mongol Emperor Chengzong 成宗 (Temür Khan, r. 1294–1307) via a prayer ceremony.[24]

These examples show that the Mongol elites believed in the magical effect of Tibetan medicine, though the healing rituals seem to have been always shrouded in mystery. In a closed environment, in the process of struggling in arduous living conditions, ancient Tibetans had accumulated abundant medical knowledge and formed a very special medicinal tradition.[25] Although due to the introduction of Buddhism and intermarriage with the Tang Empire in the seventh century, Tibetan medicine was to some extent impacted by both Indian and Chinese medicinal traditions, it has always been up to the present day a highly independent system. Moreover, thanks to the invention of the Tibetan script system in the seventh century, the ancient Tibetan medical system has been well documented and widely circulated. Both the *sMan-dpyad Zla-ba'i rGyal-po* (The Lunar King of Medicine; *Yuewang yaozhen* 月王藥診, comp. in seventh century), and the *rGyud-bZhi* (The Four Medical Tantras; *Sibu yidian* 四部醫典, comp. in eighth century) have been well preserved to this day and translated into various languages. Also, in the Dunhuang documents, some manuscripts on Tibetan medicine, probably recorded in the ninth to tenth centuries (such as S. 756, P. 127, and P. 1044), have also survived in fragments. All these surviving Tibetan medicinal documents make it possible for us to trace the history of the reception of the peacock's gallbladder.

It must be mentioned that, in addition to Tibetan medicine, another medical tradition also had great influence in the Yuan dynasty. It is Muslim medicine, also called the Huihui 回回 medical tradition.[26] The term "Huihui" refers to various ethnic groups in an area stretching from Western and Central Asia to northwestern China. Since Muslim medicine had absorbed elements of the medical traditions of the Egyptians, Indians, Byzantines, and Chinese, it was at that time considered one of the leading medical schools. Many Muslim physicians served in the Mongol Imperial Academy of Medicine; the academy was even once presided over by a Syrian physician, Ngai-Sie 愛薛 (1227–1308).[27] There are also surviving records on Muslim physicians curing Chinese commoners in the Yuan.[28] Unfortunately, the medical records and prescriptions by these physicians were very badly recorded and preserved.

Other works on exotic medicines, such as the *Haiyao bencao* 海藥本草 (Herbal Medicine from Overseas), compiled by Li Xun 李珣 (*c*.855–930), of Persian descent, and the *Hu bencao* 胡本草 (Non-Chinese Herbal Medicine), also completed during the Tang, might have preserved some accounts of Muslim physicians and their medical practices. However, on the one hand, they can by no means reflect the information of the Yuan dynasty;[29] on the other hand, both works had also long been lost. Only some fragmentary manuscripts of the *Huihui yaofang* 回回藥方 (Muslim Prescriptions), a Yuan dynasty collection of Muslim prescriptions written down in Chinese, were preserved to this day. In its modern annotated version, the *Huihui yaofang kaoshi* 回回藥方考釋 (compiled by Song Xian 宋峴), however, there is no entry addressing the peacock, not to mention its gallbladder. Thus, we should concentrate on Tibetan civilization, the only remaining possible source.

The Records on the Peacock's Gallbladder and the Peacock in Tibetan Medical, Pharmacological, and Buddhist Documents

The records on the Tibetan gurus' medical practices in extant sources mainly focus on the details and results of their healing rituals, and neither their therapeutic procedures nor prescriptions are well documented. Fortunately, however, several works of ancient Tibetan materia medica have been preserved to the present day, thus providing us with invaluable traces.

The medical book *rGyud-bZhi* (The Four Medical Tantras) provides the most evidence for this study. It is believed to have been compiled by Tibetan physicians represented by the famous g.Yu-thog Yon-tan mGon-po the Elder (708–833) in the second half of the eighth century, and has been considered to be a parallel to the *Huangdi neijing* 黃帝內經 (Inner Canon of the Yellow Emperor) in the Chinese tradition. After its initial compilation, generations of Tibetan medical experts continuously added amendments and supplements to it. In the twelfth century, g.Yu-thog Yon-tan mGon-po the Younger (1126–1202), and his students, codified prescriptions from its original version surviving to their time, and added new entries from some other sources of materia medica.[30] It was reorganized and further revised during the reigns of the fifth Dalai Lama (r. 1642–82) and the thirteenth Dalai Lama (r. 1879–1933).

In contrast to the tradition of the Chinese who considered the peacock to be a symbol of power, never to be killed for food, in the Tibetan tradition, the peacock has been generally a useful food supply since ancient times. For example, in Chapter Sixteen of the *rGyud-bZhi*, titled

"Knowledge of Food and Drink", it is mentioned that, "…there are eight sources of animal meat, belonging to the aquatic, terrestrial, and amphibious categories. The peacock, the snowcock, the partridge, the jackdaw, and the mountain pheasant all belong to the sub-category of clawed birds."[31] It seems that in Tibetan tradition, the peacock was not only edible, but also to be a source of medications. In the prologue of the *rGyud-bZhi*, it mentions that the peacock, like many other animals, is for medicine supply:

> In the Himalayas, there grow saffron crocuses everywhere, whose scent lingers in the air. All kinds of minerals and salts can be found on the rocky hillside. In the mountains rich of medicinal herbs, peacocks, jivajivas, and parrots emit musical sounds. At the foot of the mountains, there are all kinds of animals for medicine supply, such as elephants, bears, and musk deers. In a word, [the Himalayas] produce all the medications; they also embellish the mountains, presenting a splendid view.
>
> [馬拉亞] 山中到處红花满坡, 香氣繚繞, 所有山崖上礦物類盐碱類無所不全; 藥草山上孔雀, 共命鳥, 鸚鵡等發出悅耳的叫聲. 山下大象, 熊, 麝等身具妙藥的畜類也十分齊全. 總之, 那裡諸藥無所不產, 無所不全, 並以此為飾, 蔚為壯觀.[32]

Comments about the medicinal effects of the peacock can be found in different chapters of the *rGyud-bZhi*. According to this medical book, many body parts of the peacock, such as its flesh and feathers, can be used for medicinal purposes. For example, it says that "the peacock's plumes and feathers can facilitate the evacuation of empyema",[33] "its flesh can help relieve internal fever and be used for pink eye treatment",[34] and also "cure eye diseases and muteness".[35] If the peacock's flesh is combined with other medicines, it may have effects such as clearing and draining [internal fever]: "…the prescription is the combination of *radix euphorbiae lantu*, *radix paeoniae rubrathe*, peacock's flesh, and …; it is made into balls or powder for clearing and draining."[36] In the *rGyud-bZhi*, the peacock's gallbladder is also used for medicinal purposes. Differing from the peacock's flesh, however, its gallbladder is never mentioned as to be taken singly — it must be mixed with certain kinds of herbs or minerals to achieve the effect of treatment. The prescriptions containing the peacock gallbladder from the *rGyud-bZhi* are as follows:

Prescription One:
Combine aconite, black incense, and the peacock's gallbladder altogether.
By applying it to the affected part or take it orally, the symptoms of leprosy
will be relieved.

烏頭黑香孔雀膽共配,
塗或內服癩病得解除.[37]

Prescription Two:
[The prescription] is the combination of a human gallbladder, as well the
gallbladders of a bear, a monkey, a pig, a parrot and a peacock,
...
the bark of a golden cypress, borax, white mustard seeds,
faeces togopteri, and etc. It should be taken orally with cold snow water.

人熊猴豬鸚鵡孔雀膽,
...
黃柏皮與硼砂白芥子,
五靈脂等清涼雪水服.[38]

Prescription Three:
The next prescription is the combination of a bear's gallbladder, a peacock's
gallbladder, and other bitter gallbladders, *ramulus uncariae, fructus chebulae,*
the flesh of a frog, a snake, and a hedgehog, plus their livers, *calculus bovis,*
and sandalwood,
...
also *flos farfarae* etc. It should be taken orally with white sugar.

又方熊與孔雀諸苦膽,
鉤藤訶子蛙蛇刺猬肉,
及其肝膽牛黃與檀香,
...
款冬花等和以白糖服.[39]

Prescription Four:
This prescription is the combination of a human gallbladder, the gallbladders
of a bear and a peacock, *radix phytolaccae, radix curcumae,* the white and
purple *ramulus uncariae,* plus three types of aconites, *drynaria baronii,* and
crystal salt. It should be taken with snow water at dawn. This prescription is to
treat both chills and fevers, but should not be adopted if [the patient] vomits.

又方人膽熊膽孔雀膽,
商陸郁金紫白二鉤藤,
三種烏頭申姜光明鹽,
黎明一份雪水送內服,
此方寒熱共治吐則忌.[40]

Prescription Five:
Here is another prescription — the combination of the gallbladders of a bear, an elephant, and a peacock. Increase the amount of these gallbladders and the snake flesh progressively and keep them equal in amount,

...

It should be taken with the soup of *faeces togopteri* and shorea. It is considered to be remarkable especially for curing body deficiencies and muscular exhaustion.

又方熊膽象膽孔雀膽，
遞增諸膽蛇肉各等分，

...

靈脂娑羅木湯送內服，
特別體劣肌竭病稱著.[41]

Prescription Six:
Combine the peacock's gallbladder and thorns of the vervains, and double the amount of musks and *drynaria baronii* in proper order. Also, add a garlic bulb, some cheese mould, fish, a human gallbladder, and a bear's gallbladder. Take the dung ball of an eight-year-old child as the usher. Put the aforementioned medicines together and take it orally at once.

孔雀膽與荊棘萬能草，
麝香申姜依次倍增量，
蒜頭酪銹魚與人熊膽，
八齡童便為丸投之宜，
上述諸藥聚諸一次收.[42]

Interestingly, despite the fact that most body parts and inner organs of the peacock can be used for medicinal purposes, its egg seems to be harmful to the human body. The *rGyud-bZhi* mentions a method of detoxifying the poison of the peacock's egg, which recommends that the gallbladder of a motley chicken, or the egg of either a hoopoe or a skylark, can be used to treat the peacock's egg poisoning.[43] Also, it seems that the peacock's flesh can be an ingredient of some poisons if it is combined with certain medicinal materials. For example, in a part of the *rGyud-bZhi* addressing poisoning treatment, it introduces a special method of detoxification, namely "counteracting one toxin with another". The brief introduction is followed with several prescriptions as examples. One of them containing the ingredient of the peacock's flesh reads as follows: "... poisoning should be treated with poisons, ... like the combination of the chicken's liver, the peacock's flesh, and Faeces Trogopterori…" (… 毒癥當用毒為治, … 雞肝孔雀肉友五靈脂 …).[44]

The *Shel gong shel phreng* (Crystal Pearl Materia Medica), another Tibetan medical canon, which was compiled in the nineteenth century, seems to agree with the *rGyud-bZhi* on the peacock's potential toxicity — it also claims that this bird's eggs are absolute a posion; its flesh is also poisonous when being taken singly. For instance, in the part focusing on the medicinal effects of various gallbladders, it mentions that "the gallbladder of a chicken with red and white dotted feathers" can be used to treat the peacock's egg poisoning.[45] In the part discussing the medicinal effects of animal flesh, it suggests that "the peacock's flesh helps cure gallbladder diseases and detoxify the human body. However, its flesh must be combined with other detoxifying medicines and cannot be for oral administration without professional instructions" (孔雀肉治膽病, 治中毒病; 孔雀肉要與解毒藥物相配, 不可任意內服).[46]

The above examination of the *rGyud-bZhi* and the *Shel gong shel phreng* reveals a common opinion on the effects of the peacock bird in traditional Tibetan materia medica — certain body parts and inner organs of this bird, despite their potential therapeutic function when being combined with certain types of medicines properly, are basically poisonous when taken alone. Moreover, in the two authorities of Tibetan medical science which we have examined, the peacock's gallbladder can only be found in compound prescriptions for therapeutic purposes. Both clues lead us to a natural and reasonable conjecture — the peacock's gallbladder is a poison when being taken singly in Tibetan medical tradition, though this seems to have never been explicitly said.

The Image of the Peacock in Tibetan Buddhism

Although the *rGyud-bZhi* is believed to have been compiled in the eighth century, it has so far experienced several massive modifications. Since its early versions have been barely preserved, it seems impossible to affirm whether the prescriptions mentioning the toxicity of the peacock, which we have examined, had been circulated in the pre-Yuan period. Also, given that the *Shel gong shel phreng* was compiled much later, it could by no means have impacted the Mongol elites in the Yuan dynasty. In other words, although we have found textual records on the poisonous peacock's gallbladder in early Tibetan medical works, it is still far-fetched to conclude that they are the origin of the Chinese reception of this mysterious object. Moreover, given the fact that peacocks cannot survive in a cold climate, it is very difficult to believe that the Tibetan medical records on this species are based on realistic observation. In other words, ancient Tibetans were actually no more familiar with the imported birds than the Chinese. Their knowledge of the peacock must, therefore, have been derived from intercultural communications.

Among the foreign civilizations that have greatly impacted Tibet, the Buddhist canons from South Asia and Southeast Asia must be the first to be taken into account. It is well accepted that the Tibetan medical tradition, as well as some influential works of materia medica represented by the *rGyud-bZhi*, were under the deep influence of Buddhism. Thus, it would be impossible to conduct an in-depth exploration of issues on Tibetan materia medica without taking its Buddhist background into consideration. Moreover, an examination of the exotic Buddhist ideas from South and Southeast Asia, the peacock's natural habitat, may also help provide clues as to how the image of the peacock was imported into Tibetan culture.

Two Tibetan Buddhist texts relevant to the peacock, which are the *mTshon cha 'khor lo* (The Wheel-Weapon; hereafter, *WW*) and the *rMa bya dug 'joms* (The Poison-Destroying Peacock; hereafter, *PDP*), shed fresh light for this study. The two texts are early examples of the indigenous Tibetan religious literary genre known as *lojong* (*blo sbyong*), or mind training. This class of literature developed in the Kadampa (*bka'gdams pa*) school, which has been regarded as the earliest of the organized Tibetan Buddhist denominations. The original texts, authors, and translators of the two works are all unknown to modern researchers, and they seem not to be among the earliest Tibetan Buddhist canons. However, given the fact that the school was established in 1057,[47] as well as that both works were first found in the early- to mid-fifteenth century anthology of mind-training texts, the *bLo sbyong glegs bam* (The Book of Mind Training), it is almost certain that these canons were translated between the eleventh century and the first half of the fifteenth century.

This time period is an important era for the transmission of the *rGyud-bZhi* and the development of Tibetan medicine.

The two texts both employ the trope stating that, it is in the same way as the peacock dwells in a jungle full of virulent poisons, nurtures itself with poison, and develops beautiful feathers, that a Buddhist practice based on mental poisons (anger, selfishness, desire, etc.), namely, the method of enlightenment, is processed. The conception conveyed by this practice tallies with the statements on the peacock's toxicity in the two works of Tibetan materia medica which we have examined. Differing from the peacock in the Pāli or East Asian Buddhist traditions, the peacock in the *WW* and the *PDP* does not eat snakes or detoxify snake venoms; instead it wanders in a jungle of virulent poisons and eats such poisonous plants as aconite. The *WW* begins with a scene in which peacocks, while roaming through the jungle, thrive on its virulent essence. It reads as follows:

> When the peacocks roam the jungle of virulent poison,
> The flocks take no delight in gardens of medicinal plants, no matter how beautiful they may be, for peacocks thrive on the essence of virulent poison.[48]

In the commentary on the modern translated version of this text, the translator points out that the "virulent poison" was simply a literal meaning in the translation, because of its vividness and its accurate conveying of the sense. In fact, in the original text this word is *btsan-dug*, which is universally understood as a metonym for black aconite (*bong nga nag po*).[49] Aconite is a highly toxic plant best known in the West under the name of "wolfbane".[50] As Terry Clifford claims, "…it [aconite] is an important ingredient in traditional Asian medicine and is used in Tibetan medicine, mixed with other ingredients, as a treatment for, among other ailments, mental illness."[51] This proves that aconite was generally believed to be an acute poison in the Tibetan tradition, and it is by such a poison that the peacock nurtures its beauty, as a passage of the *WW* says:

> Just as the pattern of colors in a peacock's feather is due to poison, so may the afflictions be transformed into the aids to enlightenment by my taking on the physical, verbal, and mental deeds of other living beings, past, present, and future.[52]

The *PDP* reiterates this idea as follows:

Thus, the entire mass of poisons should be experienced as if it were an illusion, untrue, something that appears but is empty. Tie up the poisons into the single bond of "I" and "mine," and, like a peacock, take it as nourishment.[53]

In both verses above, the peacock does not fear the poison, but instead enjoys the poisonous plant; the growth of its attractive feathers is also catalyzed by the poison. This echoes one passage from the part of "Food Taboo" in the *rGyud-bZhi*, which reads:

Both the color and taste of poisonous food are abnormal.
If it is burned, there will be smoke, like the throat of the peacock.
Flames spin and rise, and sparks fly.
If crows see it, they will be clamorous, while peacocks will be excited;
If a dog eats it, its abdomen will be hot, and then it will vomit.[54]

It clearly states in the above passage that the burning of poisonous food may resuscitate both crows and peacocks. However, this does not indicate that the peacock is naturally compatible with the virulent poison. As a simile about the peacock and heroes (generally, Bodhisattvas) in the *PDP* shows, the various hardships undergone by the heroes are made at the risk of their own lives, like that of the peacock:

Therefore, this is the heroes' happy way of life: to endure hardship come what may, even at the risk of one's own life. This is the heroes' actual practice: part one of *The Elixir Made from Poison*.[55]

It is beyond the scope of this study to provide a complete survey of the images of the peacock in Tibetan Buddhism. What is more, though it is tempting, it still needs more evidence and a further examination to draw the conclusion that the opinions on the peacock in Tibetan medical tradition is derived from the *WW* and the *PDP*, the two texts we have examined. Nevertheless, we have proved that there is an implication in such texts that the peacock is poisonous, a tradition possibly originating from an era earlier than the *WW* and the *PDP*. In a word, the symbol of the "poisonous peacock" in Tibetan medical tradition resonates with its Buddhist background; the tradition of the "poisonous peacock" can be probably traced back to an era long before the Yuan dynasty.

Conclusion

By now, through an extensive examination of extant textual sources, we have brought forward a "Tibetan-origin hypothesis" for "the peacock's gallbladder", as an allegedly lethal poison. Actually, the influence of the *rGyud-bZhi* and Tibetan medicine did not reach most regions of the Mongolian territory until a relatively late period. The Gelug school of Tibetan Buddhism was introduced extensively into Mongolian territory along with the Tibetan medical tradition in the sixteenth century, when the *rGyud-bZhi* finally entered Mongolian society and began to circulate among common people. Around the eighteenth century, this work was translated into Mongolian.[56] However, its influence on the Mongol elites happened much earlier, even before the establishment of the Mongol Empire.

In previous sections, we have demonstrated how the concept of "the peacock's gallbladder" as a poison reached China through the dissemination of Tibetan medicine and Buddhism in the Mongol imperial court and among the elites. How, then, did this concept enter the realm of recognition of the Chinese people? Extant historical sources lead to a possible theory concerning the interactions between the Mongol elites and Chinese physicians in the imperial court. On the one hand, in the Yuan dynasty, the cultural exchanges among different ethnic groups were unprecedentedly active. As is well known, Tibetan Buddhism greatly influenced the Mongol imperial court, and played a pivotal role in political life, remaining unsurpassed up to Ming and Qing.[57] Under these circumstances, the East Asian Heartland and Tibet, both under Mongol rule, naturally communicated with each other much more frequently than before. The Mongol rulers, to some extent, also helped create a medium for cross-cultural exchanges. As the highest caste of the empire, the Mongol imperial house and social elites, unsurprisingly, possessed the ability to disseminate the cultural information and practices that had been received and inherited from the Tibetans. The aforementioned famous story "Princess Agai and the Peacock's Gallbladder" may not be a pure fabrication; instead, it reveals a highly possible reality — the legend of the fatal peacock's gallbladder spread among the Mongol elites, who were under the powerful influence of the Tibetan medical tradition. The transmission of this story, in turn, lodges the idea of the mystical poison "peacock's gallbladder" in the public mind of Chinese people.

On the other hand, during the Yuan dynasty when the subjects of the Mongols were racially segregated, Chinese physicians serving in the court may have played an unusual role in intercultural exchanges. Valerie Hansen mentions these potential cultural disseminators in her book:

> The Mongols' decision to suspend the civil service examination had the greatest effect on educated Chinese families. . . Under the Mongols, the sons of many officials turned to the study of medicine instead ... If very successful, one could even be appointed a court physician.[58]

There is the possibility that these Chinese physicians, as cultural disseminators, wittingly or not, introduced the elements of the Tibetan medical tradition into Chinese culture.

This chapter has restricted itself to an exploration of the Tibetan origin of the peacock's gallbladder, but we feel that the research may have wider-reaching implications. As stated in the introduction, this chapter also aims to offer a new approach to tracing Sino–Tibetan cultural exchanges, as well as to re-examine certain preconceived opinions on Sino–Tibetan relations. The Tibetan origin of the peacock's gallbladder is indubitably an example illustrating our proposed approach. Through this hypothesis we indicate clearly that the communications between cultures in medieval and late imperial China were strong, even if these interactions were indirect, and even if the route of communication no longer survives.

NOTES

1. For the original Chinese play, see Guo Moruo, *Kongque dan* 孔雀膽 [The Peacocks Gallbladder] (Shanghai: Xin wenyi chubanshe, 1954).
2. *Guoxue baodian* 國學寶典 database, <http://www.gxbd.com> (accessed 18 June 2012).
3. Ibid.
4. Ibid.
5. Ibid.
6. Ibid.
7. See *Taishō Tripiṭaka* (electronic edition 2011), (accessed 18 June 2012).
8. *Guoxue baodian* (accessed 18 June 2012).

9. Some scholars hold the opinion that the earliest record of the peacock in Chinese literary works came from the appellation "*konggai*" 孔蓋 mentioned in "Jiuge" 九歌 (Nine Songs) attributed to Qu Yuan 屈原 (339–278 BC). However, Edward Schafer claims in *The Golden Peaches of Samarkand: A Study of T'ang Exotics* (Berkeley: University of California Press, 1963) that the appearance of "*konggai*" only indicates that Chu nobles had obtained some feathers of the peacock. Still, more information is needed to solve the problem of the earliest Chinese sources regarding the peacock.

10. *Guoxue baodian* (accessed 18 June 2012).

11. The exact date of this poem is unknown. However, two clues make it possible to date this poem. First, this poem is first seen in *Yutai xinyong* 玉臺新詠 [New Songs of the Jade Terrace], a collection of poetic pieces which was compiled in the first half of the sixth century by Xu Ling 徐陵 (507–83). Second, according to the preface attached to this poem, the love story happened at the end of the Jian'an 建安 period of the Eastern Han. Therefore, one can draw the conclusion that this poem was composed sometime between the third and mid-sixth centuries.

12. Schafer, pp. 97–99.

13. See *Taiping guangji* 太平廣記, vol. 461, in *Guoxue baodian*, (accessed 18 June 2012).

14. See also *Xian yu jing* 賢愚經 [Sutra of the Worthy and the Stupid], vol. 42, in *Taishō Tripiṭaka* (accessed 18 June 2012).

15. Such as Faxian 法賢, trans., *Fuoshuo zuishang genben dale jingang bukong sanmei Dajiao Wang jing* 佛說最上根本大樂金剛不空三昧大教王經 [The Greatest Original Sutra on the *Vajrasattva* of Great Bliss: The Great King of Tantras with Concentration on Non-Emptiness], in *Taishō Tripiṭaka* (accessed 18 June 2012).

16. Valerie Hansen, *The Open Empire: A History of China to 1600* (New York, London: W.W. Norton & Co., 2000), p. 335.

17. Su Nuo 蘇諾, *Puti shuxia de zang yixue he menggu yixue* 菩提樹下的藏醫學和蒙古醫學 [Tibetan and Mongolian Medicine under the Bodhi Tree], (Beijing: Minzu chubanshe, 2001), pp. 23–24.

18. Based on the suggestion of 'Phags-pa, Kublai Khan ordered the Yuan bureaucratic system to adopt the 'Phags-pa script. However, as Hansen has pointed out, because of its cumbersomeness, the Mongols mainly adopted instead, after they had conquered Central Asia, a writing system loaned from the Uighur script, which is still used in the Inner Mongolia Autonomous Region of China. Meanwhile, their Chinese subjects still adhered to their own Chinese writing system throughout the Yuan dynasty. For more information regarding the Mongolian writing system, see Hansen, p. 351.

19. Giuseppe Tucci and Walther Hessig, *Xizang he Menggu de zongjiao* 西藏和蒙古的宗教 [*Les religions du Tibet et de la Mongolie*], translated by Geng Sheng 耿昇 (Tianjin: Tianjin guji chubanshe, 1989), pp. 383–84.

20. For a comprehensive study of the geographic origins of Tibetan Medicine, see Frances Garrett, "Critical Methods in Tibetan Medical Histories", *Journal of Asian Studies* 66, no. 2 (2007): 363–87.

21. See Su, *Puti shuxia de zang yixue he menggu yixue*, pp. 9–11.

22. Sagang Sechen 薩崗彻辰, *Menggu yuanliu* 蒙古源流 [The Origin of the Mongols], translated by Daorun Tibu 道潤梯步 (Hohhot: Neimonggu renmin chubanshe, 1980), p. 191.

23. The Fifth Dalai Lama, *Xizang wang chen ji* 西藏王臣記 [Records of Tibetan Kings and Officials], translated by Liu Liqian 劉立千 (Beijing: Minzu chubanshe, 2002), p. 65.

24. See *Yuan shi* 元史 (Beijing: Zhonghua shuju, 1983), 15. 4519.

25. Another view is that the tradition of Tibetan medicine was established by Bon guru gShen-rabMi-bo, who has also been claimed to be the founder of the Bon religious tradition of Tibet. See Cai Jingfeng 蔡景峰, *Zang yixue tongshi* 藏醫學通史 [A Comprehensive History of Tibetan Medicine], (Xining: Qinghai renmin chubanshe, 2002), p. 21.

26. The preference of the Mongol rulers for Arabo-Persian medicine was recounted in Joseph S. Alter, "Rethinking the History of Medicine in Asia: Hakim Mohammed Said and the Society for the Promotion of Eastern Medicine", *Journal of Asian Studies* 67, no. 4 (2008): 1165–86, esp. 1175–76.

27. Ngai-Sie was originally from Porum (Syria) and served in the Mongol court. In the reign of Emperor Taizong (1229–41), Ngai-Sie was appointed as an official in charge of astronomy, calendrical calculations, and medical care. He was greatly favoured by the Mongol rulers, was made the Duke of Qin, and eventually granted with the posthumous title of Grand Master.

28. See the *Nancun chuo geng lu* 南村輟耕錄 [Records Taken at the Southern Village after Farm Work] by Tao Zongyi 陶宗儀 (1329–1410), in *Guoxue baodian* (accessed 18 June 2012). Tao mentions that the Muslim physicians healed children and horses with their amazing medical skills.

29. For more information on Muslim medicine, see Yi Guangrui 伊光瑞, *Neimenggu yixue shi lüe* 內蒙古醫學史略 [A Brief History of Inner Mongolian Medicine], (Beijing: Zhongyi guji chubanshe, 1993), pp. 96–104.

30. g.Yu-thog Yon-tan mGon-po, *Sibu yidian* 四部醫典 [The Four Medical Tantras], translated by Li Yongnian 李永年 (Beijing: Renmin weisheng chubanshe, 1983), p. 6.

31. Ibid., p. 47.

32. Ibid., pp. 3–4.

33. Ibid., p. 60. The original Chinese text reads: 孔雀翎毛排肺膿.

34. Ibid. The Chinese translation reads: 孔雀肉可解毒治赤癜.

35. Ibid., p. 48. The Chinese translation reads: 孔雀肉治眼病音啞老.

36. Ibid., p. 378. The Chinese text reads: 又方狼毒赤芍孔雀肉, 黃連寒熱靈脂爐甘石, 轉機丸散隨宜作清瀉.

37. Ibid., p. 434.

38. Ibid., p. 377.

39. Ibid.

40. Ibid., p. 379.

41. Ibid.

42. Ibid.

43. Ibid., p. 381.

44. Ibid., p. 384.

45. The compilation of the *Shel gong shel phreng* was completed by De'u dmar dge bshes bsTan 'dzin phun tshogs in 1835. It was first printed in 1840.

46. De'u dmar dge bshes bsTan 'dzin phun tshogs, *Jingzhu bencao* 晶珠本草 (*Shel gong shel phreng*; Crystal Pearl Materia Medica), translated by Mao Jizu 毛繼祖 et al. (Shanghai: Shanghai keji chubanshe, 1986), p. 9. The Chinese translation reads: 孔雀肉: 孔雀肉治膽病, 治中毒病. 孔雀肉要與解毒藥物相配, 不可任意內服. 馬雞肉和膽可代孔雀肉和膽.

47. See Michael J. Sweet and Leonard Zwilling, *Peacock in the Poison Grove*, translated and commented upon by Geshe Lhundub Sopa (Boston: Wisdom Publications, 1996), p. 1. It is believed that the school was founded in 1057 by 'Brom ston rgyal ba'i 'byung gnas (1005–64), who composed this text based on the teachings of his master, the great Indian scholar-saint Dīpaṁkaraśrījñāna. The latter is better known as Atiśa (986–1054), whose arrival in western Tibet in 1042 is generally regarded as one of the greatest landmarks in the history of Tibetan Buddhism.

48. Ibid., p. 59.

49. Ibid., pp. 32–33.

50. Ibid., p. 19.

51. See Terry Clifford, *Tibetan Buddhist Medicine and Psychiatry: The Diamond Healing* (Delhi: Motilal Banarsidass, 1994), pp. 199–200.

52. Sweet and Zwilling, p. 107.

53. Ibid., p. 197.

54. g.Yu-thog Yon-tan mGon-po, p. 51.

55. Sweet and Zwilling, p. 193.

56. g.Yu-thog Yon-tan mGon-po, p. 7.

57. For a detailed discussion on this topic, see Zhao Gaiping 趙改萍, *Yuan-Ming shiqi zang chuan fojiao zai neidi de fazhan ji yingxiang* 元明時期藏傳佛教在內地的發展及影響 [The Development and Influence of Tibetan Buddhism in Yuan-Ming China], (Beijing: Zhongguo shehui kexue chubanshe, 2009), pp. 53–80.

58. Hansen, p. 335.

12

TRANSFORMATION OF THE YUNNANESE COMMUNITY ALONG THE SINO–BURMA BORDER DURING THE NINETEENTH AND EARLY TWENTIETH CENTURIES

Yi Li

The Chinese province of Yunnan was officially brought under the administrative control of Imperial China during the Yuan Dynasty through the Mongol army's southwest campaigns. However, the central government's exertion of control in this remote periphery was not as strong as that in the northern or eastern parts of Imperial China. In many aspects, Yunnan maintained its frontier identity at a crossroads between East, South, and Southeast Asia. The traditional caravan trade that linked China and India can be traced at least to the Han Dynasty,[1] and it remained a vital channel of interaction and exchange for the region throughout history, despite occasional interruptions such as the Sino-Burmese War (1762–69).[2] Even with an increasing Han population and an intensified process of Sinification from the Ming Dynasty onwards, many areas were governed by native officials, who often held multiple, but nominal, loyalties to remote power centres in China, Siam and Burma well into the nineteenth century,[3] a feature which has been identified more with Southeast Asian polities than with their counterpart based in Beijing.[4]

However, in the late eighteenth century, this balance was abruptly interrupted by the arrival of the European colonial powers. The expanding northeastern frontier of the colonial state of British India (or of its predecessor until 1857, the East India Company) was directly confronted by Imperial China's southwest periphery. Unlike contemporary confrontations along the southern and eastern coasts of China, Yunnan experienced neither wars nor concessions of its territories. Nevertheless, the colonial presence challenged the free-flowing tradition of the frontier, and to some extent, defined Imperial China's southwest border immediately prior to the fall of the Qing Dynasty.

The current study looks at one group from this frontier region, the Han Yunnanese, who traditionally sojourned between western Yunnan and Upper Burma. In response to the approaching colonial presence — and from 1886 onwards, with the newly established colonial rule in Burma — this group underwent a communal transformation with reinforced or newly created identities, which reflected the demarcation of political borders and the delineation of ethnic boundaries in one of the remotest peripheries of Imperial China and in its southern neighbour, Burma.

Securing the Colonial Frontier

British interest in the Sino–Burmese frontier was clear long before the actual extension of its rule to Burma. Michael Symes, on his first embassy visit to Ava in 1795, met the Governor of Bhamo, the traditional Sino–Burmese border town, who claimed to have visited Beijing twice on a "very fatiguing"[5] journey of three months. Symes was told that although "the Birmans have not liberty to pass at will into the Chinese territory, or the Chinese into that of the Birmans", the Governor himself had the "power to grant passports", something "of the Chop, or seal, which he was accustomed to affix to such papers".[6] If there had been any border control up till that time, it would appear that any such control was rather nominal and loose, as the local head of a border town could

FIGURE 12.1

Illustrative Map of Western Yunnan and Upper Burma in the Late Nineteenth Century and Early Twentieth Century

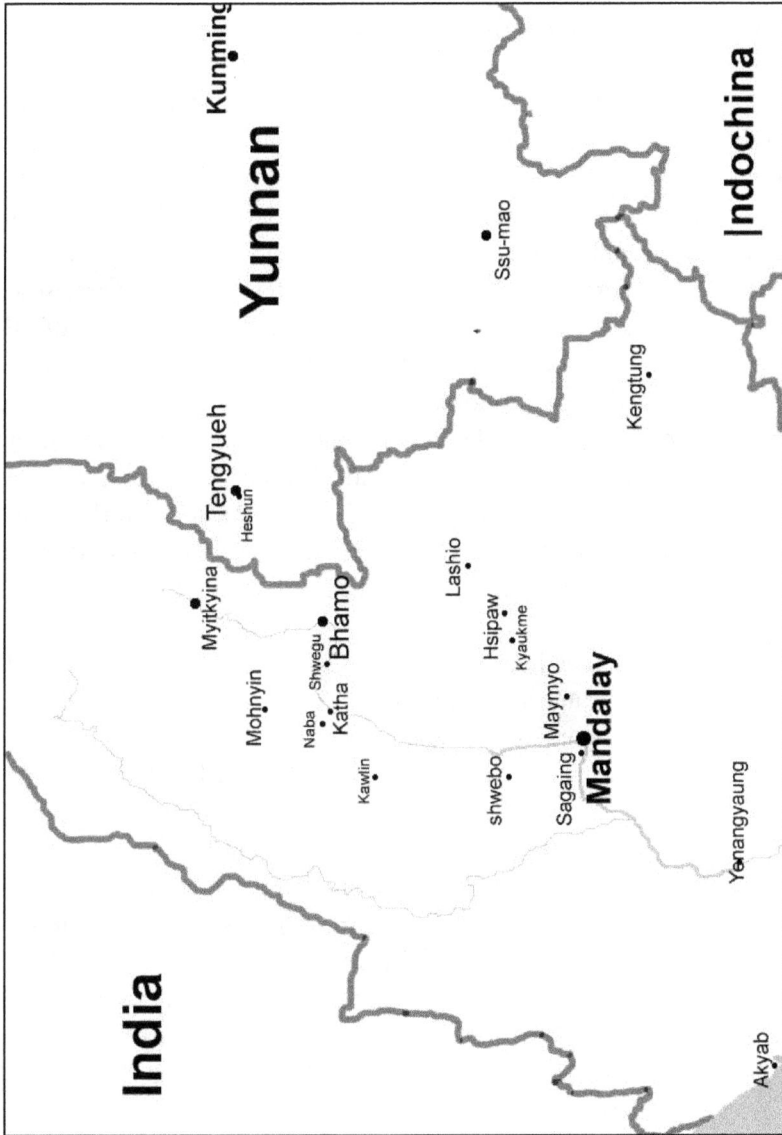

seemingly act independently when dealing with a third-country official such as Symes.

Symes' expedition was one of many British frontier expeditions launched in the years of imperial expansion, with clear territorial and commercial ambitions in this part of the world, spanning from northwest and northeast India, central Asia, and Tibet, to northern Burma and southwest China. As a well-tested practice in the British imperial project, these expeditions collected and digested local knowledge in a format that was comprehensible to the imperial readership, and integrated these geographical and ethnographical landscapes into the intellectual map of the empire, thus preparing for the imperial wars, sovereigns and trade that would undoubtedly follow.[7] In the case of the Burma–Yunnan frontier, the process that transformed a historically caravan-friendly frontier into a colonial borderland can be traced to the early nineteenth century, after the East India Company had become established in India and the annexation of coastal Burma had taken place following the first Anglo-Burmese War (1824–26). As a natural extension of British India's northeastern frontier, this area was a vast expanse of territory, about which the British had been keenly taking notes for some considerable time.

Different routes had been tried around Bhamo, all driven by the aim of finding a through route to connect the imperial-held territorial lands on the British world map; namely, northeast India, central Burma, and the southern and eastern coasts of China. British rule in Lower Burma and its presence in the Burmese capital provided a better channel through which to obtain information from the locals. In 1836, Captain Hanney, whose journey was mentioned by Pemberton,[8] visited Bhamo and Mogoung from Ava, the capital of the Burmese Kingdom, by travelling upstream along the Irrawaddy. In 1837, Dr Griffith crossed the Patkoi range (the Patkai hills of the Indo–Burmese border) and the Hukong Valley (Hukang Hegu 胡康河谷, present-day Hukawng Valley in the Myitkyina District of Myanmar) from Suddyah. In Patkoi, he met Dr Bayfield, who was sent by Colonel Burney, Resident at the court of Ava.[9] Bayfield's trip from Ava to Patkoi was via Bhamo, thus marking the completion of the northern-corridor route between India and Burma.

It was also in 1837 that Captain McLeod made the journey to Kenghung (present-day Jinghong 景洪) from Moulmein, then the administrative centre of British-occupied Burma, and thus provided another option for reaching southern Yunnan through Tai polities in northern Thailand and the Shan states.[10] In fact, throughout the nineteenth century, the frontier had been approached by colonial explorers from various directions. Thomas Cooper, who advocated an Indo–Tibetan route over the Burma–Yunnan route,[11] summarized the situation at this frontier in 1871:

> At the present time the Chinese province of Yunnan is attracting attention in its geographical, commercial, and political relations with the adjacent countries. It has been, so to speak, attacked from three sides, and that almost at the same time, by explorers acting independently of each other; viz.: the French expedition from Saigon, on the south; Major [E.B.] Sladen's party, on the Burmese or western side; and, last and least, an attempt was made by myself to reach Talifoo from Atenze, on the northern frontier.[12]

One British base used for this frontier exploration was Bhamo, which was, historically, a minor polity surrounded by the Kachin hills in northern Burma. Bhamo was known to local Chinese communities as Xinjie 新街 ("New Street", implying its commercial prominence), as opposed to Old Street or old Bhamo, which was nearby.[13] It was sometimes also referred to as Jiangtou cheng 江頭城 ("Riverhead Town"),[14] although its actual location at that time is still the subject of debate. Bhamo, along with Tengyue 騰越 (also known as Moumein, present-day Tengchong 騰衝) in western Yunnan, were the termini of a well-explored Yunnan–Burma caravan route in the northern part of this frontier.[15] Previous Chinese dynasties did make some effort to assert their sovereignty over the border region, by using, of course, Chinese protocol. For example, in the area of Myitkyina, a stela was erected by a military minister of the Ming Dynasty, Wang Ji 王驥, during his frontier pacification campaign over Tai headmen in Tengyue and the surrounding areas in the 1440s. It reads, "Only until the stone is rotten and the sea is dried, can you possibly cross this river",[16] thus attempting to deter indefinitely any external ambitions over this conquered territory. A Weiyuan garrison 威遠營 was stationed in Bhamo, during the Toungoo–Ming wars in the 1580s–90s, led by Baoshan–Tengyue military officials Deng Zilong 鄧子龍 and Liu Ting 劉挺.

After the opening of the Chinese treaty ports and of the heartland of the Yangzi River, passages from Shanghai to Bhamo (and further south into Burma) were explored extensively. A.R. Margary, working in the British consular service in China, travelled from Shanghai to Bhamo to meet another British expedition under Colonel Horace A. Browne in 1875. In February 1876, on their way to Manwyne, the team was attacked and Margary was killed.[17] Undeterred, many others followed the same route, for example, Captain A.M.S. Wingate in 1898,[18] Scottish geologist Logan Jack in 1901, who had previous experience in Australia,[19] and an American traveller, William Geil, in 1903.[20] In 1906, Reginald Johnson, a Scot working in the colonial service in Hong Kong and China, who later became the tutor of the last Qing emperor, also managed to reach Mandalay from Peking in northern China.[21] By means of presentations to academic societies or the publication of their travelogues, many of these travellers introduced their journeys to the British public. Such publicity increased public interest and attracted more resources, all of which, in turn, facilitated further exploration and, in the case of Burma, its final annexation in 1886.

These colonial penetrations inevitably invited strong reactions from local actors, including the Han Yunnanese, the subject of this study. One example involves an 1868 Sladen expedition. In 1868, Albert Fytche, the Chief Commissioner of British Burma, who controlled all the areas along the coast of the Bay of Bengal and the Irrawaddy Delta at the time, proposed an expedition from Bhamo to Tengyue. The journey was approved by Calcutta, and the team was to be led by the British political agent in Ava, Major Sladen. Burmese King Mindon (r. 1853–78) provided the logistical support for the team.[22]

Fytche emphasized the great commercial potential of routes to southwest Yunnan, whose "commercial highway",[23] he believed, would allow the British to reach neighbouring Szechuen and Kweichow, "the wealthiest and most populous provinces in China",[24] where the majority of products traded in Canton were produced. This was also seen as important for the regional imperial competition. Precisely in the year 1868, a French Mekong expedition, starting out from Saigon under the leadership of Doudart and Garnier, arrived at Ssu-mao (present-day Simao

思茅), the terminus of another Sino-Burmese caravan route that was not far from Tengyue.

Thus, the British expedition was seen not only as necessary, but also as urgent. By early 1868, a team of British officers and engineers, along with Burmese staff, was already in Bhamo, ready to commence its journey along the ancient caravan route. According to descriptions by contemporary British explorers, Bhamo had a distinctively Chinese flavour. Anderson, the naturalist for the 1868 expedition, described the town as having two portions, one Chinese and the other Shan. The Chinese quarter was in the middle of the town with fifty to sixty houses, whose enterprising residents had "regulate[d] the cotton market".[25] They also sold:

> Manchester goods, long-cloth, Chinese yarns, ball tea, opium, spices, preserved oranges, jujubes, walnuts, chestnuts, raisins, apples, potatoes, beans, watermelon seeds, betel-nut, salt, flint, gypsum, yellow orpiment, vermillion from Talifoo, copper wire, lead, bees-wax, coarse sugar, sugar-candy, twine, catgut, and many articles of less importance.[26]

The landmark of the Chinese quarter was the Chinese temple:

> A neat little temple and theatre in one, consisting of an outer and an inner court terminating in the temple itself, which contains another court, their holy of holies. The entrance to the first was through what was a novelty to us, a circular doorway. The court is paved throughout, and lies at a lower level than the one immediately above it, which appears to be the orthodox fashion adopted in Chinese temples. The theatrical stage is over the entrance to the second court, and faces the religious part of the building, which, in its turn, is raised above the court immediately below it. The court of the sanctuary has a covered terrace round its three sides with recesses off two of them, containing seated figures nearly life-size, with rubicund, almost fiery faces, having black beards and moustaches of formidable cut and dimensions. They are all, in accordance with a Chinaman's just appreciation of the value of rupees, carefully protected from dust and injury by being placed in square boxes, which I ought to dignify with the name of shrines, closed in front with almost opaque, gauze netting. A few priests live in a court-yard at the side of the building which is built entirely of brick, and after the Chinese grotesque idea of architectural beauty.[27]

This temple's circular doorway, constructed in a Chinese style, impressed Anderson and many later Western visitors. The temple was dedicated to the God of War (also the God of Fortune), Guandi, a popular god among Han residents of the Yunnan frontier, perhaps due to this region's easy exposure to warfare of all types and among all ethnicities, and perhaps also because of Guandi's patronage of merchants. The temple's last renovation was carried out in 1806 — presumably at an old site of worship for Yunnanese merchants of jade, silk, and cotton. That site might have started to function from at least the early decades of the seventeenth century, but it was disrupted previously by the Sino-Burmese War. In addition to halls dedicated to Guandi and other deities, a stage for folk performances[28] and a Chinese school were also established in the temple's compound, functioning and being regarded as the de facto Tengyue Association in Bhamo.[29] It was also at this spot, popularly known as the "joss-house" among the Europeans, that the Chinese mercenary Set Kyin (his Chinese name was Jin Guoyu 金國玉) was assassinated by his followers in 1885.[30]

The Bhamo Chinese gave an apparently amicable reception to the team. As observed by both Anderson and Sladen, the local Chinese headman had considerable influence and good connections among his fellow countrymen, Burmese, Kachins, Shans, and other locals from Mandalay to Tengyue and the vast unknown in between. He invited the British to a feast of "grand style"[31] in the temple. A "hospitality of our new Chinese friends"[32] deeply impressed both Anderson and Sladen.

> We sat round a table on which a very complete dessert of twenty five dishes had been previously arranged. Tea was handed round, and each guest, in addition, found a veritable teapot at his side, filled with the strongest samshoo. The dessert being removed, fresh and substantial signs of hospitality evinced themselves in the appearance of nine separate dishes of cooked meats and vegetables, which we were forced by good breeding to attack with chopsticks.[33]

The expedition, however, was quietly opposed. Speaking of the difficulties of the journey seemingly impossible to overcome, the Chinese hosts tried to discourage their guests from undertaking the expedition by plying them with Chinese dishes and *samshoo*, "a kind of ardent spirit made in China from rice".[34] It did not work, and the British left Bhamo, only to find that the Chinese objection to their expedition became more apparent. The only Kachin chief who was willing to help admitted his great reluctance, as he had "Chinese friends" both in Bhamo and in the country to the east, all of whom urged him not to provide any assistance.[35] Furthermore, there was a legendary robber, Chief Lees-hee-ta-hee,[36] who could stop the team at any time if it trespassed into his territory, a shadowy danger that lingered throughout their journey.

Three months later, in March 1868, information came to light regarding the team's Chinese interpreter — a half-Chinese, half-Burmese man, Moung Shwe Yah — who had been assigned to the team by the Burmese king. Thought to be "eminently useful on account of his local and varied experiences",[37] Shwe Yan, Sladen found out, had received

> ... advice all along.... [to] murder me at a convenient season, and take possession of the cash chest and other Government presents of which I had charge ... His private efforts to thwart and confound my plans having failed at Bhamo, he bethought him of the dastardly expedient of robbery and bloodshed, (so Ponlyne says) but in this too he missed his mark, and, fearing exposure, chose rather to return in confusion to Bhamo than let it be supposed by the Burmese Government that after all he might have been secretly aiding in the fulfilment of our undertaking.[38]

All these obstacles placed in the British expedition's path by the Chinese were attributed to a conflict of commercial interests by the team. Sladen and Anderson claimed that the Chinese in Bhamo, Ava, Tengyue, and the surrounding area had a firm grip on the whole of Yunnan-Burmese trade at that time, and it was natural for them to want to keep "to themselves their present petty earnings",[39] which was assured if the British effort to "open out to all the overland routes between Bhamo and South Western China"[40] failed.

However, if commercial interests were the priority for the expeditions of the British commissioners and agents, it was not entirely true of their Chinese opponents. Sladen blamed the Burmese who gave him trouble. Lees-hee-ta-hee was said to have received the endorsement of the Burmese king, and Shwe Yah "was specially told off to our assistance by the King of Burma".[41] The British thus blamed the trouble caused by the Chinese on the Burmese, understandably since during these decades they were still competing with the independent Burmese Kingdom, based in Upper Burma, for the control of all of Burma.

Upon the conclusion of the 1868 frontier expedition, Fytche managed to persuade the Indian Government, as well as King Mindon, to create the post of British Deputy Resident in Bhamo. In 1869, a certain Captain Storer was the first to hold this position, marking the start of the British presence in this border town. In December 1885, the British army occupied Bhamo during the Third Anglo-Burmese War. In 1886, the annexation of Upper Burma was completed, making the entirety of Burma the newest province of British India. In the following few decades, the British presence advanced even further. In 1897, a British consulate was established in Ssu-mao, in 1899, in Tengyue, and in 1902, in the provincial capital of Yunnanfu (present-day Kunming 昆明).

Ramifications of Communal Identities

With the securing of the colonial frontier and the establishment of foreign institutions, the frontier landscape and the lives of its multi-ethnic residents underwent a rapid change. From the 1890s onwards, officials from both sides started the border demarcation process, which lasted till the very end of the period of colonial rule.[42] For the Yunnanese along the border, what was more significant than the delimitation of the physical border was a communal reconfiguration with a divided identity, if not loyalty. A choice had to be made: either to be the loyal subjects of the Middle Kingdom on one side of the border, or immigrants (and subjects of a European empire) on the other. Under these conditions, some began to reinforce their attachment to the Chinese emperor and fully adopted a Chinese identity. Others, based on pre-existing communal foundations, decided to build a migrant community centred on Wa Cheng 瓦城 (Mandalay), the centre of this newly defined Yunnanese migrant community in British Burma that fitted into the colonial ethnic infrastructure.

Imperial Intelligence

Like their compatriots who took sea routes to Nanyang 南洋, the Chinese plying the Yunnan–Burma caravan routes often spent the majority of their lives in Burma. The practice of such travellers having both Chinese and Burmese wives was so common that many of the residents were of mixed blood. In fact, the streets in front of the Amarapura Yunnanese temple, or the "Chinese quarter", as described by some contemporary British travellers, has been occupied by these mixed children and their descendants to the present day. The same could be seen in villages and towns in Tengyue, where Burmese grandmothers with completely Han lifestyles lived well into the twentieth century.[43] The ethnic boundary, if there was one, was rather blurred and easily transgressed.

Some of the children, often boys, were sent back to Yunnan by their fathers to receive a classical Chinese education. Through education, these young men were raised and aspired to become true Chinese Mandarins, and they threw themselves into the Chinese gentry system without much reference to their foreign background. In the face of colonial rule, however, some took advantage of this background for their China-oriented outlook by gathering intelligence on British activities, for example. By doing so, they promptly identified themselves with the long-established, albeit waning influences from Beijing in the form of growing patriotic enthusiasm.

One example is a late-nineteenth-century Heshun 和順 man named Zhang Chenglian 張成濂, who came from a merchant family that had been trading cotton and silk in the Burmese capital for generations. According to a widely circulated Tengyue local story, Chenglian was born in Burma and educated in the Confucian classics under scholars in Tengyue. He passed the provincial examination in 1879, earning the title of *juren* 舉人 . In an attempt to further this career path, he began to prepare for the national examination in Beijing. At this point, Chenglian was spotted by a Tengyue frontier official and was persuaded to work as a spy for the emperor by utilising his family ties in Burma; an alternative way to serve the country and no less important than going to Beijing to earn a higher degree title.[44] Inspired by this mission, Chenglian went back to Burma, posing as an ordinary Tengyue businessman, travelling back and forth between Tengyue and Mandalay, a route very familiar to his friends and families, and he started to send information back.

In 1891, using his local knowledge, Chenglian assisted in a borderland survey report by providing much-needed information for Chinese diplomats during the negotiation of the Sino–British border agreements in 1892 and 1894.[45] In his later career, Chenglian continued to be a member of the Mandarin gentry and fully immersed himself in the Middle Kingdom's officialdom. As a provincial examinee, he witnessed the first political campaign by the reformists, led by Kang Youwei in Beijing during the 1895 national examination, known as Gongche shangshu 公車上書. He spent several years as county magistrate in Guangdong and Guangxi. Influenced by the reformists' ideas, he was later demoted and sent to Xinjiang, and remained on this northwest frontier with Russia and central Asia, an unfamiliar location compared to his tropical homeland, until his death. His Burmese wife, it was said, followed him throughout China; she was respected by his Mandarin colleagues as *Mian saosao* ("Burmese sister-in-law") and was renowned for her Burmese culinary skills.[46]

During his Burmese days, it was said that Chenglian contributed to the flight to Yunnan of some Burmese nobility after the annexation. In 1890, finding that the British planned to survey the borderland, Chenglian reacted swiftly. Under his arrangement, his Chinese relatives became guides and interpreters for the British teams, just as Shwe Yan had done for Sladen decades before.[47] They successfully gathered first-hand information from the British and duly reported back to Yunnan. Chenglian's brother, Zhang Chengyu 張成瑜, followed one British team for seven months from Mandalay to the area of the Jiulong River (in Sipsongpanna) in the southern part of the frontier.[48] His nephew, Zhang Dexin 張德馨, followed another team up from Bhamo to the north of Myitkyina along the Irrawaddy for four months.

As in the attempted assassination of the 1868 expedition, and many more before and after that particular case, the advance of a European colonial force prompted Chinese reactions that were motivated neither by purely commercial loss nor by orders from the Burmese court, as the British liked to think. The revenue from the southwest Yunnan trade was comparatively insignificant to the provincial, let alone national, treasury.[49] But the British penetration and then the establishment of colonial institutions, and the resulting threat to the Chinese sovereign created tremendous confusion for regional government officials and travelling merchants alike, and invited a great confrontation.

Throughout his mission, Chengyu kept a diary in Burmese, which he translated into Chinese prior to his death in Bhamo. During a meeting between the British and the local chief, he wrote:

> This headman does not totally forget China. But presently the Chinese officials and the generals are disappointing; it is as if they are sleeping. Now the enemy [the British] has been over our border already and tried to lure and ally with this headman, but nowhere can I see the military and diplomatic reactions of China. The enemy is so unscrupulous; are our Government officials waiting to be killed by the thunder?[50]

Dexin, on his Bhamo–Myitkyina trip, found that the British planned to advance into what was traditionally Chinese territory and tried to dissuade them. One day, he secretly went to see the local headman and warned him:

> You and your brothers have benefited from China for many generations, why do you welcome the British into China today? ... Though you have moved to this place, you had better be loyal to China and find a way to stop the British now... otherwise, you and your brothers might lose your lives.[51]

Meanwhile, he also told the Chinese porters hired by the team:

> The British behave so badly, and believe the misleading Burmese guide, without understanding the practical difficulties (of going into China). If anything happens, we should be prepared. We are all Chinese and should retain our loyalty. If we meet the Chinese armies there, we must take the chance to attack the British to show our hidden loyalty, which might bring our families honour.[52]

His suggestion was unanimously supported by his fellow countrymen, who had been complaining extensively about their British employers.

Over the years of the colonial presence, showing loyalty to the emperor was evidently attractive to a whole range of people, including provincial Qing officials, Han Chinese — educated or not and mixed blood or not — and native officials with multiple tributary orientations. In 1886, the Chinese in Myitkyina reported that Wang Ji's stela had been pushed into the Irrawaddy by the British, an action that was understood as expressing the unapologetic ambition of the colonizer.[53] In Bhamo, the foundation stone of the Weiyuan garrison was discovered and photographed by local Chinese and Burmese monks, after which a memorial pavilion in Chinese style was erected on the site.[54] Sojourning Yunnanese near Mandalay also visited ancient sites where the last Ming emperor, Yongli 永曆, was said to have been captured,[55] collecting details of his last days.[56] Such archaeological activities closely knitted with history and literature had always been a cultivated hobby favoured by Chinese gentry scholars.[57] By carrying out this activity in the now British colony, the Yunnanese demonstrated their orientation towards China in a way that not only integrated Burma into historical China's imperial map and cultural sphere, but also acted as an avowal, for both themselves and their community, that they were Chinese.

A Migrant Community

Meanwhile, the process of community-building among the Yunnanese in Burma accelerated, now with a renewed agenda under British rule. Based on existing institutions, a Yunnanese migrant community started to take shape, with increasing numbers of typical Chinese communal institutions that replicated those found in many other parts of the region, such as temples, burial lands, associations, and schools.

The establishment of such associations was more than a continuation of precolonial, communal building activity.[58] Under the changing administrative system in Upper Burma, the Yunnanese responded by developing communal temples, burial lands, associations, and schools, in such a way that an increasingly clear image of the Chinese could be identified and demonstrated to differentiate the Yunnanese from their non-Chinese neighbours. Such clarification was necessary for them to fit into the ethnic pigeonholes that were allocated to them by the colonial ethnographic infrastructure. There was no more space for freeing migration and ambiguity. As colonial subjects, they needed, so to speak, to tick a box, choosing from among indigenous races, Indian castes, or other Asiatic migrants. These were the limited options that were clearly defined in the census forms and other government documents. Under this classification system, the Yunnanese had no other choice but to become a part of the Burmese Chinese migrant communities.

The greatest impact of colonial rule in shaping the Chinese experience, however, was the opening up of Upper Burma to the Hokkien and

Cantonese from Rangoon on the one hand, and Lower Burma and the coastal areas to the overland Yunnanese on the other. Historically, the Yunnanese had travelled as far south as Tenasserim and Chiang Mai by caravan routes.[59] Chinese from other parts of China were also involved in cross-border trade in Bhamo well before the British colonial period.[60] However, it was under British rule that such mobility and inter-regional interaction reached an unprecedented level, especially in the twentieth century.

Under British rule, the Cantonese and the Hokkien now came to the north in large numbers with the expansion of colonial projects. In 1893, a Yunnan-born merchant who had been in Mandalay since the King Mingdon era, and had been serving as a municipal commissioner in the town since 1888, estimated that among the Mandalay Chinese population, 30 per cent were Yunnanese and 70 per cent were Cantonese.[61] Cantonese construction workers built railways as far north as Myitkyina, and they went to many other towns in Upper Burma to construct government buildings and markets. The Cantonese were particularly active in the trade of precious stones from northern mines, working closely with the Yunnanese, utilizing their better command of the English language, their familiarity with global commercial practices, and their closer connection through regional networks with Nanyang, Hong Kong, and Chinese ports. At least by the end of the nineteenth century, Cantonese jade merchants had organized their own association, Kunxing Tang 崑興堂 ("Jade Prosperity Hall"), on Han renjie 漢人街 ("Chinese Street", present-day 80 Street) in Mandalay, a few steps away from the Mandalay Yunnan Association. The cooperation between the Cantonese and the Yunnanese in the jade business, although with regional competition and prejudice against each other, is well remembered today by an elderly Mandalay Cantonese man.[62]

On the Hokkien side, this northward movement can be illustrated by the family experience of Taw Sein Ko 杜誠誥, Government Archaeologist and Examiner in the Chinese Language, who was a Mandalay resident. Taw's father was an Amoy native who operated a shipping business along the Burmese coast in the 1840s.[63] He married a Shan woman, and Taw Sein Ko was born in 1864 in Moulmein. Later, the family moved to Mandalay and Bhamo, under the rule of King Mindon. Despite heavy governmental duties in Rangoon, the colonial capital, Taw's official address, up till the 1920s, was the Peking Lodge on West Moat Road near the former royal palace in Mandalay.[64] The Taws could not possibly have been the only Hokkiens in the Burmese capital and Upper Burma during the 1860s. When the Mandalay Hokkien temple, Hock Kheng Keong 福慶宮, opened in 1908, the Hokkien community must have already been well established.

By the 1920s, Mandalay was a place seen to be as much Yunanese as Hokkien and Cantonese. In 1926, a Heshun businessman, Yin Zhaorong 尹兆榮, was urged by his fellow Heshun youth to adopt a modern style for his younger brother Zhaofu's wedding. Yin Zhaorong was not particularly interested, as he had seen this new wedding style in Tengyue and thought it not impressive. However, the youth insisted: "We Yunnanese have never ever practised this new wedding style in Mandalay, and we need this to establish a new trend. Otherwise, it will be living proof that we Yunnanese are too conservative, as the Cantonese and the Hokkien always say."[65] Convinced perhaps by this appeal to subtle regional competition, Yin Zhaorong finally agreed to invite Chinese, Burmese, and Indians to the Yunnan Association's grand hall for a tea party and organized a car procession around the town for the newly-weds, which cost him 2,800 rupees in total, for this "new" wedding ceremony. Even so, Yin Zhaorong was still cynical about this innovation. He wrote a Chinese classical poem afterwards:

Mingala zaun[66] is the Burmese word for wedding.
All the respectable guests are dressed properly.
A k'weq [cup] of coffee and a plate of moún [cake].
This is all about the new civilisation.[67]

Regional rivalry was undeniable, but it is important to note that, in 1926, the Yunnanese tended to compare themselves with the Hokkien and the Cantonese, instead of with other ethnicities living next to them. There certainly were more interactions than formerly, when they had been relatively isolated from other Chinese migrants and had felt a greater attachment to the Burmese and other local peoples. Even Yin Zhaorong had to acknowledge the magical healing power that the Hokkien tea (possibly) had for his father, who had fallen ill upon arriving in Mandalay for his younger son's wedding. The tea he purchased might have been brought over to Mandalay by his Hokkien countrymen,[68] if not from Yunnan (as both locations were famous for their high quality tea).

In the meantime, the Yunnanese, whose traditional homeland was firmly rooted in the area between western Yunnan and northern Burma, also captured the opportunity to explore the southern territory. Upper Burma remained a strong and reliable backyard that was well integrated into the lives of these old Burmese hands, but the cosmopolitan port city of Rangoon provided much greater potential. This was especially attractive to the merchants, the veterans of the Yunnanese community. With expanding businesses, they began to find it increasingly necessary to have a presence in Lower Burma to fully utilize its superb commercial and transportation facilities.

The life experience of Li Xianhe 李先和, a Tengyue-born merchant, illustrates this transregional and transnational mobility. Born in 1851, Li Xianhe lost his father and other senior family members in the Panthay Rebellion (the Chinese Muslim rebellion from 1856 to 1872, based in central and southern Yunnan) while still a child. Typically for a frontier resident, he moved to Bhamo and engaged in the precious stone business. With peace restored and business going well, Li Xianhe settled his family back in Yunnan, purchased land, built houses, and arranged for the education of his younger brothers and children. Li Xianhe himself remained in Burma and married a Burmese woman, Daw Pwu, perhaps from an influential family under King Mindon. Together, they funded Shwe In Bin, a teakwood monastery in Mandalay renowned for its excellent craftsmanship, for their son's *shinpyu* (initiation ceremony as a Buddhist novice).[69] Established as a Yunnanese merchant in Mandalay, a successful example of a pattern enjoyed by generations before him, he was able to explore the possibilities of a larger operation that only the new colony could provide. The precious stone business was headquartered in Mandalay, with branches in Genong 格弄 (probably the Hpakan area) for jade and Mogok for rubies, with retail networks in Yunnan, Burma, Fujian, Guangdong, Jiangsu, and Zhejiang, no doubt taking advantage of the port of Rangoon. Later, Li Xianhe also ventured into the tea trade (at which he failed) and acquired rice mills in the delta, in addition to continuing to trade in jade and rubies with Shanghai and Guangdong. One

FIGURE 12.2

Tomb of Li Xianhe, outside the West Wall of Shwe In Bin Monastery, Mandalay

Source: Photo taken by the author, 2008.

of his sons managed a family shop in Guangzhou and died there, and his other children and grandchildren became well established and married into the families of high-ranking Burmese colonial officers.[70] By the time of his death in 1917 in Rangoon, his connections with southern and eastern Chinese ports were particularly extensive, benefiting from his relocation to Lower Burma.[71]

If in precolonial times the Yunnanese were but another local people freely wandering on the Yunnan–Burma frontier, in the colonial period in places like Rangoon they established themselves in a new identity as immigrants, because they were a non-indigenous group that were seen by others to require a clear social definition and communal boundaries. In this colonial cosmopolitan centre, the Yunnanese met the British and the Indians as well as other Chinese, and, to a lesser extent, their old acquaintances such as the Burmans, Shans, and Kachins. It provided a space for them to mingle with their fellow Chinese — the Cantonese and the Hokkien — with whom they might not have had a chance to intermingle back in China. In this way, the creation of a multi-ethnic colonial state facilitated the formation of a communal identity for its immigrants.

Conclusion

Separated by high mountains and mighty rivers, Tengyue and its surrounding areas in western Yunnan had always been more closely tied to Burma than to the rest of China, due primarily to its geographical adjacency. Burma under colonial rule maintained this closeness, which was further enhanced by modern transportation technologies that were brought over by the British. Especially upon the completion of a railway extension to Katha (1895) and Myitkyina (1898), the Tengyue route became even more convenient and was preferred by many from western Yunnan who wanted to go to eastern and northern China. These travellers often went by rail to Rangoon, then transferred to steamers to reach the Nanyang region and then coastal China, and then they continued northward, if necessary. Before the fall of the Qing Dynasty, young Confucian examinees made long-distance journeys by taking the steamship from Rangoon to Tianjin to arrive at the capital, Beijing, instead of the more demanding overland option via Kunming, the provincial capital, and the rest of interior China.[72] In 1895, after succeeding in the national-level Confucian examination in Beijing with a *jinshi* 進士 title, a Tengyue native, Cun Kaitai 寸開泰, took the sea route to go home and was welcomed by his fellow countrymen in Mandalay. He attended a banquet held at the Mandalay Yunnan Association, accompanied by Mandarin-attired Chinese men and Burmese dancing girls.[73] Other young graduates extended their journeys to Japan to undertake overseas studies in Japanese universities, bringing back not only modern technologies but also revolutionary and reformist ideologies. In the 1920s, the coffin of a Yunnan community leader from Mandalay, an early member of the Tongmenghui, Cun Haiting 寸海亭, who had died in Shanghai, found its way back via Hong Kong, Rangoon, and Mandalay, so that he was eventually buried in his home village of Heshun.

What is more, the mountains provided a natural obstacle in southwestern Yunnan, which helped to stop the advance of the Japanese army in 1942 towards Yunnan, whilst Tengyue was the only area in southwest China, together with Burma, that fell under Japanese occupation during the Second World War and saw one of the fiercest battles during its recapture by the Allies later.

However, as this research suggests, such geographic, commercial, and social connections developed during the colonial era were not a simple continuation of the precolonial frontier and its free exchange. With the border clearly defined and secured, interactions now thrived as a cross-border international exchange. As a result, both the Yunnanese in imperial China and in British Burma developed a clearer image of their own identities, as shaped on various levels by imperial, colonial, and communal institutions. Together, these communities put the finishing touch on the map of southwest Imperial China.

NOTES

1. Zhang Qian 張騫, the Han envoy to Central Asia, noticed that Southwest Chinese products (cloth and bamboo sticks) on sale in the local market had been imported from India, thus suggested the existence of an overland trade route linking India and China, very possibly via Burma. This story is mentioned in Sima Qian 司馬遷, *Shiji* 史記 [Historical Records] (Beijing: Zhonghua Shuju,

1982), vol. 123, *Dayuan liezhuan* 大宛列傳 [Treatise on the Dayuan] and *Ban Gu* 班固, *Hanshu* 漢書 [History of the Han] (Beijing: Zhonghua Shuju, 1962), vol. 61, *Zhangqian Liguangli zhuan* 張騫李廣利傳 [Biographies of Zhang Qian and Li Guangli].

2. During the reign of Emperor Qianlong, war broke out between the Qing and the Toungoo dynasties. This was followed by a prohibition of cross-border trade for the next decade, but eventually the ban was lifted.

3. Charles Patterson Giersch, *Asian Borderlands: The Transformation of Qing China's Yunnan Frontier* (Cambridge, MA: Harvard University Press, 2006).

4. The Southeast Asian geopolitical pattern of Mandala is best described in O.W. Wolters, *History, Culture and Religion in Southeast Asian Perspectives* (Singapore: Institute of Southeast Asian Studies, 1982).

5. Michael Symes and Henry Glassford Bell, *An Account of an Embassy to the Kingdom of Ava in the Year 1795*, Vol. 2 (Edinburgh: printed for Constable and Co., and Hurst, Chance and Co., London, 1827), p. 91.

6. Ibid.

7. For this process in British India, see Christopher Bayly, *Empire and Information: Intelligence Gathering and Social Communication in India, 1780–1870* (Cambridge, NY: Cambridge University Press, 1996).

8. John Anderson, *A Report on the Expedition to Western Yunnan via Bhamo* (Calcutta: Office of the Superintendent of Government Printing, 1871), pp. 54–56.

9. Ibid.

10. House of Commons Parliamentary Papers (HCPP): 1868–69 (420), East India (McLeod and Richardson's journeys), "Copy of papers relating to the route of Captain W.C. McLeod, from Moulmein to the frontiers of China, and to the route of Dr Richardson on his fourth mission to the Shan provinces of Burma, or extracts from the same", 10 August 1869.

11. For Cooper's explorations on overland access to Tibet from Yunnan and Assam, see Thomas Thornville Cooper, *Travels of a Pioneer of Commerce in Pigtail and Petticoats: or, An Overland Journey from China towards India* (London: John Murray, 1871); for Cooper's death in 1878 as the British Resident at Bhamo, see Rutherford Alcock, "Address to the Royal Geographic Society", *Proceedings of the Royal Geographic Society of London* 22, no. 5 (1877–8): 346.

12. Thomas Cooper, "On the Chinese Province of Yunnan and its Borders", *Proceedings of the Royal Geographic Society of London* 15, no. 3 (1870–71): 163–74.

13. Old Street may also be Kaungton (Laoguan tun 老官屯), which was mentioned during the Sino-Burma War in the Qing Chronicles.

14. This name appears in sources from the fourteenth-century *Yuanshi* 元史 [History of the Yuan] onwards. One reference mentions a "Grand Ming Street outside of Riverhead Town" 江頭城外有大明街. See Zhu Mengzhen 朱孟震, *Xinanyi Fengtu Ji* 西南夷風土記 [Record of the Mores and Customs of the Southwestern

Barbarians] (Shanghai: Shangwu Yinshuguan 商務印書館, 1936). Possible locations of Jiangtou Cheng are: Bhamo, a town opposite Bhamo, Katha, Myikgyina, or other places along the Irrawaddy. Regardless of which, it is agreed that it is an important post where the trade route meets the river.

15. Giersch calls this frontier area the Northern Crescent, as opposed to the Southern Crescent linking Ssu-mao, Kenghung, Kengtung, and Chiangmai.

16. Author's translation of 石爛江枯, 爾乃得渡.

17. The Browne Expedition was another major British attempt to develop a through route between Burma and China, after Sladen's 1868 expedition. It was abandoned after Margary's death. However, it led to the Chefoo Convention of 1876, which, under the negotiations of the British Minister in Beijing, T.F. Wade, eventually granted the right to Tibet via Sichuan and further privileges in China to the British. For British diplomacy in China before and around the time of the Chefoo Convention, see James C. Cooley, *T.F. Wade in China: Pioneer in Global Diplomacy 1842–1882* (Leiden: Brill, 1981). For the Margary Affair, see Wang Shen-Tsu, *The Margary Affair and the Chefoo Agreement* (London: Oxford University Press, 1940).

18. A.M.S. Wingate, "Recent Journey from Shanghai to Bhamo through Hunan", *The Geographical Journal* 14, no. 6 (1899): 639–46.

19. Logan Jack, "From Shanghai to Bhamo", *The Geographical Journal* 19, no. 3 (1902): 249–74.

20. William Geil, *A Yankee on the Yangtze* (London: Hodder & Stoughton, 1904).

21. Reginald Johnston, *From Peking to Mandalay* (London: John Murray, 1908).

22. Captain Williams was the engineer of the team (later replaced by Gordon), Dr Anderson the naturalist, and Captain Bowers and Messrs Stewart and Burn were representatives of the commercial interests of Rangoon.

23. Albert Fytche, "Memorandum", in *Official Narrative of and Papers Connected with the Expedition to Explore the Trade Routes to China via Bhamo*, by E.B. Sladen, Robert Gorden, and Albert Fytche (Rangoon: British Burma Press, 1869), p. 10.

24. Ibid.

25. Anderson, p. 217.

26. Ibid.

27. Ibid.

28. For a further description of this stage and performances in the late 1920s, see Walter Harris, *East for Pleasure: The Narrative of Eight Months' Travel in Burma, Siam, the Netherlands East Indies and French Indo-China* (London: Edward Arnold & Co., 1929), pp. 23–26.

29. "Bamo guandimiao shiji" 八莫関帝廟史記 [Historical Records of the Guandi Temple in Bhamo], in *Qingfugong baizhounian qingdian tekan* 慶福宮百周年慶典特刊 [Special Memorial Edition for the Centennial Anniversary of Kheng Hock Keong], (Rangoon, 1961), pp. 6–7; and Yin Wenhe 尹文和, *Yunnan Heshun qiaoxiangshi gaishu* 雲南和順僑鄉史概述 [A Brief History of Yunnan

Heshun Village as Homeland of the Overseas Chinese], (Kunming: Yunnan meishu chubanshe, 2003), p. 63.

30. Set Kyin was previously hired by the Bhamo Chinese merchants to protect the trade route, but he did not get the payment he had hoped for. To retaliate, he attacked the town just before the British occupation in December. This incident is known as "Jin Guoyu's Riot in Mogok and Bhamo in the Tenth Year of the Guangxu Reign". See Yin, p. 63; Geoffrey William Dawson, ed., *Burma Gazetteer: Bhamo* District (Vol. A) (Rangoon: n.p., 1912), p. 18.

31. Anderson, p. 218.

32. Sladen, Gorden, and Fytche, pp. 13–14.

33. Ibid.

34. Yule and Burnell, p. 789.

35. Ibid., p. 17.

36. This person is "Leesetai" in Anderson's report and "Li Si Tai" in the 1906 district gazetteer. Wang identified him as "Li Chen-kuo" (Li Zhenguo) 李珍國, the commander of Nantin (Nandian 南甸). He was born of a Chinese father and a Burmese mother. Wang, p. 28. Li Chen-kuo was claimed to be the murderer in the Margary Affair a few years later.

37. Sladen, Gorden, and Fytche, p. 11.

38. Ibid., p. 51.

39. Ibid., pp. 13–14.

40. Ibid.

41. Ibid.

42. The last Sino–Burmese border demarcation under British rule was conducted in the 1930s. However, due to the outbreak of the war, there was no official result thereafter.

43. Yin mentioned several examples in his home village of Heshun. See Yin.

44. Yin, p. 192.

45. Chenglian helped Yao Wendong 姚文棟 with his writing of *Yunnan kanjie choubian ji* 雲南勘界籌邊記 [The Process of Demarcating the Border in Yunnan].

46. Yin, p. 192.

47. The 1875 Browne expedition, which led to the death of Margary, also hired a Chinese interpreter, Moung Yo, whom Browne met in Prome. His Chinese name was Li Han-shing and he claimed to be a distant relative of Li Chen-kuo. Wang, p. 49. Given these circumstances, it is possible that Moung Yo acted in a similar way to Moung Shwe Yah, Zhang Chenglian, and Zhang Dexin.

48. It was written in Burmese to make it unreadable to his British and Chinese companions, and was later translated by him into Chinese in a mixed classical and colloquial style.

49. The profit could not be ignored, at least, at the local level. For example, the 1770s trade embargo after the Sino-Burmese war had significantly hurt frontier

peoples of all ethnicities, and Yunnan provincial revenue was clearly affected in the following years. Giersch, p. 108.

50. Author's translation of 觀土司尚有不忘中國之情, 奈因今日為官為將者, 何其不振作, 而睡不醒耶! 目下賊已出入境, 誘降土司, 尚不見甚將來迎甚官來使. 敵人如此猖獗, 豈非要待天雷擊死耶. Zhang Chengyu 張成渝, *Lujiang yidong zhi Jiulongjiang xingji* 潞江以東至九龍江行記 [Record of a Journey from the East of the Lu River to the Jiulong River], the twenty-seventh day of the third month of the sixteenth year in the Guangxu reign (1890).

51. Author's translation of 爾兄弟世食漢祿, 今日爾何將英人迎入境界 … 爾雖遷居異地, 宜思盡忠於中國. 盡英人慾進昔董, 君一厲害阻之 … 不然 … 恐爾兄弟難保性命. Zhang Dexin 張德馨, *Dajinshajiang Shangyou Jixing* 大金沙江上游紀行 [Record of a Journey on the Upper Stream of the Great Jinsha River], the second day of the first month of the seventeenth year in the Guangxu reign (1891).

52. Ibid. Author's translation of 英人如此胡行, 不知利害, 妄信緬響導之言, 倘有逆難, 不得不先作計較, 防其未然. 我等皆中朝赤子, 當盡忠心, 設有遇內地守邊將兵, 我等待當乘機而夾攻英人, 籍表隱忠, 或可轉邀一線之榮.

53. Yin, p. 43.

54. Ibid.

55. Yongli and his entourage fled from southern China in 1661. He was allowed to stay in Burma by the Toungoo Kingdom. However, the advancing Qing army soon captured him near Sagaing and took him back to Yunnan.

56. Yin, p. 43.

57. Perhaps this also explains, to some extent, the enthusiasm for archaeology that was shown by Taw Sein Ko, who was a self-identified Chinese classical scholar. For a recent discussion on Taw Sein Ko, see Penny Edwards, "Relocating the Interlocutor: Taw Sein Ko (1864–1930) and the Itinerary of Knowledge in British Burma", *Southeast Asia Research* 12, no. 3 (2004): 277–335.

58. The Amarapura Guanyin Temple, the main Chinese temple for the Yunnanese community in the Burmese capital, was established no later than 1773 and underwent a major renovation in 1846. As part of its communal duty, it managed the Yunnanese cemetery in Amarapura. Around 1876, the Tengyue Association was established with premises on 81 Street in Mandalay.

59. HCPP, 1868–69 (420).

60. The British also noticed "a flourishing colony of Chinese" in Bhamo by 1906, including both Cantonese and Yunnanese. *Burma Gazetteer: Bhamo District (Vol. B)* (Rangoon: Office of the Superintendent, Government Printing, Burma, 1906), p. 37.

61. Royal Commission on Opium, *Volume II, Minutes of Evidence Taken before the Royal Commission on Opium* (London: printed for H.M.S.O. by Eyre & Spottiswoode, 1894), p. 214.

62. Author's interview with a jewellery shop owner, who was also a senior member of the Cantonese association in Mandalay, and whose family business is in jade, Mandalay, November 2008.

63. C.M. Enriquez, *A Burmese Enchantment* (Calcutta: Thacker, Spink and Co., 1916), pp. 213–14.

64. *Who's Who in Burma* (Calcutta & Rangoon: Indo-Burma Publishing Agency, 1926), p. 123.

65. Yin Zhaorong 尹兆榮, *Riji* 日記 (Diary), 15 December 1928.

66. For the romanization of Burmese words, this chapter uses John Okell's system in John Okell, *A Reference Grammar of Colloquial Burmese* (London: Oxford University Press, 1969).

67. Yin. Author's translation of 們嘎拉從卜媽名, 濟濟衣冠俱上賓, 一闋咖啡一碟蒙, 原來就是新文明.

68. Ibid.

69. "Zhuming Ruiyingbing Miansi juanjianzhe Li Xianhe" 著名瑞迎彬緬寺捐建者李先和 [Li Xianhe, the Founder of the Famous Shwe In Bin Burmese Temple], in *Yunnan huiguan shilue* 曼德勒雲南會館史略 [A Brief History of the Yunnan Association], [Mandalay: Mandalay Yunnan Association, 2007], pp. 187–88.

70. For example, one of his daughters married a Burmese who worked in the colonial Financial Ministry, and another son and his children all married prominent Burmese in Rangoon. Ibid.

71. *Li Xianhe muzhiming* 李先和墓誌銘 [The Epitaph of Li Xianhe], outside the west wall of Shwe In Bin Monastery, Mandalay, carved in 1917.

72. Yin, p. 192.

73. A group picture of this activity was taken in the twenty-first year during the reign of Emperor Guangxu (1895). *Yunnan huiguan shilue*, p. 69.

13

HOW THE NORTH TRIED TO PACIFY THE SOUTH THROUGH RITUAL PRACTICES
On the Origins of the Guan Suo Opera in the Nineteenth Century

Sylvie Beaud

This chapter is an attempt to understand the sociological configuration that gave rise to the masked ritual called the Guan Suo Opera 關索劇 in the Yangzong 陽宗 Valley (Yunnan province) during the nineteenth century. Similar to the well-known *dixi* 地戲 (literally, "drama on the ground") of the Tunpu 屯堡 people in Anshun 安順 (Guizhou province), the Guan Suo Opera is considered to have been brought to the Chinese southwest by garrison soldiers. As such, the study of its birth in the region provides an understanding of the interaction and exchange between imperial military culture, i.e., the central culture, and southwestern local culture. I will show that, rather than being an example of the Sinicization of a border area, the Guan Suo Opera is the result of more complex and multilateral negotiations between Han and non-Han populations upon the establishment of imperial authority in the region.

What is the Guan Suo Opera? To the best of my knowledge, there is no historical record of the masked ritual. As will be shown in this paper, the late imperial local gazetteers at the district level were compiled before the probable date of the rise of the Guan Suo Opera. This means that what is knowable is its current form, the product of more than a century of existence and inevitable change. Nowadays, it is performed every year for the New Year festival by the men of the three lineages Gong 龔, Li 李, and Zhou 周 of Xiaotun 小屯 village. They perform rituals to exorcize pestilence in a drama that partly consists of acting out the battles of generals of the Three Kingdoms. The eponymous "Guan Suo" represents a tutelary figure for the villagers. He is a unifying figure, simultaneously a social emblem and protective god. The character is known mainly thanks to a chantefable, the *Biography of Hua Guan Suo* (*Hua Guan Suo zhuan* 花關索傳), excavated from a grave near Shanghai in 1967.[1] Guan Suo is not a historical figure, in contrast to his supposed father, the famous Guan Yu (d. 219). In the current version of the *Romance of the Three Kingdoms*, Guan Suo is described as a general who has been sent as the vanguard to Yunnan during the campaign to pacify the Southern Barbarians, led by Zhuge Liang, in AD 225. This campaign is historical (though Guan Suo's involvement is not). According to the villagers in Xiaotun, Guan Suo established his camp at the location of their village. If this belongs to the realm of myth, traces of Guan Suo in the southwest of China nevertheless do exist in the topography: these are mainly to be found in the names of places (Guan Suo zhen 關索鎮, i.e., "township"), of mountain ridges (Guan Suo ling 關索嶺), and of temples (Guan Suo miao 關索廟). The foundation of at least some of these temples seems strongly connected to the implementation of garrisons at the beginning of the Ming Dynasty (1368–1644). According to Anne McLaren, a specialist in Chinese vernacular literature, the cult of Guan Suo was encouraged by the Ming central government in order to legitimate its authority in the region by reminding the local people of the old conquest by Zhuge Liang and his armies.[2] Guan Suo is not only a military figure; he is also known by bandit or rebel nicknames, for example "Sick Guan Suo-Yang Xiong" in the novel the *Water Margin* (*Shuihu zhuan* 水滸傳) or "Rivalling Guan Suo" in historical records.[3]

As an anthropologist, I rely mainly on contemporary data, i.e., those that were collected during two years of fieldwork in Yangzong Township from 2005 to 2007. The range of written primary sources available is limited. I have therefore relied heavily on local gazetteers as well as on pertinent secondary sources. This approach is meant to help us understand not primarily the historical origins of the Guan Suo Opera, but rather the way in which practitioners view it and have transmitted the memory of its origins. It gives us a glimpse of how the Han living in the margins of present-day China perceive their position with respect to the centre and define themselves in relation to their neighbours over time.

In Xiaotun village, it is very common to hear that "the Guan Suo Opera dates back to the Three Kingdoms, three hundred years ago" (while the Three Kingdoms actually corresponds to the third century, or more than 1,700 years ago). Yet the respondents who juxtapose these different dates and periods are actually not totally ignorant of the chronology of imperial history, so how is it that they seem to mix time up in this way? My research started with the findings of Chinese researchers many of whom suggest that the Guan Suo Opera took shape during the Daoguang era (1821–51). I have tried to reconstruct its history following this prior research. The major difference from that research is that the main informant, Gong Xianggeng 龔向庚 (1909–2001), died in 2001 at the age of 92. Since my first time in the field was in 2002, I was unable to interview him. Thus I had to rely on second-hand sources (written documents and information given by other informants) regarding his contribution. I use several kinds of data: the studies written by local researchers (mainly civil servants from the Cultural Affairs Office), the works of Chinese and foreign historians, and, above all, the various discourses circulating in Xiaotun village. Previous research did not place much weight on the points of view of the members of other lineages other than the Gong, mainly because Gong Xianggeng had such a long career in the Guan Suo Opera, and such a strong will to preserve it, that he naturally became the dominant point of focus. Nonetheless, it is worth considering what other villagers have to say about their practice.

Interestingly, the particular history of the three lineages that are involved in the Opera provides an alternate view of its origins and shows the diversity of the population that inhabited the valley at the time. Thus, the accounts of these three lineages offer an understanding of the relationship between the various populations, Han and non-Han, during the nineteenth century.

Three Accounts on the Origins of the Guan Suo Opera

An External Origin

The following is an account of the origin of the Guan Suo Opera according to Gong Xianggeng, collected in the 1980s:

> Xiaotun village is located south of the Yangzong valley, at the foot of the mountains. Once the mountains are crossed one arrives in the Chengjiang 澄江 valley, the district government's city. According to legend, during the Southern Campaign [AD 225], Guan Suo was sent as a vanguard by Zhuge Liang and established his camp here [i.e., present day Xiaotun]; that is why the place was called Xianfengying 先鋒營 [the Vanguard camp]. During the Panthay rebellion the place was used for the storage of cereals [for the imperial troops] so the name was changed into Xiaotun [the Small garrison]. At the beginning of the Qing Dynasty, some of the Gong lineage families moved from Laowangshiyan 老王石岩 of Dongshan 東山 village [about one kilometre away from Xiaotun] and settled here. Later on, an epidemic erupted in Xiaotun, affecting humans and cattle. All medicine failed to eradicate it. People invited *huadeng* 花燈 [flower lanterns] drama, *banda* 搬打 [local martial art] troupes[4], dragon dancers in order to expel pestilence, but without result. A geomancy master from another region passed by the valley and told the people that the geomancy of the place was "the five tigers drive the goats" [*wuhu nianyang* 五虎攆羊]. Only by "playing Guan Suo" would they manage to preserve the balance of the place and drive away evil influences. In the Guan Suo Opera there are the five tigers — generals — and they can ensure good harvest and prosperity of the cattle. So the villagers sent Gong Zhaolong 龔兆龍 and Li Chenglong 李成龍 to look for a place "playing Guan Suo." They eventually found a troupe playing Guan Suo in Datun 大屯 village in the Lunan 路南 area and invited them to come to Xiaotun to teach the villagers how to play Guan Suo. The Xiaotun villagers learned promptly. At the beginning they had no masks, so they sent someone to Kunming to order some. Since then, the Guan Suo Opera has been transmitted through generations in Xiaotun.[5]

The aged actor Gong Xianggeng provides a few key points regarding the Guan Suo Opera's origins. The first point lies in the exorcist function of the opera: epidemics are commonly seen as sent onto the population by demonic gods. Ritual performances to ease epidemic gods were thus popular responses to sanitary disorders.[6] According to Gong Xianggeng, while all medicine and the usual song and dance performances failed to eradicate the epidemic, the Guan Suo Opera came as the ritual solution. The second point is that it came from outside the region. Gong Xianggeng evokes a certain "Datun village", the precise location of which remains unclear since this name was widely used as a name for garrison villages, and the Lunan area can be equally understood as the actual Lunan township (Shilin district, located to the northeast of the Yangzong township) or as a generic geographical term meaning "the South of the circuit". It is, however, highly significant that Datun, literally "big garrison", appears as the complement of the Guan Suo Opera's village name Xiaotun, meaning "small garrison". This suggests a potential relation between the two, as well as a common military origin, as shall be confirmed hereafter.

The Reference to a Nanjing Ancestry

Apart from the Gong lineage's account, there is "a Li account" as well, mainly represented by Li Bencan 李本燦, the person currently in charge of the Opera. According to Li Bencan's point of view, the story of the two masters from Datun was invented by Gong Xianggeng. His own discourse is less elaborate than Mr Gong's. He simply says that his ancestors played the Guan Suo Opera and transmitted it to him. Now he is in charge of transmitting it to the younger generations. Li Bencan's account provides two main elements that differ from Mr Gong's information: the Guan Suo Opera originated with soldiers from the Liushu wan 柳樹灣 area in Nanjing, and this happened at the time of his great-great-grandfather.

The reference to soldiers coming from the Liushu wan area in Nanjing corresponds to the military campaigns under Zhu Yuanzhang (1328–98), the Ming Dynasty founder. These campaigns are often presented as being the main source of the Yunnanese (Han) population. Yang Shiying 楊士英, writing a history of the Yangzong population, says that a tombstone from the Yang lineage (members of which still currently live in the township capital) attests to the transplantation of the Ma family into what was to become Mazhuang 馬莊 (literally, the domain of the Ma) as a corollary of the campaign of Mu Ying 沐英, who was one of Zhu Yuanzhang's main generals.[7] Local gazetteers indeed mention such a campaign and the official encouragement of civilians to establish themselves in the region:

Ming Dynasty, Taizu reign, Hongwu era [1368–99]:

- 14th year [1382], Fu Youde 傅友德, Marquis of Yingchuan 潁川, received the order to go take control of the South; he departed with Lan Yu 藍玉, Marquis of Yongchang 永昌, and Mu Ying, Marquis of Xiping 西平.
- 17th year [1385], migration of the inhabitants of the central regions to establish themselves in Yunnan.[8]

Nonetheless, the importance of this migration should not be overstated. Fang I-chieh, researching the population of Heshun (Yunnan province), of whom ninety-six per cent are now officially registered as Han, and noting the frequent reference to the same migration wave, warns:

> We may assume that the Heshun people, *like other marginalized groups, try very hard to link themselves with an imagined centre, the locus of authority in Beijing or Nanjing, and seek to identify themselves with the higher-ranking ethnic group, the Han Chinese*... [emphasis added]
> However, looking at the Heshun case more closely, we find that local identity is more complex than this and results from a subtle interweaving of official and local concerns.[9]

James Lee's study of immigration in the southwest goes even further into the debate: it argues that the idea of migration corresponded to a collective answer to the need for auto-identification for population groups.[10] Indeed, as far as the people in Yangzong are concerned, the migration from Nanjing has been important — as elsewhere — not only in terms of the size of the population that settled in the area, but also in terms of its impact on the memory of the generations that followed, to the point that later waves were also referred to as "from Nanjing".

Thus, Li Bencan's account shows that the affiliation to Nanjing migrants is still a strong reference for a fraction of the population nowadays and relates the particular Li lineage's ancestry to a military and external origin.

Indigenous Ancestors

Contrastively, members of the Zhou lineage provide a distinct discourse on their lineage's origins. The following excerpt is taken from a conversation with Zhou Zilong 周自龍:

> My brothers and sisters died during the great famine of 1958–59, of starvation and disease. Me, I was born in 1961, everyone thought I would not survive, but ultimately, I am the only one of the eight children that survived. When I was young my paternal grandmother was still alive, but my grandfather was dead. He had been addicted to opium. At that time, everyone was growing opium in Yangzong. According to what my father told me, our family is from here. Did my ancestors come from another place hundreds of years ago? I do not know.[11]

In Xiaotun, as in Yangzong in general, almost all the villagers identify themselves as Han, but some of them claim that their ancestors belonged to populations that are nowadays categorized as "minority nationalities" (*shaoshu minzu* 少數民族). They do not necessarily refer to the same ethnic group, and in fact, it is very likely that various groups occupied the valley over time. Nonetheless, the main discourse argues that their ancestors were Yi, who later became Han. It is known that Yangzong's former name was Qiangzong 强宗, which also designated the population living in the Yangzong valley. It was called Qiangzong bu 强宗部 (*bu* 部 is "tribe"). At the time of the Dali kingdom (938–1253), Qianzong bu was also an administrative division.[12] There is a mention of this "Qiangzong bu" on a stele dating from AD 971, erected in Qujing 曲靖. The title given to the French translation is "The Oath of the 37 Lolo Tribes".[13] This text tells us that part of the population of Yangzong comes from the same branches of ancestors as the ones now categorized as Yi 彝 (the Lolo, or former Yi 夷). According to various sources, Qiangzong was changed to Yangzong to follow the local pronunciation. Even though it is not possible to identify the origins of former populations in Yangzong, the sources agree on the presence of non-Han populations, and, as such, it is completely understandable that some of the actual villagers claim a non-Han ancestry.

The Zhou do not have a particular discourse on the origins of the opera; they usually quote Gong Xianggeng's account when questioned on that point. In other words, they do not suggest any alternative version that might present a claim for a local origin for the practice. From this one can infer that it may indeed have been brought from outside, as stated both by the Gong and the Li representatives. What remains to be clarified, then, is when the arrival of such a military mask opera took place.

Attempts to Date the Guan Suo Opera's Origins

In the above account collected by Yang Yingkang 楊應康, Gong Xianggeng says that "at the beginning of the Qing Dynasty", some families of the Gong lineage settled in Xiaotun. In another publication, the collector writes that this temporal expression corresponds to the Shunzhi era (1644–61), that is, the reign of the dynasty's founder.[14] Ueda Nozomu 上田望, a Japanese specialist in Chinese literature, notes that some researchers give the Shunzhi era as the starting point, while others give the Kangxi era (1662–1722).[15] Qiu Kunliang 邱坤良 argues that the Guan Suo Opera started between the Daoguang and Tongzhi eras (1821–51 and 1862–74 respectively).[16]

Those in charge in the district's Cultural Affairs office, who had researched the Guan Suo Opera, did not find any proof of the existence of the practice in the Shunzhi period (1644–61, the earliest period mentioned). They then turned to investigate another element of Gong Xianggeng's account: the names of the persons involved. The aged actor indeed said: "So the villagers sent Gong Zhaolong and Li Chenglong to look for a place 'playing Guan Suo'". These two men, Gong Zhaolong and Li Chenglong, have thus been considered to be the first generation of Guan Suo players in Xiaotun. Trying to find out during which period these two men lived, they found the answer on a stele, discovered near Xiaotun village and nowadays included in the village's main temple.[17] The inscription, regarding a dispute over the temple's land, was carved in 1827 and mentions the name of Gong Zhaolong among the witnesses of the property judgement. Even though the inscription says nothing about the Guan Suo Opera itself, it is by relying firstly on these two pieces of data, Gong Xianggeng's account and the stele inscription, that the former director of the Chengjiang Cultural Affairs Office claims that the Guan Suo Opera started during the Daoguang era, about two hundred years ago.[18] His view matches that of several other researchers including Gu Feng and Ueda Nozomu.[19] Others favour a later origin date. For instance, Xue Ruolin, a specialist in popular drama, states that the Guan Suo Opera arrived in Yangzong along with migrants from Zhejiang during the Xiangfeng era, 1851–62.[20] In short, while they draw from the same informant, the authors come up with different interpretations of his words. Thus the sole Gong account appears insufficient to date the Guan Suo Opera's origins.

Similarly, it is difficult to discover precisely when Li Bencan's ancestor arrived in Xiaotun, but a tentative estimate is possible. Nowadays, the legal age for marriage is twenty years of age for women and twenty-two for men, which is rather late (it was eighteen and twenty respectively before 1980). We know that marriage used to occur much earlier, particularly in the countryside, especially before the first marriage law was passed in 1950 (nowadays in Yangzong, it is not unusual for a couple to live as husband and wife for a while before regularizing the marriage when they reach the legal age). From another perspective, the historian Nicola Di Cosmo tells us that the average age for entering military service for banner men (ethnic Manchu) under the Qing was thirteen years old.[21] With this in mind, I calculate the time of a generation as an average between thirteen and twenty-two, i.e., eighteen years. Since Li Bencan was born in 1925, I estimate that his great-great-grandfather might have been born around 1853. This means he may have arrived in Yunnan in or after but probably not before 1866.[22]

It is clear then, that according to the accounts of the two oldest actors alive in the 1990s, it is very unlikely that the practice originates earlier than the Daoguang era. Thus it appears that what happened during *and after* this era might be of particular importance for understanding the context in which it took shape.

The nineteenth century saw major upheavals in Yunnan in particular. Three main factors radically changed Yunnanese society at the time: migrations and economic development, epidemics, and finally, the Panthay Rebellion. These factors created social unbalance which led to the need for a radical ritual solution, and this need may very likely have played a part in the establishment of the Guan Suo Opera.

Migrations, Epidemics, and Rebellion: The Troubles of the Local Society

Mines, Trade Development, and Rapid Population Increase

From the mid-eighteenth century onward, the population in Yunnan increased very rapidly. Concerning the population of the Yunnan only, Michel Cartier estimates that it was about 2.3 million in 1750 and 7.4 million in 1850. That is to say, the population more than tripled within a century.[23]

Migration waves were of various kinds: farmers looking for land, but also migration resulting from the expansion of trade and industry, as well as of criminals sent into exile (*chongjun* 充軍).[24] Sending criminals to the empire's margins was not a new practice during the eighteenth and nineteenth centuries. Similarly, agricultural migrations remained relatively limited due to the tools and techniques in use at the time, which were adapted only for certain types of lands.[25] The new phenomenon, which makes up the major part of the migration between 1750 and 1850, is connected to economic and trade development in the province.

The economic transformation of the Yunnan and Guizhou region was essentially a consequence of the government policy in support of copper mines. This support intensified from 1723, after the Japanese Tokugawa regime stopped exporting copper to China.[26] Cartier considers that the opening of copper mines in Yunnan was the catalyst for significant migration as well as the assimilation of the indigenous population.[27] However, it was not only due to copper: tin, lead, and silver exploitation were all subject to intensification at that time.

The development of the mining industry caused not only the migration of miners but also that of merchants and workers transporting Yunnanese products. These migrants mainly came from Sichuan, Jiangxi, and Hunan provinces, and later, after 1910, from Guangdong and Fujian.[28] Reflecting the interests of the central state, emperors tried to control these migrations and to protect local indigenous populations up until the beginning of the nineteenth century. But the imperial ideology changed radically during the Daoguang era as the emperor strongly supported the colonization of Xinjiang.[29] As a consequence of these important migrations and the imperial ideology, the Daoguang period gave rise to increasing social tensions. Disputes over land, property, and exploitation multiplied.

The context of economic development gave rise not only to increasing demographic pressure on the land, but also to an intensification of traffic along the caravan routes. This second factor facilitated the transmission of bubonic plague, which spread into western Yunnan at the end of the eighteenth century.[30] The large number of epidemic outbreaks during the Daoguang era is one of the arguments on which Chinese researchers base their claim that the Guan Suo Opera, which supposedly eradicates epidemic demons, took shape at that time. They rely on documentation from the *Chengjiang Gazetteer*, 1847.[31] Although the gazetteer does indeed mention a concentration of epidemics during the Daoguang period, the records stop a few years before the end of the era (1847). In fact, these citations correspond only to the first wave of the epidemic.

Bubonic Plague in the Second Half of the Nineteenth Century in Yunnan

In Carol Benedict's study of the origins and development of the bubonic plague in the nineteenth century — the outbreak that was to become the third greatest pandemic in history affecting all continents — she particularly focused on the situation in Yunnan province where the outbreak began. Benedict shows that the bubonic plague appeared as early as 1772 in western Yunnan and caused a first epidemic wave lasting until 1830, reaching the central and eastern parts of Yunnan during the first decades of the 1800s. As far as the region of Yangzong (belonging to the Heyang district at that time) is concerned, she mentions outbreaks in Heyang in 1806, 1825, and 1830. The *Chengjiang Gazetteer* also records the outbreaks of 1806 (Jiaqing era) and 1830 (Daoguang), but does not mention a plague in 1825 (that outbreak is included in the *Yunnan Gazetteer*).[32] However, the *Chengjiang Gazetteer* records two other plagues, which appear not to have been recorded in the provincial documents that Benedict used for her study, one in 1831 and another in 1839.

A second epidemic broke out between 1854 and 1898. The plague started to reach Guangxi and Guangdong provinces in 1860, and then kept spreading eastwards. During this period, the Chengjiang area was particularly badly affected in 1872–73, at the end of the Panthay Rebellion.[33]

Thus, I suggest we should at least examine the possibility that the practice took shape during the second wave of the epidemic, that is, around 1872–73. The date corresponds to the last years of the Panthay Rebellion, when the government sent troops and money to support the imperial army in order to put an end to the rebellion. This quasi civil war had such tremendous consequences for the local society that it seems unnatural to exclude it from the various reasons why the people of Xiaotun were searching for a social and ritual response to their troubles, such as the Guan Suo Opera.

The Panthay Rebellion (1856–73)

The entire Yunnan province was devastated by the Panthay Rebellion that erupted in 1856 and lasted until 1873, leaving the population decimated and exhausted. In his book devoted to the rebellion, David Atwill gives a panoramic view of Yunnan provincial society in the nineteenth century.[34] He shows that the population was divided by the imperial administration into three categories, labelled with three ethnonyms: Yi 夷, Hui 回, and Han 漢. None of the people labelled this way formed a homogenous whole: the generic term Yi was used to name many different ethnic groups who had nothing in common, only that they were neither Han nor Hui.[35] The term Hui, at that time, was not equivalent to "Muslim" but possessed a broader meaning corresponding to an ethnicity based on shared cultural and economic activities (mainly caravans, trade, salt wells).[36] Finally, among the Han, there was an important distinction made between the old Han (who had been established in Yunnan since before the eighteenth century, were largely assimilated to local society, and had adopted a Yunnan-centred perspective) and the recent migrants who maintained strong regional identities.[37]

According to Atwill, the Yunnan ethnic landscape was directly related to the province's topography. He describes the province as being made up of three main regional zones: the east, the west, and the south. Three main ethnic groups occupied the east of Yunnan: the Yi 彝 (a different character from the previous "Yi") in the contemporary designation, who appeared as "Lolo" or "Luoluo" in nineteenth-century sources, the Zhuang, and the Miao. In the western region, which is particularly mountainous, there were the Lisu and the Yeren (present-day Jingpo) along with other Tibetan populations, while the Minjia (Bai, probably descendants of old Han migrants assimilated to locals) were established in the Dali basin, and the Naxi around Lijiang city. The south was dominated by the Thai (Dai) — sometimes called Baiyi in the texts — as well as by the Woni (Hani).

The geographical division at that time is important to keep in mind when considering the relations between groups and the notion of locality. The boundary between the south and the east was located around the Dian Lake and the road to Guizhou. In other words, Chengjiang and its region were at the juncture of the two zones, belonging to the south. It should be noted that James Lee, further dividing the province into micro-regional zones, included Chengjiang in the centre, along with the provincial capital.[38] At the edges of the two macro-regions or in the central micro-region, Chengjiang and its surrounding areas were strategically important places. Moreover, the highest-ranking religious figure in the region, Ma Dexin 馬德新, was a man from Chengjiang who was still living there. He was not a rebel leader, but, as a respected religious figure, he played an important part as an advisor and mediator between the different factions.

There is of course a great deal more to be said about the rebellion which is beyond the scope of this paper, but what is important for the present contribution is the rebellion as it pertains to the sociological situation of the Yangzong region at the time of the supposed birth of the Guan Suo Opera.[39] One should remember that many indigenous populations, as well as Han people were also connected to the Hui leaders of the uprisings. This shows that there were increasing tensions between the imperial authority on the one hand, and the local leaders (*tusi* 土司) and their subjects on the other. The historian Patterson Giersch analyzed the sultanate of Du Wenxiu 杜文秀 established during the rebellion as follows: "It may prove to be that the Panthay regime represented an older vision of Yunnan. This was a vision of multiple, diverse communities, drawn together under imperial rule, yet flexible enough to allow an orientation toward Southeast Asia through the caravan routes."[40]

Fighting was not the only reason for the brutal decrease in the Yunnan population — epidemics, famine, and emigration were also contributing factors. While Cartier estimated that the Yunnan population was about 7.4 million around 1850, Atwill estimated that it was less than five million in 1874.[41] Words are insufficient to describe the damage caused by almost twenty years of fighting during the course of the war. The rebellion had started after massacres of Hui people in Kunming in 1839, 1845, and 1856 carried out with the approbation of the Qing administration. Many more massive executions took place during the years of the rebellion. To escape the massacres, some Hui hamlets converted to Han. Even today the names of these villages remain typical of their past Hui identity: some Hui people in Yunnan informed the anthropologist Kevin Caffrey that villages named Ma 馬, Ding 丁, or Na 納 — all common patronyms of the Hui people — attested to the phenomenon.[42] During the last years of the rebellion, when imperial troops occupied the rebel cities, Emile Rocher, a historical witness, mentioned forced conversions. Among the humiliations and abuses visited on the population was eating pork and raising pigs, which became the only way for Muslims to survive.[43] Once they had started to behave like Han, they could not go back: they "became Han" (*biancheng Hanzu* 變成漢族).[44] In the Yangzong valley, at least two villages bear names that could refer to Hui origins: Ma zhuang and Dingjia zhuang 丁家莊 (literally, the "domain of the Ma" and the "domain of the Ding family"). It is possible that these villages were formerly Hui villages. Nowadays, several Hui families live in the township capital and many more in the district capital, including a certain number of civil servants. What should be noted from the situation of the Hui villages and people is the flexibility of categories of identity: according to Caffrey,

> ... the notion that these ethnic categories were changeable would have been available to people under duress, and the notion remains commonplace in the stories some Hui tell about themselves. Similarly, many Han have also at times become non-Han.[45]

To put an end to the rebellion, troops and funds were sent to support the imperial forces on the spot.[46] When the imperial troops gained control of the region, the old garrisons were reactivated. After the imperial forces took the city, a fraction of the troops was left there.[47] It is worth noting that Gong Xianggeng mentioned this in his account of the origins of the Guan Suo Opera. It is significant that the name of Xianfeng ying (Vanguard Camp) was changed into Xiaotun (Small Garrison) at this very time. Some of the troops may have stayed there after the rebellion. Detailed information about the armies' movements and routes is lacking. However, Dzengsĕo, a Manchu soldier who took part in the campaign against Wu Sangui's rebellion in the seventeenth century and who went to Yunnan, provided information about the daily life of soldiers in the Qing army. He also gave indications about the route of the army from the eastern China to Yunnan. Dzengsĕo mentioned three "Guan Suo ling" mountain ridges and a Guan Suo temple on the way to and from the site.[48] The first two mentions might have referred to the same place, of which the author noted that there was also a temple devoted to Kongming 孔明 (Zhuge Liang) at the ridge. The translator of the diary, Nicola Di Cosmo, comments in his introduction that it is perfectly clear that the soldiers worshipped Kongming and Guan Suo.[49] The soldiers even erected a statue of Kongming on the way back.[50] This rare account "from inside" suggests that, despite the passage of two centuries, the cult of Guan Suo promoted under the Ming Dynasty was still alive three centuries later under the Qing, and not only among the Han, but also among the Manchu. Absent any evidence to the contrary, it seems likely that it was still active in the nineteenth century as well.

The presence of imperial authority was strengthened in the region with the establishment of troops in garrisons in Yunnan to quash the rebellion, but it did not resolve the social and political tensions that were troubling the province before 1856. On the contrary, tensions with the Hui continued to intensify, and many of the rebels who did not flee to Burma or Southeast Asia became bandits. Other revolts broke out among the indigenes at the local level and continued until the end of the century. Atwill concluded his book as follows:

> The sustained presence of non-Hui resistance — well after the rebellion was supposedly suppressed — contradicts the claims of Cen Yuying and others that the rebellion had been entirely a Han–Hui affair. Rather, the Panthay Rebellion in many ways was the final battle in a centuries-long process to formally and firmly orient Yunnan toward central China.[51]

I argue that it is in this enlarged perspective that the origins of the Guan Suo Opera should be investigated. Indeed, these eighteen years of war changed radically the configuration of the province, at least in terms of population. Chengjiang city was badly affected and the place partly occupied by soldiers. The Hui villages became Han in the vocabulary of the time and remained so in the contemporary categorization of *minzu* 民族, or "nationalities". It is noteworthy (and now very understandable) that the Guan Suo Opera took shape in circumstances that Atwill considers the result of a long process of the establishment of central authority in Yunnan, and this tends to confirm the idea that Guan Suo consists of a symbol of the central authority.

Conclusion

To conclude, the Daoguang era indeed constituted an important period for the local society in Yangzong, and for the whole province more generally. It corresponded to a rupture in the control of the movements of migrants. The different kinds of plague that may have created the need for a common ritual were also numerous at that time. But the administrators and researchers of this phenomenon have been relying on limited sources that failed to explain the views of the other villagers.

After the Panthay Rebellion, not only was the region left partly depopulated, but the ethnic landscape was also greatly modified. This can be explained partly by the malleability of categories, as well as by the plural signification of the notion of the "Han" at the time. The category of "Han" included people who had arrived from China's central regions and had been established in the area for a very long time (some surely at the beginning of the Ming Dynasty), as well as recent migrants who called themselves Han, including Hunanese, Sichuanese, etc. To call oneself Han was a way to unite under the same label as people who claimed a Chinese identity, being closer or farther from a genealogical perspective. This was sustained by the elaboration of a Yunnan dialect (distinct from the languages of the non-Han populations), mainly transmitted through oral literature and theatre that took shape progressively and on which the Yunnan Han identity could be based.[52]

The situation in Yangzong was in many ways similar to the ethnic tripartition that Atwill describes for Yunnan province as a whole. As Giersch noted, despite the efforts of the imperial government to control migrations and to keep new migrants separate from the local population, such segregation never worked in Yunnan.[53] Thus, in Yangzong, between the (potentially) Hui villages, the garrison villages and the autochthonous villages, the population seems to have been (and for a long time) diverse. The Guan Suo Opera has its origins in a complex ethnic background inherited from historical population movements. These populations had to coexist and collaborate after more than a decade of war and duress, and the Guan Suo Opera may have contributed to the creation of links between the villages.

Despite some differences of views in the way the practice was brought to their village, the discourses of the informants Gong Xianggeng and Li Bencan share several important elements, such as the fact that the practice came from "outside" and had been brought by the military. This point is less explicit in the Gong discourse, but the mention of Datun (Big Garrison, which is the complement of Xiaotun, Small Garrison) favours this interpretation. The researchers also confirm these points, no matter whether they rely on Gong Xianggeng's account or re-trace the chronology of the practice themselves, following the history of the Guizhou *dixi*. The practice probably did not take shape overnight, and might have incorporated some local pre-existing local practices as well, but it seems very likely that it was carried by soldiers who worshipped Guan Suo, at least up until the seventeenth century. The fact that Xiaotun was already a garrison place may have helped the implementation of this new ritual.

From all of this, we can suggest that the potential origins of the Guan Suo Opera might be found around 1872–73, at the end of the Panthay Rebellion, when the second peak of the epidemic devastated the region in the Tongzhi era, as mentioned in the *Guan Suo Opera Gazetteer*.[54] This period is not so far from my own tentative calculation relying on Li Bencan's genealogy. Moreover, it also corresponds more or less to Gong Xianggeng's account, at the point at which he connects the name of Xiaotun to the Panthay Rebellion and the reactivation of its garrison function.

The notion of "reactivation" indeed is central to the process and helps with our understanding of the way people talk about the past. The new military settlers reproduced, even though under different conditions, the establishment of the garrison troops which had arrived under the previous dynasty. It is not surprising, then, that people talk about the second wave of military implementation (Qing) in the terms of the previous one (Ming), which, as shown above, was often reduced to its emblematic scheme of soldiers and migrants from Nanjing. In the discourse of the Xiaotun villagers these models are conceptualized in the terms of Guan Suo's mythic role as a figure who came as a vanguard general during Zhuge Liang's campaign to pacify the south, and who established his camp in their village. Thus one pacification campaign is conceptualized in reference to a previous one. Migrations and military colonization are put in the same terms. The diachronic references encase one another like nested boxes and tend to give the impression of being synchronically associated. Then the questions raised by the accounts of people who were seemingly suggesting that the Three Kingdoms referred to three hundred years ago can be answered: they certainly did not confuse the Three Kingdoms period of the third century with the three hundred hundred years that separate the twenty-first century from the Qing Dynasty. Rather, the more recent period is being conceptualized in the terms of an older period, which is itself conceptualized in terms of an older one, and so on, and the result is that it ends up symbolically referring to the Three Kingdoms period.

As for China's relations with her southern neighbours in nineteenth-century Yangzong, old Han Chinese relying on a Yunnanese identity, new Han migrants, non-Han people, as well as garrison soldiers, all lived together and established notably ritual relationships. Affected by the same plagues, they united under the Guan Suo banner in order to eradicate epidemics and rebuild the social network within the valley. According to the actors, the Guan Suo Opera would visit every village and put it under its divine protection.

What remains unclear is how much the Qing central authorities supported the worship of Guan Suo as a way to re-establish peace in the region and legitimate the central government's presence in the localities of Yunnan, as the Ming government did. But it seems that, somehow, the central government and the various ethnic populations at the borders found a common emblem, though bearing different meanings for each, in the figure of Guan Suo. It is probably thanks to the perceived ritual efficacy of the Guan Suo Opera that the relationship between the different agents could be established and subsequently re-contextualized on a regular basis. As a result, the Chinese imperial authority found a way to re-legitimate its presence in the border region after the chaos of the rebellion, as it had done centuries earlier under the Ming Dynasty. Military operations were of course central to the process, but what probably gave it longevity was the establishment of ritual relationships between the villages.

NOTES

1. For an English translation of the chantefable, see Gail Oman King, *The Story of Hua Guan Suo — Hua Guan Suo Zhuan* 花關索傳 (Tempe: Arizona State University, 1989).
2. Anne E. McLaren, *Chinese Popular Culture and Ming Chantefables* (Leiden: Brill, 1998).
3. McLaren, pp. 243–47; King, p. 15.
4. It should be noted that even though I use "troupe" to designate these drama and martial art groups, the Chinese term (*dui* 隊) does not distinguish between a military troop and a theatrical troupe, and in the case of the local circumstances, both would apply.
5. Collected by Yang Yingkang in Hong Jiazhi 洪嘉智, ed., *Guan Suo xi zhi* 關索戲志 [The Guan Suo Opera Gazetteer], (Beijing: Wenhua yishu chubanshe, Yunnanjuan congshu, 1992), p. 81. I designate this version "official" because it is the one given in the official, Beijing-sponsored book on the Guan Suo Opera. Other versions (by the same informant) are mentioned in other publications that will be referred to later, and I also collected oral versions during my fieldwork. The above fully translated version is the most detailed.
6. See for instance the description of rituals for Marshal Wen in Paul R. Katz, *Demons Hordes and Burning Boats: The Cult of Marshall Wen in Late Imperial China* (New York: State University of New York Press, 1995), pp. 143–74.
7. Yang Shiying 楊士英, "Yangzong jumin laiyuan ji Mosuoman de hanhua" 陽宗居民來源及麼些蠻的漢化 [The Origins of the Yangzong People and the Sinicization of the Mosuo Barbarians], in *Chengjiang senshi ziliao* 澂江文史資料 [Documents on Chengjiang History and Culture], edited by Wenshi ziliao bianji weiyuanhui 文史資料編輯委員會 (Chengjiang: Wenshi ziliao bianji weiyuanhui, 1990), p. 84.
8. *Daoguang Chengjiangfu zhi* 道光澂江府志 [Gazetteer of Chengjiang Prefecture in the Daoguang Era], 1847, Book III, "Historical Events".

9. Fang I-chieh, "'Talking' Landscape: The Culture Dynamics of *Rushang* (Confucian Entrepreneurs) in a Peripheral Migrant Hometown in Yunnan", *The Asia Pacific Journal of Anthropology* 11, no. 2 (2010): 194. My emphasis; bibliographical references excluded from the quotation.

10. James Lee, "The Legacy of Immigration in Southwest China, 1250–1850", *Annales de démographie historique* (1982): 280.

11. Fieldwork notes, Xiaotun village, 23 July 2005.

12. *Daoguang Chengjiangfu zhi*, Book V, "Historical Sites".

13. Fernand Farjenel, "Le serment des 37 tribus Lolos", *Extraits du Journal Asiatique* (1910).

14. Yang Yingkang 楊應康, *Chengjiang fengwu zhi* 澄江風物志 [Chengjiang Scenery Gazetteer] (Kunming: Yunnan renmin chubanshe, 2004), p. 237.

15. Ueda Nozomu 上田望, "Unnan Kan Saku gi to sono shûhen" 雲南關索戲とその周辺 [The Guan Suo Opera of Yunnan and Its Environment], *Kanazawa daigaku chûgokugogaku Chûgoku bungaku kyoshitsu kiyô* [Journal of the Office for the Study of Chinese Language and Literature of Kanazawa University] 金沢大学中国語学中国文学教室紀要 6 (2003): 71.

16. Qiu Kunliang 邱坤良, "Guan Suo yishi yu Guan Suo xi yi Yunnan Chengjiang Xiaotun 'wan Guan Suo' wei li" 關索儀式與關索戲劇以雲南澂江小屯 '玩關索' 為例 [The Guan Suo Ritual and the Guan Suo Opera: A Case Study of "Playing Guan Suo" in Xiaotun Village, Chengjiang District, Yunnan Province], in *Minjian xinyang yu Zhongguo wenhua guoji huilun wenji* 民間信仰與中國文化國際會論文集 [Proceedings of the International Conference on Chinese Culture and Popular Beliefs], edited by Hanxue yanjiu zhongxin 漢學研究中心 (Taipei: Hanxue yanjiu zhongxin yekan lun zhu lei di 4 zhong, 1994), p. 594.

17. The full script of the stele is reproduced in Hong, pp. 121–22.

18. Yang, p. 237.

19. Gu Feng 顧峰, "Yizhi dute er yi you de nuoxi: Guan Suo xi" 一支獨特而移有的儺戲: 關索戲 [A Peculiar and Changing *Nuoxi* the Guan Suo Opera], in *Zhongguo nuo wenhua lunwen xuan* 中國儺文化論文選 [Collection on the Chinese *Nuo* Culture], edited by Guizhousheng minzu shiwu weiyuanhui wenjiaochu 貴州省民族事務委員會文教處 (Guiyang: Guizhou minzu chubanshe, 1989 (1985]), p. 277; Ueda, p. 72.

20. Xue Ruolin 薛若鄰, "Guan Suo xi yu Guan Suo" 關索戲與關索 [The Guan Suo Opera and Guan Suo], in *Yunnan nuoxi nuo wenhua lunji* 雲南儺戲儺文化論集 [Collection on Yunnan *Nuo* Drama and *Nuo* Culture], edited by Yuxi diqu wenhuaju 玉溪地區行署文化局 and Yunnansheng minzu yishu yanjiusuo 雲南省民藝術研究所 (Kunming: Yunnan minzu chubanshe, 1994 [1984]), pp. 163–64.

21. Nicola Di Cosmo, *The Diary of a Manchu Soldier in Seventeenth-Century China, "My Service in the Army" by Dzengsěo*, with introduction, translation and notes by Nicola Di Cosmo (London, NY: Routledge, 2006), p. 26.

22. If we calculate that eighteen years constitutes a generation, Li Bencan's father would have been born around 1907, his grandfather around 1889, his great-grandfather around 1871 and his great-great-grandfather around 1853.
23. Michel Cartier, "La croissance démographique chinoise du XVIIIᵉ siècle et l'enregistrement des Pao-chia", *Annales de démographie historique* (1979): 23. See also James Lee, "Food Supply and Population Growth in Southwest China, 1250–1850", *The Journal of Asian Studies* 41, no. 4 (August 1982): 711–46.
24. Fang, p. 198.
25. Lee, "Food Supply", pp. 719–20.
26. Ibid.; Carol Benedict, *Bubonic Plague in Nineteenth-Century China* (Stanford: Stanford University Press, 1996), p. 25.
27. Cartier, p. 21.
28. Lee, "The Legacy", p. 296. Sylvie Pasquet highlights the same provinces with the exception of Fujian. She also adds Hubei and Shaanxi provinces. See Sylvie Pasquet, "Entre Chine et Birmanie. Un mineur-diplomate au royaume de Hulu, 1743–1752 (première partie)", *Études chinoises* VIII, no. 1 (printemps 1989): 63.
29. Patterson C. Giersch, *Asian Borderlands: The Transformation of Qing China's Yunnan Frontier* (Cambridge, MA: Harvard University Press, 2006), p. 220.
30. Benedict, p. 29.
31. *Daoguang Chengjiangfu zhi.*
32. *Yunnan tongzhigao* 云南通志稿 [Draft Gazetteer of Yunnan Province], 1901, in Benedict, p. 20.
33. Benedict, pp. 36–71.
34. David G. Atwill, *The Chinese Sultanate: Islam, Ethnicity and the Panthay Rebellion in Southwest China, 1856–1873* (Stanford: Stanford University Press, 2005).
35. Ibid., pp. 23–5.
36. Ibid., pp. 34–47.
37. Ibid., p. 26.
38. Lee, "Food Supply", p. 731.
39. Atwill
40. Giersch, p. 219.
41. Cartier, p. 23; Atwill, p. 185.
42. Kevin Caffrey, "Who 'Who' Is, and Other Local Poetics of National Policy: Yunnan Minzu Shibie and Hui in the Process", *China Information* 18, no. 2 (2004): 262.
43. Émile Rocher, *La province chinoise du Yün-nan* (Paris: Ernest Leroux, 1880), p. 187.
44. Caffrey, p. 262.
45. Ibid.

46. During the first years of the rebellion, Yunnan was not a main concern for Qing imperial authority, which was already overwhelmed with two other rebellions that had broken out at the same time (1851): the Nian in the north and the Taiping in the south. It was only after these two were over (the Taiping in 1864, and the Nian in 1868) that central authorities were able to send military support to Yunnan. Rumours of massacres of Hui perpetrated by the imperial representatives reached the north-western provinces as well and caused another revolt (called the Dugan revolt) affecting Shaanxi, Gansu, Ningxia, and Xinjiang between 1836 and 1877. In the south-west, the Miao population had rebelled as early as 1853 in Guizhou province. See Gabrielle M. Vassal, *In and Round Yunnan Fou* (London: William Heinemann, 1922), pp. 30–70; Atwill, pp. 178–84; Yunnansheng difangzhi bianzuan weiyuanhui 雲南省地方志編纂委員會, ed., *Yunnansheng zhi* 雲南省志 [Gazetteer of Yunnan Province], *juan shou* 卷首 [vol. 1] (Kunming: Yunnan renmin chubanshe, 2004), p. 145.

47. For the account on the Chengjiang region, cf. Rocher, p. 152.

48. Ibid., pp. 65, 75, 76.

49. Ibid., p. 42.

50. Ibid., p. 82.

51. Atwill, p. 190. Cen Yuying 岑毓英, a man from Guangxi, helped the imperial army to put an end to the rebellion. He quickly became a member of the imperial administration in Yunnan. Among other positions, he became prefect of Chengjiang in 1861 and eventually governor of the province until the end of the rebellion. Cf. Ibid., p. 173 ff.

52. Lee, "The Legacy", p. 303.

53. Giersch, p. 211.

54. Hong, p. 13.

14

REALMS WITHIN REALMS OF RADIANCE, OR CAN HEAVEN HAVE TWO SONS?
Imperial China as *Primus Inter Pares* among Sino-Pacific Mandala Polities

Andrew J. Abalahin

The present King of Cochin China is the true heir and direct lineal descendant of the ancient royal house of Siam, which was extirpated by the Burmans around the year 1750; and as the present Siamese government is weak and distracted, it has for some years been considered a very probable occurrence, that he will soon find or take an opportunity of asserting his claims to the throne of Siam. Though this Prince has derived great assistance from the French in his dominions, on many occasions, he is obviously jealous of all European interference and can only be considered under the influence of the maxims of Chinese policy... . It is not... probable that any thing more than a very limited and hampered trade would ever be permitted with Cochin China; and this will be the more apparent if we consider the humiliating and slavish manner in which all traffic still is, and has been, carried out with both

Cochin China and Siam. ... It is obvious that trade of this type is by no means accommodated to the habits of Englishmen.

— Stamford Raffles, letter to Lord Minto, 1811[1]

There are three possible methods of dealing with the threat posed by proximate concentrations of Power — destruction and dispersal, absorption, or a combination of the two ... Destruction ... is the least desirable. More satisfactory is the method of absorption.... In theory, absorption is seen as the voluntary submission of neighboring kingdoms to the supreme Power of the ruler. One finds, therefore, in the classic description of the great kings of the past that *raja séwu negara nungkul (sujud)* — the kings of a thousand kingdoms offer submission to them. Significantly, the glorification of the ruler does not mention his prowess in battle, as might be the case with a European medieval monarch....

— Benedict Anderson, "The Idea of Power in Javanese Culture"[2]

The Master said: "Governing with excellence (*de* [also potency, power, virtue]) can be compared to the North Star: the North Star dwells in its place, and the multitude of stars pay it tribute."

— Confucius, *Analects*, 2.1 (trans., Roger T. Ames and
Henry Rosemont, Jr.)[3]

Little did Raffles, the future founder of British Singapore, understand that the role he would be playing in East and Southeast Asian courts was that of an inferior luminary paying tribute to imperial or royal "North Stars". Japan, he lamented, was even more vigorous in enforcing the "maxims of Chinese policy" than China itself.

How different would eastern Asia be within less than a century! It went from Englishmen begging to have emperors and kings open trade to them, griping all along about how the Asians opposed (the newly minted dogma of) "free trade", to Asians now rejecting the "maxims of Chinese policy" — in the 1880s, Japan, newly again "Imperial", forced Korea's Chosŏn kingdom to become the "Great Han Empire". This was so as to wean it off of vassalage to the Qing Empire and thus render it amenable to Japanese colonization. How could declaring "independence" ever mean rendering oneself liable to losing freedom? By what audacity could Imperial China's vassals have ever dared to emulate the "maxims of Chinese policy"?

This chapter seeks to re-evaluate questions of suzerainty and sovereignty in the "traditional" (pre-twentieth century) Eastern Asian (East Asia + Southeast Asia) multi-state system. It continues the inquiry I began in two earlier articles: "Sino-Pacifica: Conceptualizing Greater Southeast Asia as a Sub-Arena of World History" (*Journal of World History*, December 2011) and "*Intsik, Sangley*, and *Chinese*: The Politics of Sinonymy in Southeast Asia and Beyond" (forthcoming). In the first, I argue for viewing East Asia, Southeast Asia, and parts of Inner Asia as a single macro-region, "Sino-Pacifica", whose coherence can be traced back to the Neolithic period. In the second, I examine patterns of naming "Chinese" in Southeast Asia and beyond in order to assess the strength of an ethnic identity (hence of the depth of nationalism) among Chinese and in so doing identify a major substantive difference between Sino-Pacifica and Indo-Mediterranea[4] (Western Afro-Eurasia) that dates back to the Bronze Age: ethnicity has been *less* important an identity marker in Chinese history than in Western Afro-Eurasian history due to the perdurant hegemony of the "Chinese" state and of "Chinese" civilization within Sino-Pacifica. In the present chapter, I analyse the nature of Sino-Pacific states, Imperial China and its southern and eastern neighbours, in themselves and the character of their interactions with each other. In so doing, I discover yet another substantive difference between Sino-Pacifica/Eastern Asia and Indo-Mediterranea/Western Afro-Eurasia: Imperial China, its pioneering the modern bureaucratic state notwithstanding, was to a certain extent a mandala polity[5] like those for which Southeast Asia is renowned, a *primus inter pares* among Sino-Pacific mandala monarchies — Sino-Pacifica was a mandala of mandala states, a galaxy of galactic polities while Indo-Mediterranea oscillated between Imperia and Commonwealths.[6]

Did the Chinese get Funan *Right*? Comparing Chinese, Southeast Asian, and European Polities

I would like to begin my approach to the broad questions of state sovereignty within a multi-state system by considering a much narrower one: did the Chinese chroniclers get the proto-Khmer polity of Funan (first to sixth century CE) *right*, actually *not* misperceive and misrepresent it?

We read in surveys of early Indianized Southeast Asia that Chinese accounts have given us the "misleading impression" that Funan was a coherent kingdom: Chinese record-keepers "organized" their information about what was actually a "multiplicity of non-institutionalized states" under the rubric of "Funan" (and later of "Chenla").[7] By "state coherence", present-day scholars mean that a state is defined by defined borders — supposedly the *Chinese* definition of a state. Has not the Great Wall, that supreme border marker, been what has defined the Chinese empire as a state from the time of its founder, Qin Shihuang? Does not the very character for *guo* 國, the Chinese word for "state", include the "enclosure" radical, indicating "walled-ness", "bounded-ness" as the *sine qua non* of a Chinese-style state? Funan (which, by the way, seems to have the Khmer word for mountain, *phnom*, behind it), up-to-date scholarship tells us, was anything but a coherent Chinese-style kingdom but rather a blanket term for a number of upgraded chieftaincies in the Mekong Delta region. In other words, Funan was a collection of small-scale Southeast Asian-style mandala polities. But what if the Chinese writing those accounts did not think of *guo*, of statehood, in terms of a bounded territorial entity, in terms of what is, after all, the modern European-derived notion of the state? What if those ancient Chinese conceived the state more in the terms comparable to the Sanskrito-Southeast Asian *negara*, statehood defined by a walled *royal centre*? Could they then have gotten Funan "right"?

Conventional scholarship on Southeast Asia regularly draws a contrast between the structure and dynamics of the traditional Southeast Asian polities on the one hand and those of Western *and Chinese* ones ("states proper") on the other. China is vaunted for its pioneering bureaucracy, at least the "truly modern", systematically meritocratic, variety, whereas in Southeast Asia, Angkor, Pagan, and Borobudur are marvelled at for being erected supposedly with hardly any bureaucratic apparatus at all, conjured into monumental being by networks linking royal courts, aristocratic clans, monasteries, and villages.[8] China and Southeast Asia are characterized as enjoying two totally different ratios of people to land: in China, as in Europe, *land* is the scarce resource that the state must occupy and guard (hence the crucial role of walls — or fences — in open country), while in Southeast Asia *people* are the scarce resource that political actors, state and non-state, must attract or capture (hence the importance of the walled palace-city or citadel as the focus for the gathering of followers and slaves — albeit there was never a stark distinction between "free" and "slave" as in Western contexts).[9] The high ratio of people to land has, it is thought, permitted Western and Chinese states greater freedom to apply coercion on subjects since the latter cannot "vote with their feet" and abscond to "empty" hinterlands.

Now, Chinese statecraft *initially* evolved in a landscape that for a long period had yet to be filled in with human settlements, still possessing an open frontier that was "empty" but for scatterings of non-Chinese/ pre-Chinese "barbarians".[10] *Guo* in Shang times, in fact, referred only to the citadel of a ruler.[11] While Legalism may have expounded the efficacy of material rewards and physical punishments, Confucianism, which would become the bureaucratic empire's dominant ideology, emphasized the need for rulers to display virtue (*de*) so as to draw the voluntary submission of subjects and potential subjects. A nineteenth-century Vietnamese scholar not only disparaged the idea that physical objects (in his case, bronze pillars) could mark the boundary of a state but also questioned the very notion of marking state boundaries at all. Paraphrasing the Confucian classic the *Greater Learning*, he asked, "When one has virtue, one will have people and land. Who can limit this?"[12] Such words could make for a concise definition of the "philosophy" of the *Southeast Asian* mandala state. Chinese empires were the pioneers not only of bureaucracy, Bin Wong reminds us, but also of the welfare state; they saw catering to the material and educational/moral needs of their subjects as their business long before Western states began to.[13] In this, they showed a political calculus no different from that of Southeast Asian rulers who are ever mindful, on their far smaller scale, of staying on the right side of the thin line between squeezing willing subjects and driving them away.

The notion that Chinese and Southeast Asian notions of the state may not have been so different after all leads me to another question: How could this way of viewing the matter influence our view of how China and Southeast Asian (and other) "tributaries" related to each other? We clearly do not find in pre-twentieth-century Eastern Asia anything like the modern international state system, derived from the European historical experience, one that envisions a community of legally equal, absolutely sovereign, territorially demarcated states. Rather, what we find is a hierarchically structured Sino-centric or Sino-tropic multi-state order. What we observe is a galaxy of galactic polities, a mandala of mandala states, with Imperial China at its heart. No less than for Southeast Asian kings and other "men (and women) of prowess", the capacity to attract followers was the mark of a virtuous, truly legitimate ruler for the Son of Heaven; he (and in one case, she) was expected to draw tributary missions from as far as possible. *Tianxia*, "All Under Heaven", a common designation for the Chinese empire, was, after all, a *boundless* writ.

The unbounded, universal sovereignty proclaimed for China's emperor was, of course, a political fiction, just as the equality of states that is the foundation of the modern European-derived international system is a legal fiction. However, both frame a discourse through which state actors of unequal power can press for their interests. The difference between the two multi-state systems derives from the contrasting fates of their respective charter polities (to extend an idea of Victor Lieberman's[14]), the Qin-Han empire and the Roman empire. The question is often pondered: How would the history of the West have been different had the Roman Empire survived as the Chinese empire did? However, we need to remember that the Roman Empire *did* survive, not merely as an ever-shrinking Byzantium in the East but also as an ever growing Papacy in the West. Just as the Mongols were filling out their world empire with the conquest of the Southern Song, the papacy was extending a concrete institutional framework over Western and Central Europe, a true resuscitation of Roman imperial unity down to the level of the country parish and, if weakly, the peasant mind. The Western idea of national sovereignty, of a community of legally equal states, emerged as a rejection of an actual continent-wide Papal imperium.

In Eastern Asia, the dynamics were different. The overweening weight and scale of the Chinese empire (but for some eras of fragmentation) among the polities of the region meant that a discourse positing the equality of states could hardly ever arise. At the same time, the Chinese empire's dominance was not institutionalized in administrative structures that extended deep into the remote fastnesses of Eastern Asia. Therefore, for "vassal states", there was little reason until the modern era to reject a hierarchy positing China as centre or summit. In such a context, without a discourse of equality among states, how then did states assert themselves? Let us look at a particular anecdote, one from a state that did arise out of a rejection of direct Chinese imperium.

The Ever-Assertive South: Vietnam, Nan Yue, and Chu

In 1803, China's emperor gave Vietnam its name. The ruler of that southern tributary, Nguyễn Phúc Ánh (regnal name, Gia Long), the "Cochin Chinese prince", "sole surviving heir of Ayutthaya", of whom Raffles complained, had petitioned Beijing to recognize the name he had chosen for his country: "Nam Việt". The Qing court, however, took umbrage at this name. It recalled the memory of an ancient kingdom, Nam Việt (*Nanyue* in Mandarin, "Southern Yue") that included not only northern Vietnam but also the contiguous Chinese provinces of Guangdong and Guangxi (its capital, indeed, had been Guangzhou, then called Panyu).[15] The name implied a potential claim on Qing territory. "Yue" by itself might have been even more provocative: it was a classical blanket term for "barbarian" peoples dwelling from the Red River delta all the way to the Lower Yangzi, already for several centuries a core region of the Chinese empire.[16] In replacing "Nam Việt" ("Southern Yue") with the neologism "Việt Nam" ("South of Yue"), the Qing emperor was insisting that Nguyễn's realm had always been "to the south of China" and never been "the south of China" (as indeed the Nguyen family's ancestral domain lay to the south of the historical limit of Chinese rule).[17]

Why, might we speculate, did Nguyễn set upon "Nam Việt"/"Nanyue" in the first place? Perhaps it was precisely to affirm his accepting vassal status to the Qing. The original Nanyue was established in the wake of the collapse of the Qin dynasty not by any non-Chinese Lingnan lord but by a former Qin official, a native of Hebei, Zhao Tuo. For a number of decades, his descendants acknowledged the suzerainty of the new and relatively weak Han dynasty while maintaining de facto autonomy.[18] Having just prevailed over the Tây Sơn, a peasant rebellion so powerful as to have been able to repel a restorationist Qing invasion, Nguyễn probably saw nothing better than a relationship with the Qing like that of Nanyue to the Han.

In a conference paper, Erica Brindley has shown what might really have been at stake for the Qing court in Nguyen's resurrecting the name "Nam Việt". While presenting themselves to the Han court as kings (*wang*) subordinate to the Han emperor (*huangdi*), the Nanyue rulers styled themselves "emperors" in their own right to their largely non-Sinitic subjects.[19] According to the *Hanshu*, the third Nanyue ruler, one who had himself paid homage at the Han capital and taken a concubine from Hebei, upon his investiture by the Han emperor "hid the seals of his forebears" that named them "emperors".[20] Having just suppressed the White Lotus Rebellion at great cost in terms of resources but more importantly of prestige, a sedition-sensitive Qing court might have seen ancient Nanyue as providing a precedent for insubordination rather than for submission.

The Nguyễn court gave in and, when corresponding with Beijing, referred to its country as "Việt Nam". However, in its own internal communication, Nguyễn officialdom came to use an even more assertive name than "Nam Việt": "Đại Nam", the "Great" or "Imperial South". This phrase explicitly rejected the connotations of the name "Annam", the "Pacified South" (as the Tang dynasty had dubbed its province in northern Vietnam, a name the French would later apply to their colony in central Vietnam). "Imperial South" paralleled the expression "Nam Triều", the "Southern Court", whereby the Vietnamese state styled itself as comparable in dignity to the "Bắc Triều", the mere "Northern Court" of its Qing suzerain — a Manchu and no more "Chinese" than a Nguyễn. Two years after the Qing bestowed the name "Việt Nam", Nguyễn Phúc Ánh even referred to his state as *trung quốc*, the "Central State", China's *own* self-appellation (*Zhongguo*).[21] (This only should remind us that the most common current name for China in Chinese does not in fact refer to "*a* China", i.e. to a specific geographic space, at all!)

In *Beyond the Bronze Pillars*, Liam Kelley stresses that elite "Southerners" (as he prefers to dub them rather than anachronistically as "Vietnamese") embraced the idea of the centrality of China while at the same time asserting their own country's dignity as a comparable "domain of manifest civility", where the same Confucian norms held sway. The Nguyễn court's terminological "duplicity" can be put into a longer historical perspective by looking at the catalogue of names used by "Southerners"/Vietnamese for their own kingdom and for the "North"/China (as recorded in the envoy writings produced between the late sixteenth and early nineteenth centuries that Kelley studies). On the one hand, Vietnamese elites called China the "Esteemed Kingdom" (Thượng Quốc) and the "Inner Lands" (Nội Địa) and referred to their own country by the "colonial name" of An Nam, the "Secure" or "Pacified South" when communicating with the Chinese court or with envoys from other tributary states (most notably Korea, *Andong*, "the Pacified East"). On the other hand, they called China the "Northern Kingdom" (Bắc Quốc) and Vietnam the "Southern Kingdom" (Nam Quốc), language that appears to deny China the monopoly over "centrality". Even more self-assertive was to identify Vietnam as the "Celestial South" (Thiên Nam),[22] which calls to mind the Japanese term for their own — divine — emperor, the "Celestial Emperor", *tennō*, a term whose Chinese equivalent, *tianhuang*, was reserved for Taoist deities[23] (China itself merely had a mortal "*Son* of Heaven", *Tianzi*).

In order to assert the dignity of their own state in the face of a far more powerful and advanced Chinese empire, the Japanese deployed a more exalted term for their ruler than the Chinese applied to theirs (*tennō* rather than *kōtei*/*huangdi*). The Vietnamese contented themselves with applying the same term (*hoàng đế*) while also deploying the term *vương* ("king") when alternatively conveying submission to the Chinese emperor. Furthermore, in addition to the Sinitic *hoàng đế* and *vương*, they also called their ruler by the native term *vua*; this term conjured up a whole different set of associations than those called up by the "lofty" Sinitic titles, presenting the ruler as an approachable father figure to his people (comparable to the protective *vua bếp*, the kitchen god, who shared the intimacy of the peasant home).[24]

Parallel vocabularies of kingship, Sinitic and "native", can be traced as far back as the Chu state of the Zhou era. Long before the ascendancy of Qin, Chu had come close to seizing the leadership over the Central States that had once belonged to the Zhou. Expansive Chu evolved into a mirror of the Zhou, assembling a vast alliance of states matching and rivalling the one nominally under the Zhou but in reality dominated by Jin, Qi, or another ephemerally ascendant northern state. Chu imitated the features of the early Zhou polity, including a professional bureaucracy to administer its core royal domain. Chu's imitation (and surpassing) of the Zhou model was so successful that Li Xueqin speculates that the Zhou chroniclers refrained from describing its institutions in detail out of loyalty to the Zhou court, since it alone and no mere "vassal" state was fit to boast of such a sophisticated apparatus.[25]

The playing at submission was not kept up: in the eighth century BC, the Chu ruler assumed the title of *wang* ("king") that heretofore had been the unique prerogative of the Zhou ruler among all the rulers of the Central States, setting a precedent that all the other major states would follow. This "usurpation" of the Zhou title, one of the landmarks of the transition from the Western Zhou to the Spring and Autumn period, may have been merely to bring Chu into line with the practice of non-Zhou states such as Wu and Yue, whose rulers had never been called anything but "king". At the same time, beside *wang* Chu continued to use its own indigenous term for "king", *xiong*, which, Barry B. Blakeley speculates, could also have been the term for "(royal) clan head", and whose logograph suggests a role in sacrifices involving wine (the title's placement *before* the ruler's name ["King X"] rather than after it as in Chinese language practice ["X King"] likely reflects the Chu language's having a Southeast Asian-type grammar).[26]

Such parallel vocabularies of kingship have counterparts elsewhere in the Sino-tropic sphere. We have already mentioned the Japanese case. The monarchs of Indicized Siam, whose indigenous titulature proclaimed them awesomely as the "Lords of Life" (*chao chiwit*), consistently sought investiture from the Chinese as mere "kings" until almost a decade after the first Opium War.[27] Javanese monarchs to this day style themselves "Pakubuwono", the "nail" around which the "world" revolves. The Mongol title "Chinggis Khan" (applied to that genius of empire-building, Temüjin) meant "universal" or "limitless sovereign".[28] The Qing rulers drew on multiple conceptions of sovereignty, Manchu, Mongol, and Tibetan as well as Chinese, that exalted their status above the mere mortal.[29]

Flying, Refugee Mandates: Korea

The only Sino-Pacific people who seem not to have invoked a vocabulary for kingship that matched the claims of the Chinese emperor were the Koreans, who knew only too well how much they depended on China as their protector against third parties such as the Jurchens or the Japanese. And yet, under the Chosŏn Dynasty (especially during the first years of the Qing Dynasty when Koreans looked with dismay upon China's new Manchu masters as barbarians), Koreans prided themselves on being more (Neo-) Confucian than Confucius's race itself and thus perhaps saw themselves for a time as the *moral* centre of the world.[30]

In certain ways, Chosŏn *was* the fullest embodiment of Confucian ideals and thus just as or even more deserving of the Mandate of Heaven after the fall of the Ming. The society was, at least potentially, the most immersed in Confucian indoctrination: the per capita availability of Confucian academies (*suwon*, in Mandarin *shuyuan*) was almost ten times higher than in China.[31] Seemingly paradoxically, the feudal character of Chosŏn meant it was actually closer to Confucius's ideal, the Western Zhou polity. The Korean ruler never called himself *huangdi* ("emperor") any more than the Zhou sovereign/suzerain ever did (in the latter's case this would have involved time travel — it was Ying Zheng of Qin, liquidator of the Six Warring States, who put two ancient characters together to create the new title, to mean "universal monarch"). The monarchs of Chosŏn and of Zhou were both simply *wang* ("king"). A Korean scholar-reformer commented that the king was like the head of a dance troupe — no more personally indispensable than that, the dance of state could go on if a king had to be (bloodlessly) replaced.[32]

In part because they were still grateful for the Ming intervention that helped deliver Chosŏn from Toyotomi Hideyoshi's brutal invasions (which intervention was of such a scale that it is thought to have pushed the Ming Dynasty definitively towards its eventual collapse), Koreans did let on that they did not have complete confidence that the Mandate of Heaven had come to rest with the Qing. In Beijing, Chosŏn representatives dared to sport Ming fashions, and back in Seoul the court sacrificed at shrines dedicated to the Ming dynasts and even continued to mark time by the regnal year of Chongzhen, the last Ming emperor.[33] By these, they suggested that the Mandate of Heaven had devolved by default to Chosŏn.

The question arises: Why did the expansionist Qing state, one of the great "gunpowder empires" of the early modern era, never contemplate annexing Chosŏn in the way it did Tibet or Xinjiang (or in the way the early Ming regime occupied Đại Việt)? Kirk W. Larsen offers three reasons: 1) *Andong* (the "Pacified East", cf. *Annan*/Annam, the "Pacified South" — northern Vietnam's name while a province of the Tang empire) was already "pacified", already provided by its native rulers with a model Confucian state; 2) Andong as a tributary yet autonomous state was a convenient buffer against a proven dangerous Japan; and 3) a tributary relationship with Andong/Chosŏn was the most convenient way to manage trade not only with it but also with silver-exporting Japan (less urgent now that silver was flowing in from the Americas via Manila).[34] For Chosŏn, the tributary system was as much about *limiting* contact with China as about earning access to it — protective of their own polity, economy, and even culture, Chosŏn elites did not regard unregulated exposure to China as a thing to be desired.[35]

The question still remains: Why did the Qing not attempt to subjugate Chosŏn as the Sui and Tang — at enormous cost — had tried to subjugate Chosŏn's remote predecessor, Koguryŏ? Why *did* the Sui and the Tang see it as so crucial to vanquish Koguryŏ? I venture that this was because Koguryŏ, unlike steppe confederacies or any other states, was a viable candidate for the Mandate of Heaven, which after all was never reserved for "ethnic Chinese" (fully a member of which, in any case, the Northern Zhou-Sui-Tang elite was not). Koguryŏ was a Manchuria-based state like the later Jin and Qing but one that was already "Sino-civilized" (deriving ultimately from Han commanderies in northern Korea such as Lelang). Moreover, Koguryŏ's ally Paekche was a maritime power that could have threatened the shipment of Jiangnan rice to the northern capitals and frontier — hence the need for the Sui to dig the inland Grand Canal.

Heavenly Sovereigns: Japan

One of the regrettable effects of the area studies demarcation of an "East Asia" separate from a "Southeast Asia" has been to obscure something otherwise quite obvious: in terms of political evolution, Korea has more in common with distant Vietnam than adjacent Japan. Alexander Woodside discusses the comparability of the "three mandarinates", China, Vietnam, and Korea while leaving Japan aside (it had no equivalent bureaucracy until the samurai settled down into serving as domain clerks during the

Pax Tokugawica). Northern Vietnam and northern Korea were equally parts of the Han empire at a time when agriculture and metallurgy, much less any substantial influence from China's urban civilization, were still new to Japan (during the Tang period, northern Vietnam would remain under Chinese rule, while Korea/Silla and Japan/Yamato would become satellites of Chang'an).

How did peripheral Japan, backed up against the Emishi, Ainu, and the cold ocean, partake in the Sino-centric world order? The relationship varied over the centuries. At first, it was largely second-hand, through Korean states, mainly Paekche. Japanese rulers may have been, and certain specialist clans definitely were, Korean in ancestry. Japanese maintained an enclave on the southern tip of the peninsula: Mimana (called "Kaya" by the Koreans, in the area of the old Samhan confederacy).[36]

After an initial flurry of state-building tributary missions, Japan by the late Heian period turned inward and focused on digesting the legacy of an idealized China, a China of the classics,[37] rather than on facing the real, contemporary China of proto-capitalist/proto-industrial economics, of a meritocracy nurtured by print culture, and the dangers of a multi-state system including overweening barbarian "Sons of Heaven". Much later, the relatively weak Ashikaga shogunate, increasingly beleaguered in its headquarters in the Kyoto district of Muromachi, in an age of greater commercial dynamism and sophistication, accepted satellite status within the Sino-centric world order — the shogun obtained investiture as "king" (*koku-ō/guowang*) of Japan. As soon as Hideyoshi completed the "re-"unification of Warring States Japan begun by his erstwhile master Oda Nobunaga, he immediately launched a vast enterprise aimed at conquering the centre of the world, i.e., Ming China via Chosŏn Korea. This hubristic adventure failed, but the Tokugawa-era Japanese still sought to put their own island realm at the centre of the world. As Marcia Yonemoto writes, the "centrality" to which the Japanese now aspired was no longer geopolitical or philosophical but something more abstract. As did the Koreans of Chosŏn, with regard to their own state, the Japanese saw that the Mandate of Heaven was no longer in the hands of the rulers of China, since these were now Manchu "barbarians", but rather had passed to Japan.[38]

Late Tokugawa thinkers like Aizawa Seishisai, no longer saw "centrality" in terms of conformity to specific norms originating in China. For them, Japan, with its rigidly hierarchical social order, not only better embodied Confucian ideals, but was also the "Divine Land" — its supreme position in the world would be reinforced by selective adoption of "Dutch learning". The virtue of Japan lay in its unbroken line of emperors tracing their ancestry back to the sun goddess Amaterasu, something China with its dozen-plus dynasties and plethora of local regimes could never match.[39]

Thus in Eastern Asia we have five (or four and one-half or three and two halves) "domains of manifest civility": China, Vietnam, Korea, Ryukyu, and Japan. The three major "tributaries" asserted themselves *vis-à-vis* China in distinctive ways:

1) Vietnam posited a world with two courts, a Northern and a Southern one, its own;

2) Faced from the thirteenth to the nineteenth centuries with a China first ruled by world-sovereigns of nomadic descent, then by "Sons of Heaven" of peasant and Buddhist millenarian origin, and most recently by Sino-khans of Manchurian backwater fisher-forager-farmer ancestry, Korea strove to become the perfect realization of Confucian kingship in the world; and

3) Japan redefined centrality as possessing a Mandate of Heaven permanently invested in a divine dynasty.

Our understanding of the Sino-centric world order then can be given greater nuance, recognizing the following broad categories:

1) The territory under the direct rule of the sovereign of China (named after a dynasty, most recently, the Great Ming Country or the Great Qing Country);

2) The ex-colonial "domains of manifest civility", the Confucian mandarinates of Vietnam and Korea;

3) Japan, a partaker in Sinitic civilization but only incompletely since it lacked a mandarinate;

4) Tributary states in Southeast Asia (mandala polities) not Sinitic in civilization: Burma, Siam, Java, Malacca, Sulu, etc.

5) Adversarial states (often receiving tribute *from* China) in Inner Asia: Tibet during the Tang period and the steppe confederacies from the Han period onward.

Ryukyu, Nanzhao/Dali, and the Xinjiang oasis states represent special, intermediate cases, and the chieftainships of Yunnan and elsewhere, though technically part of the Chinese empire, were more exotic to China proper than were Korea, Vietnam, or even Japan.

Axes of the Cosmos and Palaces of Language: Siam and Java

Southeast Asian states participated in the tributary system but were also oriented towards non-Sinitic civilizations for their sources of high culture. In any case, they figured themselves "centres of the world" in their own right — generally as members of Indic (Sanskrit) or Islamic cosmopoleis. Siamese rulers presented themselves as Theravada Buddhist *cakravartin* monarchs ("he who sets in motion the Wheel of the Law").[40] They, however, at least during the early years of the Chakri Dynasty (until some decades after the First Opium War) communicated with the Qing court in Classical Chinese and adopted Chinese official names, *Tae Hua* for Rama I and *Tae Chia* for Rama V (Chulalongkorn). The Javanese monarchs, combining indigenous, Indic, and Islamic notions of kingship (*ratu, raja, sultan*) identified themselves by names such as "Pakubuwono", the Nail of the Universe (i.e. the Nail/Axis around which the Cosmos revolves").

Java, for its part, seems to have served at various points of its history as an alternative Central State or Celestial Kingdom within Sino-Pacifica. In early times, Java was famed as a source of magical or mystical power. Cham culture shows clear Javanese influences,[41] and the prince who would found Angkor spent part of his youth a hostage on Java.[42] The dynasty, the Sailendra, that ruled Srivijaya, Southeast Asia's premier trading polity, also dominated Java for a time, erecting the world's most impressive didactic exercise in stone, the Borobudur. Much later, East Java-centred Majapahit would gain control over the route to the Spice Islands. Finally, if we accept Ann Kumar's meticulously argued thesis, Java was the mother civilization of pre-Sinified Japan (late Yayoi-early Kofun periods).[43] In any case, halfway there, a rather Javanized form of Malay culture seems to be behind the early Philippines's Laguna Copperplate Inscription.[44]

One peculiar phenomenon needs to be noted here. In terms of one linguistic feature, China differs radically from its southern and eastern neighbours, its former vassals in the tributary system. The languages of the ex-tributaries display complex systems of honorific language, by far the most baroque in all the world.[45] Javanese is the most developed case with common vocabulary items offering variants in three or more politeness levels. Both Korean and Japanese among other things change verb inflections according to politeness level. Vietnamese and Thai have complex pronoun systems designed to define status differences. Even gender hierarchy or at least difference is marked: in Thai, by gender-specific sentence-final particles and in Japanese, by gender-specific vocabulary sets. All this luxuriant linguistic apparatus served and, to an extent, still serves to articulate a feudal social order. The Chinese language is, by contrast, relatively egalitarian. It seems as if the massive meritocratic and proto-capitalist realm at the centre of Sino-Pacifica could afford linguistic egalitarianism since it availed itself of massive coercive forces, both bureaucratic-police and market-driven. The much smaller tributaries, dominated by hereditary aristocracies, cohered, on the other hand, in some part by the sheer force of linguistic etiquette.

These nomenclatures of kingship cast the Sino-centric tributary system in a different light. Rather than simply submitting passively to the universal sovereignty of Chinese emperors, "barbarian" states figured themselves as centres of the world in their own right, either as alternative but equally legitimate embodiments of Confucian ideals or as supreme authorities within their own indigenous (actually, usually Indic) ideological frameworks — or, as in Vietnam's case, they did both.

This was even more ironic since many of these rulers were themselves or were descendants of what Magnus Fiskesjö calls "entrepreneurial Chinese" (or specifically Chinese "political entrepreneurs") who exploited the discourse of a "Chinese vs. barbarian" dichotomy in order to position themselves in the profitable role of mediator between the two spheres.[46] Zhao Tuo, the founder of Nanyue, began as a renegade Qin general, and Wiman, the founder of the first authenticated kingdom in Korea, was a refugee from early Han political restructuring.[47] Centuries later, the dynasties of Ayutthaya and Bangkok would be partially of Chinese merchant family descent,[48] Chinese-native mestizos would evolve into the elite of the modern Catholic Philippines,[49] and acculturated Islamized Chinese and their descendants would easily be absorbed into the Javanese aristocracy until the Dutch VOC for its own political purposes started to insist that they "stay" Chinese.[50] The examples could be multiplied, and much of the history of state formation in Southeast Asia (and to a significant extent also in Inner Asia and Northeast Asia) can be understood in terms of local or immigrant "men of prowess" building their power in great part on privileged access to the Chinese court and the Chinese market (the quest for which was very often the same game). The power of these political entrepreneurs derived from affirming Sino-centrism and subverting it at the same time.

Mandalas, Imperia, Commonwealths, Cosmopoleis

As I stated in the introduction, my aim in this chapter is to argue for a structure or dynamic that distinguishes Sino-Pacifica (Sino-centric/Sino-tropic Eastern Asia) from other world regions. This structure or dynamic that defines Sino-Pacifica is, as I have stated, that of the mandala.

First, I would like to comment on the complexities of comparing Chinese and Southeast Asian polities with European ones. Both Chinese and Southeast Asian cultures have regularly served as the Other for the modern West. Sometimes, China and Southeast Asia have been viewed, on the other hand, as broadly similar to the West, compared to other regions, particularly India.

The European observers of the early modern era did not find the Chinese particularly exotic — they were "as white as we are", they said. And the Japanese were even martial in a way chivalric Europeans could relate to (unlike the "effeminate Chinese"). The differences that obsessed Europeans of that period were the religious one of the "Moors" and the pigmentation one of the "Blacks" (which included the dark-skinned denizens of India). Later, Enlightenment intellectuals, fed on idealized Jesuit accounts, looked to China as the paragon of the rule of reason to which Europeans could barely imagine aspiring.

Then came the Industrial Revolution and the Opium War. As was the case with Raffles, in an age when Westerners, above all Englishmen, trumpeted the self-evident good of "free trade", China and the "maxims of its policy" came to epitomize the *irrational*. Without Islam's Abrahamic tie to the West or India's Aryan one, China became the West's ultimate Other. Without intending to denigrate China, S.A.M. Adshead would enumerate fundamental differences between "East Asia" and "Western Eurasia" (two of his four "primary civilizations", the other two being "Black Africa" and "Amerindia"): "The true East does not begin at the Suez but at Singapore, at the T'ien-shan rather than the Caucasus, and from one point of view, Calvin, St. Thomas Aquinas, al-Ghazzali, Sankra, and Tsong-kha-pa are simply permutations of a single position."[51]

On the other hand, other Western observers saw affinities between China and West-Central Europe. Oswald Spengler considered China along with Egypt to be kindred spirits to the "Faustian" culture of the post-classical West — for their sharing a devotion to the unitary state and to history, to the depths of time (to the Faustian was unique the drive into the infinities of space). The "Abendland" was closer to China than to its own supposed progenitor, the "Apollonian" culture of the ancient Greeks and Romans — who in turn shared an indifference to time depth with India (both cremated their dead, valorizing evanescence).[52]

Max Weber recognized that China had possessed "bureaucracy and the germs of capitalism" and for this was closer to the West than India.[53] Most recently, Francis Fukuyama credited China with pioneering the modern (i.e., post-tribal) state. The breakthrough to political modernity, however, was made in the West — with various manipulations of the medieval Roman Catholic Church, including its invention of the separation of church and state[54] (Harold J. Berman similarly locates the origins of modern law in the twelfth-thirteenth century papacy's reform of canon law[55]).

Southeast Asia, with its "moonlight civilizations" (Spengler's phrase for what present-day scholarship would call cases of "secondary state formation") has also served as an Other to the West despite certain points of similarity, e.g., a maritime multi-state system and the prevalence of bilateral kinship that promotes individualism over clan solidarities. Tony Day has provided a valuable survey and analysis of Western takes on the Southeast Asian state or quasi- or pseudo-state: he ended up offering a definition of the state that went beyond Weber's so as to be capacious enough for Southeast Asia's polities.[56] In the enterprise of establishing the rationale for a separate existence of a "Southeast Asia", there has been a tendency to contrast Southeast Asian state forms not only with Western ones but also, more crucially, with Chinese ones.

Of course, the great weakness of grand comparative theories is that they do not take account of interactions between civilizations. They fail to see how the features of a particular culture are a function of its place within a single world order (at least for Afro-Eurasia).

China's civilization, statecraft, and mode of interstate relations evolved in a totally different environment from that which gave birth to the Western political tradition, including inter-state relations down to the present Westphalian system. The same can be said when comparing Southeast Asian polities and Western ones, and we must remember that Southeast Asian polities developed in tandem with the evolution of the Chinese empire, if not of even earlier "Chinese" state formations. State formation unfolded in quite literally different environments: Sino-Pacifica's first states emerged in a then still-subtropical North China, whereas Indo-Mediterranea's arose in Mesopotamia, in an arid climate on a floodplain between high mountains and a vast desert.

Urbanism in early China was born in an environment in which all the essential resources were close at hand, limiting somewhat the importance of long-distance trade. Wood, significantly, was abundant — the ready availability of which underlay the region's precocity in advanced metallurgy and ceramics. Sino-Pacifica was after all the region where pottery was first invented — and here not in an agricultural society but in a sedentary fishing-and-foraging one, the Jomon cultures in Japan, and where metallophones (bells and cymbals) have been the core of musical ensembles from those of the Zhou period in China, to those of the Đông Sơn chieftainships in northern Vietnam, to the present-day gamelan orchestras of Java's courts and Bali's villages. By contrast, the urban civilizations of Mesopotamia as well as of Egypt had to import timber from stands in distant lands, the latter from the mountains of Lebanon, which trade made for the first links between the two civilizations via Syria–Palestine. Metallophones occupy a marginal place in Indo-Mediterranean musics, which are dominated by strings and winds — the eminently portable instruments of nomads.

So many phenomena can perhaps be traced back to the originary ecologies of the two "primary civilizations" — differences in: 1) the model of the state; 2) the relationship between the city and the farmed countryside; 3) the role of the earliest writing and the nature of the first state; 4) the importance of law; 5) the nature and role of supernatural forces; and 6) the further development of religious feeling.

The differences are so basic they are expressed in the very words for "civilization" and "culture". For the West, etymologically "civilization" is inseparable from the idea of the city, a type of political community (Latin *civitas* literally means "citizenship"/"citizenry"). "Politics", "politeness", even "police" all derive from the Greek word for city, *polis* (and "urbanity" from the Latin, *urbs*). "Culture" shares the same root as "cultivate" and "colony", the planting of cities, the nurturing of what until relatively recently was conceived of only in terms of city-based life. The Sinitic words for "culture" and "civilization", on the other hand, have nothing to do with urbanism. Though originally neologisms coined by Meiji-era Japanese to translate the Western concepts of "culture" (Jap. *bunka*/Ch. *wenhua*) and "civilization" (Jap. *bunmei*/Ch. *wenming*), the compounds contain the ancient logograph *bun*/*wen*, which nowadays denotes "written language" but originally referred more generally to "patterns", whether of woven cloth, of the constellations of the night sky, or of human affairs.[57] The *ka*/*hua* of the compound for "culture" signifies "transformation", culture as learned behaviour, and the *mei*/*ming* in that for "civilization" indicating civilization as enlightenment, even of a messianic or apocalyptic flavour.

"Because the gods have the dwellings of their hearts' delight' in cities, Mesopotamian cities are always sacred", writes Gwendolyn Leick, "[t]hus the Mesopotamian Eden is not a garden but a city, formed from a piece of dry land surrounded by waters. The first building is a temple. Then mankind is created to render service to god and temple."[58] In Western Afro-Eurasia, the city-state was thus in the beginning a temple-state, writing was initially developed to inventorize the goods gathered to the temple, for accounting.

How different was East Asia! There, the first writing was that of the oracle bones, communications with the ancestors. The early Chinese city was an extension of the palace of the royal family, not a super-village centred on a communal temple. Religion was focused on ancestor veneration, not on the appeasement of a pantheon of capricious deities who created human beings to work in their stead. In China from early times, the distinction between gods, ancestors, and exemplary historical figures has not been sharply drawn.

In the West (now broadly speaking), societies developed an emphasis on the rule of law. Perhaps this was to counter the capriciousness of the gods, to posit a more reliable authority. Perhaps this longing for cosmic order underlay the drive towards monotheism, for a Supreme Being above petty passions. In the "East" (that is, early China), the emphasis was different, not on rule of law but on rule of men, men of virtue, men in tune with the will of an increasingly impersonalized "Heaven" (*tian*) or a completely impersonal "Way" (*dao*). Perhaps it is only a coincidence that later, elsewhere in Sino-Pacifica, the Tagalog language, when it borrowed "*hukom*" from Arabic via Malay, turned the meaning from "the law" to "a judge". This is not to say that politics has been fundamentally different in the two regions, only that the respective discourses prefer different emphases — what sounds like an invitation to personalizing power (i.e., to corruption) in one context would be, in another, to put the onus of good governance on the individual ruler's moral being rather than on institutionalized procedures.

One last difference to note before moving on is relevant to the configuration of interstate relations. In Mesopotamia as much as ninety per cent of the population lived within the walls of cities[59] — farmers had intramural homes (an urban percentage matched only recently in some modern industrial societies). This made for a distinction between a populous urban sphere and an empty rural one — the city *was* society. In later Western societies, when the countryside was filled with villages shading off into vast hinterlands of heath and forest, the distinction between urban and rural remained absolute (the very word "country" derives from the Vulgar Latin *contrata*, "that which is opposite, that faces one as one views it", the countryside as a city-dweller gazes on it from the ramparts). In early China, by contrast, the palace-city and the countryside of villages formed a more integrated whole, with such results as a "precocious" focus by the state on popular, particularly rural peasant, welfare. In the West, after ages of cities and urban-based states essentially parasitic on rural villages, the gap only began to be bridged with the Catholic Church's extension of the parish system to rural villages in tandem with the establishment of networks of rural monasteries. It is no coincidence that the welfare and indoctrination functions pioneered by the state in East Asia were performed in the West by the Catholic Church. With Reformation and Revolution struggling to marginalize the Church, the onus for these functions was pushed on to the modern state, whose genesis not coincidentally owed much of its inspiration to a certain idea of the *Chinese* polity conveyed by Jesuit reports.

The ideal relationship between Church and State from the Church's point of view was the Spanish Philippines. There the secular authorities holed themselves up in Manila awaiting the annual galleons from Mexico laden with silver expressly destined for the Chinese market and tax-collecting state, while friars gathered often reluctant natives into townships across the archipelago, a project into which they funnelled the zeal originally intended for the conversion of China's "Celestial Kingdom" and Japan's "Divine Realm". The irony is that the Philippine natives who had been the longest to evade the temptations of urban civilization found themselves subjects of a temple-state like the first urbanites on the Mesopotamian plain. A further irony is that some Confucian literati in China were attracted to the Christianity propagated by Catholic missionaries as an alternative to Buddhist and Taoist heterodoxies for the masses: they perceived that Christianity, unlike those religions, promoted moral values consonant with those of Confucianism.[60]

Sino-Pacifica, Indo-Mediterranea, and Indo-Pacifica — each has its own characteristic state form, yet their evolutionary trajectories have never been in isolation from one another. They have all shared the experience of Empire — and done so not independently but as effects of a single phenomenon: the intrusion of pastoralist warrior aristocracies, for the most part from Inner Asia, the region abutting all three.[61]

Empire arose first in Mesopotamia: the Semitic Sargon of Akkad conquered and united the originally Sumerian city-states.[62] Outside Mesopotamia (Egypt aside[63] as well as India — the nature of the relationship among the city-states of the Indus Valley Civilization has yet to be determined), one sees in Indo-Mediterranea a proliferation of commonwealths: the Phoenician, the Greek, the Etruscan, while the Assyrians continued the project of Empire. Eventually, the Persians founded the first "world empire", stretching from the Indus to Thrace, which patrimony would be seized by the Macedonians. Another commonwealth or multi-state system was the result: the community of Hellenistic kingdoms of which Carthage, Rome, and Maurya India may be regarded as satellites or honorary members. With the unification of the Mediterranean littoral by Rome and the revival of Iranian monarchy first with the Arsacids (Parthia) and then with the Sassanians, a stable division and balance of power between two empires was established, the "Two Eyes of the World".[64] Then sprang forth the Islamic caliphate, surpassing the Achaemenids by creating a world empire that spanned from Andalusia to the Indus with the new Babylon, Baghdad, as its centre. As we near modern times, we see Indo-Mediterranea dominated by an Islamic commonwealth eventually organized into the multi-state system of Ottomans, Safavids, and Mughals. But between there erupted forth the Mongol Chinggisid enterprise, of Sino-Pacific origin, which for the first time forced together Sino-Pacifica and Indo-Mediterranea from Quanzhou to Basra to Novgorod for a few generations. After that, the medium of Empire shifted from the steppe to the sea: first, the Habsburg world empire which swallowed up the imperial projects of the Aztecs and the Incas and fantasized about converting the Chinese emperor and enlisting him in a final crusade against Islamdom and, second, the British world empire, born of a rejection of papal imperium that created a Protestant Caesaropapism, one of whose analogues was the Shi'a confessional state of Safavid Iran.

Inner Asian warrior aristocracies played a key role in state formation in South Asia and East Asia respectively. Victor Mair has argued that China's empires have been founded by northern and northwestern peoples rather than formed to defend against them.[65] This may have begun very early: the domesticated horse and the chariot from Western Asia via Inner Asia transformed the Shang polity. The Zhou also came from the frontier that would one day become the eastern terminus of the Silk Road. The Zhao state's adoption of cavalry (and trousers) from the northern "barbarians" no doubt intensified the warring of the Warring States, hastening the unification and the true founding of the bureaucratic empire. This empire-building trajectory would culminate in the Ming state whose massive maritime expeditions can be said to inaugurate the Age of Exploration and the Qing state, which became one of the greatest colonial (albeit landward-directed) empires of the early modern era.

India's history is less well documented and thus less well understood. Does an overarching imperium account for the pervasive standardization (weight and measures, city layouts, etc.) that we witness across the Indus Valley Civilization? What we do not see is evidence of a warrior aristocracy,[66] such as is elsewhere ubiquitous from Mycenae to Thebes-on-the-Nile to Anyang. In any case, the Aryans eventually brought that with them into the subcontinent. Fellow Indo-Iranians, the Persians, brought their empire into the Indus valley, and fellow Indo-European Alexander followed the vaunted Achaemenid post roads there. The Maurya Empire was then arising on the opposite side of subcontinent, near the mouth of the other great river, the Ganges. But the independent cosmopolis or a system of independent cosmopoleis, each grounded in a particular region and local language, would be the norm[67] — until Islamized Inner Asian warrior aristocracies would invade and establish more durable avatars of Empire. Finally, of course, from the sea came the British, whose Raj finally gave India a single unified bureaucratic state, though not before competition from Indian dyed cotton textiles spurred the Industrial Revolution and the British cynically deployed colonially deindustrialized India's opium to drain Qing China's silver reserves and to steal from it the economic hegemony of the world.

The mandala and the cosmopolis are not that different: I conceive the former more in terms of a political mode without specific cultural content, being either Sinitic or non-Sinitic, while I see the latter as the replication of a particular cultural model, the Sanskritic. Southeast Asian states were both at the same time: mandalas that were miniature versions of the Imperial Chinese mandala (consciously imitative in the Vietnamese case, unconsciously so in the case of, say, Angkor or Majapahit) or cosmopoleis comparable to Indian ones — Srivijaya on par with Chola, for instance. What differs among the three regions is the extent to which Empire played a role in their histories.

After the Qin-Han unification and particularly after the Sui-Tang reunification, empire was the norm for China. For India, on the other hand, division or rather a multi-state system was the norm, though the northern plain came more and more under a single state once Islamized Turkic elites established sultanates there. Southeast Asia was not to experience rule by a single power until the Japanese "co-prosperity sphere" of the mid-twentieth century. What we see there is more or less a stable multi-state system, the mainland divided among three powers, the archipelago between two:

1) A Western Mainland power (to use Lieberman's tripartite division of the mainland), taking in the Irrawaddy basin (Pagan and its successors);

2) A Central Mainland power, first centred on the Tonle Sap lake (Angkor), then on the Lower Chao Phraya basin (Ayutthaya);

3) An Eastern Mainland power, first consisting of the Cham polities along the Central Vietnamese coast and then of the expansionist Vietnamese state that absorbed them, or alternatively we could regard the Chinese provincial government of Jiaozhi as the centre of the Eastern Mainland power (in the first millennium BC *before* the Chinese conquest, the Red River valley was home to the densest population south of the Yangzi, surpassing even the delta of the West/Pear River, hence the Han decision to anchor their southern empire in the area of present-day Hanoi rather than of present-day Guangzhou) — the western edge of the South China Sea connecting the Red and Mekong deltas could then count as the Eastern Mainland's "river";

4) A power dominating the Straits of Malacca (Srivijaya, later Malacca); and

5) A power dominating Java (Old Mataram, later Majapahit).

Geography, to an extent, has determined these configurations. China has two major river systems, the northern one of which runs through an extensive plain; the two rivers run parallel to each other, their watersheds are contiguous, and they reach the sea not too far from each other. This layout has promoted unification. India, too, has two river systems, the Indus's and the Ganges's, but they run in opposite directions and debouch into different seas, partly nullifying the unitive effect of having a single northern plain. India, in effect, has had two faces, one oriented towards West and Central Asia and another to Southeast Asia and southwestern China. The mountainous southern half of India resisted incorporation into northern empires and never was unified in itself. Finally, Southeast Asia's geography made for an even more fragmented political landscape: instead of a single northern plain that could provide the basis for empire, we have four river systems: the Irrawaddy, the Chao Phraya, the Mekong, and the Red — the basins of the second and the third often dominated by a single power because high mountains do not separate them. The archipelago had, in a sense, its own "river" too, the Straits of Malacca. Java's rivers, meandering among several volcanoes, did not promote the development of all but a very fragile unitary state — the most successful, Majapahit and the VOC/Dutch Batavia, combined access to maritime traffic and inland rice production.

The other factor in the establishment of Empire, as Mair and Lieberman have noted, is the empire-building work done by Inner Asian warrior aristocracies. Is it any coincidence that the region most exposed to Inner Asia, China, was the one with the most sustained experience of Empire? The north China plain abuts the steppe along its entire length. India was much less exposed — Inner Asian pastoralists had to cross the mountains of Afghanistan to reach the Indus. With the exception of the ephemeral irruptions of the Mongols, Southeast Asia was, as Lieberman says, a "protected zone", spared the attentions of Inner Asian warrior aristocracies. However, it cannot be said that state formation in Southeast Asia was always the work of "insiders" — political entrepreneurs set up shop in lands not their own. In many cases, the state-builders were seaborne: Malays from earliest times, Bugis in the early modern period. Other "political entrepreneurs" were not: the Dai princely elites who established themselves in the Irrawaddy, Chao Phraya, and Mekong basins (the Shan states of Upper Burma, Sukhothai, Lan Na, Lan Xang, Ayutthaya). Indeed, medieval European state formation can be thought of in similar terms — the Vikings/Northmen/Normans established states from Sicily to the Ukraine — they were outsiders who became the ultimate insiders to Christendom. Europe, as much as Southeast Asia, was also, in this sense, an "exposed zone". European state-builders in the archipelago, the Spanish as well as the Dutch and the British, can be characterized as the "Mongols of the sea".[68]

In this chapter, in positing the mandala as the form of the state and of interstate relations, I have attempted to argue for the historical coherence of Sino-Pacifica and its distinctive character. In so doing, I question the absolute distinction regularly made between "modern" and "traditional" states. Our theories about the modern bureaucratic state come from Max Weber, but we must remember that his notion of the modern bureaucratic-political order was partly a fantasy — the state that he regarded as epitomizing that kind of political modernity, Wilhelmine Germany, was semi-feudal, dominated by a hereditary caste[69] descended from ex-monks, the one-time knights of the Teutonic Order, yet another example, like the England of Henry VIII onwards, of rejecting papal imperium. Similarly, we recognize a false dichotomy between the "free trade" touted by the British and the monopolism of Imperial China (and of Cochin China, of Japan, and of the Dutch VOC, in Raffles's account) — the British could not have enforced "free trade" had they not retained a remnant of mercantilism: at the very least, the willingness of the state to open up markets by force, steamboats against junks.[70]

The dynamics of the mandala state as observed on a smaller scale across Southeast Asia, I have argued, can also be observed on a larger scale in imperial China and its community of subordinate polities. Within the inherently hierarchical structure of the Sino-centric/Sino-tropic tributary system, the functional equivalent (at least for internal consumption) of a state asserting an equal status with all others was exalting one's own ruler as universal sovereign (as a Hindu *devaraja*, a Buddhist *cakravartin*, an Islamic "Shadow of God", or indeed a Confucian "emperor"). In Eastern Asia, Heaven had many sons.

NOTES

1. Lady Sophia Raffles, *Memoir of the Sir Thomas Stamford Raffles, F.R.S &c* (London: John Murray, 1830), p. 62.
2. Benedict Anderson, *Language and Power: Exploring Political Cultures in Indonesia* (Ithaca, NY: Cornell University Press, 1990), pp. 44–45.
3. Roger T. Ames and Henry Rosemont, Jr., *The Analects of Confucius: A Philosophical Translation* (New York: Ballantine, 1998).
4. The term is Ross Dunn's: "the belt of territory that extends from the Mediterranean basin eastward across South West Asia to northern India as far as the Bay of Bengal", a "place on the map" that frames a series of world-historical developments that brings together histories that have customarily been viewed apart. Ross Dunn, "Indo-Mediterranea: Rethinking World Historical Space", lecture, San Diego State University, San Diego, California, 17 February

2006). Following his lead, I conceived of a "Sino-Pacific" space alongside his Indo-Mediterranean one; I regard both as having been born of Neolithic agricultural revolutions, a Central Chinese one in Sino-Pacifica's case and a West Asian one in Indo-Mediterranea's. In this chapter, I am also proposing a zone overlapping the two, encompassing both South Asia and Southeast Asia, united by Indic civilization or, as Sheldon Pollock has argued, by the "Sanskrit Cosmopolis". See Sheldon Pollock, *The Languages of the Gods in the World of Men: Sanskrit, Culture, and Power in Modern India* (Berkeley: University of California Press, 2006).

5. Drawing on the metaphor of Hindu-Buddhist diagrams of the cosmos consisting of concentric circles (*mandala* is Sanskrit for "circle"), what scholars have called the "mandala state or polity" differs from the modern Western notion of the state by being defined by its royal centre rather than by its boundaries. Sovereignty is not uniformly potent throughout the territory, becoming progressively weaker as one gets farther and farther from the capital (i.e., the royal palace). The spheres of influence of mandala states overlap; they are not sharply demarcated from each other by borders — lesser states could belong to the mandalas of more than one more potent state. For the classic formulation, see O.W. Wolters, *History, Culture, and Region in Southeast Asian Perspectives*, rev. ed. (Ithaca, NY: Cornell Southeast Asia Program Publications, 1999), pp. 27–31.

6. For this concept, I draw on Garth Fowden, *Empire to Commonwealth: Consequences of Monotheism in Late Antiquity* (Princeton, N.J.: Princeton University Press, 1994). A commonwealth in this context is a community or network of states that share a common culture, particularly religion. Fowden identifies four such commonwealths in medieval Western Afro-Eurasia: the First Byzantine (Monophysites from Armenia to Ethiopia), the Second Byzantine (Greco-Slavic Orthodoxy), Latin Christian, and Islamic.

7. Keith W. Taylor, "The Early Kingdoms", in *The Cambridge History of Southeast Asia, Volume One, Part One: From Early Times to c. 1500*, edited by Nicholas Tarling (Cambridge, U.K.: Cambridge University Press, 1999), p. 158.

8. Kenneth R. Hall, "Economic History of Early Southeast Asia", in Tarling, pp. 202–8, 229–45.

9. Anthony Reid, *Southeast Asia in the Age of Commerce, 1450–1680, Volume One: The Lands Below the Winds* (New Haven: Yale University Press, 1988), pp. 120–36.

10. Cho-yun Hsu, "The Spring and Autumn Period", in *The Cambridge History of Ancient China: From the Origins of Civilization to 221 B.C.*, edited by Michael Loewe and Edward L. Shaughenssy (Cambridge, U.K.: Cambridge University Press, 1999), pp. 548–50.

11. The word *guo/*"state" (*kwǝk* in Old Chinese) is one of a group of related words including the word for "city moat" (*xu*, OC *xjwǝk*) and "park" or "garden" (*you*, OC jǝu^c). See Axel Schuessler, *ABC Etymological Dictionary of Old Chinese*

(University of Hawai'i Press, 2007), p. 208. Thus, with *guo* we are dealing with a similar semantic family as we see in the English words "yard" and "garden", the *gard* in the Norse Asgard, and the *grad* and *gorod* in Slavic city names. In Zhou times, within a given state's "territory" the *guoren*, the "people of the capital", were contrasted with the *yeren*, "the people of the field", the latter being non-"Huaxia" — "Man", "Yi", "Rong", "Di", "barbarians" (Hsu, p. 549). The ethnonym used by the lowland-dwelling Vietnamese for themselves today is "Kinh", literally "people of the capital" (the word is cognate to Mandarin *jing*), in contrast to non-Viet highlanders. The cultural landscape of Bronze Age North China was as ethnically diverse as that of southern China and of Southeast Asia in more recent times.

12. Liam C. Kelley, *Beyond the Bronze Pillars: Envoy Poetry and the Sino-Vietnamese Relationship* (Honolulu: University of Hawai'i Press, 2005), p. 8.

13. R. Bin Wong, *China Transformed: Historical Change and the Limits of European Experience* (Ithaca, NY: Cornell University Press, 1997), pp. 92–101.

14. Victor Lieberman, *Strange Parallels: Southeast Asia in Global Context, c.800–1830, Volume 2: Mainland Mirrors: Europe, Japan, China, South Asia, and the Islands* (Cambridge, U.K.: Cambridge University Press, 2009), p. 896.

15. Alexander Barton Woodside, *Vietnam and the Chinese Model: A Comparative Study of Vietnamese and Chinese Government* (Cambridge, MA: Harvard University Press, 1988 [1971]), p. 120.

16. At this Lower Yangzi extremity, a non-Sinitic kingdom named Yue arose that did participate in the multi-state system of the Eastern Zhou period; perhaps with the dispersal southward of its aristocracy after its annexation by the Chu state, Yue bequeathed its name to this general category of "southern barbarian". For a discussion of the identity of the Yue and of the evolution of the images of the Yue in Chinese discourse, see Erica Brindley, "Barbarians or Not? Ethnicity and Changing Conceptions of the Ancient Yue (Viet) Peoples", *Asia Major* 16, no. 2 (2003): 1–31. See also William Meacham, "Origins and Development of the Yüeh Coastal Neolithic: A Microcosm of Culture Change on the Mainland of East Asia", in *The Origins of Chinese Civilization*, by David N. Keightley (Berkeley: University of California Press, 1983), pp. 147–75, and Heather Peters, "Tattooed Faces and Stilt Houses: Who Were the Ancient Yue?", *Sino-Pacific Papers* 17 (April 1990): 1–27. Peters gives a salutary caveat against the common habit of equating archaeological cultures with modern ethnic groups — Chinese archaeologists generally presume that the Yue artifact "horizon" represents Tai people such as now inhabit Guangxi, Guizhou, and Yunnan, cf. map on page 52 of Yan Wenming, "The Cradle of Eastern Civilization", in *New Perspectives on China's Past: Chinese Archaeology in the Twentieth Century, Volume 1: Cultures and Civilizations Reconsidered*, edited by Xiaoneng Yang (New Haven: Yale University Press, 2004).

17. Woodside gives an alternative interpretation: "Việt" stood for the northern part of the country that had been under Chinese rule and "Nam", literally "the South", for the new lands added to that older core. I do not find this reading convincing since it does not fit with the meaning of comparable Chinese place names such as "Hunan", "Jiangnan", or "Minnan", which all mean "[region] to the south of X". Moreover, why would this "North + South" name have caused Nguyen's envoys to return home "in trepidation" at his displeasure (indeed, his regnal name, which combined characters that referred to Hanoi and Saigon, conveyed the same idea)?

18. Charles Holcombe, *The Genesis of East Asia, 221 B.C.–A.D. 907* (Honolulu: Association for Asian Studies and University of Hawai'i Press, 2001), pp. 148–49.

19. Erica Brindley, "Han, Yue [Viet], or Something Else? Constructions of Identity in Several Ruling Families of the Yue, ~220–100 BCE", paper presented at the Association of Asian Studies Annual Conference, Atlanta, 5 April 2008.

20. Holcombe, p. 150.

21. Woodside, pp. 18–19, 121.

22. Kelley, pp. 9 and 25.

23. My thanks to Chiou-Ling Yeh for this information.

24. Woodside, p. 10.

25. Li Xueqin, "Bronzes of the Chu Kingdom and the Chu Cultural Sphere", in Yang, p. 297.

26. Barry B. Blakely, "Chu Society and State: Image and Reality", in *Defining Chu: Image and Reality in Ancient China*, edited by Constance A. Cook and John S. Major (Honolulu: University of Hawai'i Press, 1999), pp. 53–54, 191 n.19.

27. Anthony Reid, "Flows and Seepages in the Long-Term Chinese Interaction with Southeast Asia", in *Sojourners and Settlers: Histories of Southeast Asia and the Chinese*, edited by Anthony Reid (St. Leonards, Australia: Allen and Unwin, 1996), p. 47.

28. David Morgan, *The Mongols* (Cambridge, MA: Blackwell, 1986), p. 60.

29. Pamela Lyle Crossley, *The Manchus* (Cambridge, MA: Blackwell, 1997), pp. 106–7.

30. Bruce Cummings, *Korea's Place in the Sun: A Modern History*, updated ed. (New York: Norton, 2005), pp. 54–55, 78.

31. Alexander Woodside, *Lost Modernities: China, Vietnam, Korea, and the Hazards of World History* (Cambridge, MA: Harvard University Press, 2006), pp. 22–23.

32. Woodside, *Lost Modernities*, p. 109.

33. Kirk W. Larsen, *Tradition, Treaties, and Trade: Qing Imperialism and Chosŏn Korea, 1850–1910* (Cambridge, MA: Harvard University Asia Center, 2008), pp. 38–39; and Saeyoung Park, "Multiple Chinas: Cosmopolitan Confucianism and East Asian International Relations in the Early Modern Period", paper presented at the Association for Asian Studies Annual Conference, San Diego, 23 March 2013.

34. Larsen, pp. 40–41.

35. Ibid., p. 33.

36. See Holcombe, pp. 164–93, for a detailed discussion of interactions between Peninsular and Insular North East Asia. At this early point, it is dubious to speak of contrasting categories of "Koreans" and "Japanese" — some of the "Koreans" (namely the peoples of Koguryŏ and Paekche) — had more in common at least linguistically with the "Japanese" than with their "fellow Koreans". It is the language of the people of Silla that became the basis of modern Korean, which accounts for the paucity of cognate vocabulary linking the modern Korean and Japanese languages.

37. Ivan Morris, *The World of the Shining Prince: Court Life in Ancient Japan* (New York: Knopf, 1969), pp. 8–11.

38. Marcia Yonemoto, *Mapping Early Modern Japan: Space, Place, and Culture in the Tokugawa Period (1603–1868)* (Berkeley: University of California Press, 2003), pp. 103–4.

39. Bob Tadashi Wakabayashi, *Anti-Foreignism and Western Learning in Early-Modern Japan: The* New Theses *of 1825* (Cambridge, MA: Council on East Asian Studies at Harvard University, 1986), pp. 22–40, 149. I am grateful to Hugh R. Clark for directing me to this fascinatingly rich work.

40. Thongchai Winichakul, *Siam Mapped: A History of the Geo-Body of a Nation* (Honolulu: University of Hawai'i Press, 1994), pp. 83–84.

41. Hall, p. 258.

42. For the exercise by "Javanese" (this name could just as easily have referred to peninsular Malays) over early Khmer polities, see Ian Mabbett and David Chandler, *The Khmers* (Oxford, U.K.: Blackwell, 1995), pp. 85–87.

43. Ann Kumar, *Globalizing the Prehistory of Japan: Language, Genes, and Civilization* (London: Routledge, 2009).

44. Antoon Postma, "The Laguna Copper-Plate Inscription: Text and Commentary", *Philippine Studies* 40, no. 2 (1992). To prove links between Central Luzon and Malayo-Javanic civilization, the LCI (whose authenticity is far from beyond question) is actually superfluous — all the evidence one needs is embedded in the Tagalog and Kapampangan languages. See John U. Wolff, "Malay Borrowings in Tagalog", in *Southeast-Asian History and Historiography: Essays Presented to D.G.E. Hall*, edited by C.D. Cowan and O.W. Wolters (Ithaca, NY: Cornell University Press, 1976). In fact, the shape of the Sanskritic borrowings indicates a specifically Old Javanese rather than Malay mediation, e.g., the Tagalog word *sigla* ("lively") relates directly to the Javanese *sigrah* rather than to the Malay *segera* ("soon") as well as does the retention of the Indic aspiration in such Tagalog words as *mukha, budhi, kutha, katha, Bathala*, etc. (Malay *muka, budi, kota, kata, betara*).

45. Cliff Goddard, *The Languages of East and Southeast Asia: An Introduction* (Oxford: Oxford University Press, 2005), pp. 19–24.

46. Magnus Fiskesjö, discussant comments for panel, "Historical, Rhetorical, and Linguistic Connections along China's Early Frontiers", Association of Asian Studies Annual Conference, Atlanta, 5 April 2008.
47. Holcombe, pp. 148–50, 165–67.
48. David K. Wyatt, *Thailand: A Short History* (New Haven: Yale University Press, 1982), pp. 65 and 142.
49. Skinner, pp. 76–78, 89–90.
50. Mason C. Hoadley, "Javanese, Peranakan, and Chinese Elites in Cirebon: Changing Ethnic Boundaries", *Journal of Asian Studies* 47, no. 3 (1988): 511.
51. S.A.M. Adshead, *China in World History*, 3rd ed. (Houndmills, Basingstoke, U.K.: Macmillan, 2000), p. 2.
52. Oswald Spengler, *The Decline of the West: Form and Actuality, Volume One*, translated by Charles Francis Atkinson (New York: Knopf, 1926), pp. 14–15, 136–38.
53. Stanislav Andreski, ed., *Max Weber on Capitalism, Bureaucracy and Religion: A Selection of Texts* (London: George Allen and Unwin, 1983), text 3, "The Confucianist Bureaucracy and the Germs of Capitalism: The City and the Guild", and text 4, "Hindu Religion, Caste and Bureaucratic Despotism as Factors in Economic Stagnation: The Caste and the Tribe".
54. Francis Fukuyama, *The Origins of Political Order: From Prehistoric Times to the French Revolution* (London: Profile Books, 2012), pp. 110–27, 229–41.
55. Harold J. Berman, *Law and Revolution: The Formation of the Western Legal Tradition* (Cambridge, MA: Harvard University Press, 1983), pp. 538–58, as quoted in Woodside, *Lost Modernities*, p. 4.
56. Tony Day, *Fluid Iron: State Formation in Southeast Asia* (Honolulu: University of Hawai'i Press, 2002), pp. 1–37.
57. Kelley, pp. 28–31.
58. Gwendolyn Leick, *Mesopotamia: The Invention of the City* (London: Penguin, 2001), p. 2. The idea of heaven as a garden is seen in the origin of the word "paradise" (Greek *paradeisos*) in the Persian word *firdaus* for "garden". Such a metaphor, we might venture, derives from a nomad's perspective.
59. Ibid., p. xviii.
60. Erik Zurcher, "Confucian and Christian Religiosity in Late Ming China", *The Catholic Historical Review* 83, no. 4 (1997).
61. Victor Mair, "The North(west)ern Peoples and the Recurrent Origins of the 'Chinese' State", in *The Teleology of the Modern Nation-State: Japan and China*, edited by Joshua A. Vogel (Philadelphia: University of Pennsylvania Press, 2005), p. 46 and Lieberman, pp. 900–5.
62. As Semites originating in the Arabian Desert whose forebears had come from north-east Africa, the Akkadian-speakers who integrated themselves into the Sumerian cities may have been another example of pastoralist outsiders becoming empire-builders in the lands of sedentary cultures.

63. Egypt stands apart in Western Afro-Eurasia and in certain ways more resembles China. We see from the earliest times a unitary state whose cities were not independent communes, a realm that saw itself as the unique home of order in the world. In any case, this realm eventually came to participate in a multi-state system created first by the Mesopotamians — Akkadian remained its lingua franca. The fusion of Mesopotamian and Egyptian civilizations through the mediation of Syro-Palestinian-Phoenician cosmopolitanism brought into being what David Wilkinson calls "Central Civilization" — "Far Eastern Civilization" was the last to be "engulfed" by it. See David Wilkinson, "Civilizations, Cores, World Economies, and Oikumenes", in *The World System: Five Hundred Years or Five Thousand?*, edited by Andre Gunder Frank and Barry K. Gills (London: Routledge, 1993), p. 221.

64. Fowden, p. 12.

65. Mair, p. 46.

66. Jane R. McIntosh, *A Peaceful Realm: The Rise and Fall of Indus Civilization* (New York: Westview Press, 2002), pp. 177–83.

67. Peter Robb, *A History of India* (Basingstoke, U.K.: Palgrave, 2002), pp. 55–58, 78–80.

68. Lieberman calls them "White Inner-Asians". See Lieberman, p. 824.

69. Woodside, *Lost Modernities*, p. 32.

70. Wong, p. 142.

INDEX

A

Abbasid Caliphate, 239
  relations between Tang Dynasty
    China and, 240
  Yang Liangyao's embassy to,
    242–43, 261
  Zhenyuan 貞元 era (785–805), 242,
    256
aboriginal settlements, 175–76
Abramson, Marc, 81
Abu Luoba (阿蒲·羅拔), 239
aconite, 284
Agai (阿蓋), Princess, 269, 286
Age of Exploration, 360–61
agricultural migrations, 325
Amarapura Guanyin Temple, 314n58
An Dương Vương 安陽王 (also
    known as Thục Phán 蜀泮), 50,
    165, 167
Angkor, 61, 62
  Cham naval attack on, 153
Angkor Wat, 151
  carvings in, 153
Anglo-Burmese War, 294
Annan tuzhi 安南圖志 [Treatise and
    Maps of Annan], 205
anti-colonial movements, 2

anti-communist forces, 2
Antony, Robert, 200
"Apollonian" culture, 355
archaeological research in Southeast
    Asia, 43, 44, 70
aromatic resins, 233
aromatic timbers, 230
Arrayed Tales 嶺南摭怪列傳
    (*The Arrayed Tales of Collected
    Oddities from South of the
    Passes Lĩnh Nam chích quái liệt
    truyện*), 161–62
  becoming traditions, 183–88
  categorizing stories, 163
  fox essence in, 173–74
  and history, 165–70
  importance of, 164–65
  othering savages, 170–79
  promotion of, 164–65
  savage tales, 179–83
  stories in, 162–63
  versions of, 170
  writing style, 164
Atwill, David, 327
Âu Lạc 甌駱
  kingdom, 49–51
  polity, 50

B

Bạch Đằng River, 204

Bà Lộ Savages (Bà Lộ *man* 婆露蠻), 177–79

Ba Min tongzhi 八閩通志, 118, 121–22

baneful spirits, in medieval China, 143

Banteay Chhmar carvings, 151, 153

Baoqing siming zhi 寶慶四明志, 224–25, 231

barbarians, 46

southern barbarians, 48, 68, 70

barbarization, Han society implications and identity, 67–72

bark cloth, 91–92

Baron, Samuel, 198

Barus camphor, 216–17

batik-patterned indigo cloth, 96

Bayfield, 294

Bayon carvings, 151–53

Bayon relief, 152

of Cham war boat, 154

Bayu state, 258

Bắc Bộ communities, bronze-casting technologies, 63

Bắc Bộ region, 46

before Chinese arrival, 49

cultural development in, 48

Iron Age archaeological record, 67

Bạch Đằng river, 146

Bạch Hạc, 177

Bencao gangmu 本草綱目 (Compendium of Materia Medica), 270, 271

Benedict, Carol, 326

Beyond the Bronze Pillars (Kelley), 345

Bhamo Chinese, 298

Bhamo–Myitkyina trip, 303

Bin Wong, 342

Biography of Hua Guan Suo (*Hua Guan Suo zhuan* 花關索傳), 317

black clothing, 95

Blakeley, Barry B., 347

bLo sbyong glegs bam (The Book of Mind Training), 283

Blumea balsamifera, 216, 220

boat competitions, 144

in southern Chinese local traditions, 149

boat racing, 155, 156. *See also* crossing competitions

Bodhisattva, 273

body culture, elements of, 100

Bokun state, 258

border demarcation process, 300

Brindley, Erica, 345

British colonial period, 305

British expedition, 296, 297, 299

British imperial project, 294

British India, 300

colonial state of, 292

northeastern frontier, 294

British political agent, 296

British rule, 304, 305

in Lower Burma, 294

bronze-casting technologies, 63–64

Browne Expedition, 312n17, 313n47

Browne, Horace A., 296

btsan-dug, 284

bubonic plague

in second half of nineteenth century in Yunnan, 326–27

transmission of, 326

Buddhabhadra 佛陀跋陀羅, Indian monk (359–429), 271

"Buddha-Molded Harbor" (Phật Đào Cảng 佛陶港), 185, 187

"Buddha-Molded Water Passage" (Phật Đào Kinh 佛陶涇), 186

bug silk, 94

Burma–Yunnan frontier, 294

Burmese Chinese migrant
    communities, 304
"Burned Field Village" (Huotian cun
    火田村), 121

C
Caesaropapism, 360
Caffrey, Kevin, 329
camphor, import from Southeast Asia
    to China, 216–22
Candana tree, 177
Cantonese, 305, 306, 309
capping ceremony, 17
Carrie Reed, 86
Cartier, Michel, 325
carvings
    in Angkor Wat, 153
    Banteay Chhmar, 151, 153
    Bayon, 151–53
"Celestial Emperor", 346
"Celestial Kingdom", 359
Central Lands, Sinitic heritage of,
    111
Central Mainland power, 362
Central States, hairstyles in, 33
Central Vietnam, 200, 206
    Thunder God in, 203
Cen Yuying 岑毓英, 330
ceramics traditions development, in
    Southeast Asia, 215
Chakri dynasty, 352
Cham culture, 352
Cham embassies to Song and Lý
    courts, 150
Cham emissaries, 148
Cham military capabilities, upgrading
    of, 151
Cham naval, attack on Angkor, 153
Champa's missions, 217
Cham region, influences in, 149–56
Cham tribute missions, 150
Chao Phraya, 363

Chaozhou 潮州, 113, 120, 123–25
Chen Fu 陳孚, cultural practices
    descriptions, 171
Chengjiang Gazetteer, 326
Chen Jinghe 陳荊和, 198–99
Chen Shangchuan 陳上川, 198
Chenshi xiangpu 陳氏香譜 [Master
    Chen's Manual of Aromatics],
    218–19
Chen Yuanguang 陳元光 (ca. 657–711),
    114, 115, 120, 132
    hybrid cults of, 126
Chen Zheng 陳政 (d. 677), 112–13,
    120–21
Cherry, Haydon, 51
China, 2
    camphor import from Southeast
        Asia, 216–22
    issue of material cultural influences
        between Southeast Asia and,
        215
    and kingdoms of the Nanhai,
        trading relations between, 2
    market, 220
    material culture, 216
    national boundaries for, 63
    Southeast Asia and, economic
        interaction between, 214
    technological knowledge and
        capabilities, 214
    Tibetan influence on, 268
    Vietnam and, 4
Chinese archaeologists, 167
Chinese chroniclers, 340
Chinese civilization
    excavation data implications,
        59–66
    interregional interaction and
        emulation, 63–66
    urbanism and political complexity,
        60–63
Chinese community, 5

Chinese cultural values, 81
Chinese cultures, 274, 287, 354
Chinese ethnography, 94
Chinese gentry scholars, 304
Chinese gentry system, 301
Chinese ideas and social
    organization, 48
Chinese identity, 331
Chinese imperial authority, 334
Chinese language, 347, 353
Chinese maritime, 204
    activities, 206
Chinese market, 354, 359
Chinese medicinal encyclopedias,
    217
Chinese mulberry, 94
Chinese-native mestizos, 353–54
Chinese pattern of tattoos, 86
Chinese peripheries, 194
Chinese pirate groups, 198
Chinese policy, 338–40
Chinese province of Yunnan, 291,
    295
Chinese-style kingdom, 341
Chinese textual accounts,
    examination of, 60
Chinese tradition, peacock in, 269–74
Chinese treaty ports, 296
Chinese-Vietnamese piracy, 200
"Chinggis Khan", 347
Chin, James K., 256
Choson dynasty, 348
Chu, 344–47
chuanqi tales, 164
Chu Đậu, 204
cinnamomum camphora, 222
ci shrine, 115, 119
Cổ Loa Middle Wall and Ditch
    Project, 53–59
Cổ Loa polity, 60, 64
Cổ Loa roof tiles, 65
    Middle Wall excavation, 57, 58

Cổ Loa site, 44–47, 49
    archaeological investigations at,
        53–59
    brand of urbanism, 62
    early form of urbanism, 61
    geographic milieu, 63
    monumental fortification system
        at, 66
    settlement, 66
    timing and development process of,
        52–53
close-cropped hair (duanfa 斷髮), 89
clothing, 91
    changing clothes, 100–2
    colour and dyed patterns, 94–97
    social fabrics, 91–94
    wearing identity, 97–100
Cochinchina, 198
Cold War, 2, 11
collaborative archaeological project,
    53
colonial ethnographic infrastructure,
    304
colonial frontier, securing, 292–300
colonial rule, 300, 301, 304, 309
    in Burma, 292
colour patterns, 94–97
combat element, crossing
    competitions, 144
communal identities, ramifications
    of, 300
Complete Book of the Historical
    Records of Đại Việt 大越史記
    全書 (Ngô Si Liên), 166, 174–75,
    185
Comprehensive Institutional Records
    (Tongdian 通典), 253
Confucian academies, 348
Confucian concept, 164
Confucian culture, 5
Confucian indoctrination, 348
Confucianism, 342, 359

Confucian literati, 7
contemporary designation, 327
Cooked Li people, clothing of, 100–1
Cooper, Thomas, 295
"co-prosperity sphere", 362
cotton cloth, 93
court-sponsored *jingdu* (競渡) events, 144
crossed legs of Jiaozhi (交趾), 83
crossing competitions
    Cham and Khmer regions influences, 149–56
    in Đại Việt, 146–49, 155
    in Yangzi Valley, 142–46
Cui Hanheng 崔漢衡, 245
cultural analysis, hairstyles, 19
cultural artifacts, 2
cultural frontier between Sinitic and proto-Vietnamese civilizations, 44
culture, 349, 350, 352, 357
    "Apollonian", 355
    Cham, 352
    Chinese, 274, 287, 354
    Confucian, 5
    "Faustian", 355
    hairstyles in Zhou, 16
    huaxia 華夏, 5, 6
    Longshan (*c.*3000–1800 BC), 65
    politico-religious, 141
Cun Haiting 寸海亭, 310
Cun Kaitai 寸開泰, 310
cut hair (*zuan fa*), 27

D
Đại Việt, 202
    army, 86
    Cham tribute missions to, 150
    crossing competitions in, 146–49, 155
    political independence, 44
    warships, 148

Dalbergia parviflora, 223, 227
Dali (大曆) era, 241, 249, 252
Daoguang period, 325, 326
Daoyi zhilue 島夷誌略, 221, 225, 226, 231
"dark-clothing people", 95
Dashi zhuan 大食傳 (Account of Dashi), 261
Datun 大屯 village, 319, 320
Day, Tony, 355
"decorated face" description, 85
de facto Tengyue Association, 298
Deng Yao group, 210n25
Deng Zhong 鄧鐘, 205
Deng Zilon 鄧子龍, 295
Di Cosmo, Nicola, 324, 330
Đại La, 173, 174
Dingjia zhuang 丁家莊, 329
Đinh Gia Khánh, 163
"Divine Realm", 359
Đại Việt sử ký toàn thư, 197
Dog Head Mountain, 187
Đông Son bronze drums, 48
Đông Son civilization, 49
Đông Son culture, 47, 55, 60
    period, 52
Đông Son period, political consolidation during, 64
Đông Son society, 46–47
    models and symbols of political authority and foreign elements, 66
    in Red River plain, 50
Dong-Xiyang kao 東西洋考 (A Study of Eastern and Western Oceans), 205, 222, 232
"down-the-line" form of emulation, 65
dragon-boat racing, 146
Dragon Lord, 187
dragon ship, 146
drynaria baronii, 281

Dryoblanops aromatica. See camphor
Duanwu 端午, 143
Du Huan 杜環, 253
Duke Huan of Qi 齊桓公, 19, 24
Duke Jing of Qi 齊景公, 30
duli clothing 獨力衣, 99
Dunn, Ross, 364n4
"dust-pan style", 31
Du You 杜佑, 252, 253
dyed patterns, 94–97
Dzengsĕo, 330

E

Eastern Asian multi-state system, 340
Eastern Han cultural elements, 68
Eastern Han dynasty, 273
Eastern Jin dynasty, 271
Eastern Mainland power, 362
Eastern Yi culture, sheared hair
    (*duanfa* 斷髮), 26
embassy, timeline of, 255–56
Emblica officinalis, 227
embroidered faces, 87
Emperor Daizong, 241
Emperor Dezong, 241, 246–48,
    266n28
Emperor Gaozong, 113
Emperor Huizong, 119
Emperor Xuanzong, 241
Empress Dowager Wei, 241
emulation, Chinese civilization,
    63–66
Engelbert, Thomas, 164
Enlightenment intellectuals, 354
"Esteemed Kingdom", 346
ethnic groups in Red River Delta,
    172
Europe, 12
    rival empires in, 1
European-derived international
    system, 343
Europe-based knowledge system, 10

Excessive Rain Pool (Dâm Đàm
    霪潭), 176
expansionary campaigns, 71

F

fabrics. *See also* clothing
    social, 91–94
faeces togopteri, 280, 281
Fan Chengda 范成大
    colour and dyed patterns, 95
    Li clothing, 97
    naked bodies, 88
    needle and brush, 87
    silk cloth, 93
    tattoo, 82, 85, 86
"Faustian" culture, 355
Faxian 法顯 (337–422), Chinese
    monk, 271
field households, 95
fifteenth-century Vietnam
    Arrayed Tales. See Arrayed Tales
    development of, 161–62
Fish Essence Crag, 187
Fiskesjö, Magnus, 353
Five Furies (Wuchang 五猖), 178,
    179
flood control, 50
foetal hair, 90
folk literature, 163
foreign bodies, 83–84
    hair, 89–91
    naked bodies, 87–89
    tattoos and scarification, 85–87
foreign camphor, 222
Foshi state 佛逝國 (southeast part of
    the island of Sumatra), 257–58
Fox Aboriginal Settlement, 176
"Fox Corpse Pool" (Hồ Thây Đàm
    狐尸潭), 175, 176
fox essence, in *Arrayed Tales*,
    173–74
"Fox Grotto" (Hồ Động 狐洞), 175

"Fox Village" (Hồ Thôn 狐村), 175, 176

French Mekong expedition, 296

Fujian connection routes by passing, 204–8

Fujian region, 126

Fukuyama, Francis, 355

Fury God (Xương Cuồng thần 猖狂神), 177, 179

Fury Men (Cuồng phu/Kuangfu 狂夫), 178

Fytche, Albert, 296

G

Gao Pian 高駢, 185, 186

Gegesengdi state, 258

Gegesengzhi state 葛葛僧祇國 (now Brouwers Archipelago in the southern part of the Straits of Malacca), 258

Geguluo state 哥谷羅國 [Qaqola/ Kakula, now the Kra Isthmus of the Malay Peninsula], 258

Geil, William, 296

Geluo state 箇羅國, 258

Giersch, Patterson, 328

"golden fangs and bronze teeth" (kim nha đồng xỉ 金牙銅齒), 179

Golden Teeth (Jinchi 金齒), 192n55

Gongche shangshu 公車上書, 302

Gong Xianggeng 龔向庚, 318–20, 322–23, 329–30, 332

Gong Zhaolong 龔兆龍, 319, 323

Great Life-Protecting Lord (Baosheng dadi 保生大帝), 126

Griffith, 294

Guangdong, 206
  coast of, 194–95
  province, 166, 169, 326

Guangxi
  coast of, 195
  province, 326

routes bypassing, 204–8

Guangzhou Bay, 207

"Guan Suo ling 關索嶺" mountain ridges, 330

Guan Suo Opera, 316–24, 326, 328, 330–34

Guan Suo Opera Gazetteer, 332

Guan Suo temple, 330

Guan Zhong 管仲, 19–20, 30

Guda state 古笪國 (present-day Nha Trang, Vietnam), 257

Guihai yuheng zhi 桂海虞衡志, 82

Guizhou province, 316

Guizhou region, economic transformation of, 325

Gulf of Tongking, 195, 205, 206
  maritime system, 202

Guo Qitao, 178

H

Hồ Aboriginal Settlement, 176

Hainanese cotton cloth, 93

Hainan Island, 194, 197
  correlations between northern Vietnam and, 199
  epidemics from, 195–202
  and Leizhou Peninsula, interconnections between northern Vietnam, 207
  local gazetteers of, 195

hair, foreign bodies, 89–91

hairstyles, 16
  descriptions of, 19
  "human-like creatures", 23
  mallet-shaped bun (*chuijie* 椎髻/ 魋結), 28–36
  sheared hair (*duanfa* 斷髮), 25–28
  types of, 17
  unbound hair (*pifa* 被髮), 19–25
  in Zhou culture, 16

Han Chinese civilization, 5

Han Chinese colonization, 59

Han dynasty, 3, 132, 166, 291, 344
Han Empire, 44, 48
hangtu 夯土 method, 64–65
Han immigrants, 68
Han imperial conquest and
    incorporation, 66
Han obsession, 71
Han period, mallet-shaped bun, 29
Hanshu, mallet-shaped bun, 30
Han society
    implications and identity,
        barbarization, 67–72
    relations with Koreans, 65
Han-Tang period in northern
    Vietnam, 67
Han-Việt graves, 68, 69
Han Yu 韓愈, 123–25
Han Yunnanese, 292, 296
"Heaven's Awe Harbor" (Thiên Uy
    Cảng 天威港), 185
"Heaven's Awe Passage" (Thiên Uy
    Kính 天威徑), 185
Heling state 訶陵國, 258
Hellenistic kingdoms, community of,
    360
Hessig, Walther, 275
Histoire du Cambodge (Leclère), 199
History of the Former Han (Ban Gu),
    170
Hải Thượng Lãn Ông, 199, 200
Hokkien community, 306
Hokkien dialect speakers, 206
Huainanzi text, 23
Huangdi neijing 黃帝內經 (Inner
    Canon of the Yellow Emperor),
    278
Huanwang state 環王國 (or Champa,
    in present-day central Vietnam),
    257
huaxia 華夏 culture, 5, 6
Huaxia peoples, mallet-shaped bun,
    32

Huihui 回回 medical tradition, 277
Huihui yaofang 回回藥方 (Muslim
    Prescriptions), 277–78
human trafficking, 202
"Hundred Barbarians 百夷", 174
Hundred Yue (Baiyue 百越), 17, 18,
    48, 68, 70
Hùng kings (Hùng vương 雄王),
    165–67, 172, 175, 177
Hồ Village, 176
hydraulic cities, 61, 62
Hyung Il Pai, 65

I

Imperial Chinese mandala, 361
imperial events, crossing competitions,
    145, 146
imperial intelligence, 300–4
*Imperially Reviewed Encyclopedia of
    the Taiping Era* (*Taiping yulan*
    太平御覽), 173
Indianized Southeast Asia, 341
indigenous ancestors, 322–23
indigo clothing, 96
Indo-European Alexander, 361
Indo-Mediterranea, 340, 356, 359, 360
Indo-Pacifica, 359
Industrial Revolution, 354, 361
Indus Valley Civilization, 359, 361
Inner Asian warrior aristocracies, 360,
    361, 363
"Inner Lands" (Nội Địa), 346
internationalism, 12
interregional interaction, Chinese
    civilization, 63–66
"invented traditions", 52
Iron Age
    colonial interactions, 67
    of Vietnam, 47–48
Iron Age Đông Son Culture
    communities, 46
Irrawaddy, 362, 363

irrigation network of Yanshou Weir, 115, 116
Islamic caliphate, 360
Islamic commonwealth, 360

J
James Lee, 321, 328
Japan, 339, 349–52
  Jomon cultures in, 356
Japanese rulers, 350
Japanese Tokugawa regime, 325
Java, 352–55
Javanese monarchs, 352
Jayavarman VII, 151, 155
Jia Dan 賈耽, 257, 259, 260, 266n28, 266n29
Jiangtou cheng 江頭城 ("Riverhead Town"), 295
jiangzhen 降真, 226–28
Jiankang empire, political culture of, 141
jiao 蛟, known also as the *jiaolong* 蛟龍, 122–24
jingdu 競渡. *See* crossing competitions
Jinming Lake (Jinming chi 金明池), 145
Jiu Tangshu 舊唐書 (Old History of the Tang), 261
Jizi 箕子, 22
Johnson, Reginald, 296
Jomon cultures in Japan, 356

K
Kai-hentai, 198
Kaihuang era, 254
Kaiyuan 開元 era, 250
Kang Youwei, 302
Khan, Kublai, 275
Khmer empire, 61
Khmer military, 151
Khmer region, influences in, 149–56

Khmer tribute missions, 151
Khmer "water festival" (Bon Om Touk), 155
King Cheng, 169
King Goujian of Yue, sheared hair (*duanfa* 斷髮), 26
King Wen, tomb of, 167
Kinh Dương, 177
Koguryŏ, 349
Korea, 347–49
Kwang-chou-wan (Guangzhou wan 廣州灣), 207, 208
Kwangtung, adjacent districts of, 200

L
Lạc kings, 165, 167
lakawood, Southeast Asian product, 222–28
Lama, Dalai, 278
Larsen, Kirk W., 349
Late Period, Cổ Loa Middle Wall and Ditch Project, 56, 57
Leclère, Adhémard, 199
Lê dynasty, 161
Lees-hee-ta-hee, 299
legalism, 342
legendary traditions, 49
Lê Hoàn 黎桓, 146, 148
Leick, Gwendolyn, 357
Leizhou dialects, 206
  map of, 207
Leizhou, local gazetteers of, 195
Leizhou Museum, 202–3
Leizhou Peninsula, 194, 195, 197, 204, 206
  interconnections between northern Vietnam, Hainan Island, and, 207
Lê Quý Đôn, 162, 164, 171
Lê Thánh Tông, 202
Lê Văn Siêu, 165–66

Lewis, Mark, 16, 20, 22
Liang dynasty, 273
Liang, Zhuge, 317
Liao Pengfei 廖鵬飛, 127
Liao 獠 people, tattoo, 85
Liao tribes, 96
Liaozi, 96, 175
Li Bencan 李本燦, 320, 321, 324, 332
Li Chenglong 李成龍, 319, 323
Li clothing, 97
Liji 禮記, unbound hair, 20
Li Mi 李泌, 246–49
Lingnan frontier, 101
  administration of, 82
Lingnan region, 146
Lingwai daida 嶺外代答, 202
Liu Kezhuang 劉克莊 (1187–1269), 117, 121
Liu Taizhen 劉太真, 259
Liu Ting 劉挺, 295
Liu Zongyuan 柳宗元 (773–819), 122–23
Li Xianhe 李先和, 307
  tomb of, 308
locus classicus, 269
lojong (*blo sbyong*), or mind training, 283
Longshan culture, 65
loop skirt, 99
loose hair. *See also* unbound hair (*pifa* 被髮)
  element of, 24
Luoheyi state 羅和異國, 258
Luoyue state 羅越國 (the southern tip of the Malay Peninsula), 257
Lý Công Uẩn, 148
Lý courts, Cham embassies to, 150
Lý dynasty, 148, 150, 156, 173
  religion, 146
Lý Thái Tổ, 173, 174

M
Ma Dexin 馬德新, 328
Mahayana Buddhist approach, 155
Malacca Straits region, 216, 217, 221, 225, 227, 232
  aromatic woods, 221–22
Malayo-Javanese world, 10
mallet hairstyle, 89–91
mallet-shaped bun (*chuijie* 椎髻/魋結), 28–36
Manchu Qing dynasty, 6, 8
mandala state, 340
  dynamics of, 364
  mandala of, 343
Mandalay Chinese population, 305
Mandalay Hokkien temple, 306
Mandalay Yunnan Association, 305, 310
Mandarin gentry, 302
man, unbound hair (*pifa* 被髮), 20
manyi 蠻夷, 18
Marcia Yonemoto, 350
Margary, A.R., 296
Marx, Karl, 13
Maspero, Henri, 48
Maternal Ancestress (Mazu 媽祖), 131
  origins of, 126–27
Maurya Empire, 361
Mauryan polity, 66
Ma zhuang, 329
McLaren, Anne, 317
medieval China, baneful spirits in, 143
medieval Chinese southern dynasties, 143
Mekong, 363
Mekong Delta region, 341
Mendu state 門毒國 (Qui Nhơn, Vietnam), 257
Mercantile Shipping Superintendency, 229, 230

metallophones, 356
miao shrine, 115, 119
Middle Period, Cổ Loa Middle Wall and Ditch Project, 56, 57
Middle Wall excavation, Cổ Loa roof tiles, 57, 58
migrant community, 300, 304–9
Mị Hầu Kingdom, 178
military exchange, with Đại Việt, 151
military patron-client networks, 141
mines, 325–26
Ming dynasty, 161, 291, 295, 317, 321, 330, 334
Ming intervention, 348
mining industry, development of, 325
"minority nationalities", 322
Minyue (閩越), 18
Miss Lin (Lin shi 林氏 or Lin furen 林夫人), 126, 129–31
moated settlements, analogous forms of, 62
Molai state 沒來國 (present day Malabar, India), 258
Moluo state 末羅國 (now Basra, Iraq), 258
Mongol army, 291
Mongol imperial court, pharmacology into, 274–78
Mongol rulers, 274, 286
Mongol Yuan, 8
monumental earthen rampart, 57
monumental fortification system, 66
Moung Shwe Yah, 299
mountain savages, 174–75
Mulan River, 118
Mulian opera, 178
"multiplicity of non-institutionalized states", 341
multi-state system, 360
Mường, 172
Murray, Dian, 200
muskwood in *Zhufan zhi*, 230, 232

myth of peacock's gallbladder, 269, 270

N
naked bodies, 87–89
Nam Việt, 344
Nanfang xaomu zhuang, 222
Nanhai Temple 南海祠/南海廟, sacrificial ceremony at, 254–55
Nanhai Trade, The, 3
Nanjing ancestry, reference to, 320–21
Nan Yue, 344–47
Nanyue rulers, 345
national festival in Cổ Loa site, 47
national-level Confucian examination, 310
naval forces at Jinming Lake, 145
naval warfare, 141, 143, 148
    Cham and Khmer, 153, 155
    tactics, development of, 153
Neolithic and Metal Age periods, 63
new history perspective, 13–15
Ngai-Sie 愛薛 (1227–1308), 289n27
Ngô Sĩ Liên, 148
Nguyễn court, 345
Nguyễn Đổng Chi, 163–64
Nguyễn Dynasty chronicle, 198
Nguyễn Phúc Ánh, 344
Nguyễn Phuong, 165–66
Nguyễn's realm, 344
Nicola Di Cosmo, 324, 330
Nihon shoki, mallet-shaped bun, 29
non-Chinese ruler, 275
Nong Zhigao 儂智高, 81
non-Sinitic culture, 128
non-Sinitic societies, 46
northern Chinese migrants, 5
northern Korea, 349, 350
northern Song, 82
northern Vietnam, 200, 344, 350, 356
    and Hainan Island, correlations between, 199, 207

Han-Tang period in, 67
Han-Việt class of elites, 68
and Leizhou Peninsula,
    interconnections between, 207
Thunder God in, 203
northward perspective, 9–10, 12

O

"Oath of the 37 Lolo Tribes, The",
    322
O'Harrow, Stephen, 52–53
oil-based camphor, Chinese
    manufacturers, 221
Opium War, 354
oracle bone divination, Shang
    traditions of, 65
oral tales, 162–63
orthodox imperial hierarchy, 119
*Outer Annals of the Comprehensive
    Mirror for Aid in Government*
    (Liu Shu), 169
Ouyang Xiu 歐陽修 (1007–72), 115

P

Palace Gates Service, 252
Panthay rebellion, 307, 319, 324,
    326–32
Panthay regime, 328
patron-client networks, 144
"peace parley" of local, 29
peacock
    in Chinese Tradition, 269–74
    Tibetan medical, pharmacological,
        and Buddhist documents, 278–82
Pelliot, Paul, 266n27
Peng Nian, 32
peripheral relationships, with
    communities, 72
'Phags-pa script system, 275
phases and chronological periods,
    Cổ Loa Middle Wall and Ditch
    Project, 55–59

Phnom Penh region, tradition of, 155
Phong Châu 峰州, 177
political community, 357
political complexity, Chinese
    civilization, 60–63
political culture of Jiankang empire
    and southern-based regimes, 141
political organization of southern
    regimes, 141
political regeneration models, 66
politico-religious culture, 141
Polu state, 258
post-Angkor period development, 155
premodern scholars, *Arrayed Tales*,
    163
pre-Sinitic traditions, 129
primogeniture-based tradition of
    imperial succession, 141
Prince Godan, 276
Prince of Liang, 269, 274
proto-Khmer polity of Funan,
    340–41
proto-Vietnamese civilization
    cultural frontier between Sinitic
        and, 44
    foundations for, 44
proto-Vietnamese history, 48
proto-Vietnamese state, formation
    of, 62
Ptak, Roderich, 200
Putian flood plain, 118

Q

Qiangzong bu 强宗部, 322
Qianyuan 乾元 era, 249
Qin dynasty, 3, 169, 344
Qing central authorities, 333
Qing dynasty, 292, 309, 319, 333
Qing imperial authority, 337n46
Qingjiao 青蕉, 126
Qingming festival, 145–46, 149
Qing territory, 344

Qin-Han dynasty, 6
Qin-Han empire, 5, 343
Qin Shihuang, tomb of, 22
Qiongzhou Straits 瓊州海峽, 196,
    204–6
Qiu Kunliang 邱坤良, 323
Quanzhou merchants, 93

R
ramie, 92–93
rampart construction, 57
    chronology, phases, and
        dimensions, 59
    stamped earth technique, 64–65
rapid population increase, 325–26
Raw Li tattoos, 86
recruiting system, crossing
    competitions, 145
"red pants", 96
Red River, 363
Red River Delta, 44, 48, 146, 161,
    165–67, 174, 194, 203, 344
    autonomous polity, 176
    ethnic groups in, 172
    political elites of, 66
Red River plain, 71
    societies in, 52
Red River Valley, 72
    early civilization in, 61
    pre- and protohistory of, 46–51
regional rivalry, 306
religion, 357–58
religious elements, crossing
    competitions, 143
Replies from Beyond the Passes
    (Zhou Qufei), 174
resinous camphor, 218, 221, 222
rGyud-bZhi (The Four Medical
    Tantras), 278–79, 282
    "Food Taboo" in, 285
    prescriptions, 280–81
    Tibetan materia medica, 269

"rising dragon", 173
    in Thang Long, 175
ritual exchange, with Đại Việt, 151
ritual regulations in society, 16
rival empires in Europe, 1
river-based naval combat, 142
Robinson, James Harvey, 13
Rocher, Emile, 329
"Rolling Wave troops" (*Lingbo jun*
    凌波軍), 145
Romance of the Three Kingdoms, 317
Roman empire, 343
Rong tribes, unbound hair, 20
rowed longboat squadrons, 142

S
sacrificial ceremony at Nanhai
    Temple, 254–55
sages, 24
Sanskrito-Southeast Asian, 341
sappanwood, 230
scarification, 85–87
scented timbers, 230–31
Schafer, Edward H., 271
Second World War, 2, 11
Seishisai, Aizawa, 351
semi-legendary traditions, 49
Set Kyin, 298
Shang culture, 65
Shang polity, 360
Shang traditions of oracle bone
    divination, 65
sheared hair (*duanfa* 斷髮), 19,
    25–28
    vs. unbound hair, 28
Shel gong shel phreng, 282
Shen Nong, 165, 175
Shenzhong Yuanfeng period (1078–85),
    219
Shiji, mallet-shaped bun, 30
Shizi state 師子國 (present-day Sri
    Lanka), 258

Shwe In Bin, 307
 monastery, 308
Shwe Yan, 299, 302
Shy Dinh providence, 197
Siam, 352–55
Siamese government, 338
silk cloth, 93–94
Sima Qian 司馬遷, 68, 70
Sinicization process, 12
Sinicized Tai-speaking elite, 172
Sinification
 processes of, 67
 unidirectional teleology of, 101
Sinitic accommodation, hybrid cults
 of, 126–32
Sinitic civilization, 46, 118
 foundations for, 44
 and proto-Vietnamese civilizations,
 cultural frontier between, 44
Sinitic culture, 130–31
 in construction process of city, 46
 of Yellow River basin, 111
Sinitic immigration, cults of,
 112–26
Sinitic leadership symbols, 66
Sinitic settlement, 112
Sinitic societies, 46
Sinitic terms for fox, 175, 176
Sino–Arabic relations, 240
Sino–British border agreements,
 301–2
Sino–Burmese border town, 292
Sino–Burmese frontier, British
 interest in, 292
Sino–Burmese War, 291, 298
sinocentric perspective, 6–9
Sino-centric/Sino-tropic tributary
 system, 364
Sinocentric texts, 48
Sinocentric tradition, 14
Sino-centric tributary system, 353
Sinocentrism, 9

Sino-Pacifica, 340, 352–54, 356, 359,
 360, 363
slash-and-burn cultivation, 171
slavery, 85–86
social fabrics, 91–94
societies
 interaction of, 44
 in Red River plain, 52
 ritual regulations in, 16
Sojourning Yunnanese, 304
Song courts, Cham embassies to, 150
Song dynasty, 80, 81, 111, 127, 169,
 178
 mallet hairstyle, 91
 tattoos, 85
Song huiyao 宋會要, 118, 119, 230
Song regime, 145
Southeast Asia, 362
 bronze, 64
 camphor import to China, 216–22
 and China, economic interaction
 between, 214
 conventional scholarship on, 341
 culture and civilization, 43
 developments in ceramics
 traditions, 215
 furniture timber, 228–33
 issue of material cultural influences
 between China and, 215
 lakawood product, 222–28
 moated settlements, 62
 primary resources for material
 needs, 214
 raw materials and natural products
 supply to China, 214
 traditional perspectives, 43
 urbanism in, 61–62
Southeast Asian aromatic. *See*
 camphor
Southeast Asian cultures, 354
Southeast Asian Neolithic and Metal
 Age communities, 62–63

Southeast Asian polities, 356
Southeast Asian-style mandala
    polities, 341
southern barbarians, 48, 68, 70, 84
    exotic lands of, 72
Southern Campaign, 319
southern Chinese local traditions,
    boat competitions in, 149
southern frontier, nakedness on, 88
Southern Man 南蠻, 18
southern military engagements, 142
southern peoples, distinctiveness of,
    140–41
southern political culture, 141
Southern Song, 83, 84, 86, 117
southern-styled political culture,
    characteristics of, 146
Southern Tang, 145
Southern Yue, 68, 70, 71
    kingdom, 51
    polity, 60
South Seas trade, 229, 231
Spengler, Oswald, 355
stamped earth technique, 64–65
state-building tributary mission, 350
Stone Dog, 202–4
Sui dynasty (589–618), Barus
    camphor, 217
Sui-Tang reunification, 361
Symes, Michael, 292

T
Tagalog language, 358
Tai people, 175
Taiping huanyu ji 太平寰宇記
    [A Record of the World During
    the Taiping Era], 82
Taizong emperor, 82
"Tale of Heavenly King Đổng, The",
    story, 168
"Tale of Nanzhao, The", story,
    168–69

"Tale of the Fish Essence, The",
    story, 185–88
"Tale of the Fox Essence, The",
    story, 173–75
"Tale of the Hồng Bàng Clan, The",
    story, 165–68, 171, 172
"Tale of the Tree Essence", story,
    178–81
    French translation of, 181–83
"Tale of the Watermelon, The", story,
    168, 183–85
"Tale of the White Pheasant, The",
    story, 169–70
Tang culture, 7
Tang dynasty, 81, 83, 240, 241, 244,
    262
    Nanhai Temple, 255
    overseas trade in, 250
    Sui institution, 254–55
    tattoo, 85
Tang Huiyao 唐會要, 249, 260
Tang imperial court, 144
Tang period, 216, 217
Tang slave market, 85
Tantric Buddhism, 275
tattoos, 25–28, 85–87, 100
    tools of, 87
Taw Sein Ko, 305
tax revenues, 81–82
Teutonic Order, 364
Thailand developments in ceramics
    traditions, 215
Thăng Long, 174
    court, 202
    "rising dragon" in, 175
thermoluminescence analysis, of roof
    tiles, 59
Thunder God, 202–4, 211n39
Tianbao 天寶 era, 244, 249, 255
Tianxia, or All under Heaven, 13
Tibetan Buddhism, 268, 275
    peacock in, 282–85

Tibetan civilization, 275, 278
Tibetan culture, 268, 269, 283
Tibetan forces, 7
Tibetan medicine, introduction of,
    274–78
Tibetan religious literary genre,
    283
Tibetan script system, 277
Tibetan troops, 242, 245, 249, 261
Tiluoluhe state 提羅盧和國
    [Djerrarah, present-day Abadan,
    Iran], 258
Tiyu state 提鼠國 [Diul, present-day
    Diudul on the Kathiawar
    Peninsula, India], 258
Tokugawa-era Japanese, 350
Tongdian 通典 [Comprehensive
    Institutional Records], 253
Tongking Gulf, 205, 206
    trading zone, 204
Tongking–Hainan–Leizhou Peninsula,
    200
Tongking society, 199
Tonle Sap, 153, 155
Tonqueeners, 197
Toungoo–Ming wars, 295
trade development, 325–26
traditional caravan trade, 291
traditional perspectives, 43, 48
transgressive connotations of
    unbound hair, 20
Trevelyan, G.M., 13
tribals black clothing, 95
tribute-bearing emissaries, 150
tribute missions, 159n21, 159n22
Trần dynasty, 206
Trần Thế Pháp, 162
tropical southern cloth, 92
Trung Sisters, 68
Turco-Mongol, 4, 7
twentieth-century scholars, Arrayed
    Tales, 163

U
Ueda Nozomu, 323
Uighur script, 288n18
unbound hair (pifa), 19–25, 89
    vs. sheared hair, 28
"unified" Chinese dynasties, 141
universal history perspective, 10–12
urban civilizations of Mesopotamia,
    356
"urban emulation", 66
urbanism, 60–63, 356, 357

V
Vân Đồn, 204–6
Văn Lang kingdom, 49–50
Vietnam, 194, 344–47, 349, 351
    and China, 4, 10
    developments in ceramics
        traditions, 215
    and Hainan Island, correlations
        between northern, 199, 207
    internal affairs, 8, 9
    and Leizhou Peninsula,
        interconnections between
        northern, 207
    national boundaries for, 63
    prehistory in, 47
Vietnamese ceramics, brown painted
    wares of, 204
Vietnamese Hùng Kings (Hùng
    vương 雄王), 49
Vietnamese scholars, 163
Vietnamese traditions
    Cổ Loa site, 50
    examination of, 60
    potential challenges and biases,
        51–53
    Sinocentric views in, 49
Vietnam's Trần dynasty, 206
Việt bodies, descriptions of, 85
Việt elite, 171–72, 175, 176, 179
Việt formal clothing, 98

"Việt Nam", 344
Việt tattoo, 85
Việt territory, 83–84
Việt Thường, 169–70
Vu Duy Chí, 199
Vu Quỳnh, 162, 164, 183, 184

W
Wa Cheng 瓦城 (Mandalay), 300
Wang Chong 王充, 30–31, 33
Wang Ji 王驥, 295, 303
wangliang 罔兩, 89
warfares, 143
Warring States
    period, 62, 66
    unbound hair, 20
water-borne trade, 141
water management, 61–62
wearing identity, 97–100
Weber, Max, 13, 355
Wei Man 衛滿 (Korean, Wiman),
    29
Western Di, mallet-shaped bun, 30
western Guangxi, 95, 96
Western Mainland power, 362
Western political tradition, 356
Western scholarship, vocabulary of,
    4
Western societies, 358
western Yunnan, 307
    and Upper Burma, map of, 292,
    293
West Lake, 175, 176
Westphalian system, 356
white clothing, 94–95
"White Crane" (Bạch Hạc 白鶴),
    177
White Dragon-Tail (Bạch Long Vĩ
    白龍尾), 185, 187
White Lotus Rebellion, 345
"White-Robed Savages" (Bạch Y man
    白衣蠻), 174

Whitmore, John, 202
Wingate, A.M.S., 296
Winzeler, Robert, 60
Woodside, Alexander, 349
wrapped clothing, 99–100
Wuchuan 吳川 district, 196
Wu Sangui, 330
Wu Tao 吳夲, 126–31
Wu Xing 吳興, 115, 117–19,
    124–26
    hybrid cults of, 126
    local impact on cult of, 121
Wuyue 吳越, 17–18
    culture, sheared hair (*duanfa*), 26
Wu Zixu 伍子胥, 20, 22, 24, 26

X
Xianfeng ying, 330
Xiangpu 香譜, 218, 220
Xiaotun 小屯 village, 318
Xingyuan 興元 era, 241, 245, 246
Xinjie 新街 ("New Street"), 295
Xiuxing benqi jing 修行本起經
    (*Cārya–nidāna*; Sutra of the
    Buddha's Origins; also written
    Suxing benqi jing 宿行本起經),
    273
Xue Ruolin 薛若鄰, 324
Xu Xiaowang 徐曉望, 115

Y
Yang embassy, 252–55, 257, 260
    achievement and influence of,
    261–62
    sacrificial ceremony for, 255
    timeline of, 255–56
Yang group, 196, 198, 199
Yang Liangyao 楊良瑤, 240–42, 246,
    247
    sea route, 249–53, 257–61
Yang lineage, 320–21
Yang Shiying 楊士英, 320

Yang Yandi group, 196, 197
Yang Yingkang 楊應康, 323
Yang Zhi 楊志, 127–29
Yangzi Valley, crossing competitions
    in, 142–46
Yangzong 陽宗 Valley (Yunnan
    province), 326
    valley, 316, 319, 322, 329
Yanshou Creek 延壽溪, 115
Yanshou Weir 延壽陂, 115, 116,
    118
Yan Yandi group, 196–98
Yao dye patterns, 96
Yao mallet hairstyle, 90
Yao practice of rolling hair, 89
Yasodharapura (Angkor), 151
Yellow River basin, Sinitic culture
    of, 111
Yingyai shenglan 瀛涯勝覽, 228
Ying Zheng, 348
Yinhai jingwei 銀海精微, 218
Yin Zhaorong 尹兆榮, 306
Yi peoples, 18
    unbound hair, 20
Yongtai 永泰 era, 241
Yongzhen 永貞 era, 242
Youyang zazu 酉陽雜俎 (Miscellany
    from Youyang), 271
Yuan dynasty, 270, 274, 275, 277,
    278, 285, 291
Yuanhe 元和 era, 242
Yuechang (Việt Thường 越裳),
    169–70
Yue peoples, 17
    mallet-shaped bun (chuijie 椎髻/
    魋結), 28–36
    sheared hair (duanfa 斷髮),
    25–28
    unbound hair (pifa 被髮), 19–25
Yue Shi 樂史, 82
Yunlu manchao 雲麓漫鈔, 220

Yunnan, bubonic plague in second
    half of nineteenth century in,
    326–27
Yunnan–Burma caravan routes, 295,
    300
Yunnan–Burma frontier, 309
Yunnan–Burmese trade, 299
Yunnan communities, 307
    bronze-casting technologies, 63
Yunnanese identity, 333
Yunnanese migrant community, 300,
    304–9
Yunnanese society, 324
Yunnan ethnic landscape, 327
Yunnan frontier, 298
Yunnan province, 169, 316, 327
Yunnan provincial society, 327
Yunnan region, economic
    transformation of, 325

Z

zhang camphor, 220, 221
Zhang Chenglian 張成濂, 301
Zhang Chengyu 張成瑜, 302
Zhang Dexin 張德馨, 302
Zhang Guangda 張廣達, 239
Zhang Jianlin 張建林, 241
Zhang Shi 張栻, 87, 106n32
Zhang Shimin 張世民, 244
Zhangzhou–Chaozhou border area,
    114
Zhangzhou, establishment of, 114
Zhao Rugua 趙如适, 101, 226
Zhao Tuo, 31, 50, 166, 167, 169
Zhejiang Provincial Museum, sheared
    hair and tattooed bodies statues,
    33–36
Zheng Chenggong, 8
Zhenla fengtuji, 9
Zhenyuan 貞元 era, 240, 242–43,
    246–49, 256, 259, 261, 262

zhiguai tales, 164
Zhou culture
  hairstyle in, 16
  unbound hair (*pifa* 被髮), 19–20, 24
Zhou Daguan 周達觀, 155
Zhou lineage, 322
Zhou Qufei 周去非, 100
  colour and dyed patterns, 94, 96
  cotton, 93
  Li clothing, 97
  mallet hairstyle, 90
  naked bodies, 88
  needle and brush, 87
  ramie, 92–93

silk cloth, 93
  tattoo, 82, 84–86
Zhou rituals, sheared hair (*duanfa* 斷髮), 26–27
Zhou Zilong 周自龍, 322
Zhuang Xia 莊夏, 127–28
Zhuangzi text
  sheared hair (*duanfa* 斷髮), 25, 28
  unbound hair (*pifa* 被髮), 23
Zhufan zhi 諸蕃志, 83, 220, 223
  muskwood in, 230
Zhu Fu 朱輔, 98–99
  batik-patterned indigo cloth, 96
Zhuge Liang, 317, 319, 330, 333
Zhu Yuanzhang, 320, 321

NALANDA-SRIWIJAYA SERIES

1. *Nagapattinam to Suvarnadwipa: Reflections on the Chola Naval Expeditions to Southeast Asia*, edited by Hermann Kulke, K. Kesavapany and Vijay Sakhuja

2. *Early Interactions between South and Southeast Asia: Reflections on Cross-Cultural Exchange*, edited by Pierre-Yves Manguin, A. Mani and Geoff Wade

3. *Hardships and Downfall of Buddhism in India*, by Giovanni Verardi

4. *Anthony Reid and the Study of the Southeast Asian Past*, edited by Geoff Wade and Li Tana

5. *Portuguese and Luso-Asian Legacies in Southeast Asia, 1511–2011, Vol. 1: The Making of the Luso-Asian World: Intricacies of Engagement*, edited by Laura Jarnagin

6. *Portuguese and Luso-Asian Legacies in Southeast Asia, 1511–2011, Vol. 2: Culture and Identity in the Luso-Asian World: Tenacities & Plasticities*, edited by Laura Jarnagin

7. *Sino-Malay Trade and Diplomacy from the Tenth through the Fourteenth Century*, by Derek Heng

8. *Tradition and Archaeology: Early Maritime Contacts in the Indian Ocean*, edited by Himanshu Prabha Ray and Jean-François Salles

9. *The Sea, Identity and History: From the Bay of Bengal to the South China Sea*, edited by Satish Chandra and Himanshu Prabha Ray

10. *Early Southeast Asia Viewed from India: An Anthology of Articles from the Journal of the Greater India Society*, edited by Kwa Chong-Guan

11. *The Royal Hunt in Eurasian History*, by Thomas T. Allsen

12. *Ethnic Identity in Tang China*, by Marc S. Abramson

13. *Buddhism and Islam on the Silk Road*, by Johan Elverskog

14. *The Tongking Gulf Through History*, edited by Nola Cooke, Li Tana and James A. Anderson

15. *Asia Redux: Conceptualizing a Region for Our Times*, edited by Prasenjit Duara

16. *Eurasian Influences on Yuan China*, edited by Morris Rossabi

17. *Of Palm Wine, Women and War: The Mongolian Naval Expedition to Java in the 13th Century*, by David Bade

18. *Offshore Asia: Maritime Interactions in Eastern Asia before Steamships*, edited by Fujita Kayoko, Momoki Shiro and Anthony Reid

19. *Literary Migrations: Traditional Chinese Fiction in Asia (17th–20th Centuries)*, edited by Claudine Salmon

20. *Trails of Bronze Drums Across Early Southeast Asia: Exchange Routes and Connected Cultural Spheres*, by Ambra Calo

21. *Buddhism Across Asia: Networks of Material, Intellectual and Cultural Exchange, volume 1*, edited by Tansen Sen

22. *A 14th Century Malay Code of Laws: The Nītisārasamuccaya*, by Uli Kozok

23. *China and Beyond in the Medieaval Period: Cultural Crossings and Inter-Regional Connections*, edited by Dorothy C. Wong and Gustav Heldt

24. *Buddhist Dynamics in Premodern and Early Modern Southeast Asia*, edited by D. Christian Lammerts

www.ingramcontent.com/pod-product-compliance
Lightning Source LLC
Chambersburg PA
CBHW072043020426
42334CB00017B/1371